SUVs SUCK In

The Rebuilding of Iraq during a Raging Insurgency

Kerry C. Kachejian

FORTIS

A NON-FICTION IMPRINT FROM ADDUCENT

Adducent, Inc.

www.Adducent.Co

SUVs SUCK In Combat
The Rebuilding of Iraq during a Raging Insurgency

By Kerry C. Kachejian

ISBN 978-0-9845511-0-1 (hardcover version)
ISBN 978-0-9777884-5-3 (trade paperback version)
Library of Congress Control Number: 2010927003

Published by Adducent (under its Fortis non-fiction imprint)

Jacksonville, Florida

www.Adducent.Co

Published in the United States of America

Cover photo 2004 bombing at Assassin's Gate, photo courtesy Tom Jankiewicz.

About the Title

This is the first book I have written, and I really wrestled with what the title should be. In fact, coming up with a title was probably the hardest part of the entire process. (Dennis Lowery of Fortis made the publishing part really easy.)

At first, I was going to call it *Git'r Done: The Blood Sweat and Tears in the Early Days of Iraqi Reconstruction.* "Git'r Done" was a term we often used in Iraq to motivate and inspire each other to finish all the hard jobs in the face of great adversity. The former Commander of the Army Corps of Engineers, LTG Robert Van Antwerp, also used the phrase "Git'r Done" when addressing his employees. I thought he'd appreciate it. I sent Larry the Cable Guy an email to ask him about using the Git'r Done phrase, but I did not get a reply. However, some friends and colleagues thought it was overused and may confuse the reader as to the seriousness of the subject matter or the author.

I had a dozen other potential titles that I considered. I asked my friends and colleagues to give me their opinions. I made sure my teammates from Iraq got to vote, because this was their story too. The bottom line was that there was no strong opinion on any one title.

I want people to pick up the book. This is an important story—an untold piece of American military history.

So I needed a title that would distinguish this book from all others— and for it to have meaning for those with whom I served. But I also wanted the title to bring honor and dignity to our mission. Many people put themselves in harm's way trying to rebuild Iraq, and America should be proud of what they did.

Every day in Iraq, I received reports and photos about attacks on our reconstruction operations. I can't tell you how deeply painful it was to learn of each death or injury. I felt personally responsible to fix the situation. The GRD operations team and staff were aggressively seeking solutions, and we were frustrated with every new attack.

One day, our operations team received another photo of an IED attack in Bayji. The SUV in it was shredded. It was immediately clear that no one in the vehicle survived. In fact, two men supporting reconstruction operations died. LTC Jim Hampton and I looked at the photo in stunned silence. He let out a sigh, and said, "Man, SUVs suck in combat." I won't ever forget that comment. I couldn't have said it any better. I dedicated several chapters in this book to the un-armored or under-armored SUV problem—it was one of the most significant and deadly issues that we faced on a daily basis.

I still needed a great title for the book. I flipped through my chapters, and there it was staring me in the face. The Chapter, "SUVs Suck in Combat". I put it on the list of potential titles. Several people were adamant—this was the right title. They were emphatic. It was clearly their top choice. It certainly was bold and provocative. At least it made you open the book to this page.

However, I was concerned that the word "suck" in the title cheapened the book. In fact, a few people that saw the title expressed the same opinion. They were communications professionals, and some had published their own works. They strongly recommended that I change it. They were the experts, and I needed to listen. I was deeply torn, and I hesitated on using the title. I didn't want my only published work to be considered less than professional.

The clock was ticking, and it was time to publish. It was time to make a command decision. I reflected on one of my primary purposes for writing this book – to make sure the lessons we learned in Iraq are not forgotten by future generations. And the number one lesson I learned in Iraq was "SUVs suck in combat."

So there you have it. It is a provocative and emotional title. To the uninformed, it sounds humorous and crude (but to those who have served in Iraq and Afghanistan—they know the truth of it). Every time I hear the phrase, a chill goes down my spine. So I am sticking to my guns. The book is called "SUVs Suck in Combat." If you don't like it, try repeating it ten times. Get it out of your system. You should feel better.

And if you still don't like it, I'm going to blame Dennis Lowery.

Dedication

This book is dedicated to my brother, Kevin Kachejian, whose incredible life was filled with great adversity that he overcame every day. Although paralyzed from the neck down from a bicycle accident at age eleven, Kevin's determination to live an active, independent life, his strong faith, and his sincere interest and concern for others became a tremendous inspiration to our family and to the entire community of West Chester, Pennsylvania. He did what most of us with working limbs couldn't do – graduate from law school.

Few people on this earth suffered so much for so long. Yet, few people on this earth gave so much with so little. And no one faced adversity better than Kevin. His patience, courage, kindness, humility, and love for his family set a stellar example for his fellow citizens. His story is far more remarkable than mine. It is what Hollywood movies are made of. Having Kevin as my brother lifted my spirits and made every day in Iraq a little easier. Kevin passed away on August 27, 2005.

I also dedicate this book to my sister, Regina Curley, who was always there in Kevin's hour of need, particularly when I was gone serving in Iraq. Her personal sacrifice taking care of Kevin for many years was unbelievable. Although her husband had died several years earlier, leaving her alone to raise three children, Gina gave everything she had for our paralyzed brother -- out of pure love. She gave up her income, her personal life, and much treasured time with her own children to care for our brother. It is a debt that I can never repay. Gina, you rock!

Yet through all this adversity, Gina still raised All-American kids, who learned great lessons from her stellar example. And her two sons, Peter and Nathaniel, are now graduates of West Point. That's awesome.

I also want to thank my parents, Karabed "Rocky" and Helen Kachejian, who chose the harder path in life, and cared for Kevin for 31 years after his devastating accident. My father died of cancer in 1984, and my mother dedicated the rest of her life to Kevin's care. Mom died in November 2003, shortly before my deployment to Iraq. My parents taught me everything I know about selfless service.

To my wife, Alice. She tolerated my many late nights and weekends working on this book to bring it to completion. She picked up all the duties and cared for our children when I flew off to Iraq. Thank you for sticking with me during the hardest year of my life.

To my wonderful children Kent, Kara and Katie who loved their Uncle Kevin very much. Please keep him in your hearts forever.

To the West Point Class of 1982, many of whom I was honored to serve with in Iraq and Afghanistan. And to our two fallen classmates, LTC Dominic Baragona and COL Brian Allgood. "And when our work is done; Our course on earth is run; May it be said, 'Well Done'; Be thou at peace." (Verse from The Alma Mater)

To all other Americans who have fallen, in hope that we and our children may live in a safer world.

Finally, I want to remember the scores of people that died in our reconstruction operations during my deployment in Iraq. We could not have completed our mission without them.

And to four who touched me personally that I will never forget:

- **Hendrick Johannes Visagie** … aka "Fish". Our Personal Security Team member who was hit by a rocket propelled grenade in Fallujah.
- **Suna Hadi,** one of our interpreters. Her vehicle plunged into the Tigris River. I tried to save her, and I failed.
- **Lance Corporal Michael Downey:** A distant cousin and fellow patriot. He died of wounds from sniper fire. He was 21.
- **MAJ Charlie Driscoll,** my teammate, and fellow Airborne Ranger. The proud husband of Constance and new father of Grace and Claire. He was one of the finest human beings I have ever met.

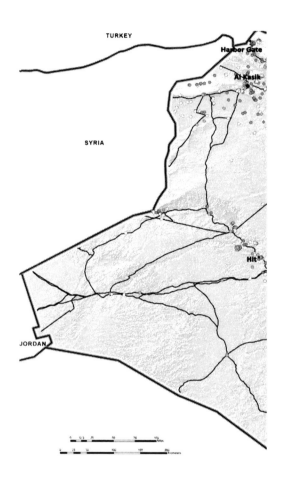

Legend

⊛ National Capital	**GRD_Projects**
▭ Country	● Health & Education
— Iraqi HWY	○ Public Works
▨ iraq_water	● Security & Law Enforcement

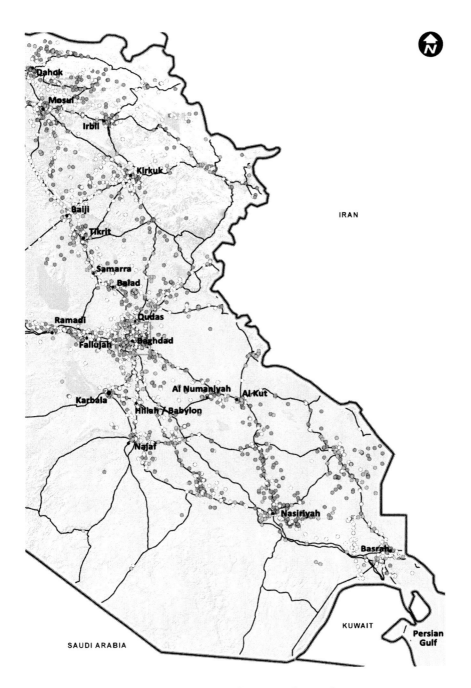

GRD Reconstruction Projects in Iraq

Map Source: U.S. Army Corps of Engineers Transatlantic Division/GRD, April 2010.

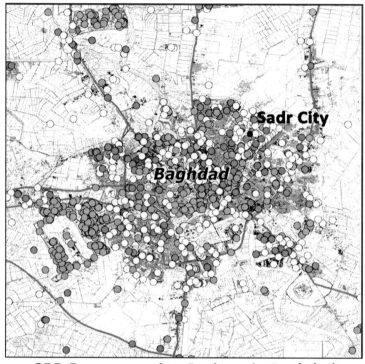

GRD Reconstruction Projects in Baghdad

Map Source: U.S. Army Corps of Engineers Transatlantic Division/GRD, April 2010.

Contents

Contents (continued)

Appendix

Acknowledgments

The Kick-Off

I never put my pen to paper until after the American Society of Industrial Security (ASIS) Conference in March of 2007. Peter Probst, a widely recognized and distinguished terrorism consultant, asked me to co-chair a panel with Dr. Anne Speckhard on the "Psychology of Terrorism". Anne was an Associate Professor of Psychiatry at Georgetown University Medical School. At first, I balked at the offer. I was not a trained psychologist, but Peter had previously heard some of my experiences from Iraq. He suggested that I use them to compliment the research that Anne had done on terrorism psychology and resilience.

The duo worked out great. I focused on describing my experiences in a terrorist-rich environment, and how it affected the mental state and the behavior of our civilians and workers. Following that presentation, Peter and Anne told me that I "had to write a book". They were insistent. I knew writing a book was a huge project, but I also knew they were right. If nothing else, I wanted to document my Iraq experience to pass it on to my children. So I am grateful to Peter and Anne for the kind words and strong encouragement. Without it, this book would likely not have been attempted.

Getting into the End Zone

I also need to acknowledge the help of Patricia Fuentes Burns, who helped me with the book's initial organization and editing. And although the draft was complete, I had no idea how to get the manuscript published. I felt like a quarterback who drove his team down to the 20-yard line but was unable to score. It was Dennis Lowery of Fortis that showed me how to get the project across the goal line. Without him, this book may not have been published.

Other Contributions

Several friends and colleagues shared stories and photographs with me to help improve the accuracy and realism of this book. They include: Scott Lowdermilk, Tom Jankiewicz, Jim Hampton, Kristine Burnell, Keith Felde, Pete Mansoor, Wendell Benner, Patrick Parker and Lisa Willover. Jay Jennings helped to assemble the appendix of the USMA Class of 1982 that have served in Iraq, Afghanistan and the Global War on Terrorism. I even had some assistance from Marty Baker, the Senior Pastor at Burke Community Church.

I also want to acknowledge John Lonnquest and Eric Reinert of the USACE History Office, who offered to share the USACE photo library and provide insights during this unique period. Some of the official photos were taken by Ross Adkins and Mitch Frazier. And I want thank Joan Kibler (USACE) and Ron Williams (Raytheon) who volunteered to review this manuscript prior to final publication. But all statements of fact, opinion, or analysis expressed in this book are those of the author and do not reflect the official positions or views of the U.S. Army Corps of Engineers, Department of Defense or any U.S. Government agency or personnel. Nothing in the contents should be construed as asserting or implying U.S. Government agency or personnel's authentication of information or endorsement of the author's views.

Introduction

Roots of Patriotism

Through the years, I've noticed Americans usually rally around fellow citizens that were held hostage. During these times, patriotism would really spike.

I first started to understand patriotism when I was a young boy watching fireworks in my hometown of West Chester, Pennsylvania. My younger brother, Kevin, was a toddler and was born on the 4th of July. He was convinced all the fireworks and celebrations were just for him. I knew there was something special about that day, when all our neighbors came together. It took a few years for both of us to finally figure it out.

In the summer of 1972, I remember watching the Munich Olympics, when eleven Israeli athletes were kidnapped and murdered. Our entire country was shocked to the core, even though no U.S. citizens were involved. I realized then that there truly was good and evil in the world, and America represented the good.

From 1979-1981, 52 Americans were held hostage in Iran for 444 days. I was a cadet at West Point, and we followed the unfolding drama in the news every day. It was a roller coaster ride of emotion, with the lowest point being the failed rescue attempt that resulted in the deaths of eight American patriots. The hostages were eventually released the day Ronald Reagan was inaugurated. They returned to the United States and spent a few days at West Point to be reunited with their families. The entire bus route from Stuart AFB to West Point was lined with yellow ribbons and American flags. I remember my friend, Mike Bruhn, recounting the powerfully emotional story of the bus ride. I was there when the American hostages arrived at the Hotel Thayer, and there was not a dry eye for miles. As cadets, we were able to meet many of the hostages and eat several meals with them in our mess hall. It was a truly uplifting experience. Our great national humiliation was finally over.

Twenty years later, one of those hostages, Paul Needham, was on the faculty at the National Defense University (NDU) when I was a student at the Industrial College of the Armed Forces (ICAF). The stories of what he endured at the hands of his Iranian captors, including mock executions, were a great inspiration to us.

In the 1970s and 1980s, Hezbollah was routinely taking hostages in Lebanon. The stories kept the nation riveted to the nightly news. The more famous hostages were Terry Waite, LTC

Higgins and William Buckley, the CIA station chief. It all peaked in October of 1983, when a Hezbollah suicide truck bomb blew up the Marine Corps barracks at the airport in Beirut, Lebanon. Two hundred and forty-one servicemen died—ninety percent were Marines. The country was enraged and shocked. Twenty years later, one of the survivors, Curt Powell, would become one of my good friends at Raytheon.

On September 11, 2001, I was a student at NDU at Fort McNair in Washington, D.C. My seminar was watching a live broadcast of both World Trade Towers in New York City burn as our fellow citizens were being cooked by a ruthless and evil enemy. From the top floor of Eisenhower Hall, we had clear line of sight to the Pentagon when American Airlines Flight 77 hit it. In each aircraft, scores of passengers were held hostage and then flown to their deaths. Our nation was shocked. I was furious. The first F-16 flying over the city was a welcome sight. I later learned that four of my fellow Raytheon employees died in the crash. A few weeks after the attack, I recorded my personal account of what happened that day.

Immediately after 9/11, I saw U.S. flags hanging on every bridge on I-95. American patriotism was surging, and I knew we were going to be OK. I don't know who put all those flags up, but I want to thank every one of them personally.

A few weeks later, an anthrax attack occurred in Washington D.C. using the postal system to deliver the deadly spores. Our ICAF auditorium (Baruch) was quickly modified to serve as an alternate location for the Congress in case the capital required evacuation.

During the repair of the Pentagon, a Chapel was built at the point of impact of Flight 77 – where 64 souls were lost. I had a chance to visit it in August of 2008. COL Mike Donovan, my friend, chose the site for his retirement ceremony. Sitting there gave us all another opportunity to reflect on our values and our common bond as Americans. After Mike left the Army, he went to work as a consulting Program Manager for the World Trade Center Redevelopment Program in New York City.

No discussion on patriotism could be complete without mentioning Pat Tillman. He was an outstanding example of a patriot. He could have continued his career as an NFL football star, but instead, he turned down a multi-million dollar contract to serve his country after 9/11. He was tragically killed by friendly fire in Afghanistan while I was serving in Iraq. To give up a life of fame and fortune—for a life of great personal sacrifice and imminent danger to help his country, speaks volumes about Pat Tillman's character. His loss was deeply painful to all of us in uniform. I suspect there are many others like Pat Tillman, but less famous, who gave it all up for the honor of serving their country in the Global War on Terrorism.

This Story

This is the untold story of the Gulf Region Division (GRD) and its critical mission to rebuild Iraq during the early tumultuous days of the Iraqi insurgency. The race to rebuild Iraq was a team effort that involved multiple government agencies, ministries and contractors. It was the Super Bowl of reconstruction—the largest and most complex project ever undertaken by our nation. We went to war with what we had, and without much of what we needed. Our mission was to stand up a new Division and simultaneously rebuild critical sectors of the Iraqi infrastructure.

I have three purposes for writing this book:

First, I simply want to tell the story of one man's experience during an important historic and political episode in our nation's history, based on the events but also filtered through my own background and personal situation. *It is a different perspective. I want you to feel like you were there with boots on the ground—and in the moment.*

Second, I want to clarify and humanize a historic and political situation that has been misrepresented and misunderstood by many. I want you to have a better understanding of the complexity and danger of Iraqi reconstruction operations. Many of our soldiers and civilians made great personal sacrifices that few of our fellow citizens would dare to endure.

Finally, a great motivation for writing this book is to make certain our country does not forget—or repeat—what we learned during this seemingly impossible period. I want to preserve the details and insights about the reconstruction of Iraq as well as share the lessons learned so that we are better prepared if ever faced with a similar situation or challenge.

* * *

While my experience in Iraq as the GRD Operations Officer (G3) involved the strategic, operational and tactical levels of warfare, I focused on the daily struggle to complete our mission.

We had a new Division that was severely understaffed. Ninety percent of our personnel were civilians—all volunteers. I was one of a handful of military personnel. We came together in Iraq on game day and began to execute our mission. We built thousands of construction projects distributed throughout a hostile country—without military vehicles, military radios and crew–served weapons. We depended on contractors for security. We drove around in combat in SUVs (the same type that you see on the street). Our unit faced daily car bombs, rocket attacks, ambushes, kidnappings and other threats.

We lost many people during the reconstruction effort—most were brave contractors who took risks every day while operating in a complex and dangerous environment. Through great perseverance, we were able to complete the mission. And for all of its incredible efforts, the Gulf Region Division was awarded the Meritorious Unit Commendation.

I have hundreds of stories to tell. And several thousand photos to back them up. I will share some of them with you. So strap in while I tell you the rest of the story. This book is about the blood, sweat and tears of rebuilding Iraq, and what it took to "Git'r Done".

Prologue

The Tough Road to Baghdad

Getting to Baghdad would be a tough, tough journey for me. And while all Americans face adversity during their lives, my family had borne far more than its share. To us adversity was a normal state of affairs, and we faced it head on. My family's collective resilience and ability to cope with tough times often amazed our friends and neighbors. But it was this very ability to cope that allowed me to leave my family even in a time of hardship.

My family's challenges can be traced back almost 100 years to a mass genocide that drove my grandparents, Aram Kachejian and Regina Hagopian, out of Armenia and to the United States. They were among the lucky survivors of the "Starving Armenians". They opened a shoe shop in Philadelphia and raised their kids during the Great Depression. I owe my grandparents the American life I know today.

I come from a long line of patriots, and many served in the military during World War II, Korea and the Cold War: Alex, George and my father, Karabed "Rocky" Kachejian; Haig and John Geovjian; Tony Klijian and Morris Arabian. They all paid their dues. In the next two generations, six more, including me, served their country in uniform during Desert Storm, Iraq and Afghanistan.

As for me, at this point I figured I had already seen the toughest part of my life. I had seen my brother Kevin paralyzed after breaking his neck in a bicycle accident at the age of eleven. I listened as my infant son Kent, in intensive care eight times, struggled to breathe and was read his last rites, and I watched him survive. I lost my father at an early age. I thought of my life as a series of character building experiences. I felt that God was good to me to help me get this far.

The months leading up to my deployment to Iraq were filled with even more challenges. It started with Hurricane Isabel hitting the North Carolina coast in fall of 2003. My wife and I had recently fulfilled a long-time dream of owning a beach house there after talking about it for ten years. Isabel devastated our home, and it would be months before it was again habitable. In the following weeks, my mother's health began deteriorating rapidly. She lived in West Chester, Pennsylvania. Helen Kachejian was the sole caregiver for my brother Kevin. She cared for him during the last thirty years while he was a quadriplegic and in doing so had neglected her own health. At seventy-one, she had stage four lung cancer, emphysema, and a mass in her heart. I stayed in West Chester for a few weeks helping my sister, Gina, take care of Kevin and watching my mother's health get worse. One night, after Gina and I put Kevin in his bed, the phone rang. It was Paoli Memorial Hospital. Mom had died. Gina and I raced back to the hospital, deeply regretting that we had left her only two hours earlier. We thought she would survive a bit longer. We wanted to be with her when she passed. A family friend stayed with Kevin, who paralyzed in his bed, wept alone.

Meanwhile, the war in Iraq was heating up, and my Army Reserve unit, the Contingency Response Unit (CRU), was being considered for deployment. I met with my teammates in Washington D.C. to assess the situation. With each passing week, the deployment was becoming increasingly certain. The Army needed our team to lead a special mission to rebuild Iraq. It was the right thing to do. It was going to happen. We all knew our lives were going to change radically and the timing couldn't be worse for me personally. The order was given. It was time to salute and execute. But each of us was concerned about how we would inform our families.

At my Mother's funeral, I approached Gina and told her I had some bad news. Now, she was thinking that my house was hit by a hurricane, our mother had just died, and we both now had to provide fulltime care for our quadriplegic brother. What could be that bad? I told her I was expecting orders to deploy to Iraq. I was still at my civilian job with Raytheon. I had missed quite a bit of work, and I was concerned that I was letting my industry colleagues down. I had always been a team player and valued my reputation as a dependable guy. So I felt compelled to attend an urgent company leadership meeting regarding business opportunities in the Middle East. On the night of my Mother's funeral, I flew to Waltham, MA. I felt horrible leaving my family before we had finished mourning. I wish I could take that decision back.

At the business meeting, I told Paul Cerjan, a retired Army Lieutenant General, that I was probably being deployed to Iraq. (In the mid-1980s, COL Cerjan was my Brigade Commander, and he was now a consultant to the company). I failed to tell him that it was confidential, and I still hadn't told my boss. When LTG Cerjan gave his presentation to the corporate leadership team, he highlighted that the Iraq War was growing, and it was hitting closer to home. He cited that even "Kerry Kachejian ...was getting mobilized." It was not the way I wanted my colleagues to hear the news, but the word was out now. I hadn't even told my wife yet.

For the next month, I drove back and forth from Virginia to Pennsylvania, sometimes round trip overnight, to help my sister with the estate and to care for my brother. I was running out of time, and we needed a better solution before I disappeared. Gina was a single parent. Her husband had died a few years earlier, and she was self-employed. Caring for Kevin continuously meant she would be virtually unemployed. And I felt I was placing the entire responsibility of Kevin's care on her by going to Iraq.

I broke the news about my pending deployment to my wife, Alice, over the Thanksgiving holiday. She took it hard and felt overwhelmed. Her family had their own health issues. Alice's mother, Elizabeth "Betty" Bush, was seventy-nine and had emphysema and osteoporosis. She was on oxygen 24/7. She lived alone in her Virginia home after her husband, Jim, a decorated WWII veteran, died two years earlier. Alice was trying to care for her mother's special medical needs while I was attending to my family in Pennsylvania. I felt guilty that I would be flying off to Iraq and abandoning my post as a father and husband.

Training Up for Iraq

Once the CRU team was notified that it was going to Iraq, we immediately began to focus on our pending mission. In the two months preceding our deployment, our team developed an intensive training program to sharpen our technical and tactical skills and to gain a solid understanding of both our mission in Iraq and the operating environment. We also needed to acquire the right personal equipment.

Meanwhile, MG Ron Johnson was selected to be the first GRD Commander. He had a reputation for being very direct and detail oriented. His task was to activate the new division in Iraq in January 2004 (Initial Operational Capability - IOC), and get it fully up and running (Final Operational Capability - FOC) in a few months. Standing up and staffing a new Division while in combat was like building an aircraft while simultaneously trying to fly it. To prepare, MG Johnson pulled the USACE staff together in Washington, D.C. in December to conduct a series of "Rock Drills". (A Rock Drill is a simulation or rehearsal, where the team talks through each step of a mission in detail. It helps the leader and staff better understand the entire picture of an operation.) In the field, rocks are used to represent units or teams, and they are moved on a terrain board to play out a pending mission. During the simulation, each team gets to see what other teams are doing. Many deficiencies or gaps in the plan are identified and then fixed. I participated in the final GRD Rock Drill to get a sense of the reconstruction mission and to become familiar with the incoming commander.

Our CRU team spent much of its time improving our individual training skills at the Transatlantic Programs Center (TAC) in rural Winchester, VA. Foremost on our "to do list" was weapons qualification, which was a critical survival skill. However, we had an immediate problem. The CRU didn't have any weapons assigned to it, nor was it authorized to have training ammunition. Fortunately, we had a resourceful logistician supporting us at TAC, Mr. Rick Bierlich. Rick was able to acquire about a dozen highly prized M-4 rifles. I don't know how he got the weapons, but I gave him an A+ on that supply action. The M-4 is a carbine version of the longer M-16 rifle. With a collapsible stock, it was easier to carry, and more suitable for urban fighting and for shooting from SUVs. That helped our team's morale.

The ammo situation was totally unacceptable, and I was very irritated. We had no time to order ammo through the Army supply system. Our unit had low priority, and much of the ammo the Army had was already being sent to Iraq and Afghanistan. We had only one opportunity to fire our M-4s at the local training range, and we needed ammo now. Submitting a justification for training ammunition and waiting on an approval would take too long, and it meant we would not adequately train on our weapons. But Rick came to the rescue again. He found a source of commercial ammo that was virtually the same as that in the Army supply system. The only catch was that we had to purchase it personally. I immediately whipped out the "Just do it" card issued to me by LTG Flowers. As the USACE Commander and the Army's senior Engineer, LTG Flowers never wanted his personnel to be paralyzed by indecision. The "Just Do It" card empowered us to act decisively. So my team all chipped in, and we bought our own ammo (since Charlie Driscoll was the junior guy on the team, I paid for his ammo) and headed off to the firing range. It wasn't the Army way to do it, but neither was going into combat without training on our weapons.

On the cold clear morning of January 20, the CRU CENTCOM team headed to a firing range run by the West Virginia Air National Guard (WVANG). Tom Jankiewicz and Scott Lowdermilk from TAC coordinated the training. We met a couple of WVANG Noncommissioned officers, who went over the range procedures and gave us a safety briefing. We had a good day, firing our M-4s from the prone position, while standing, and on the move. We were all serious about getting our weapons zeroed and improving our perishable marksmanship skills. We knew the next time we used them may well be against the enemy. By the end of the day, we were all comfortable with using our new weapons, which felt as if they were an extension of our own bodies.

During December and January, our team continued to prepare for the reconstruction mission. MAJ Mike Kiene issued us ruggedized laptop computers, updated our security clearances and acquired additional uniforms and accessories like flashlights, and pistol holsters. MAJ Chris Kolditz compiled our engineering technical and field manuals on CD. CPT Charlie Driscoll was able to get us digital map data for all of Iraq. We received numerous briefings on USACE capabilities and services that our team could "reach back" to include geospatial intelligence. We trained on satellite telecommunications equipment, so we could connect via live video to U.S. engineer experts while we were on a project site in Iraq. One potential application would be to immediately assess whether a partially damaged bridge could support an M-1 tank driving over it. Another use might be to determine if a major dam was about to fail or to relay video of a building damaged by a car bomb. We also trained on the Automated Route Reconnaissance Kit (ARRK) used to locate, photograph and record potential obstacles that could impede the movement of U.S. forces. The ARRK could be used to locate potential obstacles such as restrictive highway tunnels, low capacity bridges, road craters, cut rail lines, or mountainous slopes that would delay the movement of military vehicles. Our team was continuously busy and focused on the pending mission.

Meanwhile, we held several social events for our families. It could get lonely on both sides of the ocean during a deployment, and we wanted our wives and children to get acquainted so they could support each other while we were gone. Participating in these social events was always voluntary, and there were still a lot of mixed emotions about the pending deployment from the spouses. One outing was a family bowling day held at Ft Belvoir, and our kids had a good time.

On January 27, the CENTCOM team met in Washington, D.C. with LTG Flowers in his Command Conference room at HQ USACE. He was serving as the senior Engineer officer in the U.S. Army. LTG Flowers knew we were deploying to serve as the operations cadre for the new Gulf Region Division. He wanted to wish our team well on our pending mission and to thank us personally for our service. MG

James Cheatham, COL Walt Chahanovich, and Mike Alexander joined the small ceremony that lasted only ten minutes. COL Chahanovich was the CRU Commander who directed our team to support the Iraq mission. We cut a big cake with an Engineer Castle and the words "Good Luck" scrolled on it. In other words, "We hope you come home in one piece."

LTG Flowers (center in black) with CENTCOM Team

Two days earlier, in Baghdad, Iraq, another cake had been cut. This one was at a ceremony led by MG Johnson who was officially activating the Gulf Region Division. The deployment was now imminent.

MG Johnson cuts the cake

From Bliss to Baghdad

On February 1, our team was officially "mobilized" and flew to the CONUS Replacement Center (CRC) for Iraq at Ft Bliss, Texas. CRC was a place where small units and individuals, both military and civilian, could go through their final training, medical screening and equipment issues before departing for Iraq. It uses "batch processing" to move people through like cattle—an inefficient and impersonal process. Customer service was not part of the culture. The philosophy was, "There's a war going on—just get in line and wait an hour to get your turn. When you get to the front of the line, we'll tell you if you were standing in the correct line. Then you will move on to the next line." I was the most senior person mobilizing through CRC that week, but rank had no privileges there. The CRC barracks were drafty, austere and noisy. It had World War II era metal bunk beds with springs that creaked all night. I found a back room and thought I had some privacy but was later locked out of it. So I slept in the hallway on the barracks floor the first night.

My team reported to Ft. Bliss on the day of the Super Bowl. It raised the question, "What military planner would start our combat deployment training on Super Bowl Sunday?" He must have been a disgruntled baseball fan. At least the intent was to start the CRC training in the evening, after the game. My team wanted to watch it together. I agreed. It would be a good bonding experience and would relieve some stress. On that day, we were going to be spectators for the NFL Super Bowl—soon we were going to be blue chip players in the Reconstruction Super Bowl. But my team didn't want to watch the big game standing in the back of a musty CRC recreation room, next to a decaying sofa, in a room full of people we didn't know. I was going to treat my team better than that.

There was an Army Captain in charge of the CRC training at Ft Bliss. I met with him, and he seemed like a sharp guy. He had to train an eclectic group of several hundred civilians and soldiers that were not associated with any large military unit. Lacking organization, many of these individuals needed a very structured environment to make it through the week of training. Many of the CRC "trainees" lacked discipline and could easily stray. I was somewhat sympathetic for the Captain and his staff. Controlling the trainees at CRC was as difficult as herding cats.

A "welcome meeting" had been scheduled for 19:00 that evening. (Did I mention this was Super Bowl Sunday?) The Captain had a policy of no alcohol during training. Fine. I get it. But I reasoned that we didn't start "training" until 19:00. I was clear and unambiguous. I told the Captain that I was taking my team to the local Officer's Club to watch the Super Bowl. We were all mature seasoned officers, and I was not going to treat my team like new recruits. I was going to buy them all one beer. It was probably the last thing I could do for them before we all went into combat. I would be personally responsible for them. If he had any issue with this, I'd be happy to discuss it with his chain of command. The Captain knew he wasn't going to win this one. He replied, *"OK, Sir. You're a Colonel."* That quick and decisive reply immediately confirmed my initial impression that the Captain was a very sharp man.

That was the green light I needed. I just wanted to be forthright and address what we planned to do right up front. We were going to the O'Club, watch the Super Bowl and drink one beer. Then we'd start with the CRC training briefings. Speak now or forever hold your peace. What was the Army going to do to me—shave my head and send me to Baghdad? We were already on the way.

Team morale spiked, and we headed to the O'Club to get a decent seat. There was a spirited crowd watching the game. The only twist was that the game ran longer than expected. We had to leave the club early, but we made it to the CRC meeting on time, as we had agreed. The Patriots beat the Panthers with a last second field goal that cleared the uprights just as our first training meeting kicked off. The next day, I learned that I had won the O'Club door prize, and a picture of my team appeared prominently in the Ft. Bliss newspaper. It was a good thing we cleared the trip in advance.

CRC training started the next morning. During the following week, we conducted first aid training, fired our 9mm Berettas at the White Sands pistol range, took medical and dental exams, and were issued more equipment and uniforms. We were issued too much crap. Why we received multiple sets of cold weather gear, thermal underwear and mountain boots puzzled me. Iraq only gets severely cold in the mountains up in Kurdistan. I was going to be operating in the other 90% of the country where the temperature hits 120° F in the summer. Most of the CRU team chose to leave the cold weather gear behind.

We received dozens of briefings in a large auditorium. During a question and answer period on the "law of land combat", some civilian mentioned a recent video of a U.S. helicopter attack on Iraqi insurgents planting Improvised Explosive Devices (IEDs) in the road. I hadn't seen the video at that point, so I listened to his description. The attack helo caught two of the bombers in the open and ripped them apart. A third insurgent was hiding under a truck and was possibly wounded. When the last bomber tried to crawl away, the Americans finished him off. The civilian was convinced the Americans may have committed an unlawful act (I assume by attacking a wounded enemy), and he wanted an opinion. That's when I stood up and threw the bullshit flag. I asked if any of the enemy were raising their hands to surrender. If so, we were obligated to take them prisoner. But they were not surrendering. In fact, by crawling away from the scene of the attack, the enemy was conducting a retrograde (attempting to conserve combat power to fight another day). In my view, he was a legitimate enemy target. We don't need a bunch of lawyers reviewing every combat action we conduct. War is inherently dangerous, chaotic and ambiguous. Warfighters need to make quick tactical decisions all the time. This was clearly an enemy team trying to set up an IED ambush on Americans. But we found them first and killed them in the act. They deserved to die. And killing them probably saved the lives of several of our troops who would have been killed by their ambush the next morning. After the briefing, I had a few civilians and contractors come up to me and express their appreciation for my comments. It put an abrupt end to the debate.

Regrettably, there was no formal IED training at the weeklong CRC course held in February 2004. CRC only included a couple of IED briefings and discussions. Our team would soon learn that IED training was desperately needed. The Army recognized this need and would later expand CRC to two weeks and include much needed IED training and convoy operations. But this change occurred too late for our team to benefit. We'd have to learn about IEDs the hard way.

In addition to our CRU military team, there were a dozen or more USACE civilians at CRC that week. These civilians were also deploying to GRD to help run projects, administer contracts and perform other reconstruction related tasks. While USACE civilians were not issued weapons, they were issued much of the same equipment: chemical masks, rain gear, sleeping bags, rucksacks, body armor, etc. USACE civilians were also required to wear the Desert Camouflage Uniform (DCU). And our troops in Iraq would expect the uniform to be properly worn and respected. Most of the USACE civilians were unfamiliar with the uniforms and equipment. So CPT Charlie Driscoll volunteered to lead an "after hours" class on wear and care for uniforms and equipment for all USACE civilians. MAJ Chris Kolditz was his assistant and the rest of the team attended to pitch in. It was the first time these civilians were getting a good look at the CRU team, as our main job in Iraq would be to keep them alive. As always, Charlie conducted the training with great professionalism, and the class helped to build the civil-military relationship that would be central to the success of the reconstruction mission.

During the week of training, I interviewed another Army Reservist, Master Sergeant (MSG) David Breitbach. He had contacted the CRU and was looking for an opportunity to serve with us. Since we were near him at Ft. Bliss, we arranged to meet on post. After a thirty-minute discussion, I was convinced he had the skills and background that the CRU needed. I sent my recommendation to COL Chahanovich, the CRU Commander, in Washington, D.C. The CRU then recruited him into our unit. MSG Breitbach joined our team in Iraq later that year, and served with distinction as my Operations NCO. Another CRU soldier, Sergeant First Class (SFC) Keith Felde, served in the Iraqi Provisional Command (IPC) that preceded GRD. He would serve two additional tours in Iraq supporting reconstruction, including during my tour.

At the conclusion of the weeklong CRC course, the entire team went to dinner at the German restaurant on Ft. Bliss. The beer restriction was lifted, and we all toasted our team. Privately, I was wondering who among us might not return alive. But, my goal was to have dinner in the same restaurant with the same team upon our return.

With the CRC training complete, the next day we were off duty. The weekly CRC flight from Ft. Bliss to Iraq was still 48 hours away. Four of the members of my team were on that flight: CPT Charlie Driscoll, LTC Hal Creel, MAJ Chris Kolditz and LTC George Clarke. MAJ Bob Cabell and I would follow in the coming weeks. The CRU Advanced Party, LTC Whit Sculley and MSG Tom Jankiewicz, had already deployed in January. We were getting early reports back of daily IED and rocket attacks. It sounded like we were all in for some fireworks once we arrived.

In addition to all the training, there were other practical matters I had to attend to. I needed to plan financially for my wife and children. I quickly learned that Raytheon had great policies for Reservists. The company had over 100 Reservists activated at that time. Raytheon continued my medical plan for my family and paid a salary differential, so my family would not take a pay cut while I was gone. And my boss, Ed Woollen, was going to hold my position until I returned. Ed was a member of the Board of Directors and a distinguished Vietnam vet. I also found a USAA life insurance policy with no war clause to supplement military insurance. This took a tremendous load off my mind. It was a blessing knowing that I could provide my family with this additional insurance coverage should something happen to me. Next, I updated my will. I wanted each of my children to have a special bequeath, in case I was killed. Alice and I set up the monthly bills on auto pay, so she would spend less time writing checks each month. I signed a general power of attorney for Alice to take whatever action she needed in my absence.

At Christmas, Alice and I took the kids to visit Santa at the Fair Oaks Mall. We split our time during the holidays between Virginia and Pennsylvania. My cousin, William "Pete" Peters, and his wife, Julie, joined us. We exchanged gifts and took our traditional family photo at Grandma's house in West Chester. But Christmas felt very different. Grandma wasn't there this year. The annual family photo was missing its matriarch. And I wondered if I would be in the photo the next year. Was this my last Christmas with my family? And would Kevin survive another year?

I went on a military leave of absence from Raytheon in January 2004 and spent most of that month training up with my teammates. The deployment was becoming more real with each passing day. The insurgency was escalating, and we knew our mission would frequently put us in harm's way. As the date approached, Kevin's health took a turn for the worse. He kept getting antibiotic resistant infections. His blood pressure would swing wildly from over 200 to under 60 in a span of one minute. He was admitted into the hospital. His condition continued to degrade, and he was moved to the intensive care ward.

As my team flew on to Iraq, I delayed for a couple of weeks until my brother's outcome was certain. As the leader of the team, I was quite embarrassed. But the Army agreed to delay my flight date as Kevin, was gravely ill and on a respirator. His survival was uncertain. So I returned to the east coast until Kevin's life or death struggle played out. I would join my team a few weeks later.

It was also time to spend some quality time with friends and family. Alice recommended that I spend a special day with each of my children. It was a great idea. I took my son Kent skiing to Whitetail. I took my daughters, Kara and Katie, to Build a Bear, where we made special stuffed animals for each. Katie made a unicorn, and I recorded my voice in it so she could hear me wish her "sweet dreams" every night while I was gone. My best friend from Henderson High School, Mike Willover, flew up from Florida to meet in Virginia a few weeks before I deployed. We played high school football and lacrosse together. He knew Kevin and my family well. Mike was watching the news on Iraq, and he knew what was at stake.

On February 17, I heard that MG Johnson had fired four military and civilians in GRD. There were now major leadership gaps in the Division. I got the word that the GRD Deputy Commander, COL Schroedel, wanted me on the ground in Baghdad by March 1. After consulting with COL Bill Fritz at USACE and COL Walt Chahanovich, the departure date was pushed to March 15.

I continued shuttling from Virginia to Pennsylvania. Gina was carrying more of the personal care responsibilities for Kevin with each passing day. Every time I drove back home, I wondered what more could befall us. One day after driving back to Virginia I received news from Gina. Kevin had come off his respirator. He had come back from the brink of death several times over the last three years. It appeared he was going to cheat death again. It was a sign that I could finally go.

March 15 was departure day. I played basketball with Kent, Kara and Katie. We took a walk. Katie rode in her Barbie Jeep. I received many phone calls and visits from neighbors. We went to Dulles airport for a long farewell at the gate. A tough scene that every departing serviceman plays out. Kent, Kara and Katie held on to me. It was very hard to say goodbye. Alice was steady and helped the kids, but I knew she felt the burden of what lay ahead for her. The aircraft doors opened, a big lump grew in my throat as I walked away from my family. I was off to Iraq.

The Trip from Peace to War

It was a lonely flight. I was leaving behind everything I cherished and was entering completely unfamiliar territory. I tried to get some sleep. It was probably the most rest I would get for the remainder of my tour.

After stops in Frankfurt, Germany and Cairo, Egypt, I wound up in a large tent in the Kuwaiti desert. It was Camp Wolverine, a large Aerial Port of Departure (APOD). There were 80 soldiers in the tent, it was 01:00, and it was getting cold. Troops don't sit around at an APOD. They flow through it. At 04:00 on March 17, a USAF sergeant came in the tent and read off names. These personnel needed to board a C-130 immediately. My name was not on the list. I went to a mess tent for breakfast at 05:00 and shaved at a field latrine. I returned to the tent and was offered a ride on the 09:00 flight to Baghdad (the aircraft was from the Idaho National Guard). I dragged my bags across the parking apron and loaded the aircraft with several USACE civilians.

Inside, the aircraft was baking hot. The engines were running hard. We packed in like sardines. The woman in the jump seat across from me took her body armor off and struggled to stuff it under her seat. There simply wasn't enough room. I offered to stuff her body armor under my seat. She thanked me. I said, "No, thank you. That body armor will protect my ass when someone starts shooting through the bottom of the plane after we take off." The look on her face was priceless.

After about an hour in the air, the C-130 made several evasive maneuvers followed by a steep dive on approach to Baghdad. I believe we fired flares to distract any heat seeking surface-to-air missiles (SAMs) that may be fired during the final minutes. We landed at 10:50. I offloaded my gear and waited in a gravel parking lot for my next ride.

At 13:30, a bus arrived, and it would take us to the Gulf Region Division in the Green Zone, a protected military enclave inside of Baghdad. We had about ten civilians in the bus. They took seats by the windows. I was the senior military person onboard. The civilian security team leader asked me not to load my weapon. I was offended. I wasn't some green troop. The unstated message was that new soldiers in Iraq might unnecessarily or accidentally fire their weapon during their first Red Zone movement. (The Red Zone refers to areas not controlled by friendly forces. It is "outside the wire".) I gave the security guy a hard look and slapped a 30 round magazine in my M-4 rifle. I took charge because that's what military personnel are trained to do. The security contractor did not understand the chain of command. I told the civilians to pull the window drapes closed so they couldn't be observed or targeted by cars driving by. I took a seat by the bus door and rode shotgun, covering a sector on the right side of the vehicle. We then rode across the most dangerous highway in Iraq without incident.

We entered the Green Zone. My bags were mistakenly dropped at the Coalition Provisional Authority (CPA) in the Republican Palace. With all the looting in Iraq, I thought everything I brought was probably already being sold at a local market. I in-processed at the CPA and recovered my bags. My passport was stamped by the CPA (just in case I didn't believe I had really arrived). I ate dinner in a large ballroom that had been converted to the dining facility.

I made my way back to the GRD HQ (the building was the home of the last monarch in Iraq, King Faisal II) and found my teammate, MAJ Bob Cabell. He showed me a spare bed on the top floor of the building. I looked up at the roof and realized that it would not stop a rocket or mortar from entering. I dropped my bags. We had a fan and a lamp. The GRD Operations Center that I would run was on the lower floor. For the next six months, this would be home.

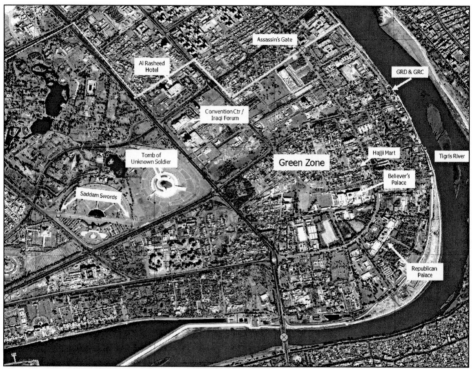

The Green Zone

1

Boots on the Ground

It was my first day in Baghdad. I was two days short of my 44th birthday. It had been a long, tough road to get to this day with the most difficult part of my journey yet to come. I was to lead an Army Reserve team from the Contingency Response Unit (CRU) that was mobilized for nine months and sent to Iraq to help rebuild the country. We were playing in the Super Bowl of reconstruction—the largest and most complex project ever undertaken by our nation. Our mission was to make operational ("stand up" in Army terminology) a new Division while also rebuilding critical sectors of the Iraqi infrastructure.

Like me, my teammates stepped out of their civilian jobs to serve our country. For the last nine years, I had been working at Raytheon, and now served as their Director of Homeland Security. As a major defense contractor, Raytheon provided defense and security solutions to the U.S. Government and our allies. My responsibilities were to develop intelligence and information capabilities to keep our nation secure and to track terrorists. It was a rewarding job, and every day I felt that I was helping to defend our homeland. Now my country called me to defend it while in uniform, as a Lieutenant Colonel and the Operations Officer (G3) of the Gulf Region Division (GRD) in Baghdad, Iraq. The timing for me was terrible. My family was facing some severe medical hardships and still recovering from a natural disaster. I was the member of the family who was trying to piece it all back together but had to leave them behind to fight a war.

* * *

My first official task in Iraq was to take part in a conference call. We had taken over one of Saddam Hussein's palaces on the Tigris River to use as our division headquarters. I sat down with other members of the division at a conference table in his extravagant home and calmly waited for our call to begin.

Suddenly, a loud explosion outside knocked us to the ground as a massive car bomb detonated nearby. LTC Joe Corrigan jumped up and hollered *"Holy shit! That's the biggest one I've ever heard!"* It seemed incredible that despite such a huge blast none of our windows were shattered. Had they been, high velocity glass fragments—like a hailstorm of scalpels—would have carved the flesh off our bodies. Fortunately, the sandbag walls outside the palace absorbed much of the blast. Unhurt, I could feel adrenaline pumping through my body. Though rocked, I was trying to gauge what had just happened by the reactions of the other men in the room. There was momentary shock, not panic. We grabbed our helmets and body armor and went outside to assess the situation. My immediate thought was, "Man, I hope they don't get much bigger than that." This was one hell of a way to welcome me to the neighborhood.

I was unfamiliar with the palace layout, so I followed Joe and MAJ Bob Cabell out of the room and toward the rear exit. Bob's eyes were wide and at full alert. Once outside, the first thing I saw was a big black cloud on the far shore of the Tigris River. I wasn't certain what had been hit, but I knew it must have been something big. Joe had his binoculars trained on the black cloud. I asked Joe and Bob what they thought the target was. Neither was sure. They mentioned there were several hotels and Iraqi Ministry buildings near the area. Then the news came from LTC Vance Purvis, the GRD Intelligence officer. The Mt. Lebanon Hotel in downtown Baghdad was no more. A 1000-pound vehicle borne IED (VBIED) had detonated next to the building. While most hotels that catered to Americans and other foreigners had a protective perimeter and blast walls, this hotel did not have any protection. That made it an easy or "soft" target. All that was left of the car bomb was a crater 20 feet wide filled with debris and water. The attack left at least 27 dead and another 40 wounded.

Blast crater

The Mt. Lebanon Hotel bombing was an early experience that convinced me of the importance of "force protection." Force protection is a series of preventative measures the military takes to mitigate attacks against our facilities. Blast walls and gate guards were fundamental force protection measures. It was something I pushed for during the rest of my tour in Iraq. Over the next six months, I would be within earshot of 150 car bombs and more than 400 rocket and mortar attacks. Our reconstruction mission would be the target of hundreds of attacks that inflicted scores of casualties all throughout the country.

Everyone's agitation over the car bombing lessened, and I realized I had plenty of work to do to get settled in my new position. It was late in the day, but I still hadn't met my boss or received direction from the GRD leadership. I met briefly with Colonel Joe Schroedel, the GRD Deputy Commander, in his office. He had already been selected for promotion to Brigadier General. Colonel Schroedel was only in Iraq for a few months to help stand up the new division. He welcomed me to GRD and immediately got down to business. Intensely focused on the mission, he had a direct leadership style. I prepared to take notes.

"Sir, I need your initial guidance," I stated. COL Schroedel replied, "You need to conduct a right seat ride (coordination to handoff duties) with Joe Corrigan. Pick his brain." Joe was my West Point classmate and had previously been responsible for GRD Plans. He was leaving Iraq soon, and I would now run the G3 shop and be responsible for the division's plans and current operations. COL Schroedel continued, "I want the division command post to look less like an office and more like a Tactical Operations Center." I nodded. I wore a Ranger Tab on my left shoulder, and that qualification meant I was tactically competent. "Ball and Hart work for you," he said. It was a statement, not a question. MAJ Jim Ball was the GRD Current Operations officer. MAJ Ray Hart was now serving as the GRD Plans officer. Since GRD was just standing up as a new division, it had a bare bones staff. I had only two other military personnel in the division operations section. We needed at least twenty more to do the job right.

"The USACE civilians are stressed," Schroedel continued. I sat up. That was bad news. The civilians, all volunteers, were the real reconstruction experts, and they made up 90% of our division staff. We needed to reduce their stress level or the flow of civilian staff may shut off. That would severely degrade our ability to rebuild Iraq. COL

Schroedel continued, *"Your top priority is to stay tied at the hip with the Chief of Staff, COL Dornstauder."*

COL Alex Dornstauder would be my boss. He was a former West Point football player, and his neck was the size of my thigh. COL Schroedel also told me to ask Command Sergeant Major (CSM) Mike Balch what he was doing to get more noncommissioned officers (NCOs) for our G3 team. CSM Balch was the senior NCO in the entire Army Corps of Engineers and was a great asset to GRD. The list grew as the Deputy Commander continued. *"Next, you should meet with Major General (MG) Ronald Johnson, to get more direction."* I got about a dozen other actions that evening; it was a fire hose of information and tasks. I scribbled down some final notes in the book that would become my combat log for the entire tour. When COL Schroedel was done I replied *"Hooah"*, an Army expression for *"I got it"*, and went straight to work.

The next day, I met with MG Johnson, the GRD Commanding General and my boss's boss. I would serve as his primary staff officer, responsible for all GRD operations. He expressed concern about my family and questioned whether I should even be in Iraq. He had been briefed on why I had arrived at GRD several weeks later than planned. I gave him a quick overview of the situation at home. In the months before deploying to Iraq, my family had experienced a number of hardships. My house was hit by a hurricane. A few weeks later, my mother died of lung cancer. My sister and I were now caring for my quadriplegic brother, who was currently gravely ill on a respirator in intensive care. Meanwhile, my wife was raising our three children while also caring for her terminally ill mother. My family situation was severe and enough to make many men bow out of a combat deployment. MG Johnson listened, and then he talked about his own family background and the personal adversity he had faced through the years. It was a rare glimpse of him that few others in his command saw. I felt he was opening up to me, sharing stories that gave us something in common. It was enough for me to identify with him, and it made me feel that I should stick it out even more. He wanted me to take a few days, re-consider my position, and decide if I should stay in Iraq or return home. I had anticipated this question, and I already knew my answer. I said *"Hooah"* and saluted as I left his office.

Two days later, I met again with MG Johnson to give him my decision. *"I have boots on the ground, and my head is in the game— I'm staying,"* I told him. I went over all my reasons. My team was here. I couldn't return to the United States and leave them in Iraq. I could not go back and face their wives and families knowing they were in imminent danger and I was not. If I left GRD now, then someone else would have to extend their tour or deploy to Iraq in my place. It was my turn to be here. And if I went home now, I would probably just be recalled to active duty again a year from now to serve here. The medical situations at home could be prolonged for many months. Yes, there was a strong possibility I was going home for a funeral sometime during my tour. I just needed to call home occasionally to keep in contact with my family. We had already worked this out. I'm here. I am not turning back. I had one more reason for staying that I didn't tell MG Johnson about. My sister had two sons that were Cadets at West Point. I wanted to try to finish this war before my nephews had to see it too.

"Now, let's Git'r Done," I finally said. MG Johnson agreed. The deal was sealed. I was staying in Iraq. "Hooah."

2

An Unbelievable Mission

Our story has never been fully told. The race to rebuild Iraq was a team effort that involved multiple government agencies, ministries and contractors. The size and complexity of the mission was only exceeded by its ambiguity and danger, particularly in the early days of the Iraqi insurgency.

It started out as 2,300 projects, but the list was dynamic. New projects were constantly added while others were dropped. The Division's infrastructure projects provided essential services such as reliable power, clean water, security, basic healthcare, transportation and education that were critical to establishing a peaceful and stable Iraq. Throughout this period, GRD continuously improved an electrical system that suffered from 35 years of neglect. But it was not until after I arrived in Baghdad that I fully understood the scope of this daunting task.

* * *

In recognition of the Gulf Region Division's exceptional performance during combat operations, GEN Casey awarded GRD the Meritorious Unit Commendation (MUC).

An extract of the MUC award justification, submitted by BG William McCoy (the third GRD Commander), follows:

"The Gulf Region Division distinguished itself through exceptionally meritorious service from 1 July 2004 to 1 December 2005. The formation of Gulf Region Division in January 2004 was a consolidation of the Corps' diverse workload in Iraq that included the Iraq Provisional Command, Iraq Reconstruction Office, Task Force Restore Iraqi Electricity, Task Force Restore Iraqi Oil, and various Forward Engineer Support Teams under one command, creating a sustainable, supportable engineer presence. The three districts, Gulf Region North in Mosul, Gulf Region South in Basrah, and Gulf Region Central in Baghdad were formed at the same time.

Whatever the mission may be or what it entails, the soldiers and civilians of this organization are always up to task. They have met every challenge and excelled past conceivable expectations. They have been faced with long hours in poor conditions, but the mission always came first, completion the only course of action. The dedication of the members of this unit and their willingness to accomplish any mission is displayed in their high state of readiness and tireless ethics."

Among the projects highlighted in the MUC award justification were:

- 730 schools
- 280 police stations
- 300 water and sewer projects
- 105 village road projects
- 230 border forts
- 90 railroad stations
- 40 public buildings
- 85 fire facilities
- 15 power generation facilities
- 1,400 electrical transmission towers
- 8,600 kilometers of power cable
- Adding 2,000 megawatts to the Iraqi national power grid
- 25 hospitals
- 155 public health care clinics
- Employing an average of 155,000 workers

The MUC Award did not mention the hundreds of attacks and scores of casualties that were part of the daily struggle to rebuild Iraq. As the GRD Operations Officer, almost every one of these events came to my attention, and they were all very painful. Each day, I felt a personal obligation to do everything possible to keep our personnel safe, so GRD could continue to complete this strategic mission. Unfortunately, the award did not cover members of the Iraq Provisional Command (IPC), Iraq Reconstruction Office, Task Force Restore Iraqi Electricity (TF RIE), Task Force Restore Iraqi Oil (TF RIO), and several Forward Engineer Support Teams (FESTs) that formed the key building blocks of GRD in 2003.

It is also important to note that GRD continued its mission for many years after the December 1, 2005 cut-off for the MUC award. By May of 2009, GRD had completed over 4,500 projects, and hundreds more were in progress by subsequent rotations of personnel. The reconstruction mission has now ended.

Enemies in Iraq

What made this mission overwhelming and almost impossible was that everything we did was inherently dangerous. There were two wars going on in Iraq. There was the one broadcast on CNN and Fox News every night involving conventional military forces. Then there was the less visible war involving the reconstruction mission.

On a typical day in Iraq, U.S. combat forces were involved in 70-110 attacks. On a peak day, there were over 120 attacks. The reconstruction war also had its daily battles. I can only remember two or three days during my tour, when our project sites, personnel, convoys or reconstruction operations were not attacked in some way. Attacks came in every conceivable form: Improvised Explosive Devices (IEDs), rockets/mortars, small arms fire, sniping, kidnappings, beheadings, repair crews ambushed, or workers threatened. Our reconstruction operations, too often, experienced all of these. Some days, I was simply a spectator in the stands. Other days, I was the coach on the sidelines, sending in the right players and calling the plays. And on still other days, I was the quarterback on the field. During my tour, I was probably within earshot of 100-150 car bombs and 400-500 rockets. I can tell hundreds of stories about Iraq—most of them are true!

In 2004, we had three clear enemies sometimes termed "anti-Iraqi forces" (AIF). They were former Ba'ath Party loyalists, Shia militiamen and Al Qaeda terrorists. You could tell which enemy was attacking you by how they did it. Some enemy attackers were in it for the money or power. Some were just criminals. Some were terrorists. It was a daily blend of bad actors, often using religion as a cover to hide their true motivations. All three enemies found coalition reconstruction operations relatively easy targets.

Ba'athists were primarily Sunnis that were loyal political followers of Saddam Hussein. Ba'athists were well-educated and previously held senior positions in the military and Iraqi society. During Saddam Hussein's rule, the Sunni Ba'athist minority suppressed the Shia majority. Under the decrees issued by Ambassador Bremer in the Coalition Provisional Authority (CPA), most Ba'athists were stripped of their former status and barred from serving in the new military or government. The CPA was cleaning house, and the Ba'athists were thrown out with the garbage. They lost control of Iraq's major oil fields in Basrah and Kirkuk. When the Iraqi Army was disbanded, many Ba'athists disappeared from public view with their weapons and ammo, and they started the insurgency in the Sunni areas of Iraq. Ba'athists had nothing to lose and everything to gain by pushing the Americans out of Iraq. They wanted to return to power and the former good life. Having the United States as a common enemy, they formed an alliance with Al Qaeda Iraq (AQI), providing the foreign terrorists with a safe haven to conduct their operations. Ba'athists were the privileged class. They were the military, political, academic and social elite. And they were tactically competent, making them smart and aggressive fighters. They often had nice cars, such as BMWs. So if a BMW raced up from behind you at 100 mph and someone popped an AK-47 out the window and sprayed your vehicle with 30 rounds, you can bet it was Ba'athists. They wanted to live another day, so they would attack and then immediately speed off. One of the things we needed in our reconstruction convoys was a sensor that could detect and track BMWs. I wanted it to tell me where every BMW was within two miles of my current position so I could be looking in the right direction and not surprised by a high-speed "drive-by" shooting.

The second enemy we faced was the Shia militias, particularly those groups loyal to Muqtada al Sadr (Muqti Militia or Madhi Army). The Shia were the majority in Iraq but were often denied education, electricity, and social services. They were sometimes brutally suppressed by Saddam. I often heard reports of mass Shia graves being found. In fact, excavating mass graves became another "engineer mission" that USACE had to support. While the Shia were initially thrilled that the United States overthrew Saddam, they had mixed loyalties and many wanted to exact revenge on the Sunnis. Many of them felt aligned with Iran, which is also predominantly Shia. Some wanted Americans to leave immediately after Saddam fell, so they could control the country. But they lacked the technical competence to run the Iraqi government, military and critical industries. Sadr City was a slum in Baghdad with 2.5 million Shia and a stronghold for militiamen. Shia militias would often start uprisings in Sadr City. I could see and hear the firefights and bombings from the GRD headquarters building. The Shia had less tactical training and would take unnecessary risks, often believing their faith would protect them from harm, or their death would make them a martyr. If a fighter stood in the street—totally exposed with an AK-47 or an RPG pointed at you, it was probably a Shia militiaman. Their tactics and marksmanship were poor. Shia militiamen often died young, but they did so with style. Exposed Shia fighters would quickly draw small arms or sniper fire from U.S. forces. It was a Darwinian process, as only the tactically competent ones would survive. For a few weeks, the Madhi Army wore white armbands as their "uniform" to distinguish them as an organized fighting force. That made targeting them much easier.

The third enemy we faced was Al Qaeda Iraq (AQI). They were mostly foreign-born terrorists that came to Iraq to fight Americans. Al Qaeda probably numbered in the low thousands at their peak strength. But their effectiveness far exceeded their numbers. A stable and prosperous Iraq was not in the interests of AQI. Their strategy was to discredit the United States and the Interim Iraqi Government, by all means possible, including disrupting our reconstruction progress. They were not constrained by the Geneva Convention. They were not held accountable for their actions by the U.N., world public opinion or the news media. AQI teamed with and paid other Iraqi groups to attack Americans. The core Al Qaeda members were ruthless and evil. They were not cowards and were totally committed and willing to die. Many volunteered to be suicide bombers. They slaughtered many innocent Iraqis if they got in their way. They bombed markets, schools and mosques to inflict widespread fear. Their strategy was to create a civil war between Sunnis and Shia to completely destabilize Iraq and force the Americans to withdrawal. That would leave Iraq open to be another terrorist safe haven. They had a propaganda arm and posted videos on the internet of beheadings and executions. They were unbelievably inhumane, and proud of it. Their senseless cruelty was later rejected by the Sunnis who eventually turned on AQI. We knew we were up against Al Qaeda if a car bomb drove up next to a convoy and detonated. Or if soon after we completed the construction of a school, all the teachers were murdered in front of their students. Drivers of reconstruction convoys were kidnapped by AQI and beheaded. If the owner of an Iraqi construction company, under contract to the United States, was followed home and murdered along with his family, it was probably at the hands of Al Qaeda. It all happened. It was the war we saw every day in our struggle to rebuild Iraq, but few in America understood what was really happening.

Diwan School Opening

As the Division Operations Officer, I did not get into the day-to-day management of individual reconstruction projects. That was the mission of senior civilians in our Programs Directorate and the Construction Division. But occasionally my travels or duties required my direct involvement in a specific program. Such was the case with one of the local renovation projects—the Diwan School.

At the end of April, the Diwan School was completed. Diwan was a two-story brick structure about a quarter mile north of the GRD

HQ. It was renovated by the Tama Design Consultancy and Construction Company, an Iraqi contractor. This was an early success story for the reconstruction mission. The project finished on time largely because it was "inside the wire." That meant that security issues at the project site were not a major problem. Projects outside the wire were prone to schedule slips due to inadequate security. The scope of the project included new electrical and lighting, generators, chiller pumps and communications drops. The final interior finish looked professional.

On May 2, Tama Design Consultancy invited GRD personnel to an opening ceremony to celebrate the project's completion. COL Alex Dornstauder and I attended and represented the Division leadership. We had a 30-minute tour of the project including the classrooms, cafeteria, offices and auditorium. During the tour, I learned that the school was famous because Saddam's daughter attended it. There were several buildings on the school grounds. At the end of the tour, Tama Design Consultancy showed us a beautiful brass plaque they mounted in front of the building commemorating the project. We were treated to a nice grilled Iraqi lunch following the facility tour. Several speakers gave remarks in the cafeteria, expressing their appreciation for being able to participate in the project. It was the first civil event I attended since arriving in Baghdad. I could only stay for an hour, but it was refreshing to see a small measure of progress in our mission. After participating in the dedication ceremony, I returned to the GRD operations center with renewed optimism. Not all the news in Iraq was bad. But the mainstream media did not cover good news, such as the Diwan School completion.

Commemorative Plaque

A few days later, Whit Sculley told me that the Diwan School project turned out so well, that it might not be used as a school. The U.N. was considering returning to Iraq and wanted to occupy Diwan as their new headquarters. The U.N. was in Iraq during the previous year, but left after a truck bomb blew up their Baghdad HQ. The top U.N. envoy in Iraq was killed. The U.N. had been strongly encouraged by the United States to set up their original HQ inside the protected Green Zone, but they refused. The U.N. did not want to be associated with the United States and the "invasion". They needed to appear separate and impartial. The U.N.'s political idealism proved tragically fatal. Realists, not idealists, were more likely to survive in Iraq.

On June 24, while the future of the Diwan School was still being debated, a rocket hit on the grounds and killed a local guard. LTC Jim Hampton and I went to the scene after the attack to understand what happened. The round hit the curb next to the guard shack and destroyed a scooter. The only good fortune was that the there was no damage to the school building.

The U.N. delayed its planned return to Baghdad, and I don't know what eventually became of the Diwan School. The war went on, the situation was constantly fluid and there were thousands of other projects that GRD had to focus on.

New GRD Headquarters Project Site

GRD was planning to move our operations out of the Green Zone, and we were building a new Headquarters complex at Camp Victory. Since this project directly affected our entire reconstruction mission, I became personally involved. I led weekly meetings to get an update on the construction progress and visited the project site. Completion of the project drove the timing of GRD's planned move. There were reports of significant quality control problems, particularly related to Iraqis hand mixing tons of concrete.

I usually went by myself to the project site. I arrived unannounced so I could get a realistic perspective of what was happening. It was always hot and dusty. The dust was like a fine talcum powder that got in your eyes and nose. I met with the senior GRD representative and the Iraqi supervisor on the site. The senior Iraqi was usually the owner of the company. He always invited me into his large tent next to the project site. We would drink tea, and he served some dates or other treats. In Iraq, drinking tea is a big cultural ritual. In many parts of the world, making progress is often about relationships, not just about bullets, contracts and lawyers.

I had great respect for the Iraqi owner. If his identity were made known, he would be considered a supporter of the United States and hunted down by our enemies. I often wondered if I would have the guts to do the same thing, if I were in his shoes. We talked about the project, and I'd begin a walking inspection. As I moved about the site, I would greet each worker with *"Assalaam Alaikum"* (peace be upon you) and touch my heart. They would reply *"Wa Alaikum assalaam"* (and peace be upon you). I was trying to bridge the cultural and linguistic gap.

Quality was a constant issue at Iraqi construction sites. This project was no different. I saw concrete inadequately mixed by hand by unskilled laborers. It caused serious construction delays. We also repeatedly emphasized the use of safety equipment to reduce accidents.

On one trip, I arrived at the project site just before an afternoon meal was served. I immediately became their guest of honor. The Iraqi contractor set up some field tables. He walked over to his vehicle and popped open the trunk. Out came a big dish of rice and meat—probably lamb. It was a hot, dusty day, and I wondered how long the meal had been in the trunk of his car. He offered me some yogurt to sip. I had just eaten, but etiquette required me to have a small second meal. It was quite good.

After departing the project site, I stopped at a new aerostat that was being emplaced at Camp Victory. The aerostat, called Saber, was a helium-filled blimp connected to the ground with a tether, flying a high-resolution video camera at 1000 feet. The ground station below it had an operator that could control the camera – pan, tilt, and zoom – to look all around the surrounding area. Electrical power and commands to control the camera were sent up the tether. Video and telemetry came down the tether to the ground station. The elevated camera was intended to detect enemy activity. I was familiar with aerostats, and I couldn't resist checking this one out. I had previously worked on the Small Aerostat Surveillance System (SASS), an Army counter-drug program. And I participated in the world's first aerostat failure review board, chaired by John S. Attinello, the famous aerospace engineer who developed the Attinello flap that enabled the era of modern aviation. I entered the ground station and talked to the soldier operating it. He was new and had little training. I had him slew the camera over to the new GRD HQ project site. It was probably five kilometers away. He zoomed in, and I could see the Iraqi laborers placing concrete and preparing rebar. It was good to know that progress continued even when I was gone.

One week, COL Joe Schroedel, joined me on the trip to the new HQ site. We walked through the new buildings and assessed the progress. We had an interpreter with us, and COL Schroedel said he wanted all the workers assembled for a few minutes so he could address them. The Iraqi construction crew gathered around. Many were low skilled and spoke little English. But they were proud of their work. COL Schroedel's speech was short, but he took his time. Each line was translated for the workers. It went something like this: *"Thank you for all the hard work you are doing to rebuild your country. This is an important time in your history. You are the ones that are making Iraq a better place for your families and your children. And I want you to know that we have left our families, to come to Iraq, to help you rebuild your country - the way you want it - so that you may have a better future. And when we are done, we will be able to go home to our families."* The body language and smiles were telling. It resonated. Joe Schroedel hit a home run with his brief and clear message. And he related it to something we all understood—our families. We left the project site and made a rare stop at the Camp Victory Post Exchange, about two miles away. We bought a few cases of soda, came back to the project site and gave them to the workers. It was a rare treat for the Iraqi workers that capped off a good day for GRD and our Iraqi partners. We made some progress.

1st Cavalry Division

The Commanding General of the First Cavalry Division (1CD), MG Peter Chiarelli, visited the GRD headquarters on April 22, 2004. MG Chiarelli brought with him his senior Engineer officer, COL Ken Cox. Both of these guys were very impressive.

The catalyst for the meeting was a recent attack on a reconstruction convoy that made General Electric pull their electrical power experts out of Iraq. The convoy had no military escort, which was typical in the early days of reconstruction. There just weren't enough troops to escort contractors. Consequently, contractors were often contractually responsible for their own security at project sites and during movements. The convoy was hit and several GE employees, possibly subcontractors, were killed. It took a while to recover the dead. GE management decided the risks in Iraq were not worth the rewards, and they pulled their personnel out of the country. This was a strategic setback for reconstruction, as these power experts were needed to commission new electrical plants.

MG Chiarelli opened the meeting by making a pledge to GRD. He would provide all available resources from the 1st Cavalry Division to escort reconstruction personnel to project sites. The GE disaster simply could not happen again. It was the first time a maneuver Division Commander made such a broad commitment to the Reconstruction mission. MG Chiarelli justified his decision by delivering a powerful message to us. *"You are the only thing that I have to throw at the Iraqi people to save my soldiers' lives."* The silence in the room was deafening. He went on to discuss how we can win battles with military forces, but needed to provide essential services to "win the peace" in Baghdad.

Sewage canal through the middle of the street in Sadr City

Chiarelli gave us specific examples of the poor state and decay of infrastructure in Sadr City, a major slum of several million Shia in northeastern Baghdad. Every morning, 1CD patrols found two or three dead Iraqis in the streets. Young men electrocuted trying to hook their homes up to nearby power lines. Public health was deplorable. The sewers were backed up. Trash was everywhere. Raw waste sat in large pools in the streets. I had recently flown over Sadr City in a helicopter, and the odor at a height of 5,000 feet was still overpowering. And there was no publicly available clean water. Sadr City was a cesspool. MG Chiarelli argued that the best way to get the Shia population supporting the U.S. was to lift them out of the squalor that they faced every day. Chiarelli was right—fixing the sewers in Sadr City became a strategic initiative that would employ many of the Shia fighters, which reduced violence and improved the local living standards.

The 1st Cav was organized in Brigade Combat Teams (BCTs). COL Robert "Bruce" Abrams, a West Point classmate, commanded the 1st Brigade Combat Team (BCT) that was responsible for security in Sadr City—a seemingly impossible task. COL Abrams came from a distinguished military family. His father, GEN Creighton Abrams, was the Army Chief of Staff in the 1970's. The M-1 Abrams tank was named in honor of his father, whose distinguished service and legendary actions in World War II included the Battle of the Bulge. COL Abrams and I were in the same company at West Point for four years, and I had only seen him once since graduation—now, in Baghdad, Iraq.

The Iraqis did not initially believe that the U.S. was committed to help them. They measured American progress and commitment every day by looking at the massive Daura power plant. There were four large smoke stacks at Daura that dominated southern Baghdad. The Americans claimed they had been rebuilding Iraq for over a year. Yet Daura still had only one smokestack billowing smoke. The Iraqis expected to see all four smokestacks working by now.

MG Chiarelli was a big believer in using reconstruction to get military-age males employed. Unemployed Iraqi men were the recruitment pool for the militias and insurgents. The U.S. wanted to hire them first.

The enthusiasm and commitment of MG Chiarelli and COL Cox was inspiring. 1CD leaders planned to embark on a massive campaign to provide essential services to Baghdad, with a main focus on the Al Rasheed District while COL Abrams would do some work in Sadr City. To support this effort, major Iraqi Relief and Reconstruction Funds (IRRF), provided by Congress, were reprogrammed. Some large projects were cancelled in favor of smaller ones that helped Commanders be more responsive to local needs. There was an imbalance of resources. While large infrastructure projects were needed, they typically took a long time to get started, creating a lag in hiring Iraqis. Smaller projects had an immediate local economic impact. The original reconstruction plan was for the U.S. to focus primarily on big infrastructure projects, while our coalition partners and other nations would connect the local villages to the infrastructure. But the rest of the world did not put up much funding, leaving a huge gap in the reconstruction plan. Consequently, the Iraqi people were largely disconnected from power, potable water, and sewers. The U.S. would now close this gap, funding smaller projects by shifting U.S. funds into the Commander's Emergency Response Program (CERP).

The 1st Cav leadership and their reconstruction model were outstanding. They established "Task Force Baghdad" to focus on providing essential services in the Iraqi capital. They teamed the 1CD's combat engineers with the GRD "builders", USAID, the State Department, contractors, and Iraqi officials to achieve "unity of effort". The efforts of 1CD Engineer Battalion Commanders, LTC Barrett Holmes (20th Engineer Battalion) and LTC Chris Martin, were critical to the success. They teamed with the GRD Area Offices, integrated the management of all the projects and shared a common operating picture of reconstruction. The Central District of GRD reorganized its Area Offices, and aligned each one with a 1CD Brigade Combat Team (BCT). The BCTs provided security, command, and control for GRD and others. And in return, each BCT Commander got a dedicated slice of GRD supporting it. CPT Chris Grose was one of the GRD liaison officers to the 1CD.

The 1CD model proved highly effective, and they were finally able to Git'r Done. The integrated team created a large public works and jobs program and hired thousands of Iraqis. One of the keys to getting the sewers flowing was providing dedicated electricity for the pumping stations. The projects included rehabilitating sewers, improving water and electrical distribution, constructing desperately needed health clinics and renovating a hospital.

The Mahdi Army, led by Moqtada Sadr, directed militiamen in two uprisings in Sadr City in April and August of 2004. Each time, the 1CD picked up weapons and successfully fought the militia. The 1st BCT lost several soldiers in April and hundreds of Madhi Army militiamen were killed. Targeting them was made easier because the militiamen wore a white armband to identify themselves. When the fighting quelled, the 1CD picked up shovels and went back to work fixing sewers and electricity. It took time, but 1CD eventually overcame significant mistrust by local Iraqis. The locals were tired of the fighting, and the construction work provided a productive alternative–a decent job that gave them dignity and earned them some respect.

Bringing essential services to Al Rasheed and Sadr City was an almost impossible task, but the 1CD persevered over many months. Water, electricity, sanitation services and health clinics were made available to hundreds of thousands of Iraqis. The efforts of Task Force Baghdad made a dramatic improvement in reducing the violence and improving the local living standards for the city's most impoverished residents. The security gains were stunning as the number of local attacks against U.S. troops fell from well over 100 per week to less than 10.

Rock Stars of Baghdad

Another aspect to our mission that made it more unbelievable, bordering on surreal, was the constant access and engagement with distinguished visitors and senior leaders. It seemed like every official wanted to play in the sand box. Scores of Official Visitors and Congressional Delegations (CODELs) flew into Iraq to get an "on the ground" assessment. Their trips were brief, and they often flew back out the same day. Their visits were so quick, and they were so well protected, I don't see how they could really get a good sense for the daily life. But, many of them could claim that they were in Baghdad, as if to imply they were combat tested experts on the war.

In industry, similar behavior is observed in many business meetings and is likened to the actions of a seagull. Fly into the meeting, squawk loudly, eat some food, take a crap, and fly off. The CODEL parade was continuous. But leaving Iraq the same day did reduce the force protection burden that VIPs placed on the warfighters.

There was another tier of VIPs in Iraq, senior military, diplomatic and political leaders that lived in or spent extended time in Baghdad. Being the Division Operations Officer, I was honored to serve with and meet many of these distinguished officials. I refer to them as the "Rock Stars of Baghdad".

The most senior engineer officer in the Army is the Commander of the U.S. Army Corps of Engineers (USACE). He is referred to as the Chief of Engineers. Given his position and the strategic reconstruction mission that his team was performing in Iraq, the Chief was a Rock Star at GRD. During the first part of my tour, it was LTG Robert Flowers. He met with my CRU team in his Command Conference Room in Washington D.C. a few days before we mobilized to Iraq. Two months later, he visited GRD in Baghdad. When LTG Flowers retired, LTG Carl Strock became the new Chief.

LTG Strock was already a Baghdad veteran, and he returned to Baghdad in August to visit the GRD civilians and soldiers.

MAJ Erik Stor speaking with LTG Strock

Other senior military commanders that I met or briefed included LTG Sanchez of CJTF-7, GEN Casey of MNF-I, LTG Petraeus of MNSTC-I, and LTG Metz of MNC-I. Many of these senior leaders were on the receiving end of a daily or weekly "Reconstruction Update" that I gave at the Republican Palace or at Al Faw Palace. I am certain they don't specifically remember me. I was one of several officers presenting briefings, and we all had short hair and wore desert camouflage uniforms.

I also had an opportunity to meet a few political leaders. On Easter Sunday, I attended services in the Republican Palace and stood next to Ambassador Bremer. At the time, he was the Interim Authority in Iraq. I had met with Ambassador Bremer when he and I were working in industry before the war and wanted to reintroduce myself. But the timing wasn't right. We were both observing a solemn religious service. He had the weight of the world on his shoulders. And I felt like I did too—I knew later that same day we would have to take a gravely wounded member of our security team, Hendrick Johannes Visagie, off life support.

The new Iraqi Prime Minister, Iyad Allawi, visited GRD in June. The GRD leadership was thrilled to meet him as he toured the Brown Palace that we occupied. But the purpose of his visit was to politely tell us to vacate our HQ building so it could become his official residence. It was his courteous way to serve GRD an eviction notice.

I briefly met Colin Powell, the Secretary of State, outside the Republican Palace when he visited in late July. A sea of soldiers and civilians were near him. Secretary Powell made some remarks along with Ambassador Negroponte and then walked around the grounds. He happened to approach me, extended his hand and said, "How are you doing, Colonel?" His presence and greeting were just inspiring. He had no idea who I was, but he saw my uniform and recognized my rank. He used the word "Colonel" as if it were my first name. I don't remember exactly what I babbled in reply, but I'm sure it was something safe like, 'It's an honor to meet you, Sir." And it was.

3

The Clash of Cultures

Skin in the Game

In 2004, Iraq had a melting pot of reconstruction personnel from numerous agencies. U.S., coalition and non-governmental organizations (NGOs) were all struggling to rebuild the country. The players came from multiple agencies, with different authorities and funding sources, and diverse amounts of experience all trying to work in a loosely federated way. No organization owned the entire reconstruction mission, and this resulted in significant interagency friction and cultural clashes. I will not pull any punches in my account of the situation.

The State Department and the U.S. Agency for International Development (USAID) probably had the personnel that were most experienced in rebuilding third world and post-conflict countries, but both of these organizations lacked the capacity, commitment and tenacity to rebuild Iraq during a broiling insurgency.

The Defense Department had the capacity and tenacity to operate in a war zone, but they had less experience determining how to rebuild an entire nation. The military historically trained its forces to kill people and break things. Then it went home. DOD exercises never focused on fixing things after the hostilities ended - often referred to as "Phase IV operations". Quite simply, the losers had to rebuild their own country.

Because DOD was willing to operate in a hostile environment and put its personnel on the ground in harm's way, it led the reconstruction effort by default. This resulted in a very steep learning curve that significantly contributed to the strategic setbacks that we incurred during the war. GRD was on the bleeding edge of the DOD reconstruction spear.

GRD carried the largest burden of the reconstruction effort. In 2004, GRD electrical projects put about 80% of the new megawatts (2200 of the 2600 MW) on the Iraqi power grid. We were transparent and openly discussed both the progress and setbacks of our projects. GRD would assume significant security risks. We traveled out into the Red Zone every day, and we drove our projects toward completion. We came from a warrior culture and suffered losses. Our mission was to lean forward in the foxhole and to Git'r Done.

The culture in USAID was vastly different. The priority was to avoid casualties at all costs. USAID employees had better living quarters, few Red Zone movements, less stress and a mandatory day off work each week where GRD had none. They were risk averse and slow to engage with boots on the ground. As a result, USAID, and many of its contractors, stayed hunkered down in their offices. They were much better at updating project plans than achieving real progress. When a program fell behind schedule, USAID would simply "re-baseline" it to make it appear to be back on schedule, which was a useful accounting technique to erase major program delays. USAID was simply not organized or prepared to execute large projects, and GRD felt it was constantly picking up their slack. GRD tried to help accelerate progress by providing some technical and management staffing to augment USAID Project Office (UPO). LTC Stephen Dunham led the twenty-four GRD personnel assigned to USAID. His role was critical to managing the relationship between USAID and GRD and sharing project data between the two organizations. He provided GRD with some visibility about USAID projects and operations.

USAID and the Ministry of Electricity would rarely disclose the status of their electrical projects, probably because they were too embarrassed. The failure to disclose interagency data made it almost impossible for RIE to get an accurate nationwide snapshot of electrical power generation. The nearby Daura Power plant was a highly visible and critical USAID project for increasing Baghdad's electrical generating capacity. Many Iraqis measured the success of the coalition reconstruction effort by seeing how many of Daura's four tall smoke stacks bellowed smoke. Only one was working, and it provided only a small fraction of the potential energy that it could. Daura was a constant reminder of USAID's inability to maintain schedule for delivering power to the Iraqi people.

At the embassy level, reconstruction personnel focused on the strategic picture. The Iraq Reconstruction Management Office (IRMO) answered major questions including: how much oil was flowing, how many megawatts of electricity were on the national grid and how many Iraqis were employed. The Embassy also focused on getting Iraqi Ministers engaged in the reconstruction mission. However, a colleague assigned to the embassy sarcastically commented, "We produce PowerPoint slides to keep the senior leadership informed".

Hiding in Iraq

I was invited to several strategic planning meetings at the Project and Contracting Office (PCO), where U.S. officials were trying to select the best regional locations that would become the main hubs for future Iraqi reconstruction. To me, reconstruction was a non-lethal weapon best aimed near where the insurgency was hot. New projects could employ young men, and keep them from becoming future recruits for the insurgents and Al Qaeda. Since Al Anbar Province was exploding with violence, my top priority was to put one or more reconstruction hubs west of Baghdad in the Sunni Triangle near Fallujah and Ramadi.

During the meeting, I was surprised when told the State Department's top priority for a reconstruction hub was in the northern city of Irbil. Irbil Province was one of the most peaceful areas of Iraq, largely free of conflict and the economy was progressing just fine without our help. I argued against the idea that Irbil should be a priority reconstruction location. It made no tactical or strategic sense. We had limited resources, and we needed to apply them at the right place.

On my third attempt to squash Irbil from the priority list, the rebuttals became increasingly direct. Irbil was the one location that the State Department demanded be on the list of major hubs. I started to read the body language in the room. Then I just spit out what I was thinking. I said something like, *"Do you mean that Irbil is a nice safe location where officials can be stationed in Iraq, yet live in reasonable comfort and avoid the dangers of the war?"* That comment drew some smiles from the warfighters in the room and made some of the civilians squirm. I knew I had just ripped the scab off that issue, and my position was now quite clear.

One of the civilians in the room explained that the U.S. needed to keep a strong diplomatic liaison in this important area. My reply was, *"OK, that's fine. Put a liaison up there, but let's put the priority reconstruction hub in Al Anbar."* I was clearly an irritant. Someone wanted my concurrence with Irbil, and I wasn't giving it up. There was a hidden agenda, and I wanted all to see it. Sometimes embarrassment can change behavior. The priority should be the reconstruction mission, not personal preferences and creature comforts.

Once I understood the rules of the game, I wasn't surprised to learn that the CPA compound in Hillah near Babylon was also on the State Department list of Reconstruction hubs. I never visited that one, but I heard it was also cozy. I am not against comfort. It helps to recruit and retain our personnel, but the primary consideration for site selection should be based on the needs of the mission. Hillah was much closer to Baghdad and deserved consideration.

Collateral Damage

During my first week in Iraq, I vaguely recalled LTC Joe Corrigan mentioning that the U.S. Embassy was to be built next to the GRD headquarters sometime later that year. It was one of hundreds of items that Joe brought to my attention as he was departing Iraq. The Embassy project was not expected to affect GRD because the plan was to have the Division move from the Green Zone to Camp Victory before the Embassy was complete. Since it was not expected to be a conflict, it was a non-issue for GRD. I had no real details on the scope of the Embassy construction project or when work would begin. When Joe left Iraq in early April, I did not even have an Embassy point of contact in case I had questions.

Well, the insurgency kicked into high gear in April and May. The transfer of power to the Interim Iraqi Government (IIG) became the focal point of the coalition effort. CJTF-7, led by LTG Sanchez, and the CPA, led by Ambassador Bremer were standing down. MNF-I, led by GEN Casey, and the IIG, led by Prime Minister Iyad Allawi, were standing up. There was a new sheriff in town, and GEN Casey told GRD that it would not move. This was a 180-degree change in our plan. GRD now planned to stay at the Brown Palace.

At this point, the construction started on the Embassy Annex next to GRD. And Baghdad had become a hot zone of attacks. Twelve-foot high concrete walls, called "Alaska Barriers", were being installed around the perimeter of the Green Zone. A new vehicle gate was being built on the GRD side of the embassy complex. The access control point into the embassy installed a vehicle trap used to stop potential attackers. Alarm bells immediately started to go off in my head. The Embassy Chancellery would be a high value target for our enemies. All vehicles waiting to get into the new embassy complex would be backed up in a line – forming right in front of the GRD HQ building, and in Baghdad, car bombs detonate at vehicle access control points all the time.

It was clear that the Embassy would be well protected by these new security measures, but in the event of a car bombing at the new gate, GRD would become ground zero. We were cannon fodder. GRD would be an unintended, but expendable, target. Our loss would be considered "collateral damage".

A 1000-pound bomb detonating next to our headquarters would potentially kill 200 USACE personnel and our support contractors from Fluor and Erinys. It would destroy the GRD and GRC headquarters and its leadership, dealing a devastating blow to U.S. strategic reconstruction operations in Iraq.

I voiced my deep concerns about the location of the embassy's access control point to COL Dornstauder. He shared my view, but neither of us were part of the original discussions with the State Department. Those were held several weeks before either of us arrived in Iraq, under the assumption that GRD would be long gone and relocated at Camp Victory. We needed to get some more facts so we could assess the impact of this looming force protection disaster.

I immediately approached the local Embassy staff, and they arranged a meeting with the Regional Security Officer (RSO). I wasn't completely sure what an RSO was, but he sounded like the embassy's head force protection guy. The staff assured me he was their top guy in Iraq and possibly the Middle East. That told me he was probably well up the food chain. Good. That meant he could make decisions.

I met the RSO at the site of the new gate that was being installed, introduced myself and asked him about the scope of the project. I had heard some details, but I had no written documents, drawings or agreements to confirm what was planned.

The RSO confirmed the Gate was going in. I told him that I was gravely concerned that a car bomb trying to get into the embassy would detonate at the gate and destroy our headquarters. He did not like my comments and his tone immediately got hostile.

He made offensive and disparaging remarks about GRD and its commander. He "knew all about our General Johnson." Then he overtly threatened that he could adversely affect my career. I listened to his rant for about a minute trying to determine if this guy was serious. I tried to hold back a big smile. I was biting my tongue trying to stay cool and stay professional. This guy was under a lot of stress, and he just didn't want any delays or push back on his security plan.

The personal threat to my career was laughable. What the hell was anyone going to do to me—shave my head and send me to Baghdad? I made it very clear the security issue wasn't only about protecting State Department employees that worked and lived inside their fortress. He and I had a fiduciary responsibility to protect all Americans, including the lives of 200 Americans in the GRD HQ. The embassy gate risked making GRD an unintended casualty.

After he fired off all his verbal bullets, I told the RSO that we needed to mitigate the risk for GRD. As planned, the security situation was currently unacceptable to GRD. I wasn't backing down, he knew it, and his offensive tone and body language started to moderate. I stated that I needed to know how many vehicles per day were expected to come through the gate, and what security procedures were planned to manage their flow.

The RSO said that embassy vehicles were "pre-cleared", and they would drive thorough GRD's outer checkpoints without being stopped or challenged. The vehicles would then continue to the Embassy checkpoint where they would be stopped at the vehicle barrier, right next to the GRD Headquarters and our trailers, where many of our senior personnel slept.

I told the RSO that the GRD gate guards were under orders to stop and search every vehicle that comes into our compound. We had spike strips and barriers at the GRD entrance. Our guards were armed and had no way of knowing if an SUV approaching our gate was visiting GRD or intended to flow past our HQ and visit the embassy. If it came up to our checkpoint at a high rate of speed, how would our guards know if it was an embassy vehicle or a hostile car bomber? We needed to mitigate this risk.

I agreed with the concept of expedited clearance of VIP vehicles, but I wanted to have one of the embassy's guards on duty at the GRD guard shack to identify clearly which vehicles were theirs. The RSO flat out refused. No embassy guard would be posted in the forward GRD checkpoint. He did not explain why. Perhaps working at the GRD checkpoint was too exposed or dangerous for embassy employees.

If the embassy would not provide a guard at the GRD checkpoint, then I needed an alternate way to notify GRD guards of an approaching embassy vehicle. I asked the RSO for a video camera and radio or phone to link the embassy security team to the GRD guard shack. He appeared to consider that option, but offered no verbal response.

We had about 15 minutes of intense discussion. At the conclusion, the RSO told me to give him a list of what additional security measures GRD needed to protect our personnel. I appreciated the offer. The RSO was going to work with us. I immediately drafted the list and sent it to his attention, but I don't think it was ever acted on. And it may have been for good reason. A few weeks later, the Prime Minister Allawi stated that he wanted GRD to vacate the Brown Palace so he could use it as his official residence.

We would wind up re-locating several blocks away in a less VBIED prone area.

Army versus Navy

The war in Iraq was fundamentally a land campaign. Air support was available for selected units, but never for our reconstruction operations. The majority of the combat effort came from our land forces – Army and Marines. During the daily Battlefield Update Assessments to LTG Sanchez and GEN Casey, I would keenly listen for how the Navy was contributing to this largely land-based fight.

The Navy was patrolling the littoral areas of the Gulf, to prevent smuggling and infiltration. The Navy also flew fighter aircraft along Iraq's oil pipelines to look for insurgents. To me, it did not sound like a good use of the aircraft. I wondered how an aircraft flying at over 300 knots could see individuals on the ground; much less determine if they had a hostile intent. Jet fighters really couldn't hover or land next to a pipeline to prevent an oil attack. However, fighters could see and report an existing oil fire, and that would improve our tactical understanding of what was happening.

To their great credit, the Navy did provide a number of skilled engineer units, called "Seabees", on the ground in Iraq to participate in reconstruction operations. And there were a number of courageous Seabees killed during my tour.

I was once asked how the Navy might provide more assistance to the Army to support reconstruction and combat the insurgency. I jumped on the opportunity. Half-jokingly, I requested that the Navy send a battleship a few hundred miles up the Tigris River and anchor it in front of the GRD headquarters. It could provide GRD waterside force protection, and it could point some big guns at potential enemies to intimidate the hell out them. To me, the battleship was effectively a floating tank. As expected, the Navy dismissed the idea, but such an act would have made the Navy significantly more relevant to the land campaign we were involved in. We could have also used some coastal patrol boats to provide security along the Tigris River.

The "Less than Brave"

As the Division Operations Officer, my duties required me to be on the road several times a week. Traveling outside the wire was an accepted risk. We had to do it to get the job done. My job had a high operational tempo, and there were few breaks. My most important duty was to keep everyone in GRD alive so we could focus on rebuilding the country.

But not everyone's job required frequent travel in the Red Zone. Many civilians stayed in the Green Zone or on Camp Victory their entire tour. Some personnel only traveled in the Red Zone twice: the day they arrived in Iraq, and on the last day when they departed Iraq. Their jobs were much safer. On the contrary, the civilian Quality Assurance representatives, who had to check on dozens of project sites throughout the country, were constantly on the road as were the RIE and RIO teams. Folks that had "Red Zone" jobs belonged to a different culture than those who had "Green Zone" jobs.

As a member of the military, I expected everyone in uniform to take prudent risks. It was a war. We were warriors. We perform our duty and are prepared to give our lives, if necessary. If our duty requires us to go outside the wire, then we must go.

Military personnel can size each other up pretty quickly. Were you living up to the warrior code or were you just avoiding risks and marking time to get home? I am proud to say that most of the military guys I worked with were warriors. The G3 shop was full of them.

But there were a few moments where the comments and the conduct of other soldiers that I served with disgusted me. I bit my lip, and I now regret it. On one occasion, a primary staff officer found out that I was traveling to Camp Victory for a meeting. The officer asked me to take some documents to the Personnel office and work on some administrative issues. Conceptually, I am OK with helping a fellow soldier, but I was working 18-hour days, and this officer was working only 12. My schedule at Camp Victory was full of meetings with senior leaders, involving strategic issues. I had no spare time to do the work of others. When I asked why they couldn't jump into the vehicle with us, the officer quietly but candidly noted that it was too dangerous to travel.

There it was. I was standing in front of a confessed coward. It was a fricking war, and we were soldiers. If GRD had a suitable replacement, we should have put this officer on the first plane back to the USA. The officer had a reputation for frequent whining, but now I had lost all respect for this person. I won't use the person's name to spare them the humiliation and embarrassment, but their reputation was widely known.

I was later asked by the GRD leadership team for an award recommendation for this officer. I was very direct and stated that if this officer came home from Iraq with a medal, it would diminish the service to all those who truly earned it. At most, this officer deserved a Certificate of Attendance. Enough said.

I heard anecdotally of others. "There is no reason for us to go out there and get killed," was attributed to a more senior officer. I didn't hear it first hand, so I will not comment further. These types of comments and incidents were rare, but when they did occur, they permanently burned in your memory.

Celebratory Fire

Iraqis know how to throw a party. And no party in Iraq is complete without celebratory fire. Americans have often seen it on the TV news - when dozens of Iraqis fire their weapons in the air as part of a ritual celebration. It's culturally accepted and a demonstration of manhood. From an American point of view, it is reckless, but also entertaining to watch. It usually happens on Thursday nights because Iraqi weekends run from Thursday to Friday. Most weddings take place on Thursday nights. On Friday mornings, you could find expended rounds laying on the road or the concrete walkways.

Gravity works in Iraq, just as it does in the United States. When small arms, like AK-47s and pistols, are fired into the air, the rounds will come back down to earth. Every week there are probably dozens of Iraqis hit with bullets fired indiscriminately into the air. Many of the random victims die because the incoming rounds often cause head wounds. Our troops were certainly not immune from being struck by the returning rounds.

I am aware of four personnel hit by celebratory fire at or near the GRD HQ vicinity. One round came through the roof of a trailer and struck the victim in the chest. Much of bullet's energy was lost flying through the air and penetrating the metal roof. As a result, the victim only wound up with a major contusion.

Another incident occurred right outside our building. Our Iraqi gardener was hit in the lower thigh with a round plunging back to earth. He was lucky—it narrowly missed his head and would have penetrated his skull. I helped carry him to a SUV that we used as a makeshift ambulance. I knew he was going to miss work for at least a week. So before he was driven off, I slipped him a $20 bill – about a week's worth of wages, so he could keep his family fed.

On the evening of May 12, LTC Vance Purvis, the Intelligence Officer (G2) came running into the Operations Office (G3). *"Kerry, you gotta see this! Get out here right now! Put your helmet and body armor on,"* he yelled.

I geared up in about ten seconds and dashed through the exit in the sandbagged wall behind my desk. Outside in the twilight I saw Vance crouching behind a sandbagged fighting position. I looked out at the horizon and there it was – an amazing display of celebratory fire. There were tracer rounds flying skywards from all over the city. There was no way a wedding could be this large, and it was a Wednesday. The scene reminded me of the CNN video of massive anti-aircraft fire on the first night of the Gulf War in 1991. While most Iraqis were firing skywards, some of the enemy were now taking advantage of all the confusion and began shooting directly at us.

Vance and I were both staring at the massive celebratory fire scene and thinking, "What the hell happened?" Uday and Qusay, Saddam's sons, were already dead. Saddam was already captured. Why were so many Iraqis firing tens of thousands of rounds in the air across the entire city?

"Vance, what's going on?" I asked.

"I don't know," he said.

"Damn it, Vance, you're the G2, figure it out. The CG will be asking me for an answer in a couple of minutes!" I yelled.

We both stayed there, behind a small sandbagged fighting position fixated by the lethal fireworks illuminating the Baghdad sky. We peeked over the top and gave each other a puzzled look. Then it began to rain bullets. The first rounds hit the concrete nearby but a few seconds later, they started hitting the roof of the HQ building and were bouncing at our feet. We both sprinted inside the building for more cover.

"You've got two minutes to figure this out," I told Vance. Vance replied, *"Hooah."* He grabbed the phone and called Multi-National Force- Iraq (MNF-I) for an explanation of what was going on.

Meanwhile I was thinking, "Who did we kill or capture?" "Did a major Al Qaeda terrorist surrender?" "Did somebody win an election?" Nothing I could think of made sense.

Vance was across the operations center on the phone asking questions to the MNF-I Force Protection team. I could hear him acknowledge the answer. He hung up and looked me straight in the eye.

"I know what happened. Iraq just beat Jordan in soccer." He let out a huge ear-to-ear smile.

I said something like, *"Holy crap! Are you kidding me?"* We're in the middle of a war, and the entire population of Iraq was watching their national soccer team. I later learned that Iraq actually beat Saudi Arabia in an Olympic qualifying tournament in Amman, Jordan. The 3-1 victory qualified the Iraqi team for the Olympics. And at the end of the game, Baghdad immediately lit up with tracer fire. It was patriotism, Iraqi style.

We had a similar incident on August 21 with massive volumes of fire. Iraq beat Australia 1-0 in soccer. The steel rain fell all around our position again. The next morning, I stepped outside my Operations Center and recovered one of the rounds. It was from a 9mm pistol.

These soccer games tended to unite the different Iraqi factions – Sunni, Shia and Kurds. For a few hours, instead of shooting at each other, they would celebrate together.

4

RIO Tour of Northern Iraq

One week after I arrived at the Gulf Region Division, LTC Mark Schneider asked me to lead a "RIO tour" of the northern Iraqi oil infrastructure. The new Deputy Commanding General (DCG) of Combined Joint Task Force 7 (CJTF-7), MG Graham from the U.K., had recently arrived in theater. CJTF-7 provided the coalition combat power for Iraq, while GRD provided the reconstruction power or "soft power". Conceptually, CJTF-7 was the big stick, while GRD was the carrot. MG Graham needed to be familiarized with the Iraqi oil infrastructure, and I was the senior GRD official that would accompany him on the tour. I'd been in country a full week now and was already considered a reconstruction veteran and an Iraqi oil expert.

Rebuilding oil and electricity were the 1-2 punch in the reconstruction strategy. I knew that RIO, at the outset of the war, was the Restore Iraqi Oil Task Force led by BG Crear. However, RIO now was re-aligned as a Directorate under GRD to provide unity of effort in Reconstruction. The same re-alignment was also happening to the Restore Iraqi Electricity (RIE) effort. At the beginning of the war, Task Force RIE was led by BG Hawkins. COL Todd Semonite was his deputy who earned a legendary reputation for his "Git'r Done" tenacity.

I was surprised that I was asked to lead this effort with such little RIO experience and at first felt uneasy. Mark explained that the other GRD principal leaders were not available. As the Division Operations Officer, I realized this was the opportunity I needed to get spun up on RIO quickly. Mark gave me a RIO "101 course" to help me understand the big picture. Touched on previously, Iraq has the world's second largest known oil reserves. Oil production was critical because it provided 95% of Iraq's income. Without oil revenue, Iraq could not pay its military, police, teachers, and administrators or provide key services to its citizens. Quite simply, without oil Iraq would not have a viable government.

Fortunately, a civilian RIO expert, who could answer any technical questions posed by MG Graham, would accompany me. We also had a Public Affairs official, Ms. Or, covering the tour. The two-day trip would start in Baghdad on April 3. I'd fly due north on Royal

Jordanian Airlines to Kirkuk, near the northern oil fields in Iraq. This chartered commercial aircraft was dubbed "RIO Air". The next morning, two helicopters would pick up our team and fly us northwest to the relatively peaceful city Irbil, where we would pick up MG Graham. Next, we'd head west toward Mosul to refuel, and then north to Harbor Gate on the Turkish-Iraqi border. After meeting with some Kurdish political leaders, we would fly southeast to Iraq's major oil refinery at Bayji. Our final leg would take us back to Baghdad.

The first day of the "RIO North" tour, I departed the GRD Headquarters early for Baghdad International Airport (BIAP). We were protecting a number of civilians during the ride. I had to leave my M-4 rifle and 300 rounds of ammo behind, since I did not have a shipping case to put it in, as required during a commercial flight. I felt naked, carrying only my M-9 pistol and 45 rounds of ammo. Once we left the main gate of the Green Zone, the convoy ride to BIAP was fast and tense—the highway was hot with daily attacks so our weapons were loaded and rounds chambered. We changed lanes abruptly and constantly to throw off the timing of a potential IED attack or ambush as we raced toward the military checkpoint at BIAP and cleared their perimeter security forces.

It was early morning when I met the rest of the RIO travel team at the airport terminal. MAJ Carlos Henderson and Navy Lt. Garnett were among the travelers. While waiting in the terminal, one of the RIO civilians, sitting on a sofa, put his feet up on the coffee table right in front of an Iraqi man and his wife. While it was a casual way to relax for Americans, it was highly offensive to the local culture. Showing someone the bottom of your shoe in the Middle East means something like "you are beneath me" or "I walk on you". I quickly walked over and politely told him to put his feet down. He recognized his error and dropped his feet. I thanked him, and he thanked me right back. We did not need to make more enemies, particularly among those Iraqis who were working with us. The episode made me realize that the potential for insult and hostility was everywhere, and we constantly needed to stay alert.

BIAP was in the process of training new Iraqi airport screeners. American trainers, presumably TSA officials or contractors, were standing next to their Iraqi counterparts at the screening checkpoint, providing coaching on what to do. Metal detectors were set up and carry-on bags were being checked. Technically, the Royal Jordanian aircraft I was flying was a commercial flight, and the rules were that we could not take loaded weapons onboard. I wondered what the inspectors were going to say about my weapon when I had to proceed through the screening checkpoint. After a twenty-minute wait, the RIO Air flight was ready for boarding. Our group moved to the security checkpoint. The RIO civilians went through the metal detectors first. Then it was my turn. I started to laugh. I was thinking, "You gotta be kidding me. I'm wearing body armor, a helmet, steel-toed combat boots, carrying a 9mm pistol, and 45 rounds of ammo. There is a good chance the metal detector will go off." And it did. It was reassuring that the metal detector found an anomaly.

The Iraqi screener undergoing training was confused. He wanted me to give up my weapon–I made it clear that wasn't happening. Giving up your weapon in combat is like giving up your child to a perfect stranger. It is an unnatural act for a soldier. I said something like, *"I'm sorry, but surrendering my weapon in a combat zone to a civilian is not part of my job description."* I was going to need my pistol when I landed in Kirkuk, so it was coming with me. The trainer paused for a moment, not sure what to tell the screener. I told them, *"Believe me if I am on this aircraft with my weapon, no one is hijacking this bird today. This will be the safest plane in all of Iraq"*. The trainer told the new Iraqi screener to just wave me through. It probably messed up all the security training he'd been given.

I continued to walk out of the terminal building and toward the two-propeller aircraft parked on the apron. I climbed the stairs, and the pilot, with a foreign accent, told me I had to give up my weapon. I refused. He brought out a lockbox, and told me he would secure it with him in the cabin. I asked the other RIO guys if this was normal practice on their chartered aircraft, and they nodded. I reluctantly locked the weapon in the box, but kept the ammo in my pocket. I stepped inside the aircraft and found a seat next to a window on the left side.

The takeoff from BIAP was exciting. The plane leaped into a steep climb, banked to the left and corkscrewed up and around the airport to escape potential small arms and surface to air missile fire. We probably made six to eight orbits around the airport until we were at a high enough altitude to fly safely on to Kirkuk. My window seat was on the inside of the upward spiral, providing great views of the airport and Camp Victory. While climbing, I could see the high security detention facility where Saddam was reportedly held. For security reasons, he was simply referred to as a "high value target".

It was a 45-minute dash to Kirkuk. When we got into the area, the plane dove sharply, corkscrewing in for a landing. It was the steepest dive I had ever experienced in a commercial aircraft. Having studied aerospace engineering at West Point, I wondered if the wings were designed to take the stress—I didn't need them sheering off during our descent. On final approach, the aircraft flared up and leveled. Out the window, I could see many dingy looking buildings, some oil production facilities, and flames of natural gas being wasted as it was burned off.

We touched down at the airbase—still in the early morning. Kirkuk was oil country for Iraq's Kurdish population. Iraq's northern oil fields were dominated by the Kirkuk field, about 600 square miles with a maximum production capacity of 900,000 barrels per day (BPD). Due to infrastructure limitations and attacks, maximum capacity was not reached. About 500,000 BPD was typical at the time. The city was a heavily polluted industrial area and reeked. The northern field had high sulfur oil, containing toxic hydrogen sulfide gas. This had to be removed before further processing or exporting was possible. (Ironically, my classmate, COL Billy Mayville, led the 173rd Airborne Brigade on a parachute assault of Bashur Airfield opening a front in northern Iraq at the beginning of the war. His brigade later helped to secure the city of Kirkuk. He soon became the de facto mayor of over two million Iraqis. It was an awesome responsibility.)

We stepped off the aircraft and were met quickly by the Kirkuk RIO team. Assigned trailers to sleep in, we dropped our gear and learned that Kirkuk was hit each night with mortars and rocket fire. Four days earlier, an "airburst" exploded over a trailer area housing soldiers from the 25th Infantry Division. Thirteen men were wounded. Two of them lost their feet.

I decided to inspect the airbase to become familiar with the layout. MAJ Carlos Henderson and Lt. Garnett joined me. I was not sure who was responsible for running the base, but it probably wasn't the Air Force—there was no golf course! There were a number of bombed out concrete aircraft revetments (shelters) in the area from the U.S. invasion.

Kirkuk appeared to lack some of the security measures that I was accustomed to in Baghdad. The only barrier separating the U.S. installation from the local population was a light-duty fence and some concertina (razor) wire. The surrounding grass was waist high, making it relatively easy for the enemy to approach the wire undetected and infiltrate the perimeter. If I were running the base, I'd cut the grass or plow earth near the perimeter fencing. I'd hire a few dozen local Iraqis to cut the grass—perhaps by grazing sheep.

Providing jobs for local residents was the best way to produce security in Iraq. The idea was to keep the military-age males gainfully employed so they didn't join the insurgents. I was certain Force Protection officials already considered all of these ideas, and there were plenty of patrols actively working outside the wire to enhance the security.

While driving around the perimeter, we saw a captured Iraqi MiG-23 fighter jet parked near the runway. We stopped near it, and I walked over and kicked the tires. There were bullet holes in the canopy. I climbed inside the aircraft cockpit, tied a red and white checkered Arabian scarf around my head, and grabbed the austere flight controls. For a few moments, I felt like a kid at an amusement park. I snapped a few pictures to send to my wife and kids. Henderson and Garnett posed for a few Hollywood shots as well.

We continued our trip around the perimeter and stopped in a building used by a local infantry unit. I dismounted and walked inside. The interior walls were framed with sheets of plywood, which were hard to find in Iraq. On one wall was a poster of the 50 most wanted Iraqi and Al Qaeda enemy. Painted across the nearby door was the motto, "Git'r Dun." While in the building, one of the infantry squads returned from a combat patrol in Kirkuk. They would often bring back captured AK-47s and bayonets, which they stored in the building. These young soldiers had a dangerous job and my utmost respect.

Git'r Dun

Riding a MiG-23 in Kirkuk

We had a few spare moments, so I stopped in the small Post Exchange (PX) operating out of some kind of trailer or a shipping container. There wasn't much you could buy in Iraq, and I was always looking for something to mail to my kids. I wanted them to remember me when I came home. I expected to find only some razor blades and sodas for sale but was pleasantly surprised. I bought my son a camouflaged backpack and paid a local Iraqi man to monogram it with his name "Kent Kachejian". I also had a couple of my patrol caps monogrammed with my name in Arabic and picked up some jewelry boxes made by local craftsmen for my two girls, Kara and Katie. Buying the gifts made me feel like I was still being Dad, even though I was far away.

When dusk fell on us that evening, so did the mortar rounds. At 20:45, an explosion rocked the trailer area. No one went to the bunker—a sign everyone was getting complacent. At 21:00, a second round hit nearby. This attack was obviously more than a one-shot deal, so we put on our helmets and body armor and headed for the bunker where we conducted a roll call. While in the bunker, a third mortar round hit. A UH-60 helicopter was launched to try to find the enemy. We knew the attackers were probably long gone, so we headed back to our trailers. But at 22:00, another mortar round landed. Over the next 40 minutes, two more detonated. At 23:15, there was another attack, and two more rounds exploded. We spent a lot of time in the bunker that evening. While there, I started to trade jokes with MAJ Carlos Henderson and some civilians to relieve stress and pass the time. We all hoped the mortars would stop soon, so we'd be able to get some much-needed sleep. The last round hit at about midnight. Even our attackers needed to go home to get some sleep.

* * *

The second day of the trip was a big travel day. We would start by flying from Kirkuk to Irbil. I slept in until 06:30, and it felt good. I cleaned up, ate some breakfast, got my gear ready and went to the flight line. I put on my body armor, helmet and earplugs and wore my pistol in a shoulder holster.

At 09:00, we departed Kirkuk in two UH-60 Black Hawk helicopters to begin the official RIO tour. We traveled with two aircraft so they could provide protection for each other. If one went down, the second bird could provide security from the air or land to evacuate personnel from the downed aircraft. Each helo had two door gunners, each manning a machine gun to provide suppressive fire.

Once airborne I could see rows of damaged and decaying concrete buildings in the area that surrounded the airfield. The original structures could have been part of a military base destroyed by the U.S. during the invasion. I could again see the tall flames in Kirkuk burning off natural gas. As we flew toward Irbil, the terrain became rolling. Green grasses were now visible. And as we crossed a wild river, the terrain became steep.

Irbil was one of the most peaceful areas of Iraq. Many State Department officials wanted to be assigned there. If you were stationed in Irbil, you'd get credit for serving in Iraq, yet live in relative comfort and avoid the dangers of the war. Enough said. I found Irbil spelled three different ways in different references and maps: Irbil, Arbil, and Erbil. Perhaps this was a way for local residents to confuse others and keep the city peacefully hidden in northern Iraq.

The terrain below us now was covered with grass that got increasingly more dense and green with each passing mile. I could see wild flowers. Spring was breaking out in northern Iraq. We flew over a mud village, and farm animals were in their pens. Small children ran out to chase our helicopters as we sliced overhead. The kids waved at us wildly, and we waved back. It was a great feeling. They reminded me of my own children, who would run screaming to me every day when I came home from work. There was genuine admiration and support from that village, and it was not an isolated incident. The scene was repeated many times during the flight. The popular support from the children gave me hope that Iraq could one day have a bright future and see America as a friend. It made our reconstruction efforts seem worthwhile.

I saw a large flock of sheep in the open rolling field. A shepherd with a staff was tending to them. It reminded me of a Biblical scene. The shepherd and his flock were removed from the modern world and the politics of his country, and the sheep were grazing peacefully. It was an image I had seen on many Christmas cards, but never expected to witness in person. Flying above this scene made it all the more surreal. I felt as though I had traveled back 2000 years in human history.

We were performing a low-level flight. Each time we approached a major power line, the pilot climbed steeply and banked hard to one side, then dove back down toward the ground. I tightened my safety harness. I didn't want to fall out of the helicopter—that would be both embarrassing—and fatal. Each pop up and banking maneuver was short and intense, intended to avoid hitting the power line, but also to minimize exposure to enemy observation and fire. I realized the power lines we were dodging were probably new ones installed by our reconstruction crews. The threat to helicopters from small arms fire and from portable heat seeking missiles was very real. We had already lost a number of them to hostile fire. (My USMA classmate, COL Brian Allgood, would tragically die when his Black Hawk helicopter was shot down northeast of Baghdad on January 20, 2007. He was the MNF-I surgeon and among the twelve people killed. His wife, Jane, was also my classmate.)

COL Brian Allgood – COL Jim Polo

We flew over a prominent ridge, and I could clearly see tank battle positions dug into the terrain. Some time in recent history, this ground was defended in armed combat. The positions were located for mutual support in a coordinated defensive line. The layout was straight out of a tactics textbook. I heard earlier reports that the Kurds fought against Saddam's forces, and Saddam had used poison gas against them. I suspected the battle positions were related to this internal Iraqi war.

As we continued to move to Irbil, the skies grew overcast, and it started to rain. When we arrived, we immediately saw the Coalition Provisional Authority (CPA) compound at the Khandaza Hotel. It looked like a pyramid-shaped resort on a large hill overlooking the city. I could understand why the State Department was so fond of this facility. We landed on a dirt road on a ridgeline leading up to the hotel. I exited the aircraft and walked up the road to greet MG Graham and his three-man U.K. security team, who were walking towards the aircraft. I saluted and introduced myself. We then boarded the aircraft and were wheels up toward Mosul. The total time on the ground in Irbil was about five minutes.

We continued our flight on to Mosul, Iraq's second largest city, with a population of about 1.7 million people. My two CRU teammates, LTC Hal Creel and MAJ Chris Kolditz, were stationed there with the northern district of GRD - Gulf Region North (GRN). Hal was the Deputy District Commander. Chris was the District Operations Officer (S3). Unfortunately, they were not located at the Mosul Airfield (sometimes referred to as Diamondback). Our RIO tour stop in Mosul would only be a brief one to refuel the helicopters, and I regretted that I would not have an opportunity to check in on them. We landed as planned. Mosul was much cooler and wetter than Baghdad. It was going to take about twenty minutes to gas up the birds. There were no bathroom facilities designed in the UH-60 helicopter. We saw a port-a-potty across the airfield and made a beeline for it. We were now ready for the next leg of the journey. So we strapped in and took off.

We climbed out of Mosul on our way to Harbor Gate and the skies started to clear, As we flew over the city I could see several mosques reaching upwards and much more blue sky ahead of us. We left the urban area, and flew over more grassland that waved with spectacular shades of green. We flew over a massive lake to the northwest of the city; its waters held back by the Mosul Dam. I later learned that the structural integrity of the dam was seriously questioned. I think it had to do with the poor site geology. It was an Iraqi problem—they should have never put the dam in that location. The United States was not signing up to fix the dam. But there was clearly some urgency for the Iraqis to act; a catastrophic dam failure meant much of the city of Mosul would be directly threatened.

Throughout the flight, the inside of the helicopter was noisy; the engine was working hard. Rotor blades chopped through the Iraqi air, and wind rushed through the aircraft as both door gunners had their windows open pointing their machine guns toward potential threats. The two pilots and the two door gunners all wore combat crew helmets with headphones on an aircraft intercom. The four crewmen could speak to each other to coordinate the flying and any shooting, if needed. However, the passengers onboard could not hear these discussions. To protect our own hearing, the rest of us wore earplugs. That meant we could only communicate inside the aircraft via hand signals. At times we would try to shout above all the background noise if something really needed to be said. You could only effectively shout to the person sitting next to you.

After crossing the lake, we flew parallel to a high ridgeline off the right side of the aircraft. It was spectacular scenery. We crossed the mountains and started our approach to Harbor Gate, a major land port of entry between Iraq and Turkey, and a few miles from the Syrian border. Much of Iraq's economy, including oil exports through Turkey, flowed through this strategic border crossing. While airborne, we could clearly see the main highway that connected both countries. Truck traffic on it was backed up twenty miles on each side of the border. Each country had serious economic, political and security concerns along this common border.

Smuggling and terrorism were pervasive problems. The price of gas was $4.00 a gallon on the Turkish side, but only 8 cents a gallon on the Iraqi side. The motivation for underemployed and war weary Iraqis to profit by smuggling fuel to Turkey was high. Many vehicles leaving Iraq were stuffed full of fuel and carrying spare containers intended for sale on the Turkish side. Scrap metal was also leaving Iraq for Turkey by the truckload. I was outraged to learn that some of the scrap being exported to Turkey was from power lines and towers that our RIE Directorate had recently installed in Iraq to improve electrical distribution.

Refugees were also leaving Iraq to find jobs in Turkey. Kurdish guerillas were mixed in with the legitimate border crossers intending to attack targets in Turkey. Turkish border guards had to be alert for all of these potential threats. The Iraqis had their own border concerns. Northern Iraq was ethnically Kurdish. The Kurds did not want Al Qaeda terrorists, military supplies or covert Turkish military forces infiltrating into Iraq. There was historical hatred between the Turks and the Kurds. I was not a scholar on the subject, but I knew a bitter rivalry existed, and Turkey had a deep economic desire to control the rich oil fields in northern Iraq. The Multi-National Security Transition Command-Iraq (MNSTC-I), led by LTG David Petraeus, was working aggressively with the Iraqi Ministry of the Interior (MOI) to improve the training of the border guards. But the guards were modestly paid, so bribery was a pervasive concern.

Meanwhile, GRD was building scores of Iraqi border forts to support their domestic security. But, no matter how hard we plan and try to synchronize the arrival of trained forces with new facilities, snags still happen. In one notable case, forts built for the Iraqi border guards on the Syrian frontier were completed, but the local Iraqi guards were not yet trained and available to occupy them. The Syrian guards reportedly crossed the border and occupied the Iraqi forts because the new forts were much better than their own facilities. Sometime later, the Syrians border guards had to be peacefully evicted.

We approached Harbor Gate slowly, so MG Graham and I could get a good aerial look at the terrain on both sides of the border. I pointed out the twenty-mile backup of truck traffic. One of the vehicles leaving Iraq was on the shoulder of the road consumed by fire. We could not determine the cause. It could have been from an enemy attack, or more likely, an unlucky Iraqi who was smoking in a vehicle stuffed with gas cans. I snapped a few pictures of the final approach.

Our two Black Hawk helicopters landed in an open field, a few hundred meters from the river separating Iraq from Turkey. The beauty of the terrain struck me. The field had knee deep rich green grass and was full of yellow and red wild flowers. A flock of sheep grazed nearby. A dozen soldiers armed with AK rifles, in uniforms that I did not recognize, surrounded our helos quickly. Based on how they carried their weapons and their body language, I assumed they were friendly forces. But in Iraq, it was often hard to tell who was on your side. I reached down and touched my ammo pouch to reassure myself that I had spare clips for my pistol. I asked the U.K. security detail if they knew who the armed soldiers were. They did not. I wished the RIO team had briefed me on this detail. My suspicion was that the troops were Kurdish Peshmerga, and this proved true. They had a reputation for being excellent fighters and saw Americans as their allies.

The author, at left, and a British Captain on the Iraq / Turkey border

COL Rollinston from the U.S. Army drove up to the landing zone and greeted MG Graham with a salute. I immediately noticed that he was not wearing body armor or a helmet—that implied we were in a relatively safe area. He told us to standby for the arrival of a Kurdish delegation that was enroute to the landing zone. A few minutes later, three Kurdish civilian leaders arrived on site with two Kurdish military officers. A host of other support personnel accompanied the Kurds. The Kurds had been abused by Saddam for many years and were now beaming at the presence of a high-ranking coalition official on their soil. Life was clearly getting better for the Kurds. The Kurdish delegation spent about twenty minutes meeting with MG Graham and our team in the middle of that field on the extreme northern edge of Iraq.

Kurdish delegation with MG Graham

There was no time in our schedule for tea drinking and socializing. We bid farewell to our Kurdish hosts and re-boarded the two Black Hawks. Within seconds, we were airborne and dashing across the Iraqi terrain in low-level flight. The door gunners had their machine guns locked and loaded. We flew westward along the Turkish and Syrian borders then turned south toward Bayji, the site of a major oil refinery and the infamous Al Fatah Bridge. Our flight path followed a single oil pipeline that ran for many miles from the Turkish border. I noticed that sections of the pipe were not complete, immediately telling me there were no exports flowing through it. And since 95% of nation's GNP income came from oil, this export pipeline was an important part of making Iraq a viable country.

We approached the RIO Camp located next to the Al Fatah Bridge and made a wide sweeping orbit about 500 feet over the Tigris River to get a good look at the scene below. The Bayji Refinery stood out prominently about a kilometer to the south. The Al Fatah Bridge crossed the Tigris here, and it was one of the few bridges bombed by the Americans during the invasion. The USAF targeting guys took out the bridge and did a damn nice job. Unfortunately, many of the oil lines for northern Iraq ran inside this bridge. If the infrastructure experts had a vote, they would definitely not want that bridge destroyed. Al Fatah was simply too important to the post war recovery of Iraq. The destroyed bridge span was now staring us in the face. Multiple severed oil pipelines emerged from the adjacent span and had melted into the Tigris River.

Al Fatah bridge damage

MG Graham and I exited the aircraft and stepped away from the noise of the rotor blades. We paused for a moment to look back at the destroyed bridge from ground level. I explained: *"Sir, the destroyed bridge span and the severed oil lines have been a major economic issue for both Iraq and Turkey. We really need to get the oil flowing again. We are about to get a detailed briefing on the project to make it happen."* Within a minute of landing a security escort team met us. They hurried us to some waiting vehicles, since they did not want the General standing exposed in the open Iraqi terrain. The threat here was obviously higher than at Harbor Gate. I noticed there was something strange about the terrain. We were on the western bank of the Tigris River, which was covered with grass and bushes. But the eastern shore of the river was dry and barren of vegetation with little sign of life. I couldn't explain it, but the near shore looked friendly while the far shore looked hostile.

The security team drove us a few hundred meters to the heavily fortified RIO camp. The camp had a few permanent buildings and about forty trailers that served as work areas and sleeping areas. Twelve foot high, concrete Alaska Barriers were placed around the perimeter of the camp to provide protective walls for the residents.

We entered a briefing room. It was a small oasis to us. It was air-conditioned, and there was water on the table. There were some maps of the area lying on the table, and all the military guys went straight for them. MG Graham got a front row seat at the map table. He and I spent a few minutes studying the map of the local area. Tactical guys always wanted to know where they were and what was around them—that's called situational awareness, and in combat, it kept you alive.

We were scheduled for a working lunch. The chow came out, and we took seats as the PowerPoint charts hit the wall. It was an hour-long tutorial on oil production and the ongoing repair project at Al Fatah. The briefing was intended to familiarize MG Graham with the major facts and issues. I sat next to him and quietly absorbed all the information being conveyed. The bottom line was that the coalition needed to rebuild the destroyed pipelines at Al Fatah to get Iraqi oil flowing again. Unfortunately, the Iraqi Minister of Transportation would not agree to rebuild the bridge. So the plan was to tunnel the pipes under the Tigris River using a technique called horizontal directional drilling (HDD). The project was important for multiple reasons. The crude oil lines from Kirkuk fed into Bayji, the largest operating refinery in Iraq. The 40-inch Iraq-Turkey Pipeline could provide Iraq with over $7 million in revenue each day. And the completion of the lines would eliminate the need for trucking fuel products throughout northern Iraq.

A HDD project was a complex undertaking in peacetime—in wartime, it was even harder. The project covered a large area and security precautions had to be taken on both sides of the Tigris River since it was a high value infrastructure target for insurgents. It later turned out that the soil conditions on the site were unfavorable to HDD operations, a fact that probably should have been detected sooner. The project spanned several years and was only partially successful in running pipes under the Tigris. The approach was too aggressive for an austere wartime environment. An easier and faster way could have been to close the gap with some tactical military bridging asset. An example would be to use some "Mabey Bridge" that was readily available in Iraq. These modular bridge segments are quickly assembled by engineer troops and pushed across the gap to complete the bridge and allow traffic to pass the same day. Once the gap was closed, we could run the fuel lines over the bridge deck and close the bridge to most vehicle traffic. Theoretically, the oil could be flowing across the river in a few days or weeks. But it's always easier making a decision as a "Monday Morning Quarterback".

The area near the Al Fatah Bridge would become the center of attention later as the major oil pipelines there experienced three successful attacks from June to August. The 40-inch pipe was blown up repeatedly. Flaming oil from the attack flowed into the Tigris River, disrupting operations at the Bayji Refinery just downstream. It was likely an inside job by saboteurs among the Iraqi security patrols.

When the Al Fatah project briefing was complete, we headed back to the aircraft. We lifted off and flew past the Bayji oil refinery on our final flight toward Baghdad. The refinery was an important part of Iraq's critical infrastructure, but alone wasn't enough; Iraq lacked sufficient refining capacity to meet its own needs for petroleum products. Consequently, while crude oil was exported from Iraq, several finished products, like gasoline, had to be imported.

We sped southwards and flew near a burning oil fire north of Tikrit, likely another oil pipeline bombed by insurgents. We entered the infamous Sunni Triangle—the general area where Saddam Hussein was captured a few months earlier. Our route flew past cities like Samarra and Balad. We followed the river valley that became lush with vegetation; there were miles of densely packed palm trees below us. It may have been a huge tree farm where the Iraqis grew dates as a crop. We were now in the historically famous Fertile Crescent—the area between the Tigris and Euphrates Rivers.

As we approached northern Baghdad, I saw the city was dusty and had sprawling outdoor markets. I noticed the high number of satellite dishes that were on the rooftops of all the buildings and homes and learned these antennas were banned in the Saddam era, but now the Iraqis were "getting connected." Given our altitude, I expected to receive small arms fire from the city, but we returned to the Green Zone unscathed.

MG Graham, Carlos Henderson and I landed at Washington LZ a few minutes later. We agreed it was a good orientation for Northern Iraq. What I learned about the Iraqi oil infrastructure during this trip would be useful in my new job as the GRD Operations Officer. Every morning I had to brief LTG Sanchez and other senior military leaders on Iraqi reconstruction, and every afternoon I prepared strategic summaries for MNF-I that were presented to the Secretary of Defense and occasionally the President. We saluted and moved on to our next mission. I immediately headed back to the GRD Operations Center. The tactical situation in Baghdad was becoming red-hot, and the next few months were going to be incredibly difficult. At least now, I had a good understanding of the role that oil played in the broader strategic picture.

Carlos Henderson and MG Graham – RIO tour complete

5

Contractors and Civilians on the Battlefield

The reconstruction of Iraq was the largest project, of its type, ever undertaken by our nation. The U.S. military could not do it alone – nor had they trained to perform the mission. It required a rapidly formed federation of organizations from DOD, State, USAID, numerous Federal Agencies and contractors.

Performing this daunting mission required a massive mobilization of thousands of contractors from several nations and U.S. Government civilians from multiple agencies. Many of them came because the opportunity to rebuild Iraq was challenging, exciting and financially rewarding. But it was also inherently dangerous. Putting that many civilians on the battlefield was a huge task and a necessary risk, but it presented a number of serious security and policy issues.

Civilians on the battlefield performed numerous functions. Thousands of civilians, both government and contractors, served in technical and administrative positions as Program Managers, Architects, Engineers, Technicians, Quality Assurance Representatives, Contracting Officers, Counsel, Interpreters and Logisticians. Another critical function was security. Due to a lack of troops, almost all security for reconstruction projects was outsourced. Contractor security teams protected convoys, escorted workers and diplomats, and guarded key infrastructure, facilities and work sites. Even the FBI was operating in Iraq collecting evidence and conducting investigations. I first learned of this when I ran into Jorge Garcia, an FBI agent and West Point classmate, at the Al Faw Palace the week I arrived.

The population of U.S. and coalition contractors exploded as billions of dollars were pumped into supporting the military and reconstruction efforts. Many foreign contractors came from the U.K., India, South Africa, Philippines, Lebanon, Kuwait, Ukraine, Iraq and scores of other countries. In response to the deteriorating security situation, security contractors began to proliferate. But demand still outstripped supply. Companies like Triple Canopy, Blackwater, DynCorps, Fluor, Kroll, ArmorGroup, Erinys, and Aegis operated throughout the country. In 2004, Task Force Shield alone had 14,000 security contractors guarding oil facilities and pipelines. As the GRD Operations Officer, I had continuous contact with civilians performing many of these functions, but foremost on my list were the security contractors. Reconstruction operations simply could not succeed without them supporting our mission 24/7.

Contractors from France, Russia and China were also interested in winning some of the reconstruction contracts funded by U.S. taxpayers. But I noticed few winners in this group. Most Americans were still fuming mad at how badly the governments of these countries maligned the U.S. at the beginning of the war. Their theatrical anti-American actions left deep scars on our bilateral political relationships. The real motivations of these countries became quite clear much later, when an investigation found they had been getting illegal kickbacks from Saddam in the U.N.'s Oil-for-Food program. Saddam had been paying them off. The U.S. invasion threatened to shut off their profitable bribery schemes. I was not involved in the selection process, but I am sure there was little interest to award major U.S. contracts to the self-serving nations that had ridiculed the United States.

I'd like to highlight the contributions of Iraqi contractors who played a huge role in rebuilding their own nation. Iraqi contractors who worked for the U.S. put their lives in real danger, and they faced constant threats. If the insurgents or foreign terrorists knew their identities, Iraqi contractors were ruthlessly kidnapped, tortured and murdered. We had to keep the identities of Iraqi contractors secret to protect them.

There were many other civilians that visited the battlefield, including the Press, Congressional Delegations (CODELs) and Official Visitors. Many of these battlefield tourists diverted critical helicopter support away from the main military effort. Entertainers helped to support the health and welfare of the troops and were always welcome.

Managing Risks to Civilians

The risks and threats that a civilian faced depended largely on where he lived and worked and what his job was. In the case of reconstruction operations, civilians were spread across Iraq. They were working in Baghdad, Mosul, Tikrit, Fallujah, Basrah, and border areas supporting over 2,300 projects, improving infrastructure sectors like Oil, Electricity, Public Works and Water, Transportation and Communication, Security & Justice, Health and Education.

Civilians that lived or worked in less secure Red Zone areas were particularly vulnerable. These were mainly contractors. The U.S. Government took precautions to provide good security for its own civilian employees. Consequently, the vast majority of civilian casualties were contractors. Near the end of my tour, the GRD Safety Officer reported USACE contractor casualties at 45 killed in action (KIA), 82 wounded in action (WIA), 12 accidental deaths, and 23 accidental injuries. Many of the accidental deaths and injuries were armed contractors that committed fratricide during a negligent discharge of their weapon (that means they accidentally shot each other). On the contrary, during this same period, USACE civilians suffered no deaths and had 6 wounded in action and suffered 12 injuries from accidents. The statistics just cited only pertain to USACE contractors. Iraq-wide, there were hundreds more contractor deaths. And these figures do not reflect scores of overt threats made against reconstruction contractors. This was all happening long before the mainstream media became aware of the story.

The enemy intentionally attacked civilians

There were several reasons contractors suffered significantly higher casualties than their Government counterparts. Contractors inherently lacked intelligence on enemy locations and activities; they had weak command & control; they had poor armor protection; they had inadequate firepower; and they exercised poor operational security. All of these factors made contractors living and working outside the wire easy targets for insurgents.

Protecting civilians became a critical issue for GRD and for me personally. Over 90% of our work force was civilian. Most civilians were not obligated to work on the battlefield. If the conditions were too risky, they could just ask to leave Iraq. There were a number of key issues we looked at when considering force protection for civilians. Should civilians wear uniforms? Where should they live? How do we protect them on project sites or during convoys? Would civilians be permitted to carry weapons? May they consume alcohol?

USACE civilians and some contractors were required to wear the same desert camouflage uniforms (DCUs) as worn by our troops. The argument for wearing DCUs was "to reduce the risk of fratricide". U.S. troops would clearly recognize that civilians in uniform were friendly personnel and would be unlikely to accidentally target them in an engagement. The counter argument was that civilians wearing uniforms were "more likely targets of insurgents and terrorists." Both arguments were valid. The better choice really depended on the tactical situation. Both the military and GRD civilians wore body armor when traveling in the Red Zone. Body armor was essential and protected the lives of everyone. Since everyone in GRD wore uniforms, body armor and helmets, at first glance, it was visually hard to distinguish the GRD military personnel from the civilians. The key difference was that the military personnel also carried a weapon, often a 9mm pistol in a shoulder holster.

GRD Headquarters Staff

Deciding where the civilians should live in a combat zone was a huge force protection issue. The safest place to live was "inside the wire". That means living inside a protected garrison or project site.

For GRD, all of our civilians lived inside the wire. Due to a lack of space on military facilities, several contractors in Iraq established their own guarded compounds. GRD's security contractor, Erinys, maintained a private compound located in the Red Zone. Given a choice, civilians will prefer to live in a hotel, because they are comfortable and have amenities. But Iraqi hotels were subject to frequent attacks and the level of security around hotels varied. The Al Rasheed was inside the well-protected Green Zone. But hotels are typically much taller than the surrounding buildings, so they were often targeted and easily hit with horizontally fired rockets.

The Al Rasheed sustained multiple rockets hits

The Sheraton Hotel was just across the Tigris River from the GRD headquarters, and it had a small military force protecting it. From my location, I had clear line of sight to the Sheraton, and it was hit with rockets several times during my tour. One attack occurred on April 14, 2004. The rocket severely damaged the building, including at least one room occupied by a USACE civilian who left for work only ten minutes before the attack. Due to their location and relative height, the Baghdad and Palestine Hotels also presented easy targets for enemy rocket attacks. The worst hotels to stay at were those that had little or no perimeter protection. These were called "soft targets" as car bombs could roll right up to the front entrance. Such was the case with the Mt. Lebanon Hotel. It was hit with a 1000-pound

VBIED on my first day in Baghdad, leaving behind a massive crater. The attack killed thirty-four civilians.

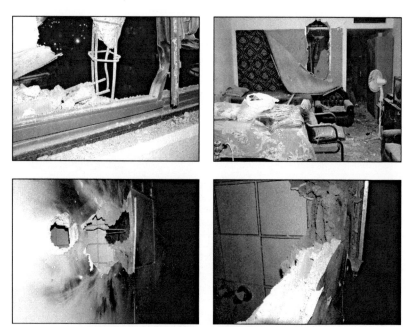

Sheraton Hotel rocket attack – room damage

Most GRD personnel were housed in a commercial trailer with several others. The trailers were thin and provided little ballistic protection. We hardened the exterior walls by stacking sandbags around the trailers to a height of eight feet. The sandbags could stop high velocity flying objects, such as bullets or razor sharp shrapnel from a nearby explosion. But there were hundreds of trailers parked inside the Green Zone that required sandbag reinforcement. So hundreds of Iraqi laborers were employed for several weeks just filling and stacking tens of thousands of sandbags around these trailers. In fact, scores of military personnel had to pull guard duty inside the Green Zone just to supervise all the Iraqi sandbaggers. At the time, we had no real solution for a rocket or mortar coming through the roof of a trailer. As with the walls, one quick and affordable idea was to put sandbags on the roof of the trailers. But heavy sandbags raised the risk of the roof collapsing on the personnel inside. So trailers remained unprotected from an aerial attack. We just bet on the "big sky, little bullet" theory–hoping that an incoming round did not hit inside the eight by ten foot space where we slept. If it did, your time was up. But the damage from the explosion would be contained by the sandbags around your trailer. Even rounds from celebratory gunfire would penetrate a trailer roof, but their entrance was far less dramatic than a 122mm rocket. Much progress was made in later years to improve "overhead cover" on key facilities, but I cannot elaborate any further.

Some civilians wanted to carry a personal weapon for self-protection. This was a major policy issue, with legal and contractual implications that quickly went into command channels. Several factors had to be considered to make the right policy determination. What was the principal duty of the civilian - security or technical? Were they working inside or outside the wire? If civilians carried weapons, were they now combatants under the Law of Land Warfare? What weapons could be carried? Would there be confusion if a civilian carried an AK-47, the same weapon often used by insurgents? What would be the source of ammunition for civilians? Standards for weapons training, regulations, and safety were other huge issues. In GRD alone, we had a couple dozen accidental discharges of weapons that killed at least 10 guards and wounded more. Would there be Rules of Engagement (ROE) for armed civilians? If armed military and armed civilians were in a convoy that was attacked, could the military direct the fires of the civilians? Would this action be a violation of the Geneva Convention? Did this make civilians armed combatants? The policies for these issues were ambiguous and probably for good reason. I even had an incident where a civilian sniper asked me for permission to engage a potential enemy target (permission was denied). And no one raised any policy issues when contractors picked up weapons to re-secure the Al Kasik Iraqi Army base after five thousand Iraqi troops deserted when two truck-bombs hit the dining facility and HQ building. This contractor action was widely viewed as self-defense. In general, the GRD policy was that security contractors could carry weapons; no other civilians in GRD were permitted to carry arms. The policy probably varied in other commands.

Hostages in Iraq

In the spring of 2004, hostage taking, seen as a profitable industry, was a widespread practice in Iraq. There was no effective law enforcement. In fact, there were cases where hostage takers presented themselves as Iraqi policemen. Many civilians, some supporting our reconstruction operations, were taken hostage. Some of the victims were offered for ransom. Foreign hostages were sometimes sold to terrorists and beheaded and others met different fates. But in combat, sometimes Murphy was on our side. This was the case of Thomas Hamill, a Kellogg, Brown & Root (KBR) employee, who was taken hostage in Baghdad, and accidentally rescued weeks later by a misguided military patrol.

The Accidental Rescue

When an Iraqi oil pipeline was attacked, we normally sent out a military patrol to verify the site of the attack, secure the repair site, photograph the damage, and report any important facts that may affect the repair. They would also recon the roads in and out of the area, to make sure no IEDs or ambushes were waiting for the pipeline repair crew. These attacks happened daily.

So when an oil pipeline was attacked on the evening of April 28, a security contractor reported the explosion and ensuing oil fire. The initial report was followed up by a telephone call with the location, a latitude and longitude expressed as a military grid coordinate. A written report of the attack was submitted the following day. One of my colleagues, LTC Mark Schneider, worked in the Restore Iraqi Oil (RIO) office, and he passed the coordinates to a military patrol. However, the initial location LTC Schneider received was wrong. The reported location was about three miles from the true location of the attack. The correct coordinates were later sent in a follow up report, but Mark did not receive them. Errors like these are common and are caused by imperfect communications systems, sleep deprivation and the "fog of war".

Consequently, LTC Schneider provided the original (inaccurate) location to the military security team. Their mission was to secure the site no later than 10:00 on Sunday May 2. The patrol drove their HMMWVs to the spot they were given, and there was no pipeline in sight. Some of the troops dismounted their vehicles to sweep the area. A shoeless, bearded man came running out of a building, waving his shirt and yelling, *"I'm an American POW!"* The patrol had found American hostage, Thomas Hamill, a Kellogg, Brown & Root (KBR) employee. He had been taken from his convoy on April 9 by insurgents. The unexpected presence of the U.S. troops caused Hamill's guard to panic, and the insurgent fled thinking it was a raid. Hamill was medically evacuated to the United States and was treated for a gunshot wound to the arm.

The details of Hamill's capture and rescue have been well documented in the news media, but it was a little known fact that he was freed because we screwed up and sent a patrol to the wrong location. So here's to Murphy—sometimes he also works against the enemy.

Another little known fact about the Hamill incident was the identity of the hostage-takers. SFC Keith Felde, who was assigned to the Iraq Provisional Command (IPC) in Baghdad (which later became GRD), filled me in on the rest of the story. Fortunately, CNN was able to film the hostage takers, who were posing with Hamill next to a vehicle. Felde realized that Hamill was seized near his location. Upon examination of the video, Felde recognized one of the hostage takers, whose face was partially covered.

Felde was convinced the hostage taker was one of the "Bee Brothers", and he immediately reported his identity. The Bee Brothers were a pair of Iraqis who did a lot of work for the coalition soon after the invasion, but the Americans had no contractual way to pay the brothers for their labor. At some point, the brothers asked to take a beehive with them for payment. Some American, presumably a sergeant or an officer, agreed. They got the name "Bee Brothers" after they were seen driving away with a massive beehive in their vehicle. Several other barters occurred, with the Bee Brothers receiving unwanted material in lieu of cash payments. Unfortunately, they were later stopped by authorities with some of these items, and arrested for stealing property. The Bee Brothers did not have any receipts to prove otherwise, and the Americans that had made the barter agreements had already rotated out of country.

So it appeared that the Bee Brothers took Hamill hostage either out of revenge for their arrest or simply as another way to make some money.

Explosion of Security Contractors

As the reconstruction mission expanded, so did the Division's need for armed security contractors.

I turned to Erinys for additional teams. Finding highly qualified security personnel was getting increasingly competitive, and the pay scales were increasing each month as the violence escalated. Many employees were on one-year contracts. As their personal contract neared expiration, they would seek a higher paying job with another security contractor. Several key Erinys personnel changed employers to support the State Department and USAID on contracts that paid better, used better armored vehicles, and traveled fewer miles across the Iraqi terrain—more pay and less danger was an attractive combination. The problem was at its worst when the Erinys contract was re-competed in combat. This was a terrible situation for GRD. No one on the Erinys team knew if they would win the re-compete, so many personnel were departing for assured jobs before the final selection. Every additional day the source selection committee took made the security personnel on the Erinys team more concerned and more likely to "jump to another contract." The lesson learned here is to avoid re-competing security contracts in combat. The Government runs the risk of losing a well performing incumbent team during the bureaucratic process.

The demand for civilian security personnel increased with each passing week. Erinys looked for innovative ways to recruit new, well-trained personnel to fill the additional security escort teams needed at GRN, GRC and GRS. The stress was showing. I looked for alternative sources, so I spoke to Brigadier James Ellery (U.K. retired) at Aegis. His company provided security for the PCO, GRD's sister organization. I knew Aegis was actively promoting more robust reconstruction security and intelligence services. I applauded this, but I had not yet seen one of their teams in operation. I thought Aegis was getting a slow start, and I was disappointed in their early progress. We needed to Git'r Done. Brigadier Ellery assured me he could provide teams. I told him I needed three nine-man teams, the first one starting in two weeks. One team was needed each in Mosul, Kirkuk and Baghdad. I did not hear back from Aegis, so I continued to rely on Erinys during my tour. (When I returned to Iraq in 2007, Aegis had clearly established a robust, professional security capability. I simply wish it were available in 2004.)

Later, Fraser Brown of Erinys reported that he had the new security teams identified and was bringing them to GRD. A few days later, Fraser brought about 22 former members of a Ukrainian parachute battalion into the GRD HQ building and introduced them as the additional Private Security Detail (PSDs). Being paratroopers, I figured the Ukrainians were trained and tough. Alex Dornstauder and I came in to inspect the new personnel. Alex asked the first question. "How many of these guys speak English?" The contract required our PSD teams to speak English. Fraser stated that they all did. So Alex started to talk to some of the new men as a test. It was clear that many of the Ukrainians had limited English skills. A few just gave us the thousand-yard stare when we asked them a simple question. Out of 22 security members, probably three or four spoke English well enough to communicate with our personnel. Fraser acknowledged the issue, and thought most of the men could be used as guards at another facility. One guy with some English skills was issued a shotgun and put on the front gate of our compound at Essayons Base. He threw the shotgun over his shoulder and marched out to his new post. Within ten minutes, he accidentally blew a hole through the roof of the guard shack. We immediately pulled him off the perimeter, and he was off the contract. Fraser and the Erinys team went back to the drawing board recruiting security teams. I knew what he was up against, and that he was resourceful. He made steady progress and was able to deliver some badly needed teams.

Another painful issue with contractors, especially foreign nationals, was getting Common Access Cards (CAC). These are DOD identification cards with built-in security features. I was told that there were 43 different types of ID cards in Iraq in April of 2004. Many military commands and Government agencies were issuing their own form of identification: Embassies, Ministries, USAID, MNC-I, U.N., etc. The CAC card was the gold standard for identity management. It was your passport to get quickly through long lines at force protection checkpoints and onto military installations. Unfortunately, senior Iraqi officials were often denied entry to U.S. facilities because the guards would only recognize the CAC cards as a valid form of ID. This infuriated the new Iraqi Government.

Getting CAC cards issued to U.S. contractors deploying through Ft. Bliss or Ft. Benning was relatively easy–getting one issued in Iraq was almost impossible and was a huge problem for GRD. Many of GRD's security personnel were non-U.S. nationals that did not deploy through Ft. Bliss or Ft. Benning. That meant they needed to be issued cards at the nearest CAC issuing facility in Kuwait. The struggle to get CAC cards was crippling Erinys, and in turn, GRD. When a CAC card machine finally arrived in Iraq a few weeks later, the government operators would only issue cards to contractors for two hours every Thursday morning. Our security teams were sleeping outside the door of the CAC facility on Wednesday nights to get a good spot in line on Thursdays. If they missed the 2-hour window, it meant another week of lost time. The situation prompted GRD to get authorization for its own CAC card machine. Scott Lowdermilk, the GRD reachback coordinator, helped to quickly work us through the approval process.

Interpreters

Few Americans in Iraq spoke Arabic, so there was a large demand for civilian interpreters. Titan Corporation was under contract to provide thousands of vetted Iraqi interpreters to U.S. forces. We had about six Iraqi interpreters assigned to the GRD headquarters. Several of our interpreters appeared to be under-utilized. So I tasked them to translate all local Iraqi news articles related to reconstruction. I wanted to get feedback on what the Iraqi people were hearing from their own press. The U.S. Press was often focused on sound bites about large car bombs and was largely silent on reconstruction progress—and the Iraqis did not read the U.S. Press.

I also heard that some of the female interpreters were looking for a husband to get a ticket out of Iraq. The leadership was on guard for any inappropriate conduct that would influence the effectiveness, morale or welfare of the unit. But we were so consumed with daily wartime operations that we simply did not see much flirting. While occasional rumors spread, the proof was harder to find. But I am now convinced that some GRD personnel likely took advantage of the situation.

Beer on the Battlefield

Alcohol consumption was another significant issue. Iraq is a largely Muslim country, but alcohol was reported to be widely available. Some impressive wine cellars were found in several of Saddam's palaces. However, by General Order, U.S. military forces and civilians accompanying them were forbidden to consume alcohol in Iraq.

Having U.S. soldiers with loaded weapons drinking alcohol was a recipe for disaster. But there was a loophole in the General Order. Anyone assigned to/with the U.S. Embassy could drink alcohol. So personnel working in the Republican Palace that supported the State Department could drink, while their peers working for the military could not. Many GRD and PCO personnel worked with reconstruction counterparts at the U.S. Embassy, so the opportunity to drink was there. MG Johnson, the GRD Commander, recognized this and issued very clear guidance for his unit. Don't even get near alcohol. The only alcohol I really saw in Iraq was alcohol-free beer approved for use at "Hail and Farewell" ceremonies.

While alcohol can improve morale, it can also lead to serious misconduct. Many contractors skirted the rules and kept their own private stash. A single armed and intoxicated contractor went out to "kick some ass" at an Iraqi police station near Al Kut, and he almost started a major conflict. And beer on the battlefield can lead to sex on the battlefield and many complicated issues. Friday nights at the Republican Palace (U.S. Embassy) swimming pool had a reputation for being wild and redefined the term "international relations." The exuberant behavior at the Embassy pool was in stark contrast with the austere life of the average soldier and the average Iraqi. I made a point to stay hundreds of yards from the pool area. These civilians got to have all the fun, while those protecting them had more serious responsibilities.

A few months after I returned home, I talked to Colonel Paul Hilton, about my experiences with contractors and civilians in Iraq. Paul worked in the Army Operations Center at the Pentagon. He and I were recent classmates at the Industrial College of the Armed Forces (ICAF). Paul asked me to brief Mr. Anderson, the Assistant Secretary of the Army, on a broad spectrum of issues related to civilians and contractors on the battlefield. I was glad to, and I did not pull any punches.

Vehicle Disabled in Downtown Baghdad

We ran daily convoy operations in SUVs to get GRD personnel to important meetings and project sites. Every one of these convoys involved contractors and civilians, which made the movements more complex and ambiguous.

I was traveling outside the wire frequently, often to Camp Victory. It was a short run, but in mid April 2004, it was an exciting one as there were continuous attacks on the main road that were often fatal. We would sometimes change our route to throw off any planned enemy attack. The problem with an alternate route was that it often took us through the heart of Baghdad. We would sometimes be caught in a traffic jam and have scores of Iraqi vehicles around us. Being boxed in traffic and immobile was a dangerous situation. We had to scan every person and vehicle near us to determine if they were potential threats. At the same time, we watched every open window and the rooftop of every building to see if an AK or an RPG was poking out. When approaching traffic jams, we would recognize the imminent danger, and our driver would throw a U-turn over the medial strip and dash off in a different direction. All the vehicles in the convoy would immediately follow suit. The lead vehicle positioned itself to block oncoming traffic to allow the others to make the radical turn. It was a well-choreographed tactical maneuver right out of the combat driving textbook, and it was a real art form.

On several trips, we had to alter our routes because one or more of the access control gates to our destination was closed. We would spend an extra 30 exciting minutes driving our SUV about ten more miles through Baghdad just to get to a point only three miles away. There was no direct route free of congestion. On one of the more memorable runs through Baghdad, our tail vehicle became disabled. The three-vehicle convoy stopped on the shoulder of the highway to try to quickly assess the problem. As the only military guy in the convoy, I immediately had to pull security while the contractors diagnosed the problem. If I tried to fix the vehicle while the contractors pulled security, it would probably violate the rules.

While we were stopped, Iraqi vehicles continued to press through the congestion and rifled past our parked SUVs. Car bombers often drove up to stopped U.S. vehicles and detonated, so we all recognized that this situation was potentially dangerous. In this situation, we had no standoff from a potential attacker. Scores of cars were racing past us, coming within a meter or two of our vehicles—it was too close for comfort. I realized we needed to immediately divert the traffic from our position. Within seconds of stopping, I jumped out of my SUV, drew my pistol, ran 20 meters upstream in the traffic flow and then stood in the nearest lane of traffic. I aggressively waved my left hand to signal approaching Iraqis to slow down and move over to the far lane. Cars raced toward me, many oblivious to my presence. Some slamming on their brakes at the last moment. I was wearing my helmet and body armor, so if they hit me, I knew I was going to mess up their front end and come through their windshield. When the Iraqi vehicles got too close, I drew a bead on them with my pistol and vigorously signaled them to change lanes immediately. Sticking a loaded weapon in somebody's face is probably the highest bandwidth communication that you can make. Essentially, it meant, "Stay the hell away from my convoy. I don't know which one of you is a suicide bomber or a drive-by shooter. Move now!" The approaching Iraqis were finally getting it.

Every minute standing on the busy highway felt like ten. Our civilian team had the hood of the disabled vehicle popped and their heads tucked in the engine compartment trying to diagnose the problem. Someone finally figured out what was wrong, and we quickly piled back in the vehicles. I jumped in the cargo area of the last SUV and played tail gunner for the rest of the ride. We got back inside the wire and headed to our compound. Mission complete. Our civilians had been successfully delivered again. I went into the GRD Operations Center, dropped my body armor, drank a bottle of water and got a tactical update from MSG Spears, the OPS NCO. It was now time to draft my daily comments for the Secretary of Defense

(SECDEF) about reconstruction progress in Iraq. I was scrambling to identify something strategic that I could report up the chain that day.

6

Ground Hog Day

Battle Rhythm

Living in Iraq was like living in the movie "Ground Hog Day". Every day a different variation of the previous day: start early, attend multiple briefings, dodge enemy rockets, eat chow, conduct a high speed SUV dash across Baghdad, drink water, visit a project site, plan for future missions, meet with key staff, eat chow, make another SUV run on the most dangerous highway in the world, witness several car bombings, stare at Medevac helicopters flying overhead and say a prayer, prepare strategic reports, visit wounded troops, drink more water, scream about needing better armored vehicles, inspect our perimeter defenses, dodge the afternoon rockets, think of better ways to protect our personnel, plan for the next morning's convoy operations, eat chow, prepare the daily division situation report, send a quick note home to family and friends, conduct a quick huddle with the operations and intelligence team, visit my battle buddy to release some stress, answer emails on three different accounts, plan special movements for the CG, drink water, and drag myself to bed sometime after midnight.

Every morning, I begin with the same basic routine. The military calls it the "Battle Rhythm" – the same daily and weekly recurring activities that are part of protracted combat operations. My Battle Rhythm began with a wake up at 05:30. I put on my uniform, threw my pistol harness over my shoulder and departed my sandbagged trailer. I started a short walk through a canyon of sandbag walls, past a large, noisy, smelly generator, and took a few deep breaths of hot dusty air. A minute later, I entered the GRD headquarters in King Faisal's home and went straight to the G3 shop to get a situation update. I'd quickly check with the bleary-eyed night duty officer for any Serious Incident Reports (SIRs) and scan scores of emails for any urgent messages.

Battlefield Update Assessment

Next, I'd jump into a SUV and drive to the Republican Palace to participate in the Battlefield Update Assessment (BUA), a daily Senior Leader update on operations in Iraq.

The BUA was a formal classified meeting attended by a hundred or so senior U.S. and coalition military personnel. All the major commanders were there, including LTG Petraeus (MNSTC-I) and other coalition General Officers. The senior leaders sat at the main table on the operations floor, focused on several large screen displays presenting the current military situation as well as live video feeds from Camp Victory and more remote areas. Dozens of staff officers from the U.S., U.K., Australia, and other coalition partners sat in tiered seating, overlooking the main table. The layout of the room reminded me of a theater or a Roman coliseum with the high-ranking gladiators in the ring at the center of attention.

The BUA's agenda included a review of each sector of Iraq, highlighting significant military and political actions in the past 24 hours: the number of patrols, raids, friendly and enemy casualties, enemy forces captured or detained, and IED attacks. It also covered any recent attacks on Iraqi leaders or infrastructure, identified visiting Congressional delegations (CODELs), and reviewed the latest status on training and equipping the Iraqi Army and Police. During the BUA, my job was to present the Reconstruction Update to LTG Sanchez or GEN Casey. I had a maximum of 3 charts and 3 minutes to convey the strategic events, usually highlighting the start or finish of a major reconstruction project. I considered it an honor to play even a small part in the daily BUA briefing. The entire world was watching everything the U.S. was doing in Iraq, and any progress with the reconstruction mission provided some hope that the war was improving. After the BUA, I'd make a quick stop at the dining facility inside the Republican Palace for some eggs, oatmeal and fruit and then hustle back to the GRD compound at Essayons Base.

Morning Attacks

About this time, the enemy would typically launch 2-4 rockets in our vicinity, hoping to hit our personnel walking to their place of duty during the morning "rush hour". They were largely ineffective, but did occasionally succeed in killing personnel or damaging vehicles, buildings or equipment. And of course, the enemy knew when and where we ate chow, so they would target these facilities, hoping to get lucky and take out a couple dozen of our people. Later that year, a rocket ripped through the roof of the Republican Palace and killed two personnel while narrowly missing BG Bostick.

Rocket attacks were daily events, and we learned to live with them. Even if one failed to explode, it would hit the ground at about 700 meters/second and send broken pieces of metal, at lethal velocities, hundreds of yards along the trajectory path. While I was pulling out of Republican Palace one morning after the BUA, a rocket smashed into the street in front of my vehicle. The violent impact sent metal fragments flying all the way to the military hospital, about a quarter mile away. If I had departed the BUA 5 or 10 seconds sooner, the round would have directly hit my vehicle, and I would have been coming home early – probably horizontally.

On another morning in June, a Navy lieutenant was hit with a Molotov cocktail and set on fire along with his SUV in the parking lot of the Republican Palace. He was badly burned. The firebomb was thrown by a kid on a motorbike. I had departed the area just prior to the incident and regretted not being nearby so I could have shot the punk. I don't think he was ever caught. The alarming part of the attack was that it happened inside the Green Zone in an area thought to be relatively secure.

Molotov cocktail attack

Battlefield Update Brief

Once back at the GRD headquarters, we'd prepare the daily Battlefield Update Brief (BUB) for our Commanding General (CG), MG Ron Johnson. COL Alex Dornstauder, the division Chief of Staff, would assemble the primary staff for a BUB rehearsal twenty minutes before the CG arrived.

A BUB: *left to right - seated in front*, LTC Purvis, LTC Kachejian; *standing*, LTC Corrigan *and seated* Maxine Shoemaker

The BUB rehearsal was essential. The CG expected each briefer to be quick, sharp and flawless during the presentation, or they risked an intense grilling. Many civilians on the staff were visibly uncomfortable with the intensity of the meeting and the rigid format of the presentation. The civilian-military mix in the staff created a clash of cultures. We were still standing up the Division and recruiting personnel while trying to rebuild the country and fight a war, so every staff section was grossly undermanned and deeply stressed. But COL Dornstauder was a master motivator. He did a phenomenal job coaching and inspiring the team during the rehearsal so they would operate like a well-oiled machine when the CG arrived.

He was always armed with dozens of anecdotes and operational examples that cut through the tension and provided a fresh perspective for the staff. When Dornstauder walked in the briefing room, you could hear a collective sigh of relief. He was the one-man cavalry coming to protect the staff, and he would make sure the team made it through the BUB alive. He could read the staff as they began to assemble around the ornate conference table that had been personally used by Saddam Hussein. To ease the tension and provide some levity during the rehearsal, he would open up with "John, your body language is killing me." It was always good for a chuckle.

When civilian staff members appeared hesitant to present bad news during the rehearsal, COL Dornstauder eloquently told them to just suck it up and do it. Don't worry about catching hell during the BUB—that is a foregone conclusion. It's like being in a knife fight. "You have to tell yourself, 'Self, I'm gonna get cut'." Once you accept that you're gonna get cut, you stop worrying about getting cut and begin to focus on what GRD needs to do to fix the situation.

When MG Johnson came in, the staff would come to attention and then give a 45-minute update on the status of Operations, Intelligence, Logistics, Personnel, Communications, Project Management, Restoring Iraqi Oil (RIO) and Restoring Iraqi Electricity (RIE). Eventually, Public Affairs and Safety were also added to the BUB lineup. I normally led off the BUB presentation and

highlighted current security issues and recent attacks on reconstruction projects and personnel.

Each day, GRD dedicated the briefing to a recently fallen soldier, whose photo and combat story were presented on our first chart. We had a solemn moment of silence, and we all reflected on the life of our fellow American and patriot. Sadly, one day, we honored a distant cousin of mine, Lance Corporal Michael Downey (pictured at left). He died of wounds several days after he was hit from sniper fire in Fallujah.

At the conclusion of the BUB, the staff snapped to attention again. After the CG departed, COL Dornstauder would keep the staff huddled, and review our performance and any major tasks that we should be working on. He would engage us with his own unique vocabulary. In many ways, he reminded me of GEN Alexander Haig, who was President Nixon's Chief of Staff. GEN Haig created many new expressions that were termed "Haiganisms". Dornstauder pioneered new linguistic expressions that will always stick in my mind. For example, he would intensely stare at the GRD staff, with deep penetrating eyes, and tell us "the staff was just a delivery system." We didn't deliver bombs; we delivered information to the Commander.

When Dornstauder wanted to describe a generic process, he would often refer to a mysterious device called a "hebenator". I always tried to envision exactly what a hebenator was. It sounded like an intriguing electro-mechanical device that was clearly more complex than a do-hicky or a thing-a-ma-jig. I checked Google, and not even the mighty search engine could define a hebenator.

If the staff had a question or an issue that was extremely important, Dornstuader would immediately offer to "call Wolfowitz VFR direct." He was of course referring to Deputy Secretary of Defense Wolfowitz. I think half the staff actually thought Dornstauder had some kind of "Red Phone" on his desk.

If the staff made a bad decision and was now trying to recover, Dornstauder proclaimed, *"We were caught in an L-Shaped ambush."* The civilians didn't get it, but the Rangers in the room knew that to be a bad situation—it meant you were now being shot at from two directions. To survive, you either need to immediately charge into the ambush or retreat and find cover. To do nothing was a decision to die. To the staff members in the room that were part of Generation X, Dornstauder was actually saying "Time to man-up, dude." If the staff was sluggish and needed to improve, Dornstauder would invoke Maslow's Hierarchy of Needs and tell us we needed to "self-actualize" so we could realize our full potential. Unfortunately, many of us were still pursuing one of Maslow's more basic human needs—sleep.

If someone continued to snivel and Dornstauder wanted to shut them up, he'd stare down his target and bark, *"OK—I got it."* And when the staff debate was over, and it was time to make a command decision, he'd announce, *"We have reached our culminating point".* Orders would then be issued. And if the CG was pleased with the BUB performance, Dornstauder would provide positive reinforcement by announcing, *"My hat is off to you."*

If the staff survived the daily BUB unscarred, we knew the rest of the day in combat would be relatively easy. Invariably, several action items would come out the BUB each morning that would take a few hours to resolve. In the meantime, the primary mission of rebuilding Iraq always needed to move forward. We had to Git'r Done.

"Mad Max" Drive in Baghdad

The next event of the day was to attend one of several meetings at Camp Victory. This involved making a round trip movement through the Red Zone in our SUVs. It was always a wild and aggressive sprint through a lawless city. Every moment in the unforgiving terrain was thrilling. Attacks could happen at any moment and from any direction. There were two kinds of drivers in Iraq – the quick and the dead. In many ways, driving in Iraq was like living in a Mad Max movie.

Preparing for a drive "outside the wire" had a ritual. Before departing, I always referred to the first rule in the Ranger Handbook—"Don't forget nothing." I'd go through the same checklist. Put on your helmet, body armor, gloves and goggles. Wearing goggles will save your eyes from flying glass if your SUV explodes. Gloves will keep your hands from catching on fire in a burning vehicle and help you to return fire. Body armor will protect your critical organs, unless of course you are hit from the side or underneath. Most of us chose to leave our throat and crotch protectors behind as they were too constraining. That meant our necks, arms, legs and peckers were expendable.

I would pack plenty of ammo, because you can never have enough. That's how Fish died. He was a member of our primary security escort team. He ran out of ammo. For me, it was seven magazines each with 30 rounds of 5.56mm for my M-4 rifle and another three clips each with 15 rounds for my 9mm pistol. I was pretty sure I could hit something with 255 bullets. The bad thing about carrying ammo was that it was heavy and bulky. But the good thing about ammo was that your load got lighter as you shot it off.

I'd continue through the checklist: inspect the vehicle equipment, conduct radio checks, and review actions to be taken on enemy contact. Make sure everyone knew the route, because you may be separated or you may have to drive if your driver is hit. Make sure there is Quik-Clot® in the glove box—a miraculous bag of shrimp shells that will quickly plug up a gaping wound and keep someone from bleeding out before they get to the hospital. It enabled wounded personnel to live through the golden hour until they received medical attention. Quik-Clot® was often missing because security guys like to take it with them rather than leave it in the vehicle. Water—take extra bottles because we are on the edge of a desert. Gas—make sure the last guy who used the vehicle filled it up. It is pretty embarrassing and extremely dangerous to run out of gas in a combat zone. I'd also check that we had a spare tire and jack. Before departing, we'd give a list of names of everyone in each vehicle to the Operations shop. That allowed us to determine who was missing if one vehicle didn't come back. Finally, I'd say a brief prayer to provide us an extra layer of protection. When the checks were complete, we'd jump in the SUVs and start "combat-driving" through the streets of Baghdad to get to our destination. We always drove fast and hard to reduce the risk of being hit by a roadside bomb or sniper.

Strategy and Planning Meetings

My weekly Battle Rhythm included an update to the Corps Commander, LTG Metz, at Camp Victory. We'd cover Iraqi oil and electricity issues and discuss what major projects were ongoing and major issues we faced. Almost all the tough issues were related to the security of personnel and project sites. We'd explore ideas about how we could do better. LTG Metz would ask us what help we needed from him. We welcomed the question.

Another weekly meeting was a two-hour session with the MNF-I Strategic Plans staff. It was led by my classmate COL Casey Haskins (pictured at right). Casey was a very confident guy who could roll with the punches. He had a remarkable gift of being able to smile in the face of great uncertainty. He was one of a handful of officers that voluntarily left the Army War College early to deploy to Iraq. A supreme selfless act. Casey always gave us useful information about the current strategic issues and plans, including the pending transfer of political power and Iraqi elections. I was enroute to a Strategic Plans meeting on May 24, 2004 when my SUV was attacked with a roadside bomb. Fortunately, I lived to talk about it.

Chow Time

Around noon, we ate some chow in one of three local dining facilities. We'd usually rotate dining facilities so we felt like we had some choice. They all generally served the same food, and the quality was pretty good for Army chow.

Good food was important for maintaining a soldier's moral. You had to keep them paid and fed. Unfortunately, the troops stationed in more remote locations in Iraq had less selection. And when the insurgents almost cut off the main supply routes from Kuwait to Baghdad in April and May, dining facilities lost all fresh foods and fell back to basic canned foods. Rumors spread that the main Republican Palace dining facility was one day away from eating MREs (Meal Ready to Eat). Real soldiers would just shrug it off, but serving MREs in the Embassy would have caused a major panic among the civilians.

Planning the Big Move

I also led a weekly planning meeting and a project site visit for the anticipated GRD move from the Green Zone (in downtown Baghdad) to Camp Victory (near the Baghdad Airport). The HQ move was considered urgent when I first arrived at GRD in March. U.S. forces were planning on "De-Greening" the Green Zone – that meant moving the military out. So we were pressing hard to build a new GRD HQ facility at Camp Victory and move to it by June. However, when GEN Casey took command of MNF-I, he told GRD to stay put. GEN Casey wanted the Division HQ to remain in the Green Zone. It was a 180-degree turn in events.

I was disappointed that the hundreds of hours of careful planning for the move to Camp Victory were now lost. But we were soldiers; we salute and execute. GRC would move on to Camp Victory, but the GRD HQ had to stay put. And the situation became more interesting later, as the Iraqi Prime Minister sought to reclaim the GRD HQ as his official residence.

Connecting to the Distributed GRD Team

My Battle Rhythm also included leading a weekly video teleconference (VTC) with a dozen operations officers and liaison officers (LNOs) assigned to different reconstruction units throughout Iraq. My CRU teammates – Chris Kolditz and Hal Creel (Mosul), Bob Cabell (Baghdad) and Charlie Driscoll (Ramadi) joined in. I looked forward to the VTC and the day we could all leave Iraq together.

During the VTC, we would discuss and solve major issues from each region. The issues varied widely. Some typical ones included:

- Determining how reconstruction convoys could get through Kuwaiti Customs faster. Sometimes the delays at the border took days to resolve. The Kuwaitis had a number of concerns related to taxing any goods departing their country. They were also concerned about the smuggling of people and drugs from Iraq back into Kuwait.
- Determining what security contractors were protecting what construction sites and what kinds of weapons and radios they used. Did each project site know who they should call if they needed a Quick Reaction Force (QRF) to rescue them?
- Establishing a classified website to share sensitive geospatial information regarding our project sites. But few of us even had a classified terminal.

Joint Civil-Military Engineering Board

I was also the GRD representative to the weekly meeting of the Joint Civil-Military Engineering Board (JCMEB). This Board was intended to de-conflict reconstruction priorities associated with different Iraqi Provinces, reconstruction organizations (GRD, PCO, USAID, AFCEE, Seabees, Tactical units), and funding sources (CERP, IRRF, DFI, AIRP, etc.).

The JCMEB meetings were frustrating for two reasons. First, they were ineffective since our project databases were marginally populated, and they were not interoperable between different agencies. At that time, no one authority owned all the reconstruction responsibilities or all the data. And some reconstruction organizations never bothered to attend the meeting. I sat in about six of these meetings with General Officers, and each week we struggled with the same basic problem. We had poor, fragmented information about all the reconstruction projects in theater. The JCMEB lacked visibility into all the projects and could not make quality decisions. At one point, I had to tell the Emperor that he had no clothes. I said, *"Sir, if we are in this meeting again next week, and we are still trying to figure out what we should do, then we have failed."* There was utter silence in the room. It was an acknowledgement that I was right. The next week the meetings were suspended.

Recruiting Staff

GRD suffered from severe personnel shortages. The Personnel Officer tracked the status of military and civilian staffing levels every day. The personnel turbulence was simply unbearable—many of our civilian experts were on 3 or 6 month tours, resulting in a 300% average annual turnover rate. By the time a civilian learned their job, they were soon preparing to return home. Every week our veteran employees left GRD, and a busload of rookies arrived.

To keep the personnel pipeline flowing, there were generous financial incentives for government civilians to serve in Iraq. But many senior civilians soon met their annual pay caps, and they would depart with much of our institutional knowledge. When I arrived in Iraq, our military strength was less than 20% of what we needed and the civilian strength was less than 40%. Some skills were in higher demand than others. The combination of short tours, austere conditions and widely reported daily attacks in the media made recruiting civilians a monumental task that consumed inordinate organizational energy. The high turnover of staff degraded GRD's ability to execute its primary mission. One highly turbulent position was the Property Book Officer (PBO), who was responsible for tracking all government owned property in the Division—throughout all sites in Iraq. In peacetime, PBOs normally held their position for at least three years. However, GRD had six different PBOs assigned in six months.

SECDEF Bullets

Every afternoon, I had to prepare a summary of up to three strategic reconstruction events that had occurred during the last day and submit them to MNF-I. This summary was referred to as "SECDEF bullets", as they were used to provide the Secretary of Defense with a daily update on the situation in Iraq.

I had to answer the question, "What strategic events happened today in Iraqi Reconstruction?" Large strategic projects took months or years to complete. While we were commissioning many new power plants, hospitals and other facilities, these major projects were not completed every day. I had a constant struggle trying to identify daily "strategic events". Our CG had the final say on the content in the SECDEF bullets, but a typical submission would read like this:

"Power Unit No. 4 of the Taiji Power Plant completed final testing and generated its maximum capacity of 17 MW during trial tests. This unit is now commissioned and on the national grid. This additional capacity is enough to power approximately 50,000 Iraqi homes."

Car Bombs and Rockets

During the early afternoon on a typical day, we would hear or see a car bombing or two, and we often had another incoming rocket attack. If the threat was nearby or imminent, I'd change the division's force protection status to RED. That meant we'd put on our body armor and helmets and herd all the civilians in the basement of the HQ building, until I could verify that the threat had passed. And you never really knew if the threat had passed. You only knew that it hadn't rained rockets in the last 10 minutes, so you ordered everybody to go back to work.

We had good telecommunications, so I could occasionally call my wife, Alice, for a few minutes to check on her and the kids. You have to make some time for family, even in combat. One afternoon, while I was on the phone, a 122mm rocket hit about 50 meters behind my office. It was a large explosion that rocked our building. I screamed for everyone to get down and get their "battle rattle" on. I yelled to the Operations NCO to get a status report from the guard force and get accountability of our personnel. After barking orders for a minute or two, I looked down at my left hand and realized I was still on the phone with Alice. I thought, "Oh, crap." I put the handset to my ear and said, *"Honey, are you still there?"* She was a bit confused and asked me what happened. I told her, *"Don't worry; we just have some noisy neighbors."*

The Baghdad Barber

Each week I tried to get a haircut; a good haircut and a crisp salute are the hallmarks of professional soldiers. But my first haircut in Iraq was high adventure.

It was late March 2004. I had been in Baghdad for a few weeks, and I desperately needed to crop my hair. The insurgency was raging, and I had little time since I arrived to break from my duties. Fortunately, the military makes things easy and hires contract barbers in a combat zone. There was no charge for the troops. We just had to wait in line. MAJ Ray Hart led me to the barbershop, which was a ten-minute walk from the GRD HQ. I walked inside and noticed two Iraqi barbers on duty. Middle Eastern music was playing on a boom box. There were four or five soldiers already seated ahead of me. While waiting my turn, I began to watch the hair cutting process.

I noticed the Iraqi barbers used a four-inch bladed razor to shave the hair off each soldier's sideburns and neck. The alarm bells instantly went off in my head. I was receiving daily reports of foreigners being kidnapped and beheaded. The idea of an unknown Iraqi putting a razor to my neck caused great concern. How did I know that this Iraqi wasn't an Al Qaeda member who got a job as a barber inside our compound? Who vetted these barbers? Were these barbers just waiting for a senior military officer to sit down so they could slit his throat? I studied the other soldiers that were ahead of me in line. None of them looked too alarmed, but they were young and probably less cautious. If I was going to get cut, I was determined to take out the barber. I checked to make sure there was a 15 round magazine in my 9mm Beretta. I went through a mental drill of chambering a round and flipping off the safety. If I needed to cap the guy, I wanted to do it quickly, before I bled out.

The troops ahead of me all survived their haircuts, tipped the barber and then left. It was now my turn. I quickly realized that there were no other soldiers left in the barbershop to back me up. I just might have to shoot two barbers while a razor was sticking out of my neck. I had plenty of bullets. I made eye contact, smiled and sat down. I didn't blink for the next 20 minutes. My hand was in contact with my 9mm pistol in my shoulder holster the entire haircut. I gave the guy my best "killer" look. I intensely watched in the mirror on the wall to keep an eye on where the barber was and what he was doing next.

At first, my hair was trimmed with an electric trimmer. But then out popped the big razor. The Iraqi was sharpening the knife blade in front of me. He had my full attention. I was thinking, maybe I should just shoot him now—a pre-emptive strike. No, that would cause too much paper work. I have to wait until he cuts me. So I started to talk to him to distract him in case he had bad intentions. He spoke some English and opened up a bit. He shaved my sideburns and neck with great care and precision. There was no ill intent. I soon realized that what really motivated these barbers was not politics or religion. It was cash. Good thing I didn't shoot the poor bastard.

The barbers' salaries were already paid by the military. Since an unskilled Iraqi laborer typically made $3-5 per day, a skilled barber probably made $10. But the troops would tip the barber $2- 5 for a good cut. By local standards, the barbers were raking it in. They each probably cleared over $100 per day and were among the best-paid workers in the country. I made sure I tipped him well, so he wouldn't want to slit my throat on the next haircut. It seemed like a good insurance policy.

Staying Fit

As the G3 of a severely understaffed division, I was consumed with my work and with constant operational demands and physical threats. Life and safety issues for our personnel came first. Taking care of me was far less important. If I had an extra 30 minutes, I would dedicate it to sleep.

On a rare day, I had some spare time, and I would work out. My options were to go to the nearby gym, or I could just go for a jog. Now running in Baghdad in 110-degree heat was bad enough. But the security inside the Green Zone was somewhat questionable, so we always ran with cell phones and pistols. It looked sort of goofy, but nobody laughs at a man running in shorts and tennis shoes while armed with a cell phone and a pistol.

Visiting the Wounded

Every day in Iraq was hard. And one of the hardest things I did was watch the MEDEVAC helicopters fly over our position. It would happen daily. I'd stop what I was doing and look up. It was the golden hour. If we could get a wounded soldier to a hospital in the first hour of their injury, they stood a good chance of living. I'd say a silent prayer that those on board arrived in time to survive and that their wounds would be quickly healed. We were paying a steep price. Watching the helo flights was the low point of my day.

About once a week, I would visit the wounded in the nearby Combat Support Hospital. Jim Hampton started the tradition in the G3 shop, and I joined in. We'd bring a soda or candy bar and stop in a few rooms to talk to the troops. To us, it was hallowed ground. One soldier, wounded in Sadr City, talked about how an Iraqi woman intentionally tried to push a baby carriage in front of an advancing U.S. tank. On another visit, we stopped in to see an Iraqi policeman who was gravely wounded while saving one of our soldiers. I was told he was presented a valor medal by an American General Officer. There were plenty of wounded. The most severely wounded were evacuated to Landstuhl Germany as soon as possible. When there wasn't enough room in the hospital, some of the less severely wounded patients stayed in large tents on the hospital grounds.

We made sure we visited any combat engineers. Almost all engineer officers start their careers as combat engineers trained on tactical skills such as minefields, demolitions and bridging. My early training also included atomic demolitions–portable nuclear weapons that were hand placed and used to blow up a major facility. Many of the combat engineers in Iraq were clearing IEDs off the roads every day. Occasionally we'd convince the hospital staff to release a couple of wounded troops so they could come to our HQ and relax. We'd get them a phone line and let them watch some TV. We had a nice view of the Tigris River. We'd return them to the hospital after a few hours before they were reported as Missing in Action. It was time well invested.

Convoy Planning

In the late afternoon, my team would hold a meeting to review vehicle convoys planned for the next morning. During this meeting, we would discuss every vehicle movement:

- Who needed to be moved and to where?
- What vehicles and security team members would be involved?
- What radios, frequencies and weapons would be required?
- What was the latest intelligence on enemy activity on the planned convoy routes?
- What actions should be taken on enemy contact?

Some of these meetings got heated as the enemy was increasing the frequency and intensity of their attacks on convoys. Our movement tactics, techniques and procedures (TTPs) were always evolving to address new threats. MAJ Cabell and MAJ Ball often argued about the best action to take. Sometimes I had to step in and referee the 150-decibel debate. It was clear both Cabell and Ball were passionate about keeping our people safe.

Evening Reports

After dinner, I started preparing the BUA briefing for the next day and had to get our Power Point slides approved by the CG. I also had to review scores of emails on three separate computer systems –

SIPR (classified U.S.), CENTRIX (classified Coalition), and NIPR (unclassified USACE). Each night, I hoped there were no surprises buried in the piles of email. But surprises happen in combat, and we saw quite a few.

Our team also prepared a comprehensive 10-page report on GRD reconstruction operations that we sent to the MNF-I Commander. It contained an update of ongoing reconstruction projects, recent attacks, the status of our critical equipment and personnel, the number of Iraqis that were employed, and major issues that needed to be brought to the attention of LTG Sanchez or GEN Casey. Those reports would be a great source for any military historian wanting a day-by-day account of GRD activities.

Battle Buddy

Several times during the duty day, I'd climb the spiral staircase to the top floor of the palace and visit COL Dornstauder. Alex and I were battle buddies. As fellow Rangers, I think we were in a competition for who could survive in Iraq with the least sleep. We shared everything we knew and constantly bounced ideas off each other.

Alex was a football player at West Point. He was as wide as he was tall and made out of steel reinforced concrete. He could accidentally crush a man just giving him a bear hug. Alex had a commanding presence and a deep penetrating gaze. As the GRD Chief of Staff, Alex had an enormous amount of responsibility, and he needed to feed and care for a mixed military and civilian staff. Alex provided top cover for the entire staff, allowing them to focus on the primary mission. On many tough days, he personally carried me over the goal line. If I had to go to war again, I would unquestionably want to serve with Alex Dornstauder.

The daily pace was relentless. I think we did more every day in Iraq than many U.S. organizations did in two weeks. My normal duty day ended between 2300 and 0100. This gave me 4-6 hours before the next "Ground Hog Day" began.

Staying Connected with Family

Staying in touch is much easier in modern war. We had relatively good access to telecommunications, including email and voice over IP (VOIP) service. Calling back to the U.S. or receiving incoming calls was almost routine. I could quickly check on my wife and kids, or contact my sister, Gina, to check on her and Kevin who was still weak but off his respirator. Being able to reach out to family on a regular basis helped me keep my sanity and focus on the mission.

USACE had another telecommunications ace up its sleeve. We had a live VTC link to anywhere in the world. On a not to interfere basis, the command allowed a monthly morale call for troops to see and talk to their families. I made use of it several times during my tour. I would look forward to the VTC for weeks. I would talk to Alice and the kids about almost anything but the actual war. There was enough stress in Iraq and at home already. There was no need to pile on. Each of my three children, Kent, Kara and Katie, got 10 minutes of one-on-one time with Daddy. I'd catch up with them on schoolwork, their soccer games and review their report cards. I missed all their birthdays, except my son's. I came home on his 12th birthday.

Other members of the CRU team also used the VTC to stay in touch. Charlie Driscoll's second daughter, Claire, was born during our tour. Our entire team was pulling for Charlie to get his VTC time, and we offered to give up our own VTC slots so he could get some extended family time. Charlie called from Ramadi. He was able to see and talk to his wife, Constance, and his daughters, Grace and Claire, once the family was home from the hospital. It was a good day for all of us.

Iraqi Sovereignty - Transfer of Power

As much as every day in Iraq was like the movie "Ground Hog Day", for me, each one had its unique moments that distinguished them from all others. Sometimes it was a spectacular attack by the enemy or a daring raid by our troops. Occasionally, the completion of a project was a memorable indicator of our progress. On other days, I was inspired by the actions of our fellow soldiers. But some days were memorable because we participated in a historical event or met with the political elite. The day the United States transferred sovereignty back to the Iraqis was one of those unique and unforgettable days.

The transfer of sovereignty to the Interim Iraqi Government (IIG) was scheduled to happen on June 30, 2004. A tremendous amount of planning and hard work went in to this milestone event. The Iraqi Ministries all had to be operating, and massive security precautions needed to be coordinated. There was great concern that many attacks were being planned by anti-Iraqi Forces (AIF) to disrupt the transfer of power and significant speculation about an Iraqi version of a "Tet Offensive".

I would receive periodic updates on the pending transition from COL Casey Haskins at the weekly MNF-I strategic plans meeting. And Casey would solicit any issues that I had about the power transfer. I expressed significant concern that the IIG might make security contractors fully subject to Iraqi laws. If so, this would have a major impact on the security of strategic reconstruction projects throughout the country. Would contractor security forces be permitted to search or detain Iraqi citizens and vehicles entering a project site? During convoys, contractor security forces used tactical driving techniques (move quickly, change lanes, etc.) as a first line of defense to evade potential IEDs, SAF, RPGs and vehicular threats. Would security contractors be stopped, searched or detained by Iraqi Police or military forces? Would contractor weapons be confiscated? This scenario was particularly concerning as the enemy had been using Iraqi Police uniforms, vehicles, and false checkpoints to deceive coalition contractors.

If GRD security contractors were fully subjected to Iraqi laws, GRD convoys and civilians would be significantly more vulnerable to attacks and kidnappings. One potential result would be security contractors pulling out of Iraq. If so, the coalition would need to use military forces to protect reconstruction personnel and project sites or all sites would be looted within hours. And there were insufficient military forces in Iraq to pick up this potential new security mission. I encouraged the CPA and MNF-I to aggressively engage the IIG, to insure that contractor security forces would be able to remain effective after the transfer of power. It was in the best interest of the Iraqi people that their infrastructure be restored as quickly as possible.

On June 28, 2004, two days before the Iraqi transfer of power, GRD planned its own milestone transition. Since its activation in January, GRD was in a transitional state called "Initial Operational Capability" (IOC), meaning it was still being equipped and staffed. MG Ronald Johnson was the Commander of GRD during this phase. He would now transfer command to BG Thomas Bostick, and GRD would officially be at "Full Operational Capability" (FOC). BG Bostick previously served as the Assistant Division Commander at the 1st Cavalry Division. His 1st Cav experience would prove important as GRD moved forward executing its reconstruction mission. BG Bostick would also wear a second hat as the Deputy for Construction in the PCO. GRD and PCO would eventually merge into a single organization to provide unity of effort.

As part of Army tradition, GRD held a farewell event for MG Johnson two days prior to the Change of Command ceremony. It was a lighthearted event in the nearby Diwan School, symbolic because it had been recently renovated by GRD. Scores of GRD staff attended, as did some of my CRU teammates, Scott Lowdermilk, CPT Charlie Driscoll, and MAJ "Baghdad Bob" Cabell. We roasted MG Johnson, and he was enjoying his final moments as the GRD Commander. The highlight of the evening was when MG Johnson performed the "BUB Dance", a new tradition GRD was adopting for its outgoing Commanders. He stood up, performed masterfully, and had the entire staff rolling with laughter. It was good medicine for all of us.

Scott Lowdermilk - LTC Kachejian - CPT Driscoll - MAJ Cabell

The sun rose on June 28. I could feel this day was going to be different. I arrived early at the Iraqi Forum, a large convention center in the Green Zone. It was the location of the GRD Change of Command ceremony. I was surprised to see Iraqi military guards outside the Forum inspecting those that entered. Then I heard the news—the United States had just transferred sovereignty to the Interim Iraqi Government. This was two days earlier than announced. Ambassador Bremer's mission was complete. Prime Minister Iyad Allawi now owned the country.

I had heard rumors that an early transfer was a possible course of action. But I never spoke a word, and I didn't know it would actually happen. The early turnover was a complete tactical surprise for many people in theater. It really threw the enemy off guard. It disrupted their operational planning. There was no event for them to attack and disrupt on June 30. The deed was done. I wished I could have seen the faces of the enemy when the news of the early transfer was announced. The historic "transfer of power" event occurred in a private ceremony, only yards from the location of the GRD Change of Command. I did not see it personally, but there was a flurry of activity in the area. Everyone felt uplifted. It was a victory. I sensed that the momentum had shifted our way. Something good was happening in Iraq that the world could see.

I had several roles at the GRD Change of Command ceremony, the most visible being escorting LTG Ricardo Sanchez, the Commander of Combined Joint Task Force-7 (CJTF-7). LTG Sanchez had operational control of over 130,000 U.S. and coalition troops in Iraq. He was the "Reviewing Officer" at the ceremony, and he would pass the GRD flag from Johnson to Bostick.

LTG Sanchez's military convoy pulled up outside the Iraqi Forum. He stepped out of his vehicle. I saluted and introduced myself. I walked with him for a few minutes toward the large auditorium where the ceremony was. I congratulated him on a brilliant move. The early transfer of power had completely disrupted the enemy. He had a huge grin on his face. He knew the coalition had succeeded with its deception.

Escorting LTG Sanchez

The Change of Command was conducted flawlessly with MAJ Erik Stor as the master of ceremonies. The color guard and band from the 1st Cavalry Division supported the event, posting the colors and playing the National Anthem, Engineer Song and the Army Song. LTG Sanchez, MG Johnson, BG Bostick, and CSM Balch took the stage; remarks were made, and the ceremony closed.

MG Johnson and CSM Balch

BG Bostick

We then went to the incoming Commander's reception in a large room inside the Forum where most of us got to meet BG Bostick for the first time. Cake and sweets were served. LTG Sanchez stayed in the area for a few minutes. We had a chance to talk about home and families while the media was snapping photos in the distance. After about an hour, it was time to "ruck up" and go back to the war. COL Dornstauder and I stepped outside and looked up. The new Iraqi flag was flying outside, so we stopped for a quick photo to remember this historic day.

I immediately began seeing many more Iraqi police and military on the streets. They were increasing their capability, although they still had a long way to go.

COL Dornstauder with the new Iraqi flag

7

Attacks on Reconstruction

Invisible War

Improving security was the primary mission of the coalition's combat forces. Improving the Iraqi economy was the primary focus of the reconstruction mission. However, the enemy's strategy was to disrupt and discredit, by all means possible, any security or economic progress. Quite simply, the enemy's objective was for our respective missions to fail.

The mainstream media heavily covered the ongoing battles in the Iraqi streets involving our combat forces. But there was a parallel war ongoing that had little visibility. This war involved widespread and determined attacks against the national reconstruction effort. When a new project was completed and announced to the media, an attack on the site or the work force usually followed. This was a common occurrence for power plants. In one case, a few days after the announcement of the opening of a renovated Iraqi school, all the teachers were murdered.

The ruthless and evil nature of our enemy was unbelievably shocking. While many attacks on reconstruction targeted major projects and the critical infrastructure, the enemy also targeted the civilians and workers that supported the reconstruction mission. I was at a loss to figure out how to stop the carnage. During the early days, attacks on project sites and workers were highly visible to GRD, less visible to the combat forces and almost invisible to the American public.

Attacks on Physical Infrastructure

The two most important sectors of the Iraqi national infrastructure were oil and electricity and the physical facilities for both of these were attacked daily. Water (drinking water and wastewater sewers/treatment) was another sector that gained importance. The enemy was determined to prevent fuel and essential services from being delivered to the Iraqi people. If the economy and the daily lives of the average Iraqi did not improve, the U.S. and the Iraqi

Government would have little credibility and support from the Iraqi people.

Much of the responsibility for selecting individual reconstruction projects fell to the Program and Contracting Office (PCO). The PCO selected the lead contractors for rebuilding the different infrastructure sectors. Scores of other companies participated as subcontractors. Having a broad mix of companies participating was helpful as no single contractor had the capacity to do it all. When some failed, other construction firms could be called in to continue the mission. Once selected, the PCO handed the projects and lead contractors to the GRD for actual construction. Mr. Bob Slockbower and LTC Dan Patton were heavily engaged from a GRD/PCO perspective. In 2004, many of the lead infrastructure contractors were just getting started. Parsons / Parsons Brinkerhoff led the Electrical sector. Foster Wheeler led the Oil sector, and CM2Hill / Parsons led the Public Works and Water effort. Berger/URS led three infrastructure sectors: Transportation and Communications; Buildings, Health, Education; and Security and Justice. AECOM served as the Integrating Contractor, trying to coordinate across all the sectors.

Infrastructure security was a huge challenge, and there were no easy solutions. The lack of security throughout Iraq had a major impact on reconstruction costs, schedules, and even quality. Thirty percent of costs were allocated to providing security to protect our personnel and project sites—and for good reason. In August of 2004, GRD had 37 attacks on project sites, 16 attacks on personnel, and 5 attacks on reconstruction convoys. These attacks included IEDs, rockets, mortars, RPGs, small arms fire, threats to our work force, and other asymmetric attacks, including kidnappings.

The enemy attacked infrastructure daily, but they seemed to adapt and rotate target sets every week. This kept the security response off balance and continuously guessing what target was next. One week it was attacks on oil pipelines, and the next week it was electrical power lines. Other targets that followed included military facilities, markets, schools, police barracks, and bridges. The rapid changes made it difficult to establish a trend before the next target change occurred. It was a frustrating period.

The security strategy was to get the Iraqis to lead the infrastructure protection mission, and coalition forces would support them. Major General Jim Molan (Australia) was the coalition leader for Civil Military Operations (CMO). His team monitored the status of key infrastructure and coordinated security responses with Iraqi

Ministries and other authorities. The CMO would assist the host nation, upon their request.

Oil Infrastructure

Rebuilding and protecting the oil sector was critical because it provided 95% of Iraq's income. Without the $50-70 M per day in export revenue, Iraq could not pay its military, police, teachers, and administrators or provide key services to its citizens. Without oil income, Iraq would just be another Afghanistan.

But Iraq was blessed with the world's second largest known oil reserves; proven reserves were about 100 billion barrels (BB), and it was potentially as high as 200 BB. That represents about 16% of Middle East reserves. There was great concern that Saddam would torch his oil fields during the U.S. invasion in March 2003, much as Iraq did during the first Gulf War in 1990. Anticipating this, Task Force Restore Iraqi Oil (TF RIO) was stood up under BG Robert Crear, prior to the March 2003 invasion, to get the Iraqi oil infrastructure working as soon as possible. (TF RIO later became the RIO Directorate under the GRD in 2004. COL Emmit "Lem" Du Bose was the RIO Director, and LTC Mark Schneider served as the Deputy Director.) The RIO team used chartered flights (Royal Jordanian Airlines) to quickly and safely move oil workers around the country. These flights were dubbed "RIO Air."

Iraq has two distinct oil production areas. The southern fields near Basrah are dominated by the Rumaila field (5,600 square miles). These fields are in the Shia dominated area of Iraq, near the Iranian and Kuwaiti borders. This area has a production capacity of 2.4 million barrels per day (BPD), but typically produces less when attacked or due to poor maintenance. The southern field produces the best quality oil, and much of it is exported via offshore terminals in the Gulf. The northern fields in the Kurdish area are dominated by the Kirkuk field (600 square miles). This area has a production capacity of 0.9 million BPD, but like the southern field, often produces much less due to attacks or poor maintenance. The northern fields produce high sulfur oil that contains toxic hydrogen sulfide gas. This must be removed before further processing or exporting it through Turkey.

Prior to the invasion, Saddam used 80,000 men to protect the Iraqi oil infrastructure. With the disbanding of the Iraqi Army, there were insufficient trained Iraqi troops and police to protect oil pipelines and production facilities. But the coalition wanted to make the Iraqis increasingly responsible for their own security. Consequently, the Ministry of Oil (MOO) protected the oil infrastructure with a 14,000-man contractor guard force called Task Force Shield (TF Shield). TF Shield had limited authority. It could observe and report oil attacks, but the security contractors were not authorized to engage the enemy to prevent or disrupt pipeline attacks.

On average, there were three significant attacks each day on the oil infrastructure. Refineries were typically attacked with IEDs, rockets and mortars, or an occasional drive-by shooting of the gate guards. Oil pipelines were more exposed, less protected and easier for the enemy to hit. Typical pipeline attacks included strap-on IEDs, RPGs and small arms fire. In addition, some Iraqis simply made their livelihood by tapping the pipeline and selling the stolen oil on the open market. At the time, we found it was much easier to repair damaged oil pipelines than it was to protect them. This meant the MOO needed to have a responsive oil repair capability. The enemy knew this, and saboteurs often had an IED or ambush waiting for the pipeline repair team. We lost several repair crews and, given the mounting casualties, fewer civilians were willing to join the next team. Through attrition, the Iraqis eventually ran out of qualified repair crews.

The 40-inch Al Fatah pipeline near Bayji was hit in June, July and August 2004 in the same spot. Three attacks in a two-month window were beyond coincidence. When this pipeline was hit, flaming oil flowed a few hundred yards downhill and entered the Tigris River. Only a mile or so downstream was the water intake for the Bayji refinery. So a pipeline attack at Al Fatah not only cut off oil flowing from the Kirkuk oil fields, it also shut down the refinery. This area was patrolled by several U.S. and Iraqi organizations, but none were able to stop the attacks. There was strong speculation that the saboteurs were among the Iraqi patrols.

Attacks on refined fuel were relatively common. Although Iraq could produce plenty of crude oil, it had inadequate refining capacity to meet its own needs. Thus, refined fuel actually had to be imported to Iraq, much of it arriving in truck convoys. The fuel convoys and storage areas made easy targets for insurgents.

At one point, the coalition paid local Iraqi leaders to secure the pipeline that was running through their tribal areas. The idea had great merit, but it failed because of U.S. procurement regulations. Rules required an open competition by multiple bidders for the local security contracts. This meant that local Iraqi rivals had to compete for the security work, in a winner-take-all competition. Winners had performance incentives and were provided bonuses if they had no attacks in their sectors. But there was no Rule of Law in Iraq. The losers of these competitions began attacking the pipeline to reduce the relative power and financial rewards paid to the winners. We forced our acquisition rules down the throats of Iraqis, and we created new enemies. The cost incurred in money and lives undoubtedly far exceeded the savings achieved by our "fair procurement process." The lesson learned was that we simply couldn't impose U.S. peacetime contracting standards in a contingency environment. We needed flexible, common sense contracting practices that best supported our national security objectives.

Al Fatah pipeline fire

Several years later, pipeline exclusion zones (PEZ) were set up on key segments of the oil distribution system. A PEZ prevented unauthorized personnel from getting close enough to the pipeline to damage or steal from it. A PEZ would include anti-vehicle trenches and berms, concertina wire and guard towers to deny access to the pipeline area. The first PEZ was completed in 2008 on the Kirkuk –

Bayji line. It was the most successful investment made in Iraqi oil security. The project paid for itself in just three days.

Attack on Oil Platform

I remember one significant attack on Iraq's main offshore oil platform by two suicide boats. Fortunately, this attack was not successful, but did result in U.S. casualties.

On April 24, 2004, the enemy launched a daring suicide boat bomb attack on Iraq's main off shore oil terminal. This attack was on a critical and strategic node in the Iraqi infrastructure. Initial reports also mentioned close combat fighting and small arms fire on the platform. But initial combat reports can be vague and confusing—it's often hard to separate the facts from speculation. Given that GRD had the Restore Iraqi Oil (RIO) mission, I thought the repair of this offshore oil facility might become an urgent project that we would be directed to undertake immediately. I expected my Commanding General to call me for a status report, and I had little information to offer other than open source reporting on CNN. I needed more facts.

Oil platform

I had little experience with offshore oil platforms and did not know how much damage could occur during such an attack. I had several immediate questions. It was late, and I had no one else in the Ops Center to turn to for more information. Then I recalled that Vice Admiral (VADM) Tim Josiah, former Chief of Staff of the U.S. Coast Guard (Retired), might be able to help me assess the situation. He was a former industry colleague working on homeland security issues for Raytheon in Rosslyn, Virginia. VADM Josiah knew something about offshore platforms and had even been to some of the facilities in the Arabian Gulf. I did not know what time it was in the United States, but I picked up the phone and called him. I asked him if he had seen the open source reports of an attack on Iraq's offshore oil platform and began asking him a series of questions: If such an attack were to occur, what could be the scope of the damage? What was the worst case? What was the likely case? What impact would it have on oil export operations? What if a tanker was offloading at the time of the attack? Could a shipping channel be blocked? Has a similar attack ever occurred?

VADM Josiah walked me through the scenarios and was quite helpful in framing the situation and the potential outcomes. He emphasized the massive size of these oil platforms and that even a large bomb would likely not destroy the entire facility. We later learned that the suicide boats had failed to seriously damage the platform. However, one exploded next to the Firebolt, a patrol boat, resulting in the first Coast Guardsman killed in action since Vietnam. I was grateful that VADM Tim Josiah was available that night. His insight and perspective made a difference in the early stages of our response. I kept his number handy in case I needed to reach back for more help on future attacks.

Electrical Infrastructure

The electrical sector was critical because it was essential to drive Iraqi industry and restart the national economy. Many Iraqis measured economic progress by the availability of electricity; Saddam had used it as leverage over his people. He rewarded his allies by delivering electrical power to Sunni regions, and he punished the Shia and Kurds by denying it to their regions in Iraq.

To address Iraq's power needs, Task Force Restore Iraqi Electricity (TF RIE) was stood up in September 2003 under BG Steven Hawkins and Deputy Commander, COL Todd Semonite. USAID also had several electrical power projects. TF RIE later became the RIE Directorate under GRD and LTC Dave Press took charge. The RIE effort to improve electrical service involved generating more power and distributing it more fairly throughout the country. I was glad to see Dave Press arrive. There had been some speculation that he would not be coming to Iraq. MG Johnson told me, if Dave did not arrive, I would lead the RIE Directorate and would need a crash course in electrical power generation and distribution. As it turned out, Dave and his sidekick, MAJ Erik Stor, did an outstanding job.

Iraq's electrical system had been neglected for two decades—it suffered for several reasons, including those caused by international sanctions. The U.S. soon discovered that it inherited an old and heavily bandaged system. When U.S. forces arrived in April 2003, Iraq was only producing 3,200 megawatts (MW) of power - well below the demand of 6,500 MW. This resulted in long blackouts across Iraq. For example, Baghdad might get fourteen hours of power a day, but Basrah might get only six. Some additional electricity was imported from Iran and Turkey, but it was not sufficient to make up the deficit.

Electricity was provided free of charge to the Iraqi people, so there was no real cap on demand. The U.S. electrical goal for Iraq was 6,000 MW, coming from all sources. As the economy strengthened, more Iraqis bought appliances, satellite TVs and air conditioners. In this situation, the rising supply could never reach the faster rising demand. Iraqis were using electricity as fast as megawatts could be added to the national grid.

Under Saddam's rule, there were separate islands of electrical power within Iraq. These regional islands needed to be connected together to better distribute and balance power on the national grid. That meant hundreds of kilometers of 400 kilovolt (KV) and 132 KV power lines needed to be added. Like the oil pipelines, these major electrical power lines were easily accessed and targeted by insurgents.

The Ministry of Electricity (MOE) was primarily responsible for protecting the Iraqi power grid. The MOE's 6000-man Electric Police Security Services (EPSS) guarded key facilities and escorted repair teams. Again, the coalition policy was to have the Iraqis take the lead on security, and would assist the MOE on a case-by-case basis. There were two or three significant attacks each week on the electrical infrastructure that followed the same pattern as those on the oil infrastructure (IEDs, rockets or drive-by shootings targeting the gate guards). If the coalition put out a press release to announce the opening of a new Iraqi power plant, insurgents read it as an invitation to attack the facility. Consequently, advertising the successful completion of a new project often proved counterproductive. We had to carefully balance our reporting of reconstruction progress with our operational security needs.

Two notable examples of attempted attacks on major power plants happened in August. The Mullah Abdullah Power Plant was located west of Kirkuk. On August 1, four IEDs were found inside the perimeter of the plant near a turbine and some transformers. This was the first incident of an IED threat inside an electrical power plant that I could recall. It was a wakeup call for all of us. I strongly suspected there were insurgents operating inside the local work force. An explosive ordinance team disarmed the IEDs and our security procedures were reviewed to prevent further occurrences. On August 10, security forces caught a VBIED driving toward Qudas, the site of several new electrical power plants located about 25 kilometers north of Baghdad. I am not sure what alerted the security team to stop the suspicious vehicle, but the car bomb was detonated short of the target.

It also did not take long for us to realize that there were interdependencies between the oil and electrical sectors. Much of Iraq's electricity was produced using oil. Consequently, fuel supplies, used for running electrical generation plants, were often targeted. Blowing up an oil pipeline, storage tank or fuel convoy could also cut fuel needed for generating electricity. So insurgents, armed with some knowledge of infrastructure vulnerabilities, could disrupt two targets with a single oil pipeline attack.

Power lines ran across the barren Iraqi terrain, and were easily damaged with IEDs. Looters saw the new metal towers and electrical cables as a source of income. They would cut up both with torches and ship the scrap metal to Turkey. Sometimes high winds would also drop the towers. By late summer, the Iraqi MOE ran desperately short of spare towers and requested coalition support. The CMO team coordinated the air delivery of rapid repair towers from the U.S. to support this urgent need.

Damaged towers

I was increasingly frustrated at the loss of power lines, and I came up with an idea to counter the saboteurs. I wanted each electrical tower to be equipped with a small box at the top. The box would have a motion sensor and imager under it. The top of the box would have a solar collector for charging an internal battery and an inexpensive satellite radio. If a saboteur drove or walked under the tower, the motion sensor would wake up the camera and snap an image. The photo, along with a time stamp and its location, would be burst back via satellite to a remote monitoring facility. If the picture showed what appeared to be a real threat, an Apache helicopter or quick reaction force was dispatched immediately to kill or capture the saboteurs. A few days later, I improved the concept. I added a grenade to the contents of the box. Instead of dispatching an Apache, the operator could simply send a command back to the box. A trap door under the box would open and drop the grenade on the unsuspecting saboteurs. I thought this was a slick idea, but I couldn't find anyone to build it in the combat zone. Everyone was too busy with their 18 hour a day job.

I had another idea that I proposed to BG Tom Bostick. We could simply plant land mines around the base of the towers and then put several rows of concertina wire around the surrounding area to keep innocent people and animals out. We could then mark the area with "minefield" signs in Arabic. Most sensible people would be deterred and heed the signs. I am sure a few would test their luck. I knew this idea would get little support, as there was a worldwide movement to ban landmines. But this application was worthy of consideration. BG Bostick liked it and took the idea to MNF-I, and as I expected, the idea was rejected.

Many other infrastructure attacks occurred during my tour. But they are too numerous to recount. After experiencing a few hundred varied attacks, I felt as though I had played in the Super Bowl of critical infrastructure protection. My GRD colleagues appreciated how easily such attacks could occur in any country, including the United States.

Within a week of my return to the United States, I briefed LTG Vines, the 18th Airborne Corps Commander, on all aspects of Iraqi infrastructure at his Military Readiness Exercise (MRX) at Fort Bragg, North Carolina. He had his senior leaders, staff and a "gray beard" panel preparing for their pending deployment to Iraq. I didn't pull any punches. I laid out all the issues and gave him my perspective on the path ahead. I did not want his Corps to re-learn any hard lessons.

A few months later, I met with Rudy Holm, a Department of Homeland Security (DHS) Infrastructure Protection official. I recently had major knee surgery and my leg was in a cast. So Rudy came over to my house during lunch, and we ate a couple of Big Macs. I showed him scores of photos of major oil and electrical attacks. I spent two hours with Rudy recounting all the infrastructure security issues and the hard lessons we had recently learned. He asked good questions, and I was impressed with his professionalism. At the end of the meeting, I felt good. DHS would benefit from our experience, and they could now be better prepared to defend our own country.

Attacks on Civilians and Infrastructure Workers

While enemy attacks were often directed against physical infrastructure, sometimes it was easier to attack the civilians and workers that were critical to building and operating it. The enemy quickly recognized our dependence on civilians and used it to their advantage. Attacks on Iraqi and coalition workers were intended to degrade the infrastructure through fear and intimidation. Without these workers, essential projects and services could not be completed or delivered. The Iraqi people were often denied electricity, fuel, water and transportation because the work force was continuously coerced, threatened or killed. It was considered "asymmetric warfare." By attacking the U.S. indirectly, the enemy could discredit our security and reconstruction efforts.

Rebuilding a country under these highly adverse conditions was tough, tough work that required the full commitment of all parties. It was particularly challenging for our civilians, who had a choice in facing danger. Civilians who volunteer to work in a combat zone can always vote with their feet, and leave. Without our civilian experts and laborers, our reconstruction mission would undoubtedly fail. Our civilians and workers were all volunteers, and they were doing good things for the Iraqi people. Our work contributed to domestic stability and economic prosperity. It wasn't easy, and it was inherently dangerous. However, it was an incredibly rewarding experience to bring the hope of a better life to the Iraqi people.

The Unseen War on Workers

Work force attacks were a daily occurrence, but few outside the reconstruction mission understood clearly their serious impact. Terrorists did not sign the Geneva Convention—they were not accountable under the Law of Land Warfare. They did not have a Code of Conduct and were not restricted by any Rules of Engagement. Their tactics to create fear were limited only by their imaginations. At the same time, Iraqi Police and Military were neither well trained nor widely available, so the Rule of Law in Iraq was not firmly established or respected.

Common tactics used against workers included threats, kidnappings, assassinations, and ambushes with IEDs or small arms fire during their daily commute to and from the project sites. In August 2004, the GRD Safety Officer, Jeffrey Pfannes, reported that 45 USACE contractors had been killed and 82 more were wounded during GRD's mission. I realized that these numbers were only a fraction of the total contractor casualties because many early attacks on reconstruction crews were not well documented or reported. Furthermore, GRD was only one of several coalition organizations that were employing contractors and Iraqi workers.

Across the country, hundreds of civilians and workers were killed, and it was largely transparent to maneuver forces and senior officials. They occasionally heard about this "shadow war", but it took many months before they understood the full extent and impact on the reconstruction effort. Logistics convoys were frequently hijacked, and some of the drivers were decapitated. Terrorists would also torture their victims by using an electric drill to bore holes in their knees and joints. The enemy was unbelievably cruel and their actions were far worse in intensity and scale than the U.S. abuse that occurred at Abu Ghraib. The mainstream media rarely reported these events nor held our enemies accountable for their ghastly crimes. Terrorist conduct got a free pass, and American misdeeds were vilified.

For many months, the military command in Iraq, MNF-I, had limited visibility on what was actually happening with the security of reconstruction projects. The security contractors, responsible for protecting many of these sites and the civilian work force, did not have access to military computer networks that would allow them to quickly report attacks. As the GRD Operations Officer, I would receive an unclassified Serious Incident Report (SIR) over the internet after an attack occurred. There were often delays in reporting from remote sites due to limited internet connectivity. Most incidents were several hours old before they were reported. Some reports were several days old. Once my operations staff was informed, we would re-enter the report in the Significant Activities (SIGACTS) database on a military network used by MNF-I. Unfortunately, any incident over twelve hours old did not flash up as a new incident, but instead automatically went into a historical file that wasn't visible to commanders. Thus, key leaders weren't seeing the daily attacks. Only after the standup of the Reconstruction Operations Center in late 2004 did the reporting situation significantly improve.

Thirty percent of the cost of reconstruction was related directly to security. It was a shockingly high number, but without security, our mission would simply fail. When civilians and contractors were killed, the prevailing philosophy in the government was "just pay the next contractor more money". It was a sad reality, and I was embarrassed that the lives of contractors were regarded in such a cavalier manner.

Rush Hour Attacks

Assassin's Gate car bombing

In Iraq, we owned many islands of land called Forward Operating Bases (FOBs). The Green Zone or International Zone was one of them. Many civilian workers needed to come to these islands each day and pass through an entry control point or main gate.

At these gates, all vehicles and personnel were thoroughly inspected and searched for weapons and contraband. During the morning rush, hundreds of cars and civilians could be in the queue waiting to get through a checkpoint. Waiting in line was inherently dangerous, and it was stressful for both civilians and guards. Long lines of cars and trucks were highly visible and vulnerable to attack. In some of the worst queues, it took up to four hours to clear the gate. And we constantly feared that any one of those many vehicles was a massive bomb just waiting to detonate. One major car bomb detonated at Assassin's Gate in early 2004. Among the dead were 15 of our interpreters on their way to work. After this attack, many civilians were understandably reluctant to wait in line.

Inside the base, civilians would commute to their daily jobs. Most were on foot. Many civilians worked in a palace or the adjacent buildings. These morning pedestrian migrations were targeted with occasional rocket attacks. It made commuting in Iraq far more stressful than any rush hour in New York City or Washington, D.C.

Threats to the Work Force

By Iraqi standards, reconstruction offered a good paying and much needed job. Any job was often the only source of income for an entire family. The average daily wage for an Iraqi laborer was $3-5 per day. And many of the jobs available in Iraq did not provide steady employment. So in the eyes of many Iraqis, reconstruction jobs were highly attractive. One Iraqi, making $40 a week in reconstruction, was ecstatic about his "dream money". He never imagined he could earn this level of income. But taking these reconstruction jobs also exposed workers to great personal risk.

Before escalating to murder, terrorists sometimes started with an overt threat. The names of workers supporting a U.S. reconstruction project were posted in a local mosque. All those listed were directed to immediately quit their jobs, or they would be killed. It was in-your-face intimidation. If a father went to work to support his family, he and his family would risk death. Some of the workers were forced to report on the activities of others. The enemy used threats and coercion to turn Iraqis against their friends and neighbors. The impact of these threats was immediate. One project site with 400 workers on Monday had only 15 report to work on Wednesday. Owners of companies that had contracts with GRD were identified by terrorists, followed home from the project site, and ruthlessly killed in front of their families. Good people, who only wanted a decent job to make a better life for their loved ones, were vulnerable every day.

We had to take extensive measures to protect the identities of these brave Iraqi companies and contractors. That meant not publicly disclosing the names of the contractors. That ran counter to the coalition push to "get the word out" about reconstruction progress. We had to balance reporting on progress with operational security. Those Iraqi workers and employers that stuck with us during this period had real guts.

Iraqi workers at Nasiriyah

We talked to many workers during an inspection of the Qudas electrical power plant. They were quite grateful for their new jobs and the opportunity to make their country a better place. Some gave tearful speeches expressing their sincere gratitude. The same was true in Nasiriyah and dozens of other project sites. But universally, these workers did not want their photos taken and published in a newsletter or magazine for fear of being identified by terrorists. Many of these Iraqis did not even tell their families where they worked or what they did.

Interpreters Being Turned

Few Americans spoke Arabic, Farsi or other regional languages, so we were often dependent on local interpreters. Many interpreters were embedded with combat units to facilitate their daily operations. They would go on patrols with U.S. forces and help our troops understand what was happening and being said. The interpreters had to be vetted to ensure they were not an "insider" that could be informing the enemy on our current or planned operations. To reduce the potential of an informant or suicide bomber working in our ranks, many of the interpreters selected were Iraqi Christians.

But even reliable interpreters could be turned. During house searches, military teams would sometimes hold up a photo of a wanted insurgent or terrorist, and ask, "Do you know this person? " The translator would communicate the question in the local language. However, if the enemy found out the identity of an interpreter, they could be coerced to work against us. Instead of translating the question properly, the interpreter might say in Arabic, "Shake your head 'no'."

Iraqi Interpreter with Handgun

One day, MAJ Jim Ball, the GRD Current Operations Officer, reported that one of our female Iraqi interpreters, Jasmine, had a loaded handgun in her purse, and she brought it into our palace. We immediately questioned her: Why did she bring it? What was her intention? How did she get it through the main security checkpoint? Her answers were clear and completely understandable. She needed the pistol for self-protection. Terrorists had just killed her cousin. They knew Jasmine worked for the Americans and were now looking for her. And she was the only one in her family with a job.

To confiscate her handgun and send her home was a potential death sentence. Our initial solution was to secure her weapon when she entered our perimeter, and we would return it when she departed in the evenings. But the death threats continued to the point that she could not return home at night. She was terrified. In this exceptional case, we made temporary arrangements so she could live in our secure compound. Eventually the threats subsided, and she was able to return to her family.

Power Plant Crisis

For many months, deteriorating security disrupted critical reconstruction projects in the electrical, water and sewage sectors. At one point, the lack of security drove major companies, like GE Power Systems and Siemens, to suspend operations in Iraq. That literally shut down progress restoring the Iraqi electrical grid. During a discussion with the GRD command group, I was informed that Bechtel (a global engineering, construction, management, and development services company) had a zero tolerance policy for battlefield casualties. If an employee was injured or killed by hostilities, the manager would be immediately fired. That led to highly risk-averse behavior, like sitting in a secure compound and never visiting a project site. The poor security situation caused major schedule slippages, and many managers would continuously re-baseline their projects to make them appear to be on schedule.

In April 2004, a convoy of contractors was hit with a car bomb in Baghdad causing multiple fatalities. The GE team lost several key technicians. The survivors, who escaped the carnage, made their way back to a secure base. I later learned that they had to return to recover their own dead. The company immediately decided to pull all personnel out of the country. Without these technicians, many new power plants could not be commissioned. The withdrawal of GE personnel from Iraq became a strategic issue.

MG Peter Chiarelli, Commander of the 1st Cavalry Division (1CD), was responsible for security in Baghdad, and he was determined to fix the problem. He personally visited GRD HQ and sat down with MG Johnson, COL Dornstauder and myself to discuss how to move forward. MG Chiarelli was an impressive man. His knowledge of what was going on rebuilding Baghdad, particularly in the Al Rasheed District and Sadr City, exceeded our own. As a maneuver commander, he owned the ground and moved about it far more freely than GRD could in its SUVs. He believed that the 1st Cav could stop much of the fighting if we could just build sewers and get fresh water and electricity flowing in Sadr City. The Shia slum was never provided these essential services under Saddam. MG Chiarelli's argument was very simple and clear – the coalition's reconstruction efforts were his most valuable tool to keep his troops from being killed. Iraqi men with good jobs don't look for a fight. Reconstruction employed Iraqis and offered them greatly improved living conditions. (Over time Chiarelli's strategy proved right. Attacks in Sadr City fell from a high of 160 per week to less than five.) MG Chiarelli stated that part of the problem in the GE attack was that reconstruction contractors frequently move in his sector without the knowledge of his combat forces, so there was no military to back them up. He flat out guaranteed his Division would escort our contractors, any time they needed it. He wanted that message conveyed to GE and any other contractor operating in his area.

Armed with this security guarantee, GRD sent Major Erik Stor to Amman, Jordan to meet with senior GE officials to persuade them to return to the battlefield. It took serious negotiation with senior corporate leaders to persuade the company to return to Iraq and continue progress on major electrical projects, but GE eventually returned, and security escorts were no longer a problem. About this time, GRD began realigning its area offices to support specific maneuver units. The reorganization and re-alignment enabled better communications and coordination between the shooters and the builders. Several months later, the PMO and GRD stood up the Reconstruction Operations Center to address the broader logistics and security issues facing contractors on the battlefield.

Other Work Force Attacks

Some of the more common work force attacks involved small arms fire. Buses and cars filled with reconstruction workers traveling to and from project sites were often shot at—usually a drive-by shooting from another moving vehicle. The main gates to project sites were occasionally sniped and roadside bombs were used to kill workers driving in SUVs. (I remember a graphic IED incident near the Bayji Refinery where two workers were killed.) Another effective attack involved placing car bombs at locations where scores of laborers assembled in the mornings to find day work. Men would unknowingly gather near a parked car bomb and then be killed in a mass casualty explosion.

Logistics convoys, driving from Kuwait to Baghdad, were badly mauled by attacks in April and May. Many of the drivers supporting the coalition were citizens of India. The Indian Government asked the Kuwaiti Government to refuse to let their citizens drive into Iraq due to extreme danger. Kuwait complied, and much of our food and reconstruction material stacked up on the Kuwait side of the border. We had to repeatedly send liaison officers to the Iraq-Kuwait border to help get the logistics "unstuck".

Motorbikes were sometimes used to attack a vehicle stopped in traffic. If a window was open, a grenade might be dropped into the vehicle. If the windows were closed, a magnetic mounted explosive device could be placed on the door. The motorbike then sped off before the vehicle exploded.

One of the RIE security contractors, I think it was Corky Shelton (Fluor), decided to preemptively attack the drive-by shooters. He added a nondescript Iraqi vehicle to the back of his convoy. It looked innocuous and attracted little enemy attention. The extra car simply did not look like it was part of the SUV convoy in front of it. But lying in the back seat of the Iraqi vehicle were some friendly shooters. When a drive-by attacker closed in on the SUV convoy from the rear, our hidden shooters popped up and killed the would-be attackers. Essentially, Corky's team surprised the enemy and conducted a moving ambush on the insurgents. It was a good thing. The dead attackers were found to be packing armor piercing rounds that would have easily penetrated the SUVs.

A Complex Attack on a Police Station

Many Iraqi Police stations were rebuilt, and they often became targets. One of the more impressive attacks by our enemies occurred during the summer of 2004. From a tactical perspective, the level of planning and complexity of the attack were surprising. It reinforced the belief that some of the enemy forces we were up against were well trained.

During one of our daily staff meetings, I briefed the details of the police station attack to the CG and the GRD staff. When I concluded, the silence in the room was deafening. In preparation for the attack, the enemy was able to acquire an Iraqi Police uniform (Captain). This was not surprising in Iraq. Even U.S. military uniforms were sometimes sold in local markets. The insurgents then stole or acquired an Iraqi Police vehicle and rigged it as a car bomb. The enemy also conducted a detailed reconnaissance on the station and knew that U.S. forces in the area were on call to respond, if the police were overwhelmed.

Phase one of the attack commenced when the enemy-driven Iraqi police vehicle pulled up to the main entrance of a police station. The gate guards saw an Iraqi Police Captain in the vehicle and let it pass through the entrance. Once the vehicle was inside the compound, it drove up to the headquarters and detonated, destroying the building and causing mass casualties among the police. Iraqi first responders immediately rushed to the scene to find survivors and quickly evacuate the wounded to local hospitals / clinics. The arrival of medical, fire and police personnel on the disaster scene was anticipated by the enemy, who had the site under observation.

Phase two of the attack commenced with a rocket and mortar attack on the police compound, intending to kill as many unprotected first responders as possible. The Iraqis were overwhelmed by the successive attacks and required immediate assistance from the U.S. military. Even this response was anticipated by the enemy. The U.S. Quick Reaction Force (QRF) left its installation several miles away.

The enemy knew where the QRF would originate and what route it would take to the disaster scene.

In Phase three of the attack, the insurgents set up an ambush on the road and attacked the U.S. force that was enroute to the scene. There were upwards of twenty attackers with RPGs and machine guns ambushing the QRF. Finally, the U.S. called in Apache helicopter gunships to defeat the ambush. The attackers fled into a nearby wood line and were decimated with overwhelming firepower that killed at least 12 of the insurgents.

After learning the details of this attack, I strongly suspected the enemy had an "insider" at the police headquarters. One bad guy (who is a good actor) inside an organization can cause immense harm by revealing operational details and vulnerabilities to the enemy. Persistent insider threats provided a huge competitive advantage to our enemies throughout Iraq.

Friendly Fire

Attacks on reconstruction personnel didn't always originate from the enemy. Casualties from friendly fire, also called fratricide, have happened in every conflict. One of Murphy's Laws of combat is that "Friendly fire ain't friendly". Another term used by the military is "blue on blue" engagements, and they are mainly due to the "fog of war". The noise, confusion and fear in combat are a recipe for fratricide incidents. And reconstruction personnel were not immune. There were plenty of opportunities for fratricide in Iraq. The complex mix of U.S., Coalition, and Iraqi Army, combined with the Iraqi Police and armed security contractors, added to the uncertainty of "who was who" in a combat environment. Many of our allies used Russian weapons, like AKs and PKMs, just as the insurgents did. I personally approved the use of Russian weapons by our security contractors.

One notable incident occurred at a USMC checkpoint in Al Anbar province. A GRD vehicle pulled up to the Marine guards, stopped and was then told to proceed forward a few yards to the next checkpoint. The driver did. But something was not communicated to the machine gunner covering the checkpoint. The Marines opened fire at close range on one of our SUVs. Thankfully, this particular SUV was one of the few with Level 3 armor that stopped the rounds from penetrating and killing our personnel. Shaken, the occupants in the SUV believed they properly followed the guard's instructions. Later, the Marine guards conducted an After Action Review (AAR) of what happened to determine if they needed to change their procedures. Their only conclusion was that they "should have used armor piercing rounds". In other words, the Marines' only mistake was that they did not kill the vehicle occupants. Man, were our guys pissed off.

And given the eclectic group of armed contractors and military that were supporting GRD, we had an unacceptably high number of weapons that were accidentally fired. The military term for this was "negligent discharge". We probably had ten security guards accidentally killed at project sites due to negligent discharges. I recall an incident where a local guard accidentally fired his 30-round magazine into the concrete floor during a shift turnover. He killed three other guards nearby.

The training standards for some of the security contractors were clearly inadequate. The U.S. military was not responsible for training them. Training was outsourced to each security contractor, and there were no universal standards being enforced. The evidence of poor training started to build with each passing week. My side view mirror was shot off one day—from inside the vehicle! A few weeks later, I found an exit hole in the passenger side door of another vehicle. I inquired, but no one seemed to know how it happened. In another incident, a Ukrainian guard accidentally blew a hole through the roof of the guard shack on our perimeter. It was during his first few minutes of duty on his first day at GRD. He was inadequately trained on his shotgun. To improve safety, we enforced a zero tolerance policy. Contractors who accidentally fired their weapons immediately lost their jobs. The incidents declined rapidly.

Hard Lessons

One of the main lessons I learned in Iraq was that the U.S. could not succeed without civilians and contractors on the battlefield. Many of the military's key support functions were contracted out. But outsourcing had real limits and our enemies widely exploited these vulnerabilities. Contractors and civilians were the soft underbelly and were particularly vulnerable when working outside the wire without adequate security. Technicians, logistics convoys, and laborers all shared the same risks.

Employing Iraqis was not only important for the reconstruction mission; it was one of our best tools to improve the domestic security situation. Employing Iraqis was also essential for capacity building – training the Iraqis how to build, operate and maintain their own infrastructure. COL Joe Schroedel proposed forming an Iraqi Corps of Engineers that he called I-FEST. This new organization would enable Iraqi engineers to stand up as U.S. engineers stood down.

Finally, tracking physical attacks against Iraqi infrastructure (oil, electricity, rail, and bridges) was necessary, but not sufficient. Attacks and threats against a reconstruction work force was also an asymmetric attack against infrastructure. Reporting these incidents needs to be timely and the analysis needs to be focused on the effects.

Reconstruction Operations Center

Since the early days of reconstruction in Iraq, the security situation for GRD convoys has dramatically improved. While my Operations team worked full throttle to get better vehicles and movement standards in place in 2004, a higher level of integration was still needed to protect reconstruction personnel.

That higher need was to provide an Iraq-wide reconstruction situational awareness picture and an integrated command and control function. The GRD G3 shop lacked the capacity to make it happen. Our minimal staff was overwhelmed with just keeping the division alive. The G3 had only one officer running current operations, one officer running future plans, an Operations NCO and a Movements NCO. We were all working 16-18 hour shifts with no days off. We needed a ringer to come in, focus on the problem, and lead this strategic integration effort. So LTC Joe Schweitzer deployed from HQ USACE and joined Colonel Ted Kanamine on the newly formed GRD Strategic Planning Team to address the problem directly.

The big problem was that no single organization had responsibility for the entire Iraqi reconstruction mission. Thus, no organization or leader had all the answers. In addition to GRD, there were many other stakeholder organizations involved in rebuilding including the U.S. Embassy, Iraqi Ministers, the U.S. Agency for International Development (USAID), the Air Force Center for Engineering and the Environmental (AFCEE), Navy Seabees, MNSTC-I, and dozens of tactical military units that had hundreds of small projects throughout the country. The MNF-I Commander, General Casey, wanted to have unity of command for all Iraqi reconstruction and one "go to" guy to answer all questions. GEN Casey looked to GRD and BG Tom Bostick for those answers.

LTC Schweitzer initially traveled to Iraq in mid-2004 with the Chief of Engineers to assess the situation and determine what still needed to be done to unify the reconstruction mission. He started working with BG Bostick, the GRD staff, Mr. Charlie Hess and his PMO/PCO staff to determine how to provide a more comprehensive view of reconstruction. The goal was to produce a real-time strategic view of who was doing what, when and where. The military calls it a common operating picture (COP). If LTC Schweitzer could build a COP for reconstruction, then senior leaders could make better decisions, based on facts not on speculation.

My G3 shop was working on the immediate needs for reconstruction, and looking at urgent requirements for the next few months. We did what was needed to keep GRD alive. It was "Git'r Done", every day. LTC Schweitzer was looking at the long haul. Joe was working on what was needed to enable GRD and the reconstruction mission to thrive. My team was making the bricks. Joe Schweitzer's team was building the house.

LTC Joe Schweitzer

In late August 2004, Joe was advocating for the rapid stand up of a Reconstruction Operations Center (ROC) and working with CAPT Wray on the concept. They began information briefings to senior leaders and stakeholders. The case for an integrated ROC was compelling. The current state was an ad-hoc assembly of reconstruction command & control (C2) efforts; there were many reconstruction players that were only partially linked. As a result, no organization was in control of all reconstruction and security efforts. We lacked a common operating picture of all activities. There was no single dataset to answer inquiries from the Office of the Secretary of Defense (OSD) or Congress and repeated data calls to disparate organizations were painful. There was a lack of coordination between contractors, security escort teams, construction managers, major subordinate commands (MSCs) and military forces that were fighting the enemy. This caused both duplications and gaps in the total effort. The MSCs were unhappy with the suboptimal delivery of reconstruction projects.

The desired end state was a ROC that provided a single point of control, coordination, and deconfliction for all reconstruction in Iraq, and it would be connected to everything. The ROC would manage resources, security, and construction, as well as coordinate contractor movements and operations throughout the battlespace. The ROC would develop a single common operating picture and collect and disseminate all data. It was to provide one-stop shopping for the Chief of Mission (COM), MNF-I, MSCs, reconstruction agencies, and contractors. The ROC was envisioned to be the place in Iraq "where the President of the United States would come to be briefed on reconstruction".

The ROC's guiding principles were simple. It would use tools and components already in place. Disparate databases would be consolidated into a single one. The COM would own the reconstruction program. MNF-I would own security. The Iraq Reconstruction Management Office (IRMO) was the chief of all data. And the MSCs were major customers. The ROC would integrate all reconstruction, regardless of funding sources: IRRF, AIRP, DFI, AIRP, CERP, and Mayor's Programs. The new Ops center would be appropriate for a 4-star command and the $18 B program. It would create efficiencies by eliminating duplicate efforts, and enable improved security for personnel.

Joe did a masterful job getting buy-in for the ROC concept by incorporating inputs from all stakeholders, including: Mr. Nash (IRMO), Mr. Hess (PCO), Tony Hunter-Choat (PCO Security), Jack Holly (PCO Logistics), BG Bostick (GRD CG), Bob Slockbower (GRD SES), LTC Vance Purvis (GRD G2), myself (GRD G3), Construction sector leads, Interagency teams, BG Davidson (350th Civil Affairs), MSCs (1MEF G3, 1ID CA), MG Molan (Civil Military Operations - an Aussie), MG Stratman, MG Williamson, Pentagon Joint Staff (J-5), DOS, USAID, and multiple contractors.

The ROC concept was right on and was quickly sold. The race was on to immediately build and staff it within 30 days. The ROC would have the precision and discipline of a military ops center, with military watch officers and civilian staff manning it 24/7. It would be equipped with state-of-the-art plasma screens, vehicle-tracking systems, a communications suite equivalent to MNF-I Joint Operations Center (JOC) and connections for classified information networks (SIPR and CENTRIX).

When completed, the ROC occupied a large room with dozens of duty desks for all key participants: PCO, IRMO, GRD, MNF-I, MNSTC-I, CMOC, COM, USAID, PAO, IIG, ISF, U.N. and contractors. Special seats were designated for GEN Casey and AMB Negroponte. The ROC was integrated with the national JOC, the State Department's TOC, and other regional reconstruction operations centers (RROCs). An intelligence cell, manned by Aegis, was able to filter classified information and produced unclassified intelligence that contractors could access and use to enhance their own security. Brigadier Ellery, a retired U.K. officer, was the primary Aegis official. Other support contractors included PMW, that staffed the Logistics Management Coordination Cell (LMCC) and AECOM that supported data collection and reporting.

Joe was pushing to get the ROC concept approved in early September 2004, the same week I was departing Iraq. I never saw it stand up during my tour. But I did tour the ROC when I went back to Iraq in 2007. The before and after comparison of reconstruction operations was stunning. The ROC provided the robust staffing, the integrated information systems, and the construction, security, and logistics coordination that we so badly lacked in the early days of reconstruction. If only we could have gone to war better prepared. The ROC finally brought all reconstruction efforts together, but we had to pay a very high price up to that point. This is a great lesson learned, and we can't forget it in future conflicts.

I wish all this had been worked out before we went to war, but the Army had rarely practiced Phase IV operations (Security and Stabilization) in warfighting exercises. Our plans were to fight, win, and then go home. Reconstruction was not seriously considered as a DOD mission—it was considered a State Department issue. But we now know we need to integrate the ROC and Contractor Operations Centers (CONOCs) into our doctrine, our force structure and into our peacetime military exercises. Surprisingly little of this was covered in the new Army Counter Insurgency Manual, Field Manual 3-24.

As the ROC concept evolved, several variants were stood up. They were all networked together and over time, they became more fully integrated with the maneuver units. The National Reconstruction Operations Center (NROC) was stood up to better coordinate security and logistics. A contractor could register via a NROC website to request convoy clearances, security escorts and to coordinate movements with all tactical forces. The convoy locations could be tracked real-time using the Tapestry system. Via the NROC, the military had much better situational awareness (SA) of where the reconstruction convoys were and could respond in an emergency with a Quick Reaction Force (QRF). Regional Reconstruction Operations Centers (RROCs) were placed at key locations throughout the country and reported up to the Baghdad ROC. Aegis set up RROCs to coordinate local convoys and to provide unclassified intelligence to contractors operating in Iraq. The Strategic Reconstruction Operations Center (SROC) focused entirely on Baghdad – the center of gravity for the entire war. The term Contractor Operations Center (CONOC) emerged later. It described a class of operations centers primarily manned by and servicing the needs of contractors on the battlefield.

* * *

There were many unsung heroes in Iraq, and Joe Schweitzer was one of them. He helped the reconstruction program take a great leap forward. Perhaps someday he will write his own book on it, to complete the historical record.

8

Fish

Erinys, a British company, provided security escort teams for the GRD. Personnel included a number of security specialists from the U.K., South Africa, and the U.S. The top Erinys security team escorted MG Johnson, the GRD Commander. Many of the senior GRD leaders, including COL Schroedel, COL Dornstauder, and myself, traveled with this team in our daily operations. Hendrick Johannes Visagie was a key member of the GRD HQ security team. He was from Roodepoort, South Africa. His last name was too hard to pronounce (sounds like "Fi saki"), so we just used his nickname – "Fish".

Fish developed an innovative security tool, called a Surveillance Bus, which was used to track potential threats while a convoy was on the move. I remember watching him use it while he was riding shotgun in the SUV. I sat behind him and watched as he identified and reported potential threats every few seconds during our high-speed dashes across Baghdad. It was intense. Every parked car, every bridge overpass, every suspicious civilian, every piece of debris in the road was identified and reported to the rest of the mobile security team for immediate attention. Fish seamlessly moved from one threat to the next, processing and relaying information at an incredible rate. He was our early warning system during convoy operations.

Leave in Amman

MG Johnson had an intense operational tempo and worked long days. Everywhere he went, the Erinys security team had to have the route pre-planned and security measures thoroughly prepared. The team was essentially on duty every day from 4:30 in the morning to 10:30 at night. At this point in the war, there were no days off for any of us. Fatigue and stress were beginning to show.

One evening in early April, Fraser Brown came dashing into the GRD headquarters looking for me. Fraser was a senior manager for Erinys in Iraq. He noted that MG Johnson was imminently traveling to the United States on temporary duty to attend the annual ENFORCE Conference at Fort Leonard Wood, Missouri. The

Commander would be gone from GRD for over a week. Fraser wanted me to sign off on a document that released the Erinys security team from duty during this period. They wanted to take a few days of leave in Amman, Jordan. Fraser urgently needed approval, as the last Royal Jordanian Airlines flight from Baghdad to Amman was about to depart.

I asked several questions: who, what, when, where and why? Fraser pressed. I told him he'd have a decision inside two minutes. I was the new G3 and hadn't heard of this request. I checked with the Deputy Commander and got a thumbs up. The security team needed a break, and we agreed with the timing. I signed the approval and told Fraser to get the team back to Iraq before MG Johnson returned. Fraser blasted out of the HQ and had the security team moving to Baghdad airport. I was glad to help the team get some downtime.

Insurgency Erupts

All hell started to break loose in late March and April of 2004. Just as the Erinys team was departing Iraq on leave, the insurgency began to roar. March 31 was a particularly infamous day.

At the time, Fallujah was the most dangerous city in Iraq. A convoy was ambushed in Fallujah and four American contractors were killed—their burned and mutilated bodies dragged through the streets. Two of the corpses were hung from a bridge over the Euphrates River. The attack was headline news. The barbarism shocked us and the rest of the world. That same day, five soldiers from B/1st Engineers (1ID) were killed when their M113 armored vehicle hit an IED. In a separate incident, a DynCorps security guard supporting GRD shot himself above the knee. The next day an Erinys security guard was killed protecting the petroleum pipeline.

On April 2, LTC Joe Corrigan departed Iraq. I would now be flying solo as the GRD G3. On April 3, the Deputy Commander (Schroedel), Chief of Staff (Dornstauder) and the Command Sergeant Major (Balch) departed in a convoy of SUVs for Fallujah to attend memorial services for the five engineer soldiers recently killed Their convoy became disoriented near Fallujah. Hostile forces stalked the GRD SUVs carrying the leadership team, and it almost resulted in a tactical disaster.

In early April, there were continuous IED, RPG and small arms fire attacks on the major highway between the Green Zone and the Baghdad Airport. Burning vehicles and trucks littered "the most dangerous highway in the world". I drove through the wreckage several times, fully expecting to be engaged by enemy fire. Large sections of guardrail, chunks of concrete and twisted steel blown up by numerous IEDs, were laying everywhere on the highway. For several days, the highway was closed to all traffic except armored vehicles. Insurgents fired on several aircraft flying into Baghdad Airport, forcing the airport to close. With the Erinys team on leave in Jordan, the only way they could now return to Baghdad was via a ground vehicle. That meant they had to drive across Al Anbar province and through Ramadi and Fallujah, where the four contractors were recently ambushed and hung from a bridge. It was a recipe for disaster.

Attack near Fallujah

The Erinys team decided to take a taxi over 400 miles from Amman to Baghdad. Unfortunately, they had left their weapons, equipment and body armor behind in Baghdad, when they departed Iraq on a commercial aircraft. Now they had to drive back, through an incredibly dangerous corridor, without weapons or equipment. Once they crossed into Iraq, they would face almost 300 miles of bandits, insurgents and terrorists.

Today, I have only fragmented accounts of what actually happened. The team acquired some weapons at some point during the journey. But when they arrived near Fallujah on April 7, the gates of hell opened. The team ran into a crushing ambush. They abandoned their damaged vehicles and began to repel the attackers. Out of ammo, Fish was hit by a rocket-propelled grenade and a fragment penetrated the top of his brain exiting through his neck.

The 1st Marine Expeditionary Force (MEF) was operating in the area, and the Marines were able to extract the Erinys team. When the Erinys operations center in Baghdad got the word, they immediately sent a contractor-led Quick Reaction Force (QRF) to recover the beleaguered team. The QRF had 4-5 vehicles and about ten shooters. The enemy expected a QRF to be sent, and the insurgents set up a two-kilometer long ambush on the eastern side of Fallujah. The size and complexity of the ambush was almost inconceivable. The enemy had fifty fighters and poured 30 RPGs and sustained machine gun fire into the convoy. Two of the Erinys vehicles were destroyed. The QRF initially suffered one killed and two wounded and performed with great valor, returning accurate small arms fire and killing twenty-five enemy personnel. I could not believe the tactical outcome. The insurgents had the element of surprise, vastly superior numbers, and were shooting from covered and concealed positions, yet the contractor team decisively won the engagement. The personnel in the QRF were clearly well trained and probably former SOF guys.

Meanwhile, Fish was evacuated to the 31st Combat Support Hospital in the Green Zone. The medical team was not sure he would survive. The initial medical assessment was that Fish had a 2% chance of a full recovery and 10% chance of living. We kept him on life support in the Baghdad hospital for about a week. When I visited Fish in the Intensive Care Unit (ICU), his condition was unstable. I was told his cranial pressure was too high – peaking at about sixty. Twenty was a dangerous level and ten was normal.

Surrounding Fish in the ICU were several enemy wounded, including terrorists – receiving the same medical treatment that our soldiers and innocent civilians received. Some of them were probably wounded in the same ambush. The enemy had leather straps on their legs to restrain them from trying to fight or escape the hospital.

For Fish, hope of any recovery faded with each day. CSM Mike Balch kept vigil and provided daily updates to the GRD team. The unit also contacted Fish's family in South Africa.

The CG Returns

Limited flights into Iraq resumed. MG Johnson was returning to Baghdad Airport well after dark on the evening of April 9. The main highway from the airport was still a hot combat zone and remained closed to all traffic but combat vehicles.

The Deputy Commander and I agreed that the tactical situation was too dangerous to conduct a night movement of the CG in an SUV. Our unit had no night vision equipment and no radios to communicate directly with U.S. tactical forces. The remainder of the CG's security team was still shaken by the recent ambush. One security member personally pleaded with me not to order the movement to the airport at all. I considered the request for a few seconds, but I knew we had to meet the CG. The outbound run to the airport had to be made, but we could do it early while we still had some daylight. I considered personally leading the convoy to raise the security team's confidence level, but my absence would mean that other urgent Division actions would risk failure.

As I was considering the possible courses of action, my Operations NCO, MSG Steven Spears, stood up and volunteered to join the convoy to give them another shooter. It was just what was needed - a senior military NCO to lead the convoy and provide some seasoned leadership. I quickly agreed and asked Spears to report the convoy's progress at each checkpoint. Then we called the Distinguished Visitor (DV) quarters at the airport to arrange for the CG to spend the night. We planned to move him back to the GRD HQ at first daylight. We quickly reviewed the movement plan and communications procedures and launched the team while the sun was setting.

MG Johnson landed, and the improvised security team met him as planned. Sadly, Fish wasn't present, and there were some new faces on the team. When told he would remain at the airport and bed down at the DV quarters that evening, MG Johnson was livid. We were in a combat zone, and we could not be paralyzed. COL Schroedel and I made telephone contact with the Commander and persuaded him to stand fast until daylight. It was too risky to move at night on "the most dangerous highway in Iraq" in an SUV with a badly shaken team. A high-speed SUV movement on a closed highway at night might also result in fratricide. The Abrams Tanks and Bradley Fighting Vehicles patrolling the highway may believe our vehicles are suicide bombers and open fire on us. MG Johnson still didn't like it, but he deferred to our tactical recommendation. The next morning, the CG was transported to the Green Zone without incident. After arrival, he noted that his security team had "lost their edge". We had his team stand down for several days while Erinys re-constituted and re-trained them.

* * *

On the morning of April 10, large mortar rounds exploded near the Sheraton Hotel. I grabbed some chow in the Gurka dining facility, which had been hit with mortars the night before. A number of us then went to the hospital to visit Fish. The doctors stated that they would not operate on him again, and it was unlikely he would survive. At best, he would be in a vegetative state. We circled around the bed and prayed for Fish—it was in God's hands now. I looked around and saw that wounded enemy combatants were still being treated in the ICU alongside Fish. I wondered if one of them was responsible for his wounds.

Only One Resurrection

The next day was Easter. I awoke to mortar fire at 05:30. I went into the G3 shop and learned that a fuel convoy had been attacked in Latafya and six HMMWVs were on fire. Scott Lowdermilk came down to the operations office and reminded me that there was an Easter service at the Republican Palace. I knew I needed to go. I couldn't keep "The Big Ranger in the Sky" waiting on the day we celebrated His resurrection.

Scott and I arrived at a packed church ceremony and coincidentally stood near Ambassador Jerry Bremer, the Interim Authority in Iraq. I previously met Ambassador Bremer in a corporate business meeting a year earlier in Reston, Virginia. At the time, he worked for Marsh Crisis Consulting and was a friend of my boss, Ed Woollen. I thought how amazing it was that we were now both engaged in this momentous struggle half a world away. I didn't say a word, and Ambassador Bremer did not recognize me. He had the weight of the world on his shoulders. I was just another uniform in the room. But Scott and I did pray for Fish. And I prayed that we could end this war quickly.

Easter for Fish brought no improvement. His cranial pressure remained over 60. He had no brain activity. The doctors planned to take him off sedatives for twelve hours to see if there was any neural activity. If not, he would be taken off life support the next day. The medical staff noted that Fish's ventilator was needed for other wounded patients.

On April 12, Fish was taken off life support, and he was officially declared dead. He was twenty-nine years old. It later struck me that the life support equipment, that Fish gave up, was used to keep a wounded enemy combatant alive. There was a deep message here. Americans did hold the moral and ethical high ground. We routinely treated enemy combatants with the best possible care. But the thought of pulling Fish off life support, so a ruthless enemy could live, was very painful. And where was the news media? Rather than report on how the Americans hold the moral high ground, the media was covering something far more newsworthy – the isolated prisoner abuse at Abu Ghraib.

Easter Sunday was to be a day for celebration, but I felt little joy. I called home to talk to Alice and the kids. They had no idea what was really happening in Baghdad, and I did not intend to tell them. I also sent a note to my sister, Gina, to check on her and my brother Kevin, who was still hospitalized but would hopefully cheat death again.

Tragically, the scene of removing Fish from life support was one I replayed a year later when we removed my quadriplegic brother, Kevin, from his respirator.

Taps

GRD held a candlelight memorial service for Hendrick Johannes Visagie at 19:30 hours on April 15, 2004. The G3 shop published an Operations Order and conducted a rehearsal to make sure the staff had made all the necessary arrangements. A well-executed memorial service was the final honor we could give our fallen comrade.

Several hundred GRD and Erinys personnel attended the indoor service along the Tigris River. We placed photos of Fish, his favorite hat, his flak vest, dozens of candles, cards and some flowers on a large table decorated with white linens. Somehow, in a war zone in Baghdad, we even found someone who could play the bagpipes. Chaplain Brown offered prayers. There were several speakers, including MG Johnson, who gave an emotional eulogy. A bugler from the 1st Cavalry Division played "Taps". We sang Amazing Grace. And we played a favorite song from Fish's native South Africa. We even discretely videotaped and photographed the ceremony to share later with Fish's family.

Memorial - Hendrick Johannes Visagie

It was a dignified Candlelight Memorial Service. Very sad and very solemn. When the ceremony ended, we all quietly left. And then we went back to war.

9

21ˢᵗ Century Jousting

Any air and ground movement of a General Officer or VIP in a combat zone was operationally sensitive and had to be particularly well planned. So when the Commanding General of the GRD or one of our Senior Executives had to visit a remote project site, the pucker factor in the operations staff increased a notch or two. Long ground convoys in SUVs were particularly vulnerable to enemy attack. At this point in the war, no General or Senior Executive had been killed, seriously wounded or captured, and we intended to keep it that way. Unfortunately, BG Jeff Dorko, a GRD Commander that served in 2007, was the first General seriously wounded when his vehicle was targeted by an IED in Baghdad.

The first three District Commanders in GRD were assigned for about four months with a mission to stand up Districts in Mosul (GRN), Baghdad (GRC) and Basrah (GRS). They had the tough job of building a hybrid military-civilian organization while also constructing major projects. By the summer of 2004, all three of these District Commanders were scheduled to rotate back to the United States. Military protocol requires that a "Change of Command" ceremony be conducted to formally transfer total authority from the existing military District Commander to his replacement. The Commanding General of the Division presides over this District-level ceremony.

In early July 2004, BG Tom Bostick, the new GRD Commander, Steve Stockton, a GRD Senior Executive, and I were scheduled to depart Baghdad and travel to Basrah to attend the GRS Change of Command ceremony. The trip to Basrah was hot, dusty and punctuated with ancient history, modern engineering and some moments of high adventure.

Movement Planning

Obviously all ground and air movements in Iraq were inherently dangerous, so they required detailed planning and coordination. MAJ Jim Ball, in the GRD operations shop, was responsible for planning all phases of the VIP movement to Basrah. Now Jim was a take-charge kind of guy with a 200-decibel voice that was a highly effective non-lethal weapon. His booming conversations could register on the Richter scale. When Jim needed a helicopter to support a mission, he would just keep raising the volume until he got what he needed. If the walls of our HQ building were shaking, I knew Jim was working on getting our helicopter request approved. Rather than deny the request and suffer permanent hearing loss, the air operations guys learned to play nice and just give Jim a helicopter whenever he needed it. When I was working near Jim, I literally had to wear earplugs so I could think while drafting some daily strategic comments for MNF-I and the SECDEF.

Our destination in Basrah was 350 miles from Baghdad, which was in the British sector of Iraq. There were no refueling points for U.S. helicopters that far south. Jim's movement plan had two phases. First, we would fly in helicopters about 250 miles from Baghdad to Tallil Airbase, near Nasiriyah in south central Iraq. We would then link up with the GRS contractor security team and begin a 100-mile ground movement in SUVs from Tallil to Basrah.

The First Leg

The air movement from Baghdad to Tallil was uneventful. That means we took off and arrived on time and nobody shot at us. It was a nice 2-hour flight, and I drank a lot of water. Too much water. I wished our Black Hawk helicopter had a rest room. It was interesting to see the terrain beneath us change from urban Baghdad to fertile river valley and again to desolate desert. We even passed over a few herds of camels in the middle of nowhere. I don't understand how those poor animals could live in such bleak and thankless terrain. No wonder they spit on people.

Upon arrival in Tallil, we met COL Thomas Koning, the GRS District Commander. He was responsible for reconstruction in the southern sector of Iraq. COL Koning gave us a quick tour of Tallil Airbase and some of the local sites. In the coming months, GRS planned to relocate its HQ from Basrah to Tallil. We briefly surveyed the future GRS HQ building and climbed the stairs to the rooftop. This part of Iraq was covered with a powdery dust and had such oppressive heat it was like standing next to a blast furnace. From this elevated position, we could see the military camps of several coalition partners that were stationed on this base, including the Italians.

As the birthplace of civilization, Iraq is a very historic place. Between the ancient cultural sites and Saddam's palaces, Iraq has great potential for tourism—whenever peace breaks out. The airbase at Tallil was next to the ancient city of Ur. We could clearly see a stepped pyramid-like structure called the "ziggurat" rising in the distance. It was originally constructed about 6000 years ago and later rebuilt by Nebuchadnezzar II of Babylon in the sixth century B.C. Ur is believed to be the birthplace of Abraham of the Book of Genesis, and it was once the largest city in the world. Ur was the first Biblical artifact I had ever seen, and I found it very interesting. Unfortunately, this was as close as I would get to it. I took a mental note to read up on Ur later.

Nasiriyah Power Plant

The rooftop tour ended abruptly after about 10 minutes. It was now time to inspect a local reconstruction project site – the Nasiriyah Power Plant. So we linked up with the security escort teams, jumped in the SUVs, and prepared for the movement from the airbase to the power plant. After a short and dusty drive to the project site on rubble-filled roads, we came through the main gate and got out of our vehicles. COL Koning gave us an overview of the ongoing power plant project. Coincidentally, there was also a large water treatment facility being renovated on the same site. Fluor was the Architectural and Engineering (A&E) firm working at Nasiriyah. Their contract was to provide design-build services for construction, rehabilitation, operation, and maintenance of power generation facilities. Much of the reconstruction work force came from local Iraqi companies. As I explained previously, we learned to keep the names of these companies and their personnel unpublished to protect them.

There was an ongoing debate as to whether the Iraq Reconstruction effort should build new electrical power generation plants or simply repair the old ones. New power plants would last longer, but they also take longer to complete. New plants also required higher technical skills among the Iraqis who would operate and maintain them, which added training to the list of tasks required.

Rehabilitating older plants took less time and money, but they would not last as long. Repairing old power plants was not in the long term interests of Iraq, but with the race to restore electricity getting daily White House-level attention, hasty repairs to existing facilities was often preferred to building new ones.

The Restore Iraqi Electricity (RIE) team had to be highly innovative while they feverishly raced to put "megawatts on the grid". If I recall properly, the Nasiriyah Power Plant was 40 years old and of Russian design. Repair parts were no longer made, but the RIE team found a similar abandoned plant in Brazil, removed the needed parts, refurbished them, and then shipped them to Iraq.

Nasiriyah was my first tour of a major electrical facility since my fifth grade field trip to the Peach Bottom Atomic Power Station in York, Pennsylvania. More than thirty years later, I was now in another power plant, halfway around the world, and still wasn't really sure what I was looking at. I followed COL Koning and Steve Stockton around and listened for any smart tidbits that I could pick up. They always had some good insight. Of course, I put my engineer poker face on and did an admirable job of pretending to know what I was doing. I would repeat important facts about the reconstruction project to those that missed COL Koning's initial comments. I did so with conviction and authority, hoping to convince the guys in the back of the tour group that I really knew all this stuff! I learned a lot on that stop, but the most important lesson at Nasiriyah was yet to come.

BG "phone home"

One of the last stops on the inspection was at a very old cast iron Russian phone booth, built like a T-62 tank. The phone itself looked like it was WWII vintage. The rotary dial made it look like something that you might find in an antique store. After some prodding, BG Bostick went into the phone booth and picked up the handset, as if to place a call. I think it was a tradition that all visitors were required to do, and the pose got a few laughs from the rest of the team.

The formal one-hour inspection of the Nasiriyah Power Plant was now over, and the normal protocol was to thank the hosts in a short ceremony. BG Bostick assembled his staff and made some closing remarks alongside six senior Iraqi civilians that were leaders at the project site. We thought the brief event was now complete, but we were wrong.

One of the Iraqi contractors asked to make some personal comments. The request was a bit unusual, but quite welcome. He spoke in Arabic, one sentence at a time, and each sentence was translated into English. It was a tearful speech, and he was very passionate. He began by thanking the Americans for giving Iraqis a chance to rebuild their country. While the rest of the world had abandoned Iraq, the United States was helping to build its future. He and his fellow countrymen knew this was the truth and wanted Americans to know how much the reconstruction program meant to their country and their children. The United States was providing electricity, clean water and jobs so Iraqi men could work to improve the lives of their families. Intuitively, we all knew how important our reconstruction work was, but this emotional outpouring drove the lesson home. Not a single reporter was there to cover this remarkable story. The press was probably inside the protected Green Zone, busily working on vilifying reports about American prisoner abuse at Abu Ghraib.

High Speed Jousting

It was time to move on. The next leg on our mission was a two-hour ground movement from Tallil to Basrah. The GRD leadership team met up with the security escort team from Erinys to review the situation. We had a convoy of three SUVs. Each vehicle had a driver and at least one other shooter. The CG was in the middle vehicle, and we had to protect him. I was a shooter in the rear vehicle, and not just any shooter – I was riding shotgun. Just like they did in the old west. Since we lacked enough armored vehicles, I was in an unarmored Toyota Land Cruiser—a six-cylinder diesel that accelerated like a wounded turtle. I was thinking, "Man this vehicle sucks, but this sprint to Basrah will make a good story someday."

My driver was a South African security guy who worked for Erinys. At the time, Erinys had the primary security contract for the GRD. We exchanged names, and I promptly forgot his. More important – I wanted to know what kind of weapons he had. I had a Beretta pistol with 30 rounds of 9mm ammo, accurate to about 30 meters and not ideal for fighting off an ambush. Fortunately, he had an AK-47, an M-4 carbine and a 9mm Glock pistol. Once I determined that we were the rear vehicle in the convoy, I knew we had to be alert for fast moving vehicles that would scream up behind us (>100 mph) and try to hose us with an AK-47. It was the infamous Iraqi drive-by shooting. At first, it looked like I had to serve as the main shooter, covering any threat from 360 degrees. Of course, turning around in body armor is really inconvenient from the front seat. Fortunately, a serious looking tail gunner soon joined us. His name escapes me too, but he had a decent weapon – which, again, was much more important to me than his name. Real names didn't matter much because I grew up outside of Philadelphia, where I learned that every guy's nickname was "Buddy".

We drove off from Tallil and entered the dusty highway to Basrah, which was flat and reasonably modern with three lanes in each direction. During the Gulf War, this highway made invading Kuwait much easier for Saddam Hussein.

Once again, we lacked armor protection, so we compensated by using speed to enhance our security. We were now flying down the road to throw off the aim point of a potential attacker. Our southbound convoy was moving between 80-110 mph, depending on the traffic situation. My driver needed to keep at least one hand on the steering wheel, and he kept his pistol mounted in front of his vest for easy access. He offered me the AK-47 or the M-4, so I picked up the AK and started scanning the front and sides of the vehicle for targets. After a few minutes, I put the AK down and picked up the M-4. It was lighter, it had a collapsible stock, and I had trained a lot more with it. I saw no need to conduct on the job training with an AK in combat, particularly when fractions of a second may count. A weapon should feel like a natural extension of your body–and that meant I should be using the M-4.

Our dusty windshield was already cracked and pitted from the stress of previous ground movements. Through it, I began to observe several large U.S. supply convoys coming from Kuwait and heading north toward Baghdad. It takes a lot of logistics to keep the war effort going, and I thought somewhere in that northbound convoy were some steaks and lobsters heading for the U.S. Embassy.

Then some crazy things started to happen. People started walking out onto the highway. They looked like civilians in traditional dress, but in Iraq, you just don't know who the enemy is. What the hell were they doing walking along the highway in the middle of the desert? It puzzled me. I couldn't think of any good reason for their presence, but I could think of some bad ones. At times, it seemed like they were human squirrels crossing the road in front of us as we sped toward Basrah. We'd change lanes abruptly to avoid hitting them. Some were only an arm's length away when we screamed by. Each one was a potential insurgent that could pop out a pistol or AK as we passed. I ran a quick mental checklist. I have a full magazine with 30 rounds. One round was in the chamber—the selector switch flipped from safe to burst mode. I had my M-4 stock fully collapsed, and kept swinging it left and right to acquire these potential targets in my front sites, consciously keeping the driver out of my line of fire. The driver drew his pistol and would point his weapon with me. I was straining to see what the CG's vehicle was doing to our front. They must also see this same threat. Perhaps these Iraqis were trying to get us to stop so they could sell us something. Sorry guys, we ain't buying nuthin' today. Gotta get the CG to Basrah. I had no idea if this strange behavior was another insurgent trick to kill or capture some Americans.

It was pretty intense for about ten minutes, but we held our fire dozens of times and there were no attacks from the "pedestrians" walking in the middle of the highway.

There was still a long way to go to Basrah. In this flat desert, you can see a long way—miles and miles. To our front, we could see a steady stream of oncoming vehicles. Many of them were screaming northbound at 100-120 mph. My radar was now up. I was alert and looking for BMWs and pickup trucks. The Ba'ath Party loyalists (Sunnis) often owned BMWs and frequently used them for rear drive-by shootings with the windows down. But this was Shiite country, not Sunni country. Shiites were poorer and their militiamen sometimes hid in a pickup truck, under a canvas in the back. When they came alongside you, they'd pop up from under the canvas and let loose with a "spray and pray" 30 round magazine. When they fired at less than ten meters, something was gonna hit you. There was also the threat of a car bomb that would detonate as it passed by your vehicle. The tactics, techniques and procedures used by our enemies changed often and kept us all alert.

I was always watching for an enemy spotter on the side of the road to tip me off about an imminent attack. The spotter was the enemy's surveillance element, who would see who you were as you passed, and then alert the ambush team just ahead. They would then have a minute or two to prepare for your arrival in their pre-planned kill zone. I was particularly alert for anyone with a cell phone or parked in a "disabled car" with the hood popped up.

Between cars flying past and human squirrels walking onto the highway, every minute of the ground movement was intense. Each time we were rapidly assessing if the potential target was a bad guy or just another civilian. Our SUV had no air conditioning, and the sweat was now pouring down my face from the intense heat and the body armor. I was thinking, "Man it doesn't get much better than this."

And there it was. Way to our front were a couple of fast moving vehicles. We were rocketing southbound on a divided highway. The rapidly approaching vehicles were racing northbound– but were driving in the southbound lanes—on the wrong side of the medial strip, driving against traffic. We were on a potential collision course. Now I was thinking, "Houston, we have a problem." I immediately identified the target to the driver and swung my rifle into position. The driver pulled out his pistol, and we both put our barrels in the front windshield.

I had a few seconds and began to assess the situation. *"Hey Buddy, the front glass is not armored – right?"* I was concerned that if our windshield was bulletproof, our rounds could bounce off it and ping around inside our own vehicle. That would be bad. But if the glass wasn't armored, I wondered if the windshield would potentially shatter in our faces when we fired into it from point blank range while we were moving at 100 mph. The driver confirmed the glass was unarmored. Several more questions raced through my mind. How would our rounds deflect through the windshield? Would we accidentally shoot the CG's vehicle in front of us? Did the other vehicles in our convoy see what we saw? Would our lead vehicles engage first? Could the oncoming vehicles be VBIEDs?

Our closing speed with the oncoming vehicles was over 200 mph, and we were now prepared for a high-speed frontal direct fire engagement. It struck me that this imminent head-to-head assault was the equivalent of 21st century jousting. We were locked and loaded and just a finger squeeze away from lighting up the oncoming vehicles. If we waited to see a muzzle flash from the oncoming vehicles, it would be too late for us. We'd lose. But did we have enough information to shoot first?

We were down to 500 meters and closing. There was no slack left in the trigger. A small bump in the road would start the rounds flying. Four hundred meters. I leaned forward and tightened my sphincter. Two-fifty. One hundred. Then both oncoming vehicles blasted by our left side like Indy race cars. They were high-end Mercedes or Beemers—it was too hard to tell. But they didn't shoot, and neither did we.

Who the hell were they? I had no idea. Did those idiots even realize that we almost lit them up? The only thing that saved them was our self-discipline. I am not sure others would have been so generous. Perhaps they were U.S. or Iraqi officials using the southbound lanes to stay clear of the armed U.S. convoys in the northbound lanes.

The relief lasted about ten seconds, and we were back to scanning for targets. There was no down time on this drive. No time for idle chatter.

We started picking up signs of civilization. We could see oil facilities in the distance. Natural gas was being burned off at each oil well because the Iraqis couldn't capture or refine it. It was an amazing waste. I was once told by the RIO team that in the U.S., we could get about 45 gallons of product from a barrel of oil. But the Iraqis could only get about 24 gallons of product from the same barrel. The rest was wasted or burned off.

We continued our vigilance until we arrived at the Basrah Airport and drove inside the wire at the GRS compound. We passed the entry control checkpoint, dismounted our vehicles, removed our helmets, knocked the dust off and drank some warm water. We traded a few brief stories with the security teams in the other vehicles, and then it was all forgotten—just another day in Iraq.

GRS Tour

The GRS compound was adjacent to the Basrah Airport that was under the control of the U.K., so the British Army provided a major element of the local security. The GRS HQ was simply a collection of trailers that served as offices, barracks and a mess hall. The perimeter was protected with a trench, concertina wire and some Jersey barriers at the main gate. GRS was planning to move its operations to Tallil because the British were scheduled to relinquish control of the Basrah Airport to the Iraqis. No one trusted that the Iraqis were yet capable of protecting the Americans.

Shortly after arrival, our military colleagues from GRS greeted us. LTC Norm Grady was the Deputy Commander of GRS. He was a smart guy and was always willing to offer his opinion. MAJ Stewart Stanton was the Operations Officer. He was low key and always reliable. Grady and Stanton had more fun in store for us. While our primary mission in Basrah was the Change of Command, we first needed to inspect some more projects in the local area. This included the Sweetwater Canal, a large project designed to improve the water supply for 2.5 million residents of the Basrah and Thi Qar Provinces. Space in the vehicles was limited, so I stayed behind with MAJ Stanton and got an overview of his operations section. He spent a good portion of his time over the previous months trying to get reconstruction convoys quickly across the nearby Kuwaiti border. The Kuwaitis were concerned about border security issues related to taxes, drug smuggling and military escorts. Every week there was a new problem at the border that needed to be resolved, and Stewart was the guy we relied on to keep critical reconstruction materials flowing.

The following day, we held the simple Change of Command Ceremony led by BG Bostick. It included a U.S. flag and an Engineer flag propped up with some sandbags, some taped music, and about a dozen folding chairs. The event was held in the Iraqi desert, on a bed of crushed rock, against a backdrop of nondescript trailers. The outgoing GRS Commander was COL Tom Koning. COL Roger Gerber was the incoming commander. Mr. Parker, a civilian in desert camouflage uniform (DCU), acted as the Command Sergeant Major.

After the ceremony, MAJ Stanton escorted us to the nearby Basrah Airport where we flew back to Baghdad on a U.K. C-130 aircraft. I was pleasantly surprised at how easy it was to catch a ride with the U.K. forces. The American procedures for getting a ride on an aircraft required a formal request and approval process. At Basrah, the U.K. flight section simply told us to climb onboard. We were even permitted to walk about the cabin, something that is not typically allowed on U.S. C-130 flights. We returned to Baghdad without incident, attracting no small arms fire or surface to air missiles.

10

SUVs Suck in Combat

Clarkson – Hoffman - Jankiewicz

The most dangerous activity GRD would perform in Iraq was ground movements. The first member of the CRU team to learn this lesson was MSG Tom Jankiewicz, a member of the GRD advance party. His team was traveling in a 2-vehicle SUV convoy on the main road to the Baghdad Airport, and they were aggressively hunted by an enemy BMW trying to position itself for a drive-by attack. A high-speed chase developed, and Jankiewicz's vehicle took rapid evasive maneuvers by weaving in and out of large trucks. The enemy vehicle attempted to close in for the kill, but clipped a dump truck while changing lanes. "Jank" saw the enemy vehicle explode in his rear view mirror. Debris showered both GRD vehicles. He realized he was lucky this time and continued on with his original mission. This incident was an early indication that SUVs were easy prey in the eyes of enemy predators.

In another early incident, the GRC Commander, COL Kevin Williams, was traveling in a convoy of SUVs to a local project site. MAJ Joe Angerer was in the convoy's lead vehicle (unarmored) along with several Iraqi security men. Joe was a confident officer who had served both in the infantry and in military intelligence. He took every mission seriously and had a reputation for being rock steady. The convoy was proceeding as planned. Suddenly, an IED detonated and severely damaged COL Williams' vehicle, which overturned. Angerer and his team saw the enemy attack behind them. He knew the insurgents would quickly swarm over the occupants of the damaged vehicle and kill or capture them. His team immediately turned their vehicle around and raced back toward the enemy. The attackers did not expect the lead SUV to turn and charge them like an angry bull. When Angerer got within rifle range of the insurgents, his team dismounted, and began firing at the enemy to drive them off. The combination of surprise, speed, and decisive action paid off. All occupants were safely recovered, but there were some heart pounding moments. I was in the GRD Headquarters that day when COL Williams came in and gave an emotional and unforgettable account of the action. It was another close call for GRD, and we were lucky yet again. The lesson learned by the insurgents was "Don't mess with a guy named Angerer". However, Joe's reward for his valiant effort was to be reprimanded by a senior officer for riding in an unarmored vehicle.

Movement Standards and TTPs

Getting the right armored vehicles for reconstruction during an insurgency was absolutely necessary, but it was not sufficient. GRD also needed the right movement standards–a rulebook on how and when to move. It involved defining the conditions under which we would drive through the hostile Iraqi environment. Movement standards would prescribe what tactics, techniques and procedures (TTPs) needed to be followed to reduce the risk of enemy contact and improve our survivability when attacked.

Ideally, movement standards were control measures that would spell out:

- Responsibilities for everyone involved in convoy planning and execution
- The convoy's chain of command
- Procedures for deciding who would move and when

- The minimum number and type of vehicles that would move in a convoy
- How many weapons and shooters would be in each vehicle
- What level of intelligence preparation was needed for planned routes and enemy activities
- What communications were required in each vehicle
- What training standards and mission rehearsals were needed
- The weapons safety procedures and Rules of Engagement
- What checklists would be used before moving to insure things like spare tires, maps, water and first aid kits were in the convoys.

GRD movement standards were not clearly defined or enforced when I arrived. The decision to move was outsourced largely to the security contractor—a gross procedural error that soon became glaringly obvious. It almost caused the loss of an entire convoy with some of the division's senior leaders. The pivotal event was a wakeup call for immediate action.

Stalking in Fallujah

The insurgency had entered a new level of viciousness on March 31, 2004. Remember the four U.S. contractors that were attacked by a mob while driving through Fallujah. Their bodies were then hung from a bridge. The images were shocking.

On April 30 and May 2, 2004, seven Navy Seabees (Naval military engineers) were killed in mortar attacks in Ramadi. When fellow Engineers lose personnel, we show our respect and solidarity by sending senior representatives to the memorial service. This service was at Camp Fallujah. Traveling there meant moving through the most hostile part of Iraq. It raised the question, "Does it make sense to put a dozen other personnel at grave risk to attend the memorial service?" But it was part of the brotherhood of war. We honor our fallen.

The Deputy Commander, COL Joe Schroedel, the Chief of Staff, COL Alex Dornstauder and Command Sergeant Major Michael Balch were planning to attend the memorial service for the fallen Seabees. We had no helicopters, so getting to the service meant conducting a risky ground movement. I sensed there would be trouble that day when a member of the security escort team came into the Operations Center looking for a map of Fallujah. The guy looked stressed, checked some grid coordinates and then left. I later learned that he had planned the route thoroughly but to the wrong destination. He had just learned that the service was at a different location, and he had only a few minutes to re-plan the route. As a hastily formed USACE Division, GRD was not equipped with any of the navigation, intelligence or situational awareness systems that the rest of the Army units had. The systems that gave our troops better situational awareness of enemy and friendly activities, the "tactical internet" and Force 21 Brigade and Below Command and Control (FBCB2), were simply not part of the GRD's equipment. We did all our planning and execution using the old method–grease pencils and acetate covered paper maps.

The result of this situation was almost catastrophic. When the GRD convoy got into the Fallujah area, it took a wrong turn and got on the wrong road. The convoy quickly attracted the attention of the Sunni insurgents, which began to tail our vehicles. Everywhere the convoy traveled, it was getting the hard and evil stares of a determined surveillance. The enemy was trying to figure out who these Americans were and how they best could kill them. It was a classic predator-prey situation, and the GRD convoy was being stalked.

Our team was disoriented–not sure where they really were relative to their destination. The convoy rode out on some elevated terrain. Fully exposed to enemy observation and fire, there was no possible way to turn around, even in an SUV. The convoy was in a bad tactical situation completely canalized in a potential enemy kill zone. Hostile vehicles continued to follow the GRD vehicles. They were clearly in imminent danger, and our team only had speed and mobility for protection. Thankfully, the insurgents were unable to block the forward movement of the convoy and engage our team. The convoy eventually broke out of the restrictive terrain and made it to their destination, but they arrived much later than anticipated.

Back at the GRD Operations Center, we had no awareness that any of this drama was unfolding. I first heard about it the following day, when both COLs Shroedel and Dornstauder gave me the details. Shroedel was clear and unambiguous–our procedures and movement standards were inadequate. We had "abrogated our authority" related to tactical movements. Even though we had hired a security contractor, the division needed to take positive control from here on. We needed to fix this, and I took ownership of the task.

We immediately conducted an After Action Review (AAR) of the near catastrophic movement to Fallujah to determine what happened and how we could improve our procedures. A number of problems were identified that required corrective action. First, we had no written movement standards that I could find, only verbal guidelines. Rather than start from scratch, we obtained copies of movement standards from other military units in Iraq. We wanted to borrow the best ideas for our own use. Different sectors in Iraq had different rules for movement. For example, some regions required a minimum of two vehicles in a convoy, while most others required three. Since our projects were located throughout Iraq, we used the higher vehicle standard. We required that all vehicles have Level 3 armor protection, but we could make an exception if conditions permitted.

Next, we had to define the number of shooters and weapons. We required an armed driver and a separate shooter in each vehicle. The rear vehicle also needed a tail gunner, to protect ourselves from a drive-by ambush. The tail gunner preferably had a machine gun, as an added deterrent. Our security contractor had some Russian-made PKM machine guns for use. However, GRD had no U.S. machine guns, such as the Squad Automatic Weapon (SAW), that could be used for perimeter or convoy protection. My team submitted an urgent request for four SAWs. Scott Lowdermilk, the GRD Reachback Coordinator, and Rick Bierlich, the logistics lead at the Transatlantic Programs Center, made it happen. Within a month, each of the three Districts received one machine gun and so did the Division HQ. Morale instantly lifted, and the SAWs were used in combat within a week of their receipt.

Tail Gunner

Radio communications were the lifeline link for a convoy in Iraq. We needed reliable radio communications to perform command and control, and if a convoy was hit, to request a quick reaction force (QRF). Gary Lowe, a former Special Forces (SF) soldier on the GRD communications staff (G6), took the lead in defining and installing our communications architecture. He put his heart into getting the comms right. Redundancy was important, and we decided to require three types of radios: satellite (SATCOM), very high frequency (VHF) and high frequency (HF). In addition, an Iraqi cell phone (IRAQNA) was issued to some personnel that could be used in an urgent situation. Our radio communications were not secure, but fortunately, our enemies were not sophisticated at intercepting communications. Unfortunately, few of our hastily procured commercial communications were interoperable with coalition forces.

We required one SATCOM radio in each convoy, used for long-range communications. GRD had a mix of Thuraya (French) and Iridium (U.S.) satellite phones. The Iridium Sat phone had a broader coverage area in Iraq and was preferred. The Thuraya phones had dead zones where we could not communicate, and we could not reliably count on them (probably a satellite coverage issue). But GRD owned more Thuraya phones than Iridium phones, probably because some procurement official found that it met the spec and the government got a "good deal". We pressed to get more Iridium phones in our inventory.

Each vehicle would also need a VHF radio, with a maximum range of 10-15 miles, but much less in urban areas. It could be used to communicate between vehicles and to reach nearby GRD HQs and project sites. To extend the range of the VHF network, a series of repeaters needed to be installed throughout Iraq. The repeater sites would take months to install and were subject to theft or disruption. It was a tough and risky task to undertake. Erinys proposed to install the VHF system, and they were awarded the contract. In hindsight, this was a bad decision. At the time, communications was not a core competency of Erinys. The repeater network never became operational, and the sites were subject to attack. The enemy overran at least one site, and our frequencies were compromised. We eventually scrapped the entire concept of a VHF repeater network; it was unreliable and not sustainable.

The HF communications system was the most successful. Gary Lowe selected the CODAN HF radio based on its demonstrated performance. During early installations, there was an electromagnetic interference (EMI) problem between the HF radio and the engine electronics. The team eventually identified the source, and they were able to isolate it. However, the HF radio required a big whip antenna mounted on the front bumper. This antenna distinctively marked the SUV as a coalition vehicle and made it a "bullet magnet".

I spent many hours with Gary Lowe discussing our comms solutions and trying to identify the right path forward. We could not have succeeded without Gary's drive and determination. Once the comms were defined, we had to purchase and install the systems. The radio installation team moved from site to site throughout Iraq outfitting GRD vehicles with the new communication systems. It took several months to get the initial radios installed. The team was constantly chasing new vehicles added to the GRD inventory all around Iraq, trying to outfit them with the proper comms.

Concurrently, we had to define when GRD convoys would communicate. Our procedures were to conduct a comms checks before each convoy departed, at preplanned checkpoints along the route and at the final destinations. That way we could monitor the progress of each convoy at discreet intervals. If a radio check was late, we knew something had gone wrong with the convoy.

The next movement standard that we needed to address was intelligence. Our convoys needed intelligence on planned routes so they could select the lowest risk roads and times to move. This intelligence was available on one of the two classified intelligence networks: SIPRNET or CENTRIX. The problem was that the GRD's contractor security teams were largely foreign nationals and weren't granted security clearances. They were not authorized access to our classified networks that could provide current intelligence on potential threats.

Upon my arrival in Iraq, we had a one-man division intelligence shop (G2), led by LTC Vance Purvis, and one classified intelligence terminal in the entire division. Over several months, we built ourselves up to four or five SIPRNET terminals in the Division HQ and GRC. Our Northern and Southern Districts (located in Mosul and Basrah) did not have their own connections, so Majors Chris Kolditz and Stew Stanton would travel to a local military unit to access the intelligence picture in SIPRNET or CENTRIX. After a couple of months, we also received a CENTRIX terminal, allowing us to see the Coalition classified network. At that point, we were no longer flying completely blind.

Our intel procedures were quickly established. A long-range convoy movement request would be provided to the G2 a day in advance. This would give Vance an opportunity to review the planned route and determine if there were any known threats on the road. If some roads were too hot with enemy activity, we declared them "no go" and convoy commanders would need to plan an alternate route. Safe havens would also be identified along the route–secure locations where the convoy could pull into, if needed. Some of the ground movements covered hundreds of kilometers and crossed multiple boundaries of tactical units throughout Iraq. All of these boundary crossings needed to be manually coordinated. An easier convoy planning system was desperately needed.

GRD convoys also needed better situational awareness (SA) of threats in their immediate area while they were on the move. Most Army units connect to a wireless tactical internet that is constantly updating blue force (friendly) and red force (enemy) positions and activities. This enabled our M-1 tanks, Bradley Fighting Vehicles (BFV), Stryker vehicles and HMMWVs to get the latest SA data while driving around the battlefield. But not GRD. Once we left a secure operating base, our convoys were driving blind.

One day, Major Erik Stor came blasting into the GRD Operations Center with a potential answer to our SA problems. Erik was a dynamic and innovative guy that worked for LTC Dave Press in the Restore Iraqi Electricity (RIE) directorate. Dave and Erik were high-energy guys. It probably came from working near too many power lines. Both of them had good attitudes that were infectious. Their mission was to rebuild the Iraqi electrical grid, and doing so meant constant ground movements all over Iraq. I believe the RIE team conducted more convoys in hostile territory than anyone else in Iraq. Unlike other government and contractor reconstruction organizations in Iraq that hunkered down in a secure compound when things got hot, RIE kept moving to project sites putting "megawatts on the grid". The enemy was constantly trying to disrupt RIE's progress building large power generation facilities and the power lines that distributed the electricity throughout Iraq. RIE epitomized the "Git'r Done" philosophy, and MG Ron Johnson was constantly driving them for more results.

As MAJ Stor entered the G3 shop, he was carrying a new toy with him. Erik had a big beaming smile that said, "Look what I found!" I walked over to greet him and to see what gift he was bringing us. Erik began to brief me on a system called Falcon View. It was an Air Force geospatial and navigation system hosted on a laptop computer. On the laptop, we could see maps of Iraq and our location updated on GPS. It was immediately clear we could use it as a vehicle navigation system—a major step forward. The software also allowed us to dump files of recent significant activities (SIGACTs) onto the same map. That meant the laptop could show us where we were and what recent attacks occurred near our current position. So as our convoy was approaching a bridge underpass, our teams would know that an IED was detonated there the day before, and an RPG was fired from a nearby position a few days earlier. The system was ideal for alerting our teams to potential threats while driving through hostile terrain. My only concern was operational security (OPSEC). I turned to Vance Purvis and told him to figure out how we could use the system in our convoys without compromising classified data. Vance made some quick calls and determined how we could do it.

I immediately authorized Falcon View laptops with GPS for all GRD convoys to improve situational awareness. SIGACTs dumps had to occur before each mission. We still did not have the ability to conduct live, on the move updates, but what we were getting was leaps ahead of what we had. We could use the system to help with convoy planning, tracking, and to keep shooters alert to recent threats. I was pumped. This SA capability would save lives.

* * *

Another area I had to address was the command climate between the G3 shop and Erinys. I began working this issue within days of my arrival.

The relationship between GRD and its security contractor had to be professional and respectful. I recognized, better than many of my peers, that our security contractors were a critical part of our reconstruction team. We could not succeed without them, and I respected that they took great personal risks to protect our civilians, facilities and project sites.

Frankly, I was embarrassed that many U.S. Government personnel often viewed contractors as blood sucking capitalists who were "in it for the money". In fact, many Government civilians would not willingly deploy to Iraq unless they were also well compensated. We needed to be fair about it. Increased risk and hardship comes with increased compensation–for both Government personnel and contractors. Contractors are humans. They have emotions. They bleed just as much as Government personnel when they are wounded, and they often have to bite their tongue because "the customer is always right".

One morning I observed one of my colleagues "ripping into" the Erinys escort team. He was reprimanding them for another incident where their escort vehicles sustained some body damage. On one level, this concern made sense. All of our vehicles were leased, and the Government would likely be responsible for incidental damage. But this myopic view would result in unnecessary death. The reality was that we were in a war. The enemy hid among other moving vehicles, drove up right next to you, shot your vehicle with 30 bullets and then sped off. Short of lethal force, speed and maneuverability were the only two capabilities that Erinys had to protect our people.

I later pulled the Erinys team aside and told them I was the new sheriff in town. I trusted them to make immediate tactical decisions that were essential to protect life and improve safety. Erinys needed to drive GRD civilians to and from project sites. Their first priority was to protect American civilians. Protecting property was a lower priority. Driving in Iraq was incredibly dangerous. If a vehicle was intentionally blocking their SUV in a lane, and it appeared to be a set up for a rolling ambush, then I expected the security team to take aggressive action to evade. If flashing headlights and horns did not made the blocker move, then ramming the threatening vehicle was an acceptable evasive maneuver. I would rather have damaged vehicles than dead Americans and dead security teams.

I also made it very clear that I did not have all the answers. I considered Erinys a core element of my team and expected them to provide ideas on how to improve our operations and security. I conducted periodic reviews with Erinys leaders and provided direct feedback on their performance and our security needs going forward. I also commended their personnel for demonstrating great valor, and GRD held memorial services to honor their dead.

* * *

Another element of movement standards was defining our maintenance and logistics requirements. All vehicles needed to be well prepared before departing on convoys.

Checklists were developed to make certain a convoy was ready to depart. The list was extensive and would typically include items such as spare fuel, oil, spare tires, radios and frequencies, maps, call signs, water, flashlights, Arabic language cards, roof identification panels, medical evacuation (MEDEVAC) procedures, etc. One of the newer items on the convoy checklist was Quik-Clot®, an expendable first aid pad that was a lifesaver for severely wounded personnel.

The one area we probably fell short on was training. We should have conducted more "immediate action drills" to hone our skills during an attack. We needed to practice transferring personnel, including wounded, between vehicles while under fire and calling for QRFs so when the real deal happened, our teams could instinctively do it. We lacked a local training area to practice once we got to Baghdad, so we only conducted verbal rehearsals before departing on convoys.

* * *

The development of our initial movement standards was an evolutionary process that used the best practices from many sources. After each major convoy, the movement team would conduct an AAR. New ideas were constantly used to update our standards. After a few weeks, we had a fairly good baseline.

I briefed the Project Management Office (PMO), our sister organization that defined projects, and their security contractor, Aegis, on our movement standards, innovations and equipment. Aegis was still standing up in Iraq, and I did not want them to re-learn any hard lessons. I also wanted to encourage them to standardize as much equipment as possible, to facilitate maintenance, logistics and communications interoperability. I was pleased to see that Brigadier Ellery, a retired British officer, took extensive notes and appeared intent on adopting many of GRD's movement standards. Eventually, the PMO changed names to the Project and Contracting Office (PCO) and then merged into the GRD. Security requirements and assets became better aligned through this organizational consolidation. Having two different reconstruction security contractors, Erinys and Aegis, was not efficient, so a single contract was awarded to consolidate the effort. These changes all happened well after I left Iraq.

In summary, the development of GRD's movement standards was a step that strengthened our security posture. We simultaneously made great improvements in our vehicular communications, route intelligence, command and control, situational awareness and weapons. Improving our armor protection was still desperately needed. It took months to get all the systems in country and installed, but we finally closed a great capability gap by reducing the risk of attack and mitigating its potential effects. It wasn't pretty, but we were eventually able to "Git'r Done".

Urgent Need For Armor Protection

Having armor protection in Iraq was absolutely critical for survival. The enemy did not wear a uniform. They could blend in with the civilian population, approach you undetected, achieve the element of surprise and take the first shot. In Iraq, there was no standoff - no distance – between you and your attacker. To survive a close combat attack with no warning, you must absorb the first punch from a machine gun, RPG or IED, and then immediately disengage or decisively engage the attacker.

In 2004, it was clear that the U.S. military forces had the wrong vehicles for conducting counter-insurgency operations. The lack of armor protection on military tactical wheeled vehicles was endemic, and every day it proved deadly. The High Mobility Multipurpose Wheeled Vehicle (HMMWV) looked cool, but its "multipurpose" design meant it had many design compromises. One of them was inadequate armor protection. Few HMMWVs, designed during the Cold War, were ever intended to be on the front lines, and we were now fighting an insurgency where combat was non-linear. Everywhere "outside the wire" in Iraq was the front lines. You could even argue that we were operating "behind enemy lines".

We went to war with what we had, not with what we needed, so the Army had to find near-term armor solutions while simultaneously pursuing the long-term. In many cases, our troops improvised in the field by adding "rag armor" to their vehicles. They would weld steel plates to their doors and floors, put sandbags under their seats, and even put layers of plywood on the sides to provide better ballistic protection. So the HMMWV was being hastily modified into a poorly designed fighting vehicle. At times, our forces looked like a third world military, where every vehicle was outfitted with different expedient armor solutions.

"Rag" side armor and gunner chair added to HMMWV

Since our military already owned thousands of HMMWVs, the immediate fix for the military was to improve what we had, and then procure the right vehicles over the long term. The military was jumping through its ass trying to get as many HMMWVs "up armored" to better protect our troops. At the time, very few factory designed mine-protected vehicles (MPVs) existed in Iraq. A few years later, these vehicles became better known as Mine Resistant Ambush Protected (MRAP) vehicles.

GRD was at an even greater disadvantage than the rest of the Army. GRD did not exist at the start of the Iraq war. The Division was created on-the-fly based on the best assumptions made by the USACE staff. All military equipment, soldiers, radios and weapons were already committed to other units. The result was that GRD had no organic military vehicles, no military radios, no crew-served weapons, no IED jammers, and no military shooters to protect its own convoys. All equipment and services for GRD had to be hastily outsourced. It was a Herculean effort just to get what we had.

Our Division had a fleet of 200 SUVs, leased from Kuwait, which we used to support the reconstruction of Iraq. They were distributed throughout the country. Only 12 of the SUVs were factory armored with Level 3 protection. That meant the vehicle could probably withstand multiple 7.62mm rounds fired from an AK-47 assault rifle. If hit with enough rounds, the bulletproof glass could be penetrated. However, Level 3 protection would not protect any occupants against armor piercing rounds, RPGs or large IEDs.

We made continuous attempts to acquire more Level 3 "hard cars" but had to compete against dozens of other agencies and organizations. Demand for armored SUVs far exceeded supply. The prices for these SUVs were skyrocketing. I think leases for these vehicles were up to $15,000 per month. The remaining 188 SUVs in GRD were soft-skinned vehicles. They had no armor protection. None. Zero. For these vehicles, driving at high speed and changing routes was our best means of protection. The lack of force protection for reconstruction teams during ground movements was shocking.

Our security escort teams also improvised their own armor solutions. One approach that I will never forget was hanging body armor on the outside of the SUVs. No kidding. Several bulletproof vests were strapped to the exterior of the SUV. That approach would stop perhaps 20% of the incoming rounds and might absorb some blast or shrapnel from an IED. It was a calculated attempt to increase the probability of surviving the first shot.

Many of our supporting contractors involved in reconstruction were in the same situation–inadequate armor. And they had little or no access to intelligence on what routes were dangerous. The lack of armor protection, weak command and control, poor intelligence, and limited weapons made reconstruction convoys easy pickings for the enemy.

By August 2004, we had 45 reconstruction personnel killed by enemy action. Another 88 were wounded. Many of them died in unarmored SUVs. Every attack recorded on a Serious Incident Report (SIR) came across my desk within minutes of its receipt. I felt pain every time I read about another attack.

"Strap on armor"

The most important lesson that I learned from Iraq was "SUVs SUCK in combat".

On the left a "soft" (unarmored) SUV – On the right a "hard" (armored) SUV – they both suck in combat.

* * *

Shortly after my arrival in Iraq, the Erinys security escort team requested an urgent meeting to discuss our vehicle situation. I agreed to meet the same day. The Erinys contract required the company to provide armed security escort personnel and the Government was required to provide the security vehicles. At the meeting, the Erinys representatives were very direct and passionate. They provided multiple reasons why our current SUV fleet was completely inadequate. I believe they called the vehicle situation "insane". Erinys was very persuasive. I completely agreed with their assessment and realized that GRD was on a course destined for disaster. We had to turn this situation around now, or reconstruction in Iraq risked total mission failure. This was a pivotal meeting in the early history of the GRD.

I was determined to immediately fix the armor situation; it was our most urgent force protection issue. There was no higher priority for GRD operations. I directed LTC Jim Hampton, the GRD Anti-Terrorism/Force Protection (AT/FP) Officer, to make it happen and wanted a recommendation as soon as humanly possible. Jim was tenacious in his search for viable solutions–like a directed energy weapon. I just had to keep him pointed on the right targets. I told Jim to find an interim solution—something we could immediately adopt to improve vehicle protection. "After-market" armor kits were the most obvious potential solution, and in parallel, I told Jim to find a permanent solution. Find the right vehicle that would best enable GRD to protect its personnel and to complete its mission for the long run.

Now just because you find something you need, doesn't mean you can actually get it, so I immediately brought in Leo Hickman, our top contracting official in GRD. He was smart, innovative, and hard working. If I went to war again, I would want Leo to be my contracts guy. I told him to do everything possible to help us acquire the solution. Without hesitation, Leo stepped up and said he would absolutely find a way to make it happen quickly. He also noted that someday he would be leaving Iraq, and he wanted to be riding in a fully protected vehicle on the way to the airport. There was nothing like having some skin in the game.

I then briefed Colonel Alex Dornstauder, the GRD Chief of Staff, my boss and battle buddy; the "Rock of Baghdad". He had a huge job to keep the division staff moving forward even during the toughest days. He was fully behind the armor improvement plan and gave me all the support I needed.

With Jim Hampton taking off like a pit bull on finding the right answer and Leo Hickman blasting through the acquisition bureaucracy, I knew we had a good chance to turn this situation around. Every day counted—every life counted. We were all focused intensely on solving this urgent requirement. Jim quickly surveyed the internet for vendors that manufactured after-market armor kits for SUVs. We had a mix of vehicle types in the Division, with the predominant SUV being Toyota Land Cruisers. Jim found a manufacturer that could support us with Level 3 armor kits. But at this point in the war, the demand for these armor kits far exceeded the production capacity.

We selected the vendor and initiated an urgent procurement through Leo. Things seemed to be moving reasonably well. We were told the delivery could happen in about eight weeks from the date the order was placed. I was relieved that the quick-fix kits were on order, and we could now turn our attention to the permanent solution. I was sitting in the Operations Center one evening about three weeks after we initiated the procurement action, and I asked Jim if he had an update on the status of the order. He said we could expect delivery of the armor kits in a few more weeks. But I had been in the Army long enough to know that "Murphy" can bite you at any time or anywhere. I wasn't comfortable with the "it's on order" reply, so I told Jim to call the factory and ask them when they expected the order to be delivered. Jim picked up the phone and dialed. He got through to the supervisor. Then came the "Oh shit" moment. The factory never received the order. We asked them to check again, and we got the same reply. The factory was expecting the order and was ready to jump as soon it came in. But nothing had arrived.

The news hit us like a bolt of lightning. Somewhere, somehow, the most urgent procurement in the entire Division had fallen through the cracks. I leapt out of my chair and went directly to the contracts office to trace the order. I got to Leo's desk in less than a minute. He was out working on some other action. The workload on the contracting team in Iraq was calculated to be ten times that of their CONUS counterparts. There was over $12 billion dollars' worth of reconstruction projects planned, and we had perhaps six contracting personnel in GRD, and new contracting personnel were always rotating in and out of the country. I looked for a deputy, but the office was thin. I finally found a contracts specialist who started to dig through some piles of paper on a desk.

It took a couple of minutes, but she found it. The order for the armor kits had never left the building. I don't get mad often, but this situation was absolutely inexcusable. I went ballistic and lit into the contract specialist. I could barely control my anger. This was the most important action in the Division—people's lives were at stake. The purchase order should have been sent to the factory three weeks ago. I recall saying something like, *"This delay may cause some of our people to die because they will not be protected! I ought to put you personally in every convoy this Division runs until the armor kits arrive so you can feel our pain! Then perhaps you will have the proper sense of urgency required for this procurement! This purchase order must be sent right now!"*

I went back to the operations shop and tried to cool down. Jim and I were still stunned. Privately, I was kicking myself for not calling the factory sooner. But we could have lost another month if we had not checked at all. After about an hour, I returned to the contracts shop, and apologized to the specialist for ripping into her. But I made it very clear that this was an inexcusable failure, and someone may die as a result. We needed it fixed immediately.

That evening I prayed that no one would be killed in an SUV during this three-week delay.

I met with Leo first thing the next morning. He was personally working the procurement and had it moving. I then asked Jim to call the factory. I wanted to talk personally to the owner. The call connected, and I explained the situation with the delayed order. I asked the owner if he was watching the news every night about Iraq. All the car bombings and ambushes being reported were very real. And we had to operate in this environment to complete our reconstruction mission. I asked the owner if he understood what was at stake for us and for our nation. He assured me he did. I asked him to take whatever steps humanly possible to expedite the armor order and get it to Baghdad. He told me he could shave off time by adding a 3rd shift and pressing his workers into action. The armor kits were to be sent by express air to Baghdad, where we had set up an installation facility for our SUVs. I can't recall the name of the armor company or the owner, but his initiative and sense of urgency in supporting us probably saved several lives. Someday, I would like to thank him personally. He was a fine example of an American patriot in action.

We had a team ready to install the new armor kits at a sparse facility near the Central District Headquarters at Camp Victory. But just because we had the kits on hand didn't mean we could immediately install them. The team had never installed an armor kit, so there would be a steep learning curve. There were steel plates to add to the doors, and a rear bulkhead and bulletproof glass to install. We were concerned that the heavy ballistic glass needed to be well secured to the vehicle so it would not fly off in an accident or blast and kill the occupants. One distinct disadvantage to the armor kits was that they had no firing ports to return fire. Laying down suppressive fire during an attack was often needed to defeat or escape an ambush. We installed run-flat tires on the armored SUVs. This was an important improvement. Being stranded in an armored SUV with all four tires shot out in the middle of the road was like sitting in a coffin. Especially if there were no firing ports.

The 20 vehicles we were outfitting with after-market armor kits were spread throughout Iraq - in Mosul, Basrah and other remote sites. We had to transport these vehicles hundreds of miles to the installation facility—requiring yet another risky ground movement. We tried to time the arrival of vehicles to match the kit production rate, to prevent the installation team from sitting around waiting for the arrival of a vehicle.

Another issue was that the initial glass shipped to GRD was not Level 3. It was a Level 2 Lexan glass that would stop a pistol shot, but not an AK-47 rifle round. The manufacturer made this point clear to us before shipping. It was all they had available for the rush order, and they would send Level 3 glass later. We reasoned that having Level 2 glass was better than having no ballistic glass. It would at least absorb some of the energy of an attack. If the occupants were wearing body armor and helmets, Level 2 was considered an acceptable risk. Upon receipt of the Lexan glass, Jim Hampton and an Erinys team went out to a local firing range and conducted a test fire on some extra glass. The field-testing confirmed that pistol rounds could be stopped, but rifle fire definitely penetrated. At least we now knew for certain what we had.

The armor kits were heavy, and they grossly overloaded the vehicles. They added up to 2000 pounds of weight to a 6-cylinder diesel SUV. That meant we had gained ballistic protection but now lost speed and acceleration. Our Toyota Land Cruisers would now accelerate like a pregnant pig. Would the new armor be worth it? After some real combat engagements involving dozens of enemy rounds striking the vehicles, the answer was clearly yes. The increased weight also meant that brakes and suspensions failed after a few months. We'd need to increase the maintenance on them, but as an interim solution, the new armor enabled us to keep the mission going.

Now the SUVs we were modifying were leased. Someday, someone would need to return these vehicles to the real owner. But modifying them was an operational imperative. And after a year of hard running in Iraq, few of these vehicles would be worth much. So I also directed that the tailgates be removed. Our tail gunner was just going to shoot through it anyway. To protect the tail gunner, I directed that steel tubs be built that had Level 3 protection. I wanted the tub designed by real tail gunners. While the tubs were hastily fabricated, we stacked sandbags around the tail gunner for rear protection.

Ironically, the tail gunner improvements also solved another problem. We had a Navy Seabee Lieutenant traveling with us on one long mission. He appeared inexperienced on the M-16 rifle. I was concerned about his marksmanship and lack of weapons discipline while we were driving inside the SUV. He repeatedly swept our heads with his weapon inside the vehicle. He was an accident waiting to happen. One negligent discharge of his weapon, and he'd kill a bunch of us in the vehicle. I gave him some operational advice and some safety tips, but I was still very concerned. When we reached Kirkuk, the Lieutenant bummed a captured AK-47 off an Army squad returning from a patrol. He started posing for pictures in front of every Saddam mural he could find, often holding his newly acquired AK-47 in front of him. So I knew I now had a Hollywood wannabe, completely unfamiliar with an AK-47 traveling with us. He was probably the most dangerous man in Iraq, but we needed the extra shooter. So he became our tail gunner for that mission. His job was to sit in the back of the SUV and point his weapon toward the rear. He was loving it. He was a pretty big guy, so I figured he would also provide us additional ballistic protection. It was the best solution for all of us.

Requirements Analysis

With the after-market armor kits now on order for our SUVs, our attention quickly shifted to the long-term solution for our mobility requirements. There were three fundamental questions we needed to answer: What type of armored vehicles did GRD need? How many did we need? And when did we need them?

I convened a team of Jim Ball, Allan Williams - a civilian from our Programs Directorate, and myself to analyze our growing reconstruction requirements. We wanted to determine how many vehicles we needed and when. I told COL Dornstauder about the meeting, and he offered to join us. Now Alex Dornstauder was Ranger qualified, and he loved field planning. He was the master of the Rock Drill, and liked to review all the possible scenarios to find the best solution or course of action. Our requirements team met three times over a two-week period in the main GRD conference room. The room had a large Ba'ath Party symbol inlaid in the top of the table. Since our Headquarters was previously King Faisal's home and later Saddam's personal residence, I was sure they both held many of their own planning meetings there.

The Division's reconstruction mission was just getting underway, but growing very quickly. GRD had a hundred or so oil and electrical projects ongoing, but there were 2,300 total planned for the division, spread throughout Iraq. Each of these project sites would need to be visited periodically by convoys transporting project managers, construction supervisors, quality assurance reps, and hosts of other official personnel. And each convoy would need to have a security escort team with it. At this point, many of the 2,300 projects were still being defined so we weren't certain about the time phasing of many of these projects, nor their specific locations.

We struggled for a few minutes to come up with an approach to solve the problem. Should we select the number of armored vehicles required by GRD based on: the number of projects, the number of project managers, the distance to the project sites, or the number of available security escort teams? We weren't sure. We were brainstorming for the best approach. Alex suggested that we start with what we did know. We knew where the Division and three District Headquarters were located. We knew we had 15-20 other sites that were subordinate Area Offices, Resident Offices and Project Offices. We began allocating convoys to each of the Headquarters and field offices. Not all required dedicated convoys. If some of the offices were reasonably close, we considered them in the same operational orbit, and they would have to timeshare convoy resources. Each convoy had to have a minimum of three vehicles to comply with our security procedures.

Our analysis told us we needed 15 full time convoys and 45 operational vehicles. But we also needed spare capacity for surge effort or for replacement vehicles. Convoys needed maintenance and some would be shot up. We made some additional assumptions and the answer fell out. The minimum number of armored vehicles we needed was 54. Any less would limit the speed of Iraqi reconstruction. This analysis also determined the number of security escort teams we needed. Staffing the 15 security teams and spare personnel was the responsibility of our security contractor, Erinys. But we needed to fund them fully. These teams were expensive, and took a relatively long time to train and establish. After some more discussion, we developed a schedule for acquiring the vehicles and escort teams. The objective armored vehicles would take up to 12 months to acquire—that meant our 20 SUVs with add-on armor kits would have to last one year.

BOHICA

Just as we thought we were getting ahead of the problem, our luck changed. Central Command (CENTCOM) sent a message out to all subordinate commands wanting a survey of hard cars in each unit. I knew what that meant. There were insufficient armored SUVs in theater, and CENTCOM was looking to re-distribute them. Our reply was honest. We informed them that GRD had 12 factory-armored SUVs. But GRD needed 54 to perform our mission. And while the rest of the Army had real military armored vehicles, the few armored SUVs that GRD had were our only means of force protection.

Our entire chain of command was stunned when CENTCOM directed GRD to transfer six of our 12 armored SUVs to the Multi-National Forces-Iraq (MNF-I) Force Protection office. We vehemently rebutted. The Army couldn't provide us with infantry, military vehicles or radios to start the war, and now CENTCOM wanted to take from us the one thing we had to keep our reconstruction teams alive. Unbelievable. Complying with this order would seriously affect our Division's ability to rebuild Iraq. In fact, we would have to cease all Red Zone movements, effectively stopping GRD's reconstruction mission. And if we continued to operate in only soft vehicles, it would result in the negligent deaths of U.S. civilians. It would then become impossible to recruit any more USACE civilians who volunteered for reconstruction duty in Iraq.

CENTCOM repeated the directive for GRD to give up six armored SUVs. MG Johnson was keenly aware of the situation, and he personally told me that we could not release the vehicles. I was glad to see he was firmly in our corner. Every night in my SITREP to MNF-I, I warned of the dire consequences of this action. I also made it clear that we did not own these vehicles. They were leased. How could we transfer vehicles that we didn't own? Who would pick up the lease? The directive came down a third time with no explanation. It was clear CENTCOM did not care about our problems. They had a more important agenda. We weren't going to win, but it was our duty to argue forcefully to protect our people. Some other CENTCOM mission was determined to be more important than ours. We had taken two swings at the plate and missed. About this time, MG Johnson was preparing to relinquish command of GRD to BG Tom Bostick.

After consulting with the CG, GRD operations reluctantly told CENTCOM the division would comply. But we needed their immediate help overcoming our lack of mobility. If CENTCOM sent us HMMWVs, we would also need military drivers for them. The request was ignored. The bottom line position was, "Give MNF-I your hard cars and good luck solving your own problem." I found it bitterly offensive that the safety of our personnel and our strategic mission were not valued.

At this point, only seven of our twelve armored SUVs were operational. The other five were broken or shot up. After the transfer, our Division would be down to a single operational hard car. In a combat zone, the repairs on the other five vehicles would likely take weeks to months. The situation was embarrassing for GRD and for our nation. The G3 office re-doubled its effort to evaluate every possible course of action to overcome the division's lack of mobility.

I received further instructions for delivering the six armored SUVs. We were to transfer them to a SEAL team that was supporting MNF-I Force Protection. I was wondering what a SEAL team was doing in Baghdad so far away from the ocean. Won't their gills dry out? At least there was someone from the Navy, who was qualified with a weapon helping us fight this war.

The next day a SEAL Lieutenant came to our headquarters. I think he had an Irish last name–like Murphy. I showed him the vehicles, and we planned for a transfer the next day. The mission of the SEAL team was to protect the Interim Iraqi Government. OK, that was important stuff. I could see how it was in our national interest to do so. But someone else's poor planning with procuring armored SUVs had just screwed the GRD. LT Murphy didn't say much. He told me the vehicles would be returned by August 1. The transfer date later slipped to September 30. I was gone by then, so I don't know if the GRD ever got them back.

Murphy turned out to be a pretty slick dude. After the SEAL team would break the cars, they would sneak them back into our field maintenance facility for repairs–right under our nose. I heard he was promoted before I left Iraq. I'm glad. He had a tough job.

In hindsight, giving up the SUVs to protect the Interim Iraqi Government (IIG) was the right thing to do. The IIG and their families were constantly targeted by the terrorists. GRD's reconstruction effort would have been meaningless if the Iraqi leadership was killed. If GRD had to give up the SUVs for a lesser cause, I would have lost faith in my country. Our mission was already painful enough.

11
Wer'Wolves of Baghdad

The search to find the right armored vehicle was urgently pressing ahead. First, we had to define our operational requirements. What features should the ideal armored vehicle have to best support GRD's reconstruction operations? Given the raging insurgency and number of attacks, we were convinced that SUVs were the wrong vehicles. And HMMWVs weren't considered much better. We needed vehicles designed to operate in asymmetric combat. To help us define the requirements, I brought our security contractor, Erinys, into these discussions. Their experience in South African brush wars and driving throughout Iraq was invaluable.

Required Capabilities

Erinys gave us examples of vehicles that were much better suited for our operations, such as the RG-31 Nyala, the Mamba and the Casspir. We reviewed each of these to determine what features made them better suited. I also relied heavily on actual tactical events, such as IED strikes and ambushes, to validate GRD's vehicle requirements. Our analysis determined that size, survivability, speed, and maneuverability were key attributes needed.

The ideal vehicle needed to have sufficient passenger capacity–able to carry at least ten personnel. I arrived at this number based on current and future operations. The vehicles needed to transport reconstruction personnel as well as their security teams (two or three shooters per vehicle) and any other travelers, such as VIPs or reporters. It needed the spare seating capacity to carry additional passengers or wounded should another vehicle in the convoy be destroyed.

The vehicle's interior needed to serve as an expedient project office, if required. Many reconstruction sites lacked office facilities in the early stages of a project and sometimes office space was destroyed. This was the case at the new Iraqi Army base at Al Kasik, in northern Iraq. On August 7, 2004, two VBIEDs drove inside the perimeter and detonated near the base HQ and the dining facility, damaging both severely. Five thousand new Iraqi troops, undergoing training, panicked and fled. Reconstruction contractors from Shaw

Environmental picked up weapons and helped to re-secure the perimeter. The GRD Commander, BG Bostick, personally sent the GRN Commander, Colonel Karl Ubbelohde, to Al Kasik immediately after the attack to re-establish reconstruction leadership and command and control (C2).

Above: pictures of the VBIED attack at Al Kasik

Since IEDs were a daily threat to our convoys, GRD vehicles needed to have a bomb resistant design. Improved vehicle survivability is often achieved with a V-shaped hull that deflects the blast away from the crew compartment. The pictures of shredded SUVs sent to me every week helped shape my thinking. I vividly remembered a recent IED attack near the Bayji oil refinery where two support personnel in an SUV were killed by an IED. Based on everything I had seen, HMMWVs weren't the right survivability solution. And acquiring IED jammers wasn't likely–they were quite rare at that point in the conflict. I was told only three-star generals and above were authorized to have them.

Our convoys were also subject to attacks from a rolling or static ambush. Sometimes it was sniper fire from nearby buildings or parked vehicles. The emerging small arms threat was armor piercing rounds, so I wanted our vehicles to have at least Level 4 armor protection.

Our vehicles needed to have a speed of at least 100 KPH. We were not a combat unit. When possible, we were to avoid or drive through attacks, rather than be decisively engaged. Speed would help us to throw off the timing of an IED that was command detonated and allow us to move quickly out of the kill zone. Our vehicles needed decent speed to stay up with the SUVs that may be in the same convoy.

Good visibility and maneuverability were also important characteristics. Good visibility allowed us to see an incident developing near us and to select the best route to avoid it. One of the enemy's tactics was to box our SUVs in on a highway and then kill us while we were immobile. To overcome these situations, we needed the ability to ram or push other vehicles and to run over any nearby obstacles.

To escape an ambush, we needed excellent cross-country mobility so we could immediately turn off the road and drive through the brush. I recalled one of our convoys near the city of Hit, deep in Sunni insurgent country, encountered a Ba'ath party demonstration while driving in a village. The convoy tried to turn immediately around, but one vehicle was caught in a ditch along the road. The angry crowd overran them, dragged the U.K. driver out and shot him in the head. Any vehicle that GRD acquired would need to have good ground clearance, so we could evade attackers in these kinds of incidents.

The new GRD vehicle must also have sufficient firing ports. One of the best ways to disrupt an attack was to return fire immediately at the attacker. Having firing ports that allow the occupants to cover 360 degrees with their weapons was an important feature. Pop-out hatches would provide a firing position that our security teams could use to engage the enemy with their Russian PKM machine guns.

With the new vehicle's characteristics now defined, Jim Hampton started cracking the whip trying to find some candidate vehicles. He would give me a summary of his findings every day. We would reassess where we were, and I'd give him some more guidance. Every lead we had, Jim would jump on it. He made contact with individual vehicle manufacturers and was surveying equipment from four continents. There were candidate vehicles identified from the U.S., Canada, U.K., South Africa, Germany, and Turkey.

* * *

During this period, Jim and I drove around Baghdad to see and touch some of the vehicles under consideration. We found two candidates nearby. The U.N. had left behind some old Nyalas at Camp Victory. We found them in a storage area, but we never found an operator. We also found some local military police (MPs) in the Green Zone that had the M-1117 Armored Security Vehicle (ASV), also known as the Guardian. We spent an hour talking to the MP troops and kicking the tires. There were only a few Guardians in the U.S. inventory, but they had a good reputation in Iraq.

I also started to grease the skids with Leo Hickman and HQ USACE to start the acquisition process moving forward. I quickly learned that we could not purchase any vehicles. It was against U.S. policy to buy Heavy Armored Vehicles (HAVs), but we were permitted to lease them. I was confused. The 1st Armored Division doesn't lease its Bradley Fighting Vehicles and Abrams Tanks; they are procured by the Army. Why was GRD restricted to leasing? It sounded like a bureaucratic rule established by some bean counter to prevent procurement abuse. That crap may be well intended for peacetime, but we were in combat and American lives were in imminent danger. When we spoke to manufacturers, only a handful would even consider leasing us an armored vehicle. Some of the best vehicle providers would only sell them. We were gravely concerned that we would not be able to find a qualified vehicle that could be obtained by leasing. How could U.S. acquisition policies restrict our best options in combat? This was a moral issue, and it made no financial sense. The prices quoted to lease a vehicle for one year were about the same as the price to buy the vehicles outright. This "lease only" policy threatened to derail our efforts to get the right equipment. No one we spoke to was able or willing to change or waive the rules on GRD's behalf. Even the great Leo Hickman could not get the rules changed.

I made one last urgent appeal to Mr. Joe Tyler, a senior executive from HQ USACE, who made a staff visit to GRD. Mr. Tyler was pretty much at the top of the USACE food chain for resolving this issue. He told me there was no way to legally buy the armored vehicles. We must lease them. It had something to do with DOD policy, but I was too mad to understand the "why"—I just heard the "no". At this point, I thought the war was lost. Our own acquisition bureaucracy was going to kill our people and defeat us. Many months after I returned home from Iraq, I saw a memo from the Secretary of Defense waiving any peacetime acquisition rules that were hurting military operations in combat. It was the right decision, but we needed it much sooner.

TACOM Assistance

To expedite the selection process, I told Jim to contact the U.S. Army Tank-automotive and Armaments Command (TACOM) in Warren, Michigan to see if they could help. TACOM focused on providing soldiers with "cradle to grave" solutions for mobility, survivability and lethality.

Jim and I conducted a telecon with some TACOM vehicle experts. We explained our situation and told them we urgently needed better vehicles for our Reconstruction mission. After a few minutes, TACOM began asking questions about the Buffalo, a new counter IED vehicle being fielded to Iraq. TACOM was apparently concerned that if GRD ordered the Buffalo, it would disrupt someone else's order. I quickly realized that they didn't understand our problem, and I was irritated that they didn't listen. I explained again. *"We aren't tactical engineers. We don't need a vehicle to detect and remove IEDs. We build things. I need a vehicle to protect civilians that we transport around Iraq to rebuild the infrastructure."* I bit my tongue. I wanted to say, "I really don't care about someone else's delivery schedule. Protecting my guys was just as important as protecting someone else's guys. Who in the acquisition community was looking out for our urgent needs? Or was GRD once again left hanging out on its own?"

Relieved that we weren't going to interfere with their Buffalo production schedule, TACOM then tried to sell us the ASV. I listened politely while TACOM described its capabilities. I strongly agreed it was an impressive vehicle for MP and scout missions, and it clearly met some of the speed, mobility and protection requirements we had for GRD, but Jim and I had already determined that the ASV was a marginal candidate. After the TACOM sales pitch concluded, I spoke candidly. "The ASV is a great combat vehicle. It is well designed. But it is not what we need. Let me prove my point by asking you a few questions."

> Q1: *"Are our South African security contractors, who are not U.S. citizens, authorized to operate a U.S. combat vehicle, in Iraq?"*
> A: *"No."*
>
> Q2: *"Are our South African contractor security teams authorized to operate the weapon systems? The .50 caliber machine gun? Can they fire the 40mm MK-19 grenade launcher?"*
> A: *"No."*
>
> Q3: *"Can the ASV carry ten personnel to project sites?"*
> A: *"No."*
>
> Q4: *"Can the vehicle also serve as a field office at remote project sites?"*
> A: *"No."*
>
> Q5: *"Can I lease these vehicles?"*
> A: *"No."*

I finished my questions and paused.

The light bulb on the other end of the phone had turned on, and TACOM replied; *"Now I get it."*

I asked, *"OK. What can TACOM do to help GRD select and acquire the right vehicle?"*

"We can't help directly, but we have conducted some research and have some studies on some vehicles that can help GRD with its analysis."

I accepted the offer. *"OK. We need anything you have as soon as possible. I just lost two more guys this week near Bayji. Their SUV was shredded. We have to solve this problem now. If we have questions, we will contact you for advice."*

The bottom line was that TACOM couldn't do much to help. And we had already struck out with MNF-I and CENTCOM. Our only lifeline for support on acquiring the right vehicles was through HQ USACE. At least I knew LTC Joe Schweitzer and COL Bill Fritz, in USACE Operations, would bust their asses to help us, but that was still no guarantee of success.

The SUV attacked near Bayji oil refinery

Back in the GRD Operations office, Jim Hampton was narrowing the search. Out of about 20 candidate vehicles, only two would consider a lease. One was from a Turkish manufacturer, and it looked like a HMMWV chassis with some better sloping armor. But it was too small for our needs. The other was a vehicle called the Wer'Wolf. I think it was a South African design made by a German company. The Wer'Wolf was the only vehicle we could lease that met our operational requirements. I sensed that "The Big Ranger in the Sky" was smiling on us. He gave us a potential solution when we thought we had none. We selected the Wer'Wolf and held one final review with the security contractor and COL Dornstauder for their comments. We got two thumbs up. Now we had to acquire them.

An Urgent and Compelling Procurement

We wasted no time. The lives of our personnel were at severe risk every day. Leo Hickman stepped up again and pledged that he would find a way to make the lease happen, as soon as possible. He had the look of total commitment in his eyes. He was tired, but ready to make something happen. I knew he was on a mission, and he was "gonna Git'r Done".

We initially leased the only four Wer'Wolves available–we could have bought them for the same price. There was a funding issue. GRD was a largely reimbursable organization, and it caused a Catch-22 situation. We needed revenue gained from the completion of reconstruction work to pay for the vehicles. But we needed the vehicles first to safely complete the reconstruction projects. We needed fifty-four Wer'Wolves, but our initial order was only four. I took the four and hoped to acquire more as our reconstruction efforts ramped up.

I left GRD in September 2004, and the Wer'Wolves had not yet arrived. I heard reports later that they arrived and were being used by the Gulf Region Central district (GRC) for reconstruction projects in Fallujah and Ramadi. This was the vicious Al Anbar Province of Iraq - the home of the Sunni insurgency. I heard that GRC and the Marines operating in this area loved the Wer'Wolves. It was satisfying to know the vehicles were helping to protect our teams.

* * *

In July 2007, I met with Colonel Debra Lewis, the recent GRC Commander who had just returned to the United States. I asked her, *"What happened to the Wer'Wolves?"*

COL Lewis confirmed that GRC was using the four Wer'Wolves, and wanted them to become their standard vehicle. Reconstruction in Fallujah and other parts of Al Anbar was only possible because they had Wer'Wolves to protect our teams. She wasn't certain why, but GRC's request for more of the vehicles was denied. As popular as they were, GRC was still told they could not select more. She told me there were Wer'Wolf photos all over the GRD/GRC web page to illustrate their utility and popularity. Then she told me the rest of the story. Two Wer'wolves were badly damaged. One was hit with an RPG. The other hit by an Explosively Formed Penetrator (EFP) - the worst kind of IED. All personnel inside should have been killed, but they lived. She said there were injuries, including the GRC Deputy Commander. But COL Lewis directly credited the Wer'Wolves with saving the lives of seven or eight personnel. She was very emphatic, and thanked us for them. It was an emotional account. I felt very proud that our urgent procurement efforts made a difference, but I will always wish we had acquired many more.

A Wer'Wolf in Iraq

In August 2010, LTC Curlen Robinson provided a firsthand account of one of the Wer'Wolf attacks. On April 27, 2007, LTC Robinson set out from GRC to inspect the construction of a primary health clinic in Kandari, Iraq, a few miles east of Fallujah. He established a weekly routine of traveling to the project site. Unfortunately, the enemy knew this, and they prepared for Robinson's next visit. He was accompanied by an Erinys team and two Wer'wolves that provided site security during the inspection. Robinson already had a high level of confidence in the Wer'Wolf with its armor protection, high ground clearance, V-shaped body and its impact cooling capability (if hit with an explosive device). About five minutes into the inspection, the vehicles were put to the test. The team was attacked by mortars, small arms fire, an RPG, and possibly an IED. One of the Wer'wolves was hit repeatedly, but the other vehicle withstood the brunt of the attack. The team scrambled into the surviving vehicle, and they all returned safely to their base. The incident further increased GRD's confidence in the vehicles. LTC Robinson noted that the other Wer'Wolf incident occurred a few months earlier near Sadr City. During this attack, Navy LCDR Steve Frost was inside a Wer'Wolf that was hit by an IED (EFP). He was injured and evacuated from Iraq, but he survived.

12

Madness in Mosul

Mosul Gets Hot

There was a large highway overpass in Mosul that was the focal point of three attacks on GRN convoys. Two of these attacks occurred in late October 2004. Corporal James Gieb was riding in both convoys with an Erinys security team. The first attack appeared to be a "practice session" for the enemy. The second attack, about three days later, was more serious. On that day, the Erinys team had just delivered Wendell "Ben" Benner, an AT/FP expert, to the Baji project site to conduct a Threat and Vulnerability Assessment. The team was returning to the GRN headquarters at their Forward Operating Base (FOB Freedom) in Mosul. Ken Roger was in charge of the convoy, and he was one of the top Erinys Team Leaders in Iraq. He had recently trained his team on dismounted engagements. He wanted to be prepared in case the vehicles in his convoy were damaged, and his team had to continue the security escort mission on foot.

As the convoy approached the overpass, approximately 15 enemy fighters opened up with intense fire. The vehicles were seriously damaged. So Roger decided to halt movement and secure the nearby high ground while the vehicles were quickly inspected and their drivability assessed. Corporal Gieb and the Erinys team dismounted, and they fanned out to secure the slopes of the small rise. They soon came under enemy small arms fire. The team members instinctively returned fire and assaulted the rise. The bold move caught the enemy by surprise. Typically, reconstruction convoys would just try to outrun an attack. A dismounted counterattack was not what the enemy expected. Approximately seven insurgents were caught flat-footed, but offered some fairly stiff resistance. Corporal Gieb shot one of the enemy at very close range as he charged forward. This engagement was at about 6-8 feet. The team killed at least three enemy combatants and wounded an unknown number. The enemy was defeated, and they did not attempt another attack from this location again for over four months.

Corporal Gieb was later awarded the Bronze Star. The rest of the Erinys security team deserved similar recognition, but as contractors, their combat actions were rarely acknowledged by the Defense Department. The mainstream media, however, would have quickly criticized the security contractors had they made any tactical errors.

The third convoy attack near this overpass occurred on May 22, 2005. The three armored SUVs in the convoy were transporting the new GRN Commander and a USACE civilian. The rear vehicle, an Excursion "gun truck" with three Erinys personnel, was hit by an IED that exploded in the median. Fortunately, the IED detonated a bit early - just prior to the Excursion getting fully inside the main blast. Driving the vehicle was Harry Naude, while a teammate, Mike, rode shotgun and operated the radio. Ben Benner was in the back seat.

Unfortunately, this was a two-phased attack. A suicide car bomber was rapidly approaching the convoy from the rear. Naude tried to force the VBIED out of the way and block it from approaching the GRN Commander's vehicle. He alerted his team that the threat vehicle was not going to yield. It was immediately clear that they were facing a suicide bomber. The VBIED detonated alongside the Excursion, throwing the SUV six feet in the air. The Excursion absorbed much of the blast, thereby protecting the GRN Commander's vehicle. The Colonel's vehicle sustained damage from small arms fire and some shrapnel, but it limped back to the FOB guided by the lead SUV. The Commander's vehicle lost power 100 yards after passing through the main gate.

The armored Excursion was severely damaged. Incredibly, the three Erinys security men in the vehicle survived – but they were all wounded. Later, EOD experts determined that the VBIED was carrying five to seven 155mm artillery shells. That explained why only a few fragments of the attacking vehicle and terrorist were found.

Once again, the Erinys team demonstrated their valor during reconstruction operations. And they received little official recognition for their sacrifices. Their professionalism, bravery and modesty were part of their character. Benner's humility is reflected in the following excerpt from a recent email.

> ".....no one died except the VBIED driver. That is me on the stretcher (this photo made the papers in London) but the point is, because of the efforts of you and Jim, we had at least some armor between us and death and we made it out..... We do thank you for your efforts. Many lives were saved because of them."

Stryker team from 25th ID secures the area

The Excursion on median

Ben Benner (on stretcher) extracted from vehicle

Largest remnant of the car bomb

The Excursion absorbed much of the blast

Slugfest in Mosul

Another major attack on a GRN convoy occurred on November 10, 2004 in Mosul. Pat Parker, a member of Erinys and the 2nd in charge of the convoy, recounted the attack. Parker, a retired Master Sergeant, is a former member of the 3rd Ranger Battalion and 82nd Airborne Division.

That morning, a three-vehicle convoy was traveling from the Tikrit Area Office (FOB Speicher) to the GRN Headquarters in Mosul to participate in a reconstruction meeting. Twelve personnel and their baggage were packed in the vehicles: two USACE civilians (Mr. Sedey and Ms. McDonald), two military officers (MAJ Payne and MAJ Korth), and an eight-man Erinys security team (led by John Holloway).

The lead SUV was an armored Excursion driven by Frans Van Tubbergh, while Joe Brown manned the radio. MAJ Payne also rode in this vehicle. Vehicle two, also an armored Excursion, was driven by the Team Leader (Holloway), while Mike Jackson manned the radio. The two USACE civilians and MAJ Korth were passengers. Vehicle three, a white Ford with an add-on armor kit, was driven by Pat Parker. The Ford had three shooters: Andre Struwig, Jacques

Oosthuizen, and Tim Aranjo - the tail gunner manning the machine gun (SAW).

Prior to moving, the convoy checked for updated intelligence on the planned route. The roads were considered Green (relatively safe). Unknown to the security team, an estimated 300 insurgents were assembling in that section of Mosul. The enemy was preparing to attack several targets including the nearby Iraqi Police station. The GRN convoy was about to drive into a major kill zone.

Just before noon, the left side of the convoy was fired on by four insurgents at road level. They were armed with AK-47s. Oosthuizen returned fire, and immediately 6-8 more enemy fired from the rooftops on the right side. Simultaneously, three RPGs were fired at the convoy. Two hit just behind the last vehicle and one hit in front of it. The fire continued and intensified, with the lead and trail vehicles taking the most hits. The convoy sent a situation report (SITREP) to the GRN Headquarters, providing the location of the attack. MAJ Dansereau was manning the radio at GRN, and Ben Benner was downstairs relaying updates to the Army Tactical Operations Center (TOC).

The team did not want to be pinned down in the streets and pushed on. There was continuous fire coming from both sides as the convoy attempted to outrun the ambush. Oosthuizen engaged 6 more enemy on the left side at road level before he was hit in the upper torso in an area unprotected by his body armor. The convoy sped on as 15-20 more insurgents continued shooting from the rooftop on the right side.

There was a momentary lull in incoming fire. That meant either the convoy had moved out of the kill zone, or the enemy was re-loading their weapons to continue the attack. When the convoy approached Yarmouk Circle, another enemy team opened fire again from the left side. Vehicles one and three were taking a severe beating.

The lead vehicle had multiple hits to the engine, and it was smoking heavily. Both its front tires were flat. The driver (Van Tubbergh) reported that his vehicle was losing power fast. The middle vehicle got into position to push-assist the lead SUV. At that point, the Team Leader noticed an Iraqi Police (IP) station 100 meters to their front left. It was a potential safe haven, and it was protected by large concrete blast walls. Having already driven through 3.5 kilometers of intense enemy fire, an incredibly long kill zone, Holloway decided to lead the convoy towards the IP station.

The Iraqi Police had parked a white pickup truck in front of their compound and intentionally blocked the GRN convoy from entering. An Iraqi Policeman waved the convoy off. Holloway demanded the vehicle be moved so the GRN team could enter. An IP Colonel also denied them entrance. Holloway then radioed that the team was denied refuge, and he intended to push the obstructing IP vehicle away and enter the compound. He did. Two of the GRN vehicles entered. The lead SUV had lost all power and was left outside the compound.

Then all hell broke loose. RPGs started smashing into the surrounding blast walls and were also directed at the incapacitated vehicle. The security team provided suppressive fire as the occupants exited the dead vehicle and made a series of sprints for the IP compound. MAJ Payne and Joe Brown moved from one covered position to another. Once inside, all team members cleared their quadrants and secured any openings or gaps in the wall.

There was a mosque with a high tower adjacent to the IP station. It was directly overlooking the convoy's defensive position. Within minutes, tracer fire was plunging from the crow's nest at the top of the tower. There were at least three separate muzzle flashes firing from it. Tim Aranjo returned fire until a large explosion ripped through the inside of the tower. His well-placed rounds likely caused the denotation of an enemy RPG positioned in the crow's nest.

Meanwhile, Joe Brown, the Erinys team medic, was attending to Jacques Oosthuizen who was mortally wounded. Brown soon confirmed that Oosthuizen had died.

Having lost their commanding position in the mosque, insurgents began to approach the police station on foot to locate and target the security team. One man came out of the side street and was hiding a weapon by his side. The spotter began to point toward the two GRN vehicles and yelled to alert the other enemy. The insurgent then went into a crouch and started to aim his weapon at the Erinys personnel inside the compound. Holloway immediately dropped him with two rounds.

The enemy now increased their fire at the compound. Two more RPGs hit the abandoned SUV outside the entrance. The dead vehicle was becoming a punching bag. The enemy was wasting RPGs and ammunition by engaging it. Several more RPGs hit exposed areas of the IP station, which protruded above the surrounding blast walls.

A red sedan, with three occupants, pulled to within 30 meters of the slit in the blast-wall. Two of them exited the vehicle and looked into the compound for targets. As the insurgents were retrieving their weapons, including an RPG, Aranjo and Struwig engaged them and eliminated the threat. Another sedan with two occupants pulled abreast of the first one. Aranjo and Struwig immediately fired on the vehicle. Two insurgents with AK47s dismounted and were immediately killed. A third vehicle (white sedan) came to a stop outside the gap in the wall, and two male occupants tried to peer inside the compound. These enemy spotters were immediately targeted by Aranjo and Struwig. The white sedan reversed out of sight at great speed. Suddenly, a large truck raced towards the compound. It threatened to ram into the defensive perimeter. While 300 meters from the compound, Struwig engaged it and forced it to stop. Meanwhile, Parker supported the team's defense using a Russian-made RPK light machinegun.

The enemy continued to probe the perimeter of the compound with SAF and occasional RPGs. Every time an insurgent was hit, the enemy barrage intensified.

Holloway's security team had continuous radio communications with Erinys Security (Team 1) in Mosul at the GRN HQ. Team 1 attempted to respond as a Quick Reaction Force, but the Army stopped them at the gate. The roads were closed. The Marine and Army assault on Fallujah (2nd Battle) had driven hundreds of the enemy into Mosul, and the city's streets remained locked down for several days

Since Team 1 could not leave the FOB, a Stryker unit from the 25th Infantry Division was alerted to extract the GRN team. The Erinys team used green smoke grenades to help guide the U.S. military force to the IP station. The U.S. troops dismounted and came into the compound.

Due to the severe damage to the three SUVs, most of the GRN team boarded the Stryker vehicles for the final trip through Mosul. Holloway wanted to salvage two SUVs for later use by GRN. Consequently, Jacques's body was loaded into vehicle two, which had two flat front tires. Holloway then drove the shredded SUV the final distance to FOB Diamondback and delivered Jacques to the Combat Support Hospital.

The GRN team was in sustained contact with the enemy for over an hour. Soon after returning, the team began to train three new security members and to replace lost gear, depleted ammunition and damaged vehicles.

Later that day, insurgents posted photos of their "victory celebration" on the internet:

13

Palaces of Iraq

I heard different estimates of the number of palaces that Saddam built, ranging from fifty to eighty. During the course of my tour in Iraq, I probably visited a dozen of them, some multiple times. I never had a good definition for what a palace really was. While some were clearly places where the Iraqi elite worked, others were more likely villas or residences for the senior leadership.

A number of the Iraqi palaces were damaged or destroyed during the "Shock and Awe" bombing campaign. Others were spared and later used as headquarters for military forces or the Coalition Provisional Authority. Typically large and opulent, the ones I saw often looked like a Ritz Carlton on steroids. They had lots of marble, chandeliers and gold plated fixtures in the bathrooms. The interior sometimes felt like being in Las Vegas - without the slot machines and flashing lights.

* * *

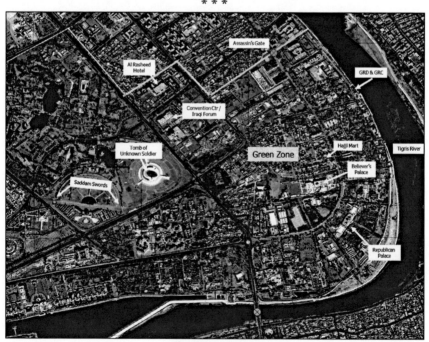

The Green Zone

Many of the Iraqi elite lived in an area of the Green Zone called "Little Venice", a wealthy residential area nestled along the Tigris River. It had palm trees, swimming pools, and ponds connected with waterways and bridges. The White and Brown Palaces that served as the initial GRD and GRC HQs were located in this area.

Prior to the invasion, there were many news reports about Saddam's Palaces. The U.S. suspected that Saddam was hiding evidence of weapons of mass destruction (WMDs) in them. I did not find any chemical or nuclear WMDs hidden in these palaces. However, the palace bathrooms might qualify as a biological WMD because the toilets often clogged, causing panic among the civilian work force and creating a stream of refugees in search of a less hostile restroom.

"Our" Palace on the Tigris River

GRC and GRD Headquarters as seen from across the Tigris (from the Red Zone)

The Palace Grounds

The first Headquarters for the Gulf Region Division was located in the Brown Palace at Essayons Base (pictured above on the right), an engineer enclave inside the Green Zone in Baghdad. The Brown Palace had a horizontal stone pattern that made it look like a multilayered brown cake. The main entrance had eight large columns in front. Essayons Base had a second palace, a white one – next door to the brown one.

The White Palace (pictured above on the left) served as the Gulf Region Central (GRC) District HQ. Both palaces provided a commanding view of Baghdad and had almost 700 feet of prime waterfront real estate along the Tigris River. These two small palaces were spared from the target list during the bombing campaign at the outset of the war.

GRD Headquarters (the Brown Palace) – front entry

History of the Palace

I never found an authoritative source with a complete account of the history of these two palaces. However, I conducted some research on site and online and have pieced together some interesting facts.

Multiple discussions with GRD personnel and interviews with Iraqi workers and translators at GRD have led to the conclusion that the Brown Palace was the home of the last Monarch of Iraq – Faisal II. King Faisal II and his family were brutally murdered nearby in 1958. The Brown and White Palaces later became two of Saddam's homes, and according to the local workers, he kept a wife in each palace. Rumored to have spent a night a week in each palace, Saddam constantly moved around Baghdad to keep from being located and targeted by U.S. forces.

In fact, the Arabic plaque near the entrance of the Brown Palace confirms much of this report. The inscription was later translated by Carolyn Handal (Raytheon Company) to English:

In the name of the Holy God.
This structure was built during the era of the King Faisal the second, God rest his sole in 1375 (~1955 A.D.). The structure was supervised during and after construction under the great

leader Saddam Hussein God bless and keep him in 1410
(~1990 A.D.).

The plaque also lists the architectural divisions that completed the renovation work.

Based on some internet searches, I believe the Brown Palace may be the former royal Azzohour Palace, but I am not certain. Unlike many of Saddam's other palaces that were built during his reign, Azzohour belonged to the kings of Iraq since 1921, and it had architectural and historic significance. Saddam renovated it in the early 1990's. After Baghdad was seized, the two palaces were occupied by the Iraq Provisional Command (IPC), a forerunner of the Gulf Region Division. It later became the first GRD Headquarters from January to September 2004.

Interior of the Palace

The Brown Palace was more of a wealthy villa than a palace. Marble, crystal chandeliers, hand woven rugs and ornate furnishings briefly describes its interior.

There were oversized wooden doors throughout the residence, starting with the main entrance. The doors were very heavy with inlaid or carved designs and had a dark brown finish. Most were double doors, providing a full opening of about six feet. The doors were probably made by craftsmen in Europe and imported to Iraq. The main foyer was about 15 feet deep and 40 feet wide. It was a main throughway of marble tile to most of the rooms on the first floor. Five heavy crystal chandeliers hung across the width of the foyer. A twelve-foot long mirrored credenza, rich with inlaid wood, stood out as a unique piece of furniture. The design had a large eight-pointed star on four of the six door panels. Other furnishings included some upholstered chairs with a lot of gold paint and trim, a mirror and a coffee table that appeared to be French style, perhaps Louis XIV. The chairs were too nice to sit on with my combat gear. The visitor waiting area had two long sofas. That's where COL Dornstauder and I met the two dozen Ukrainian paratroopers that showed up one day as a new contractor security force.

A white and black marble spiral staircase led from the foyer up to the second and third floors. A second smaller spiral staircase was located on the other end of the foyer. It was out of view and clearly for use by staff personnel that supported the palace.

There were three main working rooms on the first floor in addition to some private offices, a living area, restrooms and a kitchen. Our human resources section used the first working room. Their mission was to continuously recruit new GRD staff for both military (G1) and civilians (HR). The room, about 16 by 30 feet, had marble floors, two crystal chandeliers, and an ornate wooden ceiling with inlaid symbols and paintings. Only a color photograph could adequately present the impressive detail in the ceiling design and the overall rich appearance of the room.

The second room was larger, covering about 25 by 30 feet—was used as the Operations Center (G3) and was my office space. The Intelligence section (G2) also worked in here. This room had marble floors, three crystal chandeliers, and a colorful ceiling with ornate designs. The pink, blue, and white ceiling looked too elegant for a military operations center. Fortunately, my operations team had plenty of wall maps, flags and gun racks around the office to give it more of a martial look.

GRD Operations Center – MAJ Jim Ball coordinating a flight request

The third room, used as the Main Division Conference Room, was about 15 by 30 feet. Two large side-by-side conference tables with a Ba'ath Party symbol inlaid in the wooden tabletop were in the center of the room with a dozen matching chairs. The room also had a fireplace and three crystal chandeliers. It was likely used by Saddam and his leadership team. The GRD Commander and the senior staff held daily briefings here. We installed video teleconference capability that I used to communicate with GRD liaison officers throughout Iraq and to connect to Virginia during a live Counter IED conference. I was sitting at this conference table on my first day at GRD when a huge explosion rocked us and destroyed the nearby Mt. Lebanon Hotel.

The northern end of the building was reserved for the GRD Commander, MG Johnson and later BG Bostick. They maintained both their residence and main office in adjacent rooms. That made the Commander's daily commute to the office easy.

The final major room on the ground floor was the large industrial kitchen. It was equipped with sinks, ovens, stoves, refrigerators, and many utensils. It was sized to host large social events and not actively used by the division, except for storage. We did have some large rats that roamed in the palace at night. This kitchen was a prime hunting ground for LTC Joe Corrigan and MAJ Ray Hart who controlled the population by sponsoring a rat-trapping competition. The kitchen was a "target rich environment" for Joe and Ray.

There were multiple bathrooms in the Palace. They were all very large with marble walls and floors. The commodes, sinks and bidets were ceramic with ornate decorations and gold fixtures—some of the toilets looked like thrones! Some bathrooms had a tub or shower. This caused safety concerns, as water would always get on the marble floors causing visitors and residents to slip and fall. You had to use a squeegee to remove the water from the marble floor after taking a shower or you might kill the next guy coming into the room!

But the real problem with the bathrooms in this palace was that the waste sewage pipes were only 3-inches in diameter. Americans just eat a lot more than the rest of the world, and they tend to use a roll of paper with each flush. That meant the palace pipes clogged constantly. Consequently, flushing toilet paper was banned. People often did it anyway. That meant the pump truck had to pull up to the palace every few days to literally suck the crap out of the septic tank. Of course, every truck coming into the perimeter had to be searched for bombs. That meant some lucky gate guard had to stick his head inside the waste storage tank and inspect it for explosives. Nobody wanted that duty!

The second floor of the Palace had a similar layout, with marble floors, but was somewhat less ornate, with fewer chandeliers. The two GRD senior civilian executives (SES), Steve Stockton and Bob Slockbower, shared an office there, as did the Chief of Staff and the Command Sergeant Major. The staff elements that managed GRD programs, contracts, reach back, public affairs and geospatial support also worked on the second floor!

The third floor of the Palace was a large open storage area that was converted into a sleeping area for about a dozen GRD and GRC military personnel. It was hot, and fans were constantly blowing. We tried to keep the noise down, as some personnel worked and slept irregular hours.

* * *

The eight-pointed star, a symbol of the Ba'ath Party, was everywhere in Iraq, even in the Brown Palace. I don't understand its full significance, but I think it had more political meaning than religious. I also saw the eight-pointed star while I was in Jordan. At first glance, it looked like the Israeli six-pointed Star of David, which really confused me. But the two symbols have entirely different meanings.

GRD kept the original Iraqi palace employees on the payroll to help us maintain the building. Several of them told us stories of palace life under Saddam. One of the interesting finds in the palace was a Bible written in Arabic. One of the Iraqi employees told me that Saddam's mother was Christian, but I had no way to confirm that.

The palace also came with some groundskeepers. The palace gardener was missing for a few days. I received word in the Ops Center that he had been detained entering the Green Zone. He tested positive for traces of explosives when he was swiped by a gate guard. I immediately knew this was likely a false positive. The guy had been working with fertilizers for years, and his body would be covered with nitrates, a key component of explosives. I told our Ops team to call the appropriate authorities and explain the situation. I did not want a hard working Iraqi falsely accused of being associated with a bombing network.

Two large flagpoles stood outside each palace. I occasionally hoisted an American flag up these poles, particularly after a rocket attack—one of the most rewarding things I did in Iraq. Sometime in June or July, I met the Embassy Regional Security Officer (RSO) on our shared perimeter. He noted that the trucks at the top of the flagpoles were believed to be Ba'ath Party symbols. He strongly recommended that GRD remove these brass ornaments ASAP and definitely before GRD moved from the palace. Leaving them on top of the flagpoles would confuse and offend the new Iraqi Government. I relayed this info to COL Dornstauder and CSM Balsh. In late August, as GRD was preparing to move, a large pole truck pulled up to our HQ. I watched as a worker stood at the top of the extended bucket and used a long rod to start beating the ornaments. It must have worked, because the symbols were gone the next morning. I found the battered remains a few days later in the trash can as we were vacating the building.

The palace had a pool on its grounds. It was repaired and used for occasional celebrations on Memorial Day and the 4th of July. I got in it once for ten minutes, but I felt uneasy without my weapon.

Prime Minister Allawi Wants It Back

On June 28, 2004, the Coalition Provisional Authority (CPA) transitioned governance of Iraq back to the Iraqi people. The new leadership, called the Interim Iraqi Government, was led by Prime Minister Allawi. The new Iraqi leader soon asked U.S. Forces to turn several palaces back to his Government for official use.

On June 21, prior to the transition of power, Prime Minister Allawi and the Deputy President personally visited the GRD HQ building to discuss the transfer of King Faisal's palace back to the Iraqi Government. The palace was the traditional residence of Iraqi leaders, and would continue to serve that role. That meant the Brown Palace would become the 'White House of Iraq". The senior GRD staff assembled in the main conference room, while two GRD Senior Executives, Steve Stockton and Bob Slockbower, conducted a personal tour with the PM.

Prime Minister Allawi (in white shirt) visits GRD

Seeking a New Home for GRD

The move-out date for both palaces was set for late July. Both GRD and GRC would have to vacate Essayons Base. GRC could move to the new facility at Camp Victory, but GEN Casey required GRD to remain in the Green Zone. And there was no spare real estate in the Green Zone. It was already full. GRD was being evicted and faced potential homelessness. There was a great urgency to find a new HQ location. We looked at every conceivable alternative for workspace for our 300 personnel. I briefly considered occupying the Republican Guard Bunker under Believer's Palace. It was the #1 target in the bombing campaign at the start of the war. Believer's Palace was destroyed, but the bunker below it survived. But we continued our search for a new HQ.

Fortunately, the issue had the attention of GEN Casey and the Joint Area Support Group (JASG) that managed the Green Zone. In effect, the JASG served as the mayor of the Green Zone, specifying what units could occupy what buildings. The JASG found a potential GRD HQ site near the combat support hospital when it determined that a local medical unit was "living large", occupying far more space than was afforded to other units living in the Green Zone. The medical unit was directed to vacate a large building that was underutilized. However, the time required to relocate the medical unit and to move GRD into the building would add a few weeks to the schedule. GRD did not want to disrupt any reconstruction operations by completely unplugging. So continuity of operations during the move was the top priority. Once the medical unit vacated, GRD spent a week working 24/7 to modify the building for its needs. That included putting up and knocking down walls and updating the telecommunications, power and IT.

Each GRD staff section had an opportunity to state how much floor space they needed and their technology needs. COL Dornstauder and I devised the new space allocation plan and ended any further debate. No section got all they requested, and they just had to plan accordingly. The new GRC move date to Camp Victory was now August, and GRD's move date slipped to early September 2004. Prime Minister Allawi was gracious and patient, but these dates were now final.

Ironically, the new GRD HQ building was another former home of Saddam Hussein. This one was more modest, and certainly not a palace. My Iraqi interpreter told me the building was the home that Saddam was married in, while a field grade officer, before he became the leader of Iraq.

In our final days in the Brown Palace, I walked around and inspected each of the rooms as we vacated them. I had an opportunity to reflect on what was really happening. Our HQ had been the home of the last monarch of Iraq. And, as the new home of the Iraqi Prime Minister, it was soon to be the equivalent of the U.S. White House. It was possible that my Operations Office was going to serve as the Iraqi Oval Office. Wow.

Prior to stepping out the palace door on the last evening, BG Bostick, COL Dornstauder and I made a last walk through the nearly vacant building. Only the original Iraq furnishings remained. We took some group photos to remember how it really was. It would be something we could show our children and their children many years later.

LTC Kachejian – BG Bostick – COL Dornstauder
Final Day in the Brown Palace

Republican Palace

This was the largest and most widely known of Saddam's palaces in Iraq. The Republican Palace was located about a mile south of the GRD Headquarters. It also overlooked the Tigris River and served as the main office for senior Ba'ath Party officials. The Palace was not targeted during the aerial bombing campaign because it had potential intelligence value for the coalition if the building and documents could be seized intact. Consequently, the Republican Palace was spared damage.

The Republican Palace

After the invasion, the Republican Palace served as the HQ for General (Retired) Jay Garner of the Office of Reconstruction and Humanitarian Assistance (ORHA) and later for Ambassador Jerry Bremer of the Coalition Provisional Authority (CPA). Most of the U.S. diplomats worked here until the permanent Embassy was built.

The Republican Palace also had plenty of marble, chandeliers, large brass doors and ornate decorations on the walls and ceilings. The building originally had some large bronze heads on the roof that represented "Saddam the Warrior". These were removed by huge cranes several months after the U.S. secured the Palace. The Palace interior had a number of other interesting sites, including one of Saddam's "thrones" with a big mural behind it depicting rockets being launched, presumably at Iraq's enemies.

A large ballroom in the Republican Palace was converted to a central dining facility (DFAC) to serve thousands of troops and civilians each day. Mealtime in the DFAC was often compared to the "Star Wars" bar scene, as a mob of coalition soldiers and civilians, speaking foreign languages, wearing strange uniforms and carrying exotic weapons stood in line to feed at the trough. No two diners appeared to be from the same planet. Saddam hosted many dinners in this ballroom. At one dinner, Saddam reportedly poisoned several of his "enemies" while serving them a toast.

From a reconstruction perspective, the Project and Contracting Office (PCO) operated out of an annex located in the south wing of the Palace. The PCO and the Embassy selected and funded the projects, then turned them over to GRD. GRD's mission was to take the project and the assigned contractor and go build it. A few months after I left Iraq, the PCO Annex was directly hit by a rocket that killed two personnel and narrowly missed BG Bostick.

On the rear grounds of the Republican Palace there were hundreds of trailers where many civilians and military lived. Trailer residents were generally associated with the Embassy mission. This area was a small city, covering several acres of land. There were so many trailers in the area that I thought that a tornado or hurricane might veer toward Baghdad to strike it! Sandbag walls separated each of the trailers and protected them from flying shrapnel.

There was a large swimming pool in the rear of the Palace. It went wild on Friday and Saturday nights. Scores of Embassy employees and other civilians would drink alcohol, play loud music and play "grab-ass" while the military observed General Order #1 (no alcohol consumption) and steered clear of the area. The standards for conduct between the military and civilian personnel in this Muslim nation were starkly different.

Uday's Love Palace

Uday Hussein, the oldest son of Saddam, was a master of fear and intimidation; I read numerous accounts of his brutal and sadistic behavior. He kidnapped Iraqi women off the street and raped them. An Army officer, who defended his wife during an assault, was sentenced to death. In a separate incident, Uday reportedly beat his father's valet and food taster with a cane in a drunken rage in front of his international guests at a party. He then killed the servant with an electric carving knife. As the head of the Iraqi Olympic Committee, Uday imprisoned and tortured athletes that failed to win. In 1996, Uday was badly wounded during an assassination attempt, but survived. In July 2003, both of Saddam's sons, Uday and Qusay, were killed by U.S. Special Operations Forces in Mosul. Upon hearing the announcement, the city of Baghdad lit up with celebratory gunfire.

Uday had a passion for exotic cars, cigars, wine, heroin and women. He lived in a palace in the Green Zone, often called Uday's "Love Palace" or the "Love Shack" and reportedly flew in Swedish prostitutes on the weekends. If it was true, the women were certainly gone by the time I got to Iraq. The Love Palace was damaged during the bombing campaign. I saw it many times from the exterior, but I never went inside the damaged structure.

Al Faw Palace

Al Faw is a massive white palace near the Baghdad Airport, built on an island in the middle of a man-made lake. A causeway connected Al Faw Palace to the shore. The waters of the Tigris River were diverted to make the construction of a lake around Al Faw possible. The Palace looked like a fortress designed by an architect, not an engineer. I thought of Al Faw as the "Mother of all Palaces". And it served as the headquarters for U.S. military operations in Iraq.

Al Faw Palace

About a dozen impressive residences and boathouses lined the shore of the lake and surrounded the Palace. The lake, and hundreds of acres in the surrounding area, were reported to be the playground for the Ba'ath Party elite. I was told that the area was stocked with wild animals, such as antelope and lions. Saddam rarely left Iraq, but he could participate in an African safari on the grounds near Al Faw Palace. And U.S. Special Operations Forces reportedly dined on the antelope in the early days of the conflict.

Al Faw Palace was built to commemorate the victory of Al Faw during Iraq's bloody war with Iran during the 1980s. The Al Faw peninsula was agriculturally rich, and its oil facilities made it strategic to Iraq's economy. The Iranians seized Al Faw in 1986. Saddam vowed to recapture the city "at all costs". The Iraqis succeeded in April 1988. The walls inside the Palace are inscribed in Arabic, "Victory and glory to the warriors who freed the city from the enemy, the Persians."

Everything about Al Faw Palace was awesome - the brass doors, the columns and the chandeliers. The main foyer was stunning - with marble floors, massive columns and a ceiling at least sixty feet high. The main chandelier that hangs in this area is probably 25 feet in diameter. A large marble spiral staircase leads to the upper floors and ornate decorations cover the walls and ceilings. Sitting on Saddam's throne was a favorite photo spot for Palace visitors.

Scott Lowdermilk on the throne at Al Faw Palace

Believer's Palace

On the morning of March 26, 2004, as I was walking near the Republican Palace, I was stopped by Colonel Rick Aswell. He stated that he was the Director of Infrastructure for all of Iraq. He told me he was about to give a few visitors a tour of Saddam's national command bunker. COL Aswell said he was about to leave Iraq, and this was the last bunker tour he would give. He asked me if I wanted to tag along. All I could think was "Carpe diem, baby!" Seize the day! Let's go!

The Republican Guard Command and Control (C2) Bunker was across the street and directly under "Believer's Palace". This Palace previously served as the Ba'ath Party Headquarters. From street level, it looked just like another bombed out palace. Believer's Palace was at the top of the U.S. target list at the start of the war and was destroyed by several precision guided munitions. Yet amazingly, Saddam's bunker beneath it survived.

The remains of Believer's Palace – above the Republican Guard Command and Control bunker

A few minutes later, a dozen or so civilians showed up on the scene. I had no idea who they were. Some looked a little hesitant as COL Aswell led us into the massive building. The first part of the tour took us through the bombed out Palace. As we walked across the rubble of various ballrooms and foyers, I observed dozens of partially collapsed walls and roof segments that dangled precipitously over our heads. Those thousand pound pieces of concrete and steel were going to eventually fall, and I didn't want it to happen while I was standing under them.

From inside the Palace, I could see several entrance holes from U.S. precision guided bombs in the domed roof. The daylight illuminated two at the top of the dome. The holes were about three feet apart—not bad shooting from several miles away. Beams of daylight shot through the holes like headlights, spotlighting the rubble-strewn floor below. The acoustics in this large cavernous area were eerie. While the outer structure remained, the inside of the domed area, probably once a grand ballroom or conference area, was completely destroyed.

Sunlight from holes created by Precision Guided Munitions spotlight the rubble

The destroyed "Ballroom"

We toured a few more areas of the Palace and saw more scars from the bombing. COL Aswell stated that the Palace and bunker had already been "harvested by the Iraqi Government". The interior marble that survived the bombing had been removed and was now being re-used in new MOI / MOD facilities. The Palace and bunker had no residual value and were planned for demolition. He stated that visitors were permitted to remove a piece of broken marble or other remnants from the structure. He cautioned the group to be careful since it was a very hazardous area. That sent the civilians digging through the mountains of broken concrete and mangled steel like shoppers at a K-Mart "Blue Light Special".

Now it was time to go down into the bunker. COL Aswell told us to get our flashlights ready and to stick together The first indication that we were at the bunker entrance was the large steel blast door. There were actually two blast doors in series–both were painted navy blue with 1-meter long yellow levers used to lock them. It felt like I was entering a Swiss bank vault. Once inside the blast doors, the world got pitch black, real fast. The flashlights turned on, and we started to descend about 50 steps. The air grew thick and musty. The stairwells turned to the right at each landing. It was like walking down a large concrete stairwell in a dark hotel. At the bottom of the stairwell there was a blown out elevator shaft. The bunker reportedly had three levels, although the lower levels were later determined to be tunnels used to move between bunker segments.

The bunker was a small underground city with multiple corridors and scores of rooms. Much of it had been stripped for re-use by the Iraqi Government or looted. The primary bunker area contained an Operations and Intelligence Center, a Command Conference Room and Saddam Hussein's personal suite. I recognized the Command Conference Center from a video news clip that I had seen of Saddam before the war. There were several important functions hosted in the support area of the bunker. I found a media room where propaganda videos were made. Cut film was still lying on the floor. There were quarters for officers and enlisted soldiers, a large kitchen, restrooms, showers, a mechanical room with a large generator, and an air filtration room.

The electrical distribution room was stripped of all metal circuitry. However, lying on a nearby control panel was a set of blueprints marked "Project 551/1 Iraq Siemens AG"–the drawings were dated April 27, 1988. The design was made before the first Gulf War (Desert Storm), but I wasn't sure, when the bunker was actually built – before or after the U.N. trade embargo on Iraq.

As we moved through the bunker, we noticed it was well constructed and had multiple seismically isolated compartments. It had massive shock absorbers built between its compartments. Except for the elevator shaft, it clearly withstood a severe pounding by the aerial bombardment.

There was no doubt the Iraqis in the bunker were prepared for and expected a chemical warfare environment. We all knew that chemical weapons were considered WMDs. An entire room was dedicated to air filtration—the system likely relied on overpressure to keep outside contaminated air from penetrating the bunker. There was further evidence of Iraqi preparation for chemical warfare. Chemical protection suits, rubber boots, and atropine injector casings, used to counter nerve agents, were scattered about. It appeared as if the Iraqis had injected themselves believing that chemical warfare had already begun. Saddam may have fooled his own troops.

After the tour, I went back to GRD HQ and told the Ops team about my adventure. LTC Vance Purvis, LTC Joe Corrigan and MAJ Ray Hart were licking their chops and wanted to go see it for themselves. I told them to get their flashlights, and I would lead them in. I needed to do it the same day, or I might forget all the details and, more importantly, how to navigate inside the bunker.

The first part of my GRD "team tour" was a 75-foot climb up a prayer tower just outside the Palace. COL Aswell's tour skipped this part to save time. The tower had a tight spiral staircase. Large bullet holes pierced through the metal stairs and concrete walls–probably from a Bradley Fighting Vehicle or a .50 caliber machine gun. From above, the tower had the shape of the eight-pointed star. At the top of the tower was a commanding view of the Green Zone. The Tigris River was in the distance, as were the Brown and White Palaces, the Sheraton Hotel, the archway at Assassin's Gate, the Combat Support Hospital and the former Iraqi Intelligence Headquarters. Viewing from the other side, we could see the Republican Palace. Below us was Washington Airfield, where Little Bird helicopters were constantly active.

At Believer's Palace - *seated* Kachejian, *standing* Corrigan (L) and Hart (R)

After coming back down the tower, we walked into the ruins of Believers' Palace. Inside, I found a damaged and dusty chair and set it up on a pile of rubble. We each sat in it, and took a team photo. It is one of my favorite shots from the war. Then, we went down into the bunker and acted like kids in a toy store. I kept hearing, "Hey, look what I found!"

On a subsequent bunker tour, my pistol fell out of my shoulder holster and into an open hole in the raised bunker floor. The hole was full of water, and it was too deep for me to retrieve. Fortunately, MAJ Jim Ball was with me and had arms just long enough to grab the weapon with his fingertips in the deep dark water. I still owe Jim a cold beer for saving me from the embarrassment of losing my weapon.

MAJ Ball retrieves my weapon

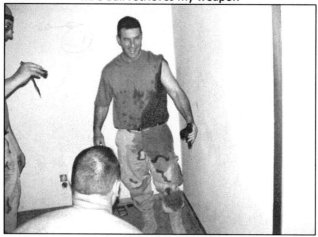
And I was one happy dude!

Over the next six months, I gave the Believer's Palace tour to many other GRD visitors. In July, I led an Officer Professional Development (OPD) tour in the bunker for two District Commanders, Colonel Carl Ubbelohde (GRN) and COL Richard Thompson (GRC), as well as Mr. Bob Slockbower (SES), LTC Mike Donovan and MAJ John Pickering. These guys needed a break from the stress of combat, and they seemed to really appreciate the tour.

I tried to schedule a broader OPD so the entire GRD staff could see the bunker. We worked only a few blocks from the site. I was certain all our engineers would want to see how the seismic design survived the heavy bombing. Unfortunately, the staff OPD tour never happened. We had it scheduled once, but it was cancelled because the war kept us too busy. I also tried to get COL Alex Dornstauder down there several times, but it just didn't happen.

When GRD had to relocate its HQ later that summer, I considered moving the Division into Saddam's Bunker. It had meeting rooms, office space, bedrooms, and was well protected from rocket attacks and VBIEDs. We were engineers, and we could quickly rehab the facility for GRD use. But there was evidence that one of the U.S. precision guided munitions (PGMs) that hit the building failed to explode. The number of PGM entrance holes in the roof exceeded the number of bomb craters in the structure. There was probably a 500 or 1000-pound bomb unaccounted for. It likely broke into pieces on impact, but we weren't certain. So we determined that occupying the bunker was an unacceptable risk to our USACE work force.

In October 2007, I returned to Baghdad with LTC Don Johantges. By now, the Joint Area Staff Group (JASG-C) had officially closed Believer's Palace and the C2 bunker because of its many dangers. Mr. Jim Proctor, the GRD Strategic Plans Manager, received special permission to conduct the educational and historic visit as a rare exception. Jim had completed several tours in Iraq and had collected quite a bit of new information about the bunker's origin, construction and its capture. He gave us a comprehensive tour that lasted almost 3 hours. I saw some new areas, and he clarified many facts. Jim provided us with a detailed map of the structure and had researched the German designer. Because the U.S. could not destroy the bunker with an aerial bombardment, Army Rangers seized it by blowing a hole in the blast doors at a hidden entrance outside the palace. We started the last tour by going through the blast doors where the Ranger raid kicked off, and we worked our way through the escape tunnel into the core of the bunker area.

It had been over three years since I had last been in the bunker. There was heavy black mold inside, and the water infiltration was much worse. The air in some areas was stifling, so we wore masks. But I saw many new areas that were helpful to my understanding. Jim gave an insightful overview of the relationship between technology and doctrine, and he served as a "myth buster" for many previously accepted bunker stories. One item in the palace, that had previously escaped me, was Saddam's black marble hot tub. And on one of the surviving walls inside the palace, Saddam had his name inscribed—above God's name. The sight of this was offensive to Iraqis and illustrated Saddam's arrogance and disrespect.

Doors to Saddam's bunker were blasted open by Army Rangers

Other Palaces

During my travels throughout Iraq, I saw several other palaces, including those in Mosul and Tikrit. One day, Iraq may have a thriving tourism industry, and I believe it will include tours of the palaces that Saddam built. These palaces may still provide some economic benefit to the Iraqi Government and many jobs for the Iraqi people who will operate and maintain them.

Palace at Mosul

14

Defending "Our" Palace

General Defenses

The GRD Headquarters enclave inside the Green Zone was called Essayons Base. It was exotic, beautiful—and dangerous. The eastern boundary was the Tigris River and across the river was the Red Zone, an area that the U.S. patrolled, but did not physically occupy. Our base had two adjacent palaces, the Brown Palace (GRD HQ) and the White Palace (GRC HQ), which shared about 210 meters of prime waterfront property and provided a commanding view of Baghdad. From our elevated position, we could see and hear combat operations occurring throughout the city, particularly on the eastern shore of the Tigris. Unfortunately, our exposed position also provided the enemy an excellent view of our facility and defenses.

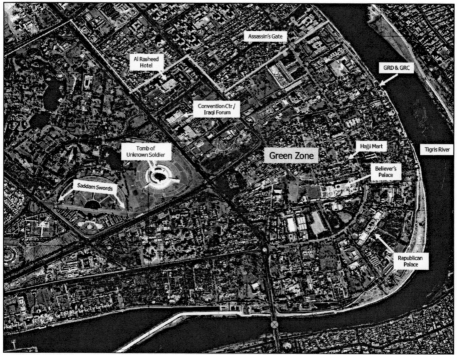

The Green Zone

The Green Zone came under daily attack from the Red Zone, typically involving rockets or mortars fired at us. During my tour, at least 400 rockets and mortars hit nearby. On one day in August, we were hit with 40 of them.

The Tigris River was 280 meters wide at this point, providing a decent security buffer, but we were still well inside the range of enemy fire from the far shore. Concertina wire was placed along the shoreline to protect against enemy infiltration from the river, but security along the Essayons Base riverfront was a constant concern for GRD.

From the palace grounds, we had a 50-yard line seat to see ongoing combat operations. Car bombings, suppressive fire from attack helicopters, and precision targeting using Air Force fighters were common sights. Sadr City was a frequent engagement area. On many days, standing behind a sandbag wall on the palace grounds with a pair of binoculars was like watching the History Channel live.

Apache flyover – headed to Sadr City

Our adjacent neighbor to the north was the U.S. Embassy Chancellery—a high value target for the enemy. The unit to our south was the 350th Civil Affairs (CA) Brigade, Commanded by BG Sandy Davidson. Civil Affairs units were part of the Army's Special Operations Command. I saw BG Davidson about once a week in a meeting or just walking around our adjacent perimeters. We had good discussions and coordinated closely on perimeter security plans. The CA brigade loaned a military radio to GRD, the only one it would ever possess, to help the division quickly communicate during perimeter security issues. The handheld VHF radio was a French-made Thompson capable of frequency hopping. We used it during several tactical threats and for conducting periodic communications checks.

I ran the GRD Operations Center on the ground floor of the Brown Palace. My desk backed up to large glass windows and doors on the riverside. In peacetime, this glass provided an impressive view of the Baghdad waterfront. But in wartime, the glass posed a serious threat to life and safety as it would become deadly shrapnel if a rocket or suicide boat bomb hit outside. To reduce the risk, we constructed a series of sandbag walls in front of the glass to protect our personnel.

Protective sandbag walls outside the GRD Ops Center

When I arrived in Iraq, the insurgency was hitting high gear. Given the degrading tactical situation, I immediately increased the security measures for Essayons Base. MSG Spears, MAJ Ball, MAJ Hart and later MAJ Bill Foos were among the few military personnel in the GRD Headquarters, and they performed many additional duties associated with security. It was unusual for such senior personnel to do so, but there were no troop units assigned to support us. We only had a handful of officers and senior enlisted personnel.

One of the security changes we made was beefing up the night shift. The limited military staff were constantly sprinting during a marathon, so we trained GRD civilians to serve as night staff duty officers (SDOs). DOD civilians were paid by the hour, and many were motivated to pull the extra duty. And there were scores of them available. Military personnel lived within yards of the Operations Center, and they could be quickly alerted. So using civilians to answer the phones and track situation reports inside the Operations Center was considered an acceptable risk.

We also increased perimeter inspections, particularly near the waterfront area. Night patrols would be conducted in full body armor with loaded weapons. For simplicity, GRD adopted the same local threat level and uniform standards in use by the nearby Brigade Combat Team (2BCT).

We strictly enforced "light discipline" to prevent our personnel and facilities from being silhouetted at night. All palace windows facing the water were covered with sheets to keep them dark. We didn't want enemy snipers looking through windows at night and targeting our personnel. At the same time, I directed that floodlights be installed along the riverfront wall to illuminate 200 feet out into the water. These bright spotlights would deter nighttime boat traffic from approaching too closely and blind any night vision goggles potentially used to observe our position.

I also requested a watchdog to serve as an early warning system along the riverfront. Man's best friend could alert us by barking at potential intruders. GRD never got the watchdog, but there were a few strays in the area. We occasionally added more concertina along the waterfront to reinforce potential weak areas.

Looking for the source of sniper fire

We occasionally received sniper fire from the far shore. During one incident, Jim Hampton and I spotted the guy. He was boldly standing on a balcony across the river, firing at a U.S. helicopter that was flying in front of our position. Next to the sniper was a young boy, perhaps 6-8 years old. It reminded me of a father teaching his son how to hunt.

MSG Spears assigned fighting positions to all military personnel living at Essayons Base. Each position was assigned a number and soldier's name. Everyone needed to know where to go if a firefight broke out. Personnel slept with their weapons and kept a minimum of 30 rounds of pistol (9mm) or 60 rounds of rifle (5.56mm) ammo with them.

Our military personnel would also conduct perimeter defense rehearsals. These drills included identifying what actions the contractor security teams would take in the event of an attack. There were some legal issues regarding armed contractors that needed to be identified and resolved. Part of our plan was to immediately move GRD civilians to the palace basement during an emergency so they would be better protected from flying bullets and shrapnel.

In the event of a night attack, I was concerned about the risk of fratricide – our own troops accidentally shooting at each other. We needed to mitigate this risk. We only had two pairs of night vision goggles in the entire division. If the enemy got inside our wire in the dark, there would be a lot of confusion. Since some security contractors and friendly Iraqi security forces used Russian weapons, the unique sound of these weapons could be mistaken for enemy forces.

In case we needed to quickly evacuate Essayons Base, all GRD vehicles were required to "combat park". That meant they would not pull into a parking space–they would back into it. Thus, all of our vehicles were always ready to make a quick departure, if needed.

Communications were another problem we needed to address. There were two separate commercial handheld radio networks being used on Essayons Base, and they were not interoperable. That meant not all of our civilian security guards and military personnel could talk to each other. GRD and Erinys used a Motorola handheld, while the DynCorps perimeter /entrance guards used Kenwood radios. To fix the command and control problem, we selected a single common radio and would simply separate users with different channels.

We also had a shortfall of some basic equipment to support GRD defenses. So I directed that we procure additional night vision goggles and pocket scopes to help us see at night, blast curtains to protect us from flying glass, and first aid kits and Quik-Clot® to treat the wounded. We also addressed many other security measures:

- We continuously updated our emergency contact lists for all GRD military and civilians. In the event of a major attack, we needed rapid accountability of our personnel.
- We outlined procedures for handling and securing classified and sensitive materials during an attack. In some cases, the materials needed to be immediately destroyed.
- We designated the underutilized kitchen in the White Palace as our Casualty Collection Point. Wounded personnel would be brought there for immediate treatment and triage.
- We published an emergency evacuation plan for GRD civilians and identified a rally point to reassemble personnel later for quick accountability.
- We were concerned about a car bomb running through the main gate to Essayons Base. So we strengthened the security procedures and barriers at the entrance.
- We opened the side gate between GRD and the adjacent 350th Civil Affairs Brigade compound. This allowed the CA Brigade to rapidly move an "Up Armored" HMMWV into GRD's perimeter to reinforce our defenses during an attack.
- We established a clear succession for Command at Essayons Base, so we always knew who was in charge if the senior leader was killed, wounded or on travel.

Our security measures could never be too good. The enemy was ruthless and cunning, so we would continuously re-assess and update our procedures. We could not afford to become complacent.

Floating Candles

The water level in the Tigris River varied seasonally, but was unusually high for several weeks in the early spring. Much of the fresh water in Iraq was stored behind dams in large lakes and was released for irrigation when needed to help farmers down river grow their crops. At one point, the water in the Tigris River was so high that it rose over the concrete embankment in front of Essayons Base. Much of the concertina wire that we installed on top of the river wall was also now under water, compromising our perimeter defenses.

I was concerned that a suicide bomber could now drive a boat across the river, over our wall and into our compound. That meant a 1000-pound bomb could detonate next to our headquarters. It would kill up to 200 USACE personnel and our contractor security force. This would be a devastating blow to U.S. strategic reconstruction operations in Iraq, and it would likely kill key members of the fragile Iraqi leadership.

The suicide boat threat was not a theoretical one. We were facing an innovative and determined enemy. Terrorists had already used two suicide boat bombs against Iraq's offshore oil facilities. It was quite conceivable that a boat bomb could be used in downtown Baghdad. This possibility kept us all on edge.

Just after sunset on a hot summer day, one of the guards came into the GRD Operations Center to alert me to something suspicious that was floating down the river. I grabbed my weapon and went outside to assess the situation.

I followed the guard to a railing along the river's edge. He pointed out into the Tigris River. In the twilight, floating down the river about 50 meters in front of our position was a paper bag secured on a small wooden float with a lit candle in it. Several other officers and NCOs joined me to observe the floating candle.

A few minutes later, another candle glided down the river and past our palace. Then came several more, all-several minutes apart. I wanted an immediate assessment of what was going on. I was straining to get a better look at the lit bags with my binoculars.

Alarm bells went off in my head. This was Iraq, and crazy things happened every day. There was a very real possibility that the candles were part of an enemy reconnaissance. It could be a test of the stream velocity and currents. The route the candles took could determine if an enemy raft, potentially with an assault team or massive IED, could be released up river and drift silently within striking distance of our headquarters. We had a quick debate about what else it could be. One of the guards stated, *"It could be a memorial ritual."*

I replied, *"That's possible. But I haven't seen this before."* It was a new thing. And this was a war. *"In the last weeks we've seen some Iraqi fishermen in a small boat anchored 150 meters from our position. They could have been an enemy surveillance team. We watched them closely for suspicious activity. The fishermen and the floating candles could be part of the same intelligence collection effort. It may look innocent, but my gut says we are being re-conned."*

Fishing was a plausible activity - there were some fish in the Tigris River. MAJ Greg Baisch managed to catch a catfish one day. But fishing just off the shoreline of Essayons Base and the U.S. Embassy compound were likely enemy surveillance methods. The combination of both fishermen and floating candles was quite unusual, and they were now "pegging my fun meter". I was determined to counter this potential threat. GRD wasn't going to be blown up on my watch.

I had LTC Jim Hampton and MAJ Bill Foos re-evaluate our defenses. We immediately took more active measures, such as increasing patrols and making their presence more visible. This was a show of strength to deter the enemy from attacking our sector of the perimeter. In the following days, we added more concertina wire to the riverfront and stacked more sandbags around vulnerable locations and windows. We had a USACE blast expert look at the standoff distance and assess the potential damage to our Palaces if a 1000-pound bomb detonated on the river's edge. He ran some blast models and recommended where more sandbags were needed to improve our protection. Sandbags are heavy, so we also had a structural engineer with us to determine how much extra weight some of the windowsills could safely support.

The vulnerability assessment team moved from room to room. We looked at the wall construction, the windows and the chairs. Flying glass kills and maims many people in a blast. To reduce the threat, I proposed we consider installing blast resistant glass or putting laminates over it. The blast experts promptly informed me that laminates were already installed. The chairs used by our civilians were another consideration. High back chairs are much safer during a blast. If your back was to the blast, the high back chair would protect your head and neck from being shredded by flying glass and debris. We repositioned desks and replaced chairs as needed.

The Erinys security team's Operation Center was in an outdoor tent next to our Palace. It had only a few sandbags around it, and these provided far less protection than what was needed. Their operations tent was dangerously exposed to enemy observation and attack. Contractually, I was told that Erinys was responsible for finding its own real estate in which to live and operate, but there were few spare buildings in the Green Zone, particularly near our HQ. Operationally, if GRD lost this security team, our reconstruction operations would be gravely impaired. Some of them had already died while protecting our civilians. I consulted with the GRD logistics team and Mr. John Shanahan, the leader of the Erinys security team.

We needed to find a more secure location for them–but somewhere still inside our compound. After a brief discussion, I decided to move the security team into the boathouse to provide some hard walls and overhead protection. It also gave them some air conditioning to escape the brutal Iraqi heat.

During my tour, I never did find out what the floating candles meant. No one had the time to research it. Years later, I learned that the Shia do have a religious ritual that uses floating candles. But given the timing and location of the candles, along with the fishermen and the high river water levels, the circumstances were entirely too suspicious to ignore. Our enemy often hid in the open and tried to blend in with normal activities.

Thankfully, a waterside attack did not occur during the last few weeks of GRD's occupancy of Essayons Base. The new HQ building was far less glamorous, but it was in a much safer location – outside the direct observation and fires of enemy personnel.

Rocket Attack on Crowded Street

Rocket and mortar attacks were quite common during my tour and were often fired into civilian populations at Baghdad markets or into our military bases. In the Green Zone, it was typical to be hit with one to three incoming rounds every day. The attacks were usually timed to inflict maximum casualties. While sometimes effective, individual rockets were often poorly aimed and hit random targets. Not knowing where the rockets would hit made them more of a psychological weapon than anything else. Rockets also disrupted our work and sleep patterns, causing fatigue.

Depending where we were, a rocket attack would send personnel scurrying into a bunker or protected area. Sometimes there wasn't any nearby cover, so you would just hit the deck if the rounds were close. If we took cover in a bunker, at least you'd meet some interesting people while waiting out the last of the incoming rounds. If you let the daily attacks bother you, they could physically drain you. It was a game of cat and mouse. For me, ninety percent of the rocket attacks were just a nuisance, disrupting our operations for a few minutes. Only explosions that were close enough to shake the ground near us were an immediate concern.

One quiet day a large explosion suddenly rocked us just outside our small compound at Essayons Base. We immediately moved the civilians into the basement of the GRC HQ building for better protection. I threw on my body armor, grabbed my weapon, and ran out to the perimeter gate to assess the situation. The gate guard reported that one rocket had exploded near an intersection just outside his position. A second rocket hit inside our perimeter, but it failed to explode.

I went to the scene of the impact expecting to find multiple casualties. LTC Jim Hampton joined me. The impact crater was still smoking. The round hit in the grass a few meters from a street that often was crowded with personnel. The wrought iron fence near the impact crater was shredded. I was surprised that there were no casualties in the street. Several of the SUVs parked along the road were severely damaged – the glass was blown out, the tires were flat, and shrapnel had sliced through the side doors and panels. I turned to Jim and said, *"I bet there is some bad news inside one of these SUVs"*. We both quickly checked the line of vehicles for potential casualties, one by one.

"This one is all clear."

"This one too."

Each vehicle we inspected was empty. It seemed like an amazing stroke of good luck. I fully expected to have many casualties from a rocket attack at this busy location at this time of day.

Just when we thought we got away clean, we spotted three more SUVs across the street that were also damaged. I hoped our luck had not run out.

We quickly moved to these SUVs to determine if there were any casualties. The first vehicle was torn up, but I gave the "all clear". Jim also gave the second vehicle the "all clear". But as I approached the last SUV, I could hear a spurting and fizzing sound coming from inside the vehicle. I dreaded that it could be the sound of arterial bleeding or someone gurgling on their blood. What was the noise coming from? A man? A woman? A child?

I looked through the blown glass window, anticipating a gruesome scene. I turned and said, *"Jim, get over here, now! I have six casualties"*. He was there in an instant. I opened the back door, and out fell a six-pack of Foster's beer. The enemy rocket had shredded it, and hot beer was hemorrhaging everywhere.

Jim and I began to laugh. This was the first real beer we had seen in months, and the damn enemy rocket took it out. I told Jim, *"We ought to give those cans some CPR!"* But after a few seconds, the last of the cans was dead. I failed to save them.

"Bastards. Attacking the beer supply is about the worst thing the enemy could do to a soldier. It's time to take the gloves off."

The SUV and the beer probably belonged to some contractor. I am sure the owner would have a hard time replacing the beer. Still, we were relieved no one was hurt during the attack, and finding humor in combat situations was a good way to manage the stress.

Jim and I stayed at the scene for a few minutes to make certain we didn't miss anything. By now, a dozen or so troops were at the scene. I said my final farewell to the six-pack and headed back toward our perimeter. We still had a mission to perform, and we couldn't rebuild the country by gawking at an impact crater.

I got back to the HQ compound and gave the "all clear". That meant the attack was over. The civilians slowly climbed out of the basement, trusting that our judgment was right. We conducted a search for the second unexploded rocket that reportedly hit in the trailer area, where some of the division's senior leaders lived. We didn't find it, which was not surprising. Unexploded rounds often hit the soft earth and buried themselves about six feet into the ground. The only evidence they usually left was a 6-8 inch diameter hole bored into the soil. After a few months of attacks, dozens of unexploded rockets were buried within a few blocks of us. The standard procedure was simply to backfill the hole with sand, and leave it in place. It was too dangerous to dig it up.

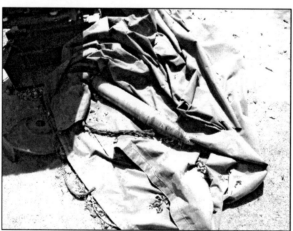
Unexploded 122mm enemy rocket

Within a day, we had largely forgotten about the incident. During the next six weeks, the location of the second rocket remained a mystery. In late August, when GRD had to move its headquarters, everything had to go. A moving crew, in the trailer area, picked up a tarp that was used to cover a generator. Out fell the unexploded 122mm "missing" enemy rocket! It was not buried. It wrapped itself in the tarp when it hit the ground. It came to rest about 10 meters from where I slept. Fortunately, it stayed dormant for those six weeks. We called the Explosive Ordinance Detachment (EOD) team and had it removed.

EOD with the unexploded 122mm enemy rocket

The Donkey Cart and the Sniper

In Baghdad, rockets were often fired horizontally into buildings and hotels. The Al Rashid and Sheraton hotels were frequently hit because they housed Americans, and they were nice tall targets. They were both easy to see and hard to miss. Sometimes the rockets were hidden in a trailer parked on the street and didn't draw much attention. The attacker often armed the rockets using a timer and a battery. By the time the rockets launched from the trailer, the attacker was long gone from the scene.

One afternoon, I received an urgent radio message from the adjacent Civil Affairs (CA) Brigade reporting that we had a potential threat on our perimeter. One of the guards had observed a donkey cart on the far shore of the Tigris River that appeared to stop and dump rockets in some bushes directly across from our position. Anticipating a rocket attack on our position, I alerted all nearby GRD military personnel. The men grabbed their rifles and took up defensive positions on the wall along the river. MAJ Bob Cabell covered the northernmost sector with his M-4. About eight other soldiers fell in, spaced at about 20 meter intervals.

I pulled out some binoculars to take a look. I could not see a donkey cart. I scanned the bushes on the far shore for any movement, but there was no one in the immediate area. Usually, one enemy team will drop off the rockets and another will come by later to set them up.

I scanned to the left about 100 meters upstream. I spotted five or six Iraqis moving in the reeds and brush armed with AKs. The armed men were in civilian clothes, and I did not know if their intention was hostile. Given the nearby report of a rocket threat, I was very concerned.

I climbed to the roof of the HQ building to get a better view. The roof was about 40 feet higher than the perimeter wall. The closest point on the far shore was 280 meters. The range to the potential threat was closer to 400 meters and probably beyond the effective range of our M-4 rifles. I mentioned to Jim Hampton that we really needed a sniper, and we quickly discussed what nearby units might have one. I continued to study the bushes and the armed Iraqis on the far shore. The Ops team started to call adjacent units on landline phones to request a sniper to support us.

I went back down to the perimeter wall to inspect our hasty fighting positions, to determine if we had any undefended sectors, and to make sure everyone had enough ammo. I wasn't sure what might happen and wanted to be ready.

We stayed in radio contact with the Civil Affairs Brigade on our right flank to discuss the developing situation. I needed to determine if the armed men on the far shore were hostile. The Madhi Army, a radical Shia group, had recently been declared a hostile force by the U.S. military and could be engaged on sight. They sometimes wore white armbands to identify themselves. It was the only enemy in Iraq that wore some type of identifying uniform, and it made targeting them much easier.

The armed men did not appear to be moving toward the suspicious bushes, but they appeared to be looking for something. I wondered if they were insurgents looking for rockets in the wrong place.

I ran back upstairs to the roof and whipped out the binoculars. There was a new man on the roof with me. I think he said he was with Erinys, but I didn't recognize him as a member of the team that supported us. He was wearing a boonie hat, some baggie trousers and had a long rifle aimed at the far shore. He told me he had the enemy in his sights and wanted my permission to shoot them.

"Who are you?"

"I'm a sniper."

"Are you in the U.S. military?"

"No."

"Are you a security contractor?"

"Yes."

My Law of Land Warfare training kicked in. I knew the military could not put civilians in harm's way or compel them to become combatants, and directing this "sniper" to engage military targets made him a combatant. It was one of those legal rules I had learned years ago. Our enemies in Iraq did not respect the Law of Land Warfare, but the U.S. Army did.

I told the civilian sniper, *"You are not authorized to engage any targets. I cannot order you or any civilian to shoot."* I continued, *"I do not know if the armed men on the far shore are hostile or if they are associated with the rockets dumped in the bushes. We are still assessing the situation. You have the right to self-defense, if necessary. Do you understand what I just told you?"*

The man looked disappointed, but replied, *"Yes."* At this point, I really wished I had a military sniper team. This cowboy could set off an international incident.

There was great uncertainty and ambiguity in this war. Mixing armed contractors and armed military on a battlefield full of insurgents and terrorists was a new dynamic. Military forces were permitted to take the offense and engage hostiles, while contractors could only self-defend. Military personnel could not put civilians between themselves and the enemy. There were legal concepts that stated that military personnel should be in an outer perimeter and the civilian guards in an inner perimeter, but no lawyer ever explained what we should do if a convoy with armed military and armed contractors was attacked or overrun by insurgents. If the defense was not coordinated and orders weren't issued, if there was no command and control, no unity of effort, everyone in the convoy might die. Except the lawyers, who would write a legal opinion after your dismembered body was dragged in the street by terrorists in front of TV cameras.

The Deputy Division Commander, COL Joe Schroedel arrived on the scene, and I gave him an update on the tactical situation. We were still unable to communicate with the local Brigade Combat Team (BCT) that was the designated quick reaction force (QRF). Schroedel told me to wait no longer and to send a courier to their headquarters. Good idea. I should have already done that. I directed the Ops NCO, MSG Spears, to send a courier immediately. We needed some military reinforcements in our perimeter and a combat patrol on the far shore to inspect the bushes for rockets.

Then I made another quick inspection of the perimeter. At each fighting position, I pointed out the bushes, and asked the men to try to assess what the armed Iraqis were doing on the far shore.

The standoff continued, but something didn't add up. The Iraqis on the far shore seemed to carry their weapons too openly to be hostile enemy militiamen. I could not see any white armbands on them, but the rockets were still a looming threat.

After about two hours, we got some answers. A military patrol had inspected the far shore and found no evidence of rockets. I wondered if the patrol looked in the right place, or if the rockets were well hidden. I was somewhat reassured but was still not confident that the threat had passed.

The BCT also reported that the armed personnel on the far shore were minimally trained Iraqi policemen, who had not yet been issued uniforms. That made perfect sense. The Multi-National Security Transition Command-Iraq (MNSTC-I), led by LTG Petraeus, was racing to stand up the Iraqi Army and the Iraqi Police. And Iraqi Police would carry their weapons openly while on patrol.

I was relieved and somewhat proud that we exercised discipline and did not engage these personnel. Killing Iraqi policemen would have been a huge international incident that our military did not need. The Abu Ghraib detainee abuse and the tragic friendly fire death of Pat Tillman in Afghanistan were still grabbing headlines, and we would have been a great follow-up story for the U.S. bashing news media had we fired at the Iraqi Police.

15

IED Attacks

In the spring of 2004, Improvised Explosive Devices (IEDs) were going off all over Baghdad. I could see or hear several every day. By the time I left Iraq, I had been within earshot of about 150 car bombs and our garrison was on the receiving end of over 400 rockets and mortars. It was a normal state of affairs. Frankly, I can only remember a few days where our Reconstruction Operations were not attacked somehow or somewhere—at a project site, on one of our convoys, or in our garrison.

A few weeks before I arrived, a car bomb exploded at the nearby Assassin's Gate, killing 45 people, including 15 of our interpreters. Iraqi workers, massing at the gate and waiting to clear security, always made a nice target for terrorists. After an attack like that, it became much harder to recruit and retain workers and interpreters. To get our Iraqi workers through the main gate more quickly, MAJ Ray Hart would meet them at the security checkpoint in the morning and escort them through, reducing their window of vulnerability.

My first car bomb attack happened the day I arrived at the GRD HQ in March. A 1000-pound vehicle borne IED (VBIED) destroyed the Mt. Lebanon Hotel across the river from our position. This massive attack gave me a very real appreciation of the threat we were up against, and it shaped my thinking about the importance of force protection.

Not all enemy IED attacks went as planned. In April, a pickup truck with a VBIED was inside the Green Zone and heading for the Al Rashid Hotel. There were many Jersey barriers in the street, arranged in a serpentine course that forced vehicles to drive slowly when approaching the hotel. The vehicle hit a speed bump, and the bomb fell out on the street. The terrorists had failed to secure their payload, and Murphy's Law works both ways in combat. The attack was thwarted, and the would-be bombers were certainly embarrassed by their incompetence. The terrorists likely thought they were on their way to heaven. Instead, they probably got a one-way ticket to Abu Ghraib prison.

IED attacks were common, and many only had limited effect. Hal Creel's convoy was hit with an IED near Mosul in April.

Fortunately, there was little damage and no casualties. Other IEDs were huge and caused mass casualties. Every time we heard a "big one", we were thankful it didn't hit us, and we counted our blessings. But we were always thinking that there was a big one somewhere out there with our name on it.

Results of an IED attack on an SUV

Since our HQ building had a commanding view of Baghdad, standing on the roof allowed us to watch history in the making. We could often locate attacks visually, particularly those across the river or near Sadr City (a slum of 2.5 million Shias). We could also observe U.S. attack helicopters and Air Force fighters, pound targets during close air support missions. I remember seeing an F-16 in a near vertical dive putting a bomb precisely on an enemy position, and then counting the "flash to bang time" to estimate my distance to the target. The speed of light–flash–is almost instantaneous. The speed of sound–bang--is about 1,125 feet per second. For example, a three-second flash to bang time meant we were 3,375 feet from the explosion.

One of the more notable IED attacks was the murder of a senior Iraqi official by a parked car bomb that was detonated just as he left the Green Zone. I heard the massive explosion and felt the powerful shock wave that carried over the blast wall. We were relatively close, but the Alaska barriers deflected much of the energy from us. In another incident, a SUV convoy escorting an American Ambassador was hit while it was leaving Baghdad. The attack used multiple small IEDs and perhaps hand grenades. Security teams returned plenty of small arms fire, but the perpetrators were elusive.

There was some good video of that attack recorded from inside one of the vehicles. I watched it numerous times to try to extract techniques for improving the security of our own convoys.

Most Americans think of IEDs as "roadside bombs". However, a large number of IEDs were placed on oil pipelines, electrical power lines and other key infrastructure. The methods of employment and targets were only limited by the imagination of our enemies. Typical IEDs were vehicle borne (VBIED), roadside bombs, or body-worn (suicide bombers). IEDs have already hit the United States: the first World Trade Center bombing (1993); Oklahoma City (1995); the Atlanta Olympics (1996); and Ted Kazinski, the infamous Unabomber, who pioneered the use of the U.S. Postal System as a bomb delivery means.

In combat, soldiers must become a fast study of the environment and its likely threats because their lives depend on it. Two months into my tour in Baghdad, I'd seen scores of IED reports, and we had been dodging them on the road every day. In the eyes of many Americans, by May 2004, I was an expert on IEDs. But it was relatively early in the insurgency and still months before DOD established the Joint IED Defeat Task Force. There were many prototype solutions coming from different agencies, but no one had developed a silver-bullet. So far, our counter IED efforts were not faring well.

The non-stop news media coverage of car bombings in Baghdad had a way of terrorizing spouses and families back in the United States. After unusually spectacular car bomb attacks, I would make a point to call Alice at home. Not to discuss the attack or even acknowledge it, I simply wanted her to hear my voice. That would reassure her that I was not among the casualties.

IED Conference with DARPA

Then an unusual offer of help came from the United States. Pete Bata, the Manager of Advanced Technology Programs at Raytheon, emailed me in Baghdad. He was setting up a workshop with the Defense Advanced Research Projects Agency (DARPA) and the Services (Army, Navy, Air Force and Marine Corps) to help Government and Industry focus on near-term solutions for the IED problem. Pete wanted some ideas to help organize and focus the workshop. What were the problems and potential solutions? How could American innovation be leveraged best to serve its warfighters?

I was honored that Pete asked for my perspective. My broad technical and operational background and my current assignment in Iraq were an ideal combination, enabling me to take a holistic look at the problem. I was engaged in protracted combat operations. I understood the capabilities of industry, and I had several engineering degrees/licenses. I had previously worked for DARPA, and I knew how the acquisition community worked. I told Pete that I greatly appreciated the contact. We desperately needed some immediate action, and I knew DARPA was innovative and agile. DARPA was the DOD's high risk, high payoff venture capital organization. And I knew the Director, Dr. Tony Tether. We had previously worked on a classified project together.

Pete's initial email led to a few phone calls to further coordinate the effort. I offered to join the planned Counter IED workshop live by video teleconference (VTC). I thought it would instill a sense of urgency in the attendees. Pete jumped at the offer, but we would need to test the video link in advance and de-conflict the timing so it would not affect ongoing operations.

I hung up the phone and began to reflect on the time I had worked at DARPA in the Electronics Technology Office from 1993-1995. I led a team that provided technical and program support to some of America's smartest people - Lance Glasser, Ken Gabriel, Eliot Cohen, Dick Urban, Nick Naclerio, Jim Murphy, and a number of others. We had a great partnership–the DARPA Program Managers understood advanced technology, and I understood its military applications. I learned a lot about microelectromechanical systems (MEMS), high definition displays, MIMIC chips, and RF technologies. I also worked on Tactical Mobile Robots, including small backpack robots called "Packbots" that were being used in Iraq to help find and destroy IEDs. DARPA funded ARPANET, the earliest version of the internet. (Al Gore never worked there.) DARPA also helped develop the Global Positioning System (GPS), stealth technology, unmanned aerial systems, and served as America's first space agency. I was excited by the possibility that my experience at DARPA might help us now defeat the grave IED threat.

The date for the workshop was set for May 18, 2004. There was a chance I would be in Mosul and might not be able to connect via VTC, so I developed some contingency plans. First, I had the G6 (Communications Staff) test the VTC link between Baghdad and Rosslyn, VA to be sure that both ends were compatible. I also planned for a telecon (no video) if I was at an alternate location. I hoped that no serious incidents would happen during the VTC, such as a rocket attack, that would cause me to terminate it early. I couldn't mitigate that risk.

Conference Prep

I had no time to formally prepare my remarks for the Counter IED Workshop. I was working 18-hour days, seven days a week and did not have a day off the entire tour. It was an exhausting pace. We were grossly under strength, trying to stand up a new division and run reconstruction operations, all during an insurgency. I kept a 3x5 card in my desert camouflage uniform (DCU) cargo pocket, and every time I had an idea, I would write it down. Eventually, I had a decent set of notes on my card, and I could improvise my comments from there. First, I should discuss the mission–what we are trying to do to rebuild Iraq. Next, I needed to describe the environment–how we live and operate. I would follow up by framing the IED problem and identifying key gaps/needs. I'd need to talk about IED attacks on project sites, on oil pipelines, on power lines and the infamous roadside bombs. I should discuss the need to secure all the ordnance and IED materials found throughout Iraq. Finally, I'd offer some potential solution approaches that were operationally viable and had a high potential for technical success.

While at the HQ for the Multi-National Corps – Iraq (MNC-I), I ran into MAJ Robert Underwood from the Army's newly formed IED Task Force. I invited him to join me for the VTC. He accepted enthusiastically, but he later was unable to attend, probably due to an operational reason.

Participants

May 18 came quickly. Before the VTC started, I decided that I wanted to motivate the audience and make them feel like they owned this problem. I chose a setting that would be psychologically powerful. I was sitting in Saddam's house, at his personal conference table. I was armed with a 9mm pistol secured in my shoulder holster. Behind me was the U.S. Flag and the map of the 2,300 project sites around Iraq. Anyone on this VTC was now inside the GRD command post and part of the team. Spectators were not allowed.

The video link went live, and I could see a room full of people. Later, I learned there were 63 participants from the government and industry. There were nine DARPA program managers from five different offices. The Army had representatives from PM SW

(Program Manager Signals Warfare), the IED Task Force, PM ECM (Electronic Counter Measure) Devices, and the 52nd, 760th and 761st Explosive Ordnance Detachments (EOD). The Navy had participants from the Office of Naval Research (ONR), EOD, and the Naval EOD Technology Division (NAVEODTECHDIV). Marines from the HQ Marine Corps and the IED Working Group attended. And the USAF sent an EOD representative.

Actual Conference Call

I had my 3x5-note card in front of me. I introduced myself and thanked the workshop participants for the opportunity to address them. Then I began to talk about our mission.

"I serve as the Operations Officer for the Gulf Region Division. We are a new unit, stood up to rebuild the Iraqi infrastructure. Our Division is only 10% military. The other 90% of our force are government civilians–technicians, logisticians and engineers. In addition, thousands of U.S., coalition and Iraqi contractors support our mission. We currently have 2,300 reconstruction projects throughout Iraq in various stages of planning and execution."

"In a war, Maneuver Commanders (infantry and armor brigades) own the ground. And they need to have the ability to destroy or employ the enemy. That is, the enemy can choose to fight against us or to work with us. Maneuver Commanders have their own lethal power. GRD is part of the team and serves as the non-lethal weapon in this fight. Along with our partners - USAID, AFCEE and the Seabees - we rebuild the infrastructure to help make Iraq a viable, self-sustaining country. Our projects include major infrastructure sectors: oil facilities and pipelines, electrical power generation and transmission, security and law enforcement facilities, healthcare, water treatment, schools, transportation and communications."

"We are now in the Super Bowl of reconstruction. It is an away game, and we have not practiced. Our civilians and local workers are in harm's way, every day. We drive around in combat zones in SUVs, and we use commercial radios to communicate. Our widely dispersed project sites (shown on the map) and predominantly civilian work force makes many of our operations 'soft targets' in the eyes of terrorists."

"American forces own islands in Iraq. Our major installations and Forward Operating Bases are essentially islands of

land, and we move between these islands primarily on roads via convoys."

"Almost all of the combat is probably occurring on only 3-5% of Iraqi terrain. Most engagements occur within 100 meters on either side of every road. Most of the tactically relevant areas that need to be secured are linear: roads, oil pipelines, power lines, borders, rail, and telecommunications. Unfortunately, our surveillance sensors are not optimized to persistently stare at linear features. They are designed to look at points and broad areas, not long linear features. Consequently, we have major surveillance gaps."

"OK. Now let me try to frame the IED and force protection problem. There are 3 major tactical environments associated with our reconstruction operations: in garrison, at project sites, and ground movement."

"While in garrison and at project sites, we are typically inside a guarded perimeter and the threat of IED attack is much reduced. Occasionally IEDs get inside the wire. More often, there is a car bomb or suicide bomber near the main gate, where workers usually await security screening before entering the access control point. The most common type of attack in garrison and at project sites is indirect fire (IDF). The enemy usually launches 107mm or 122mm rockets or mortars into our positions and tries to kill or terrorize personnel, particularly civilians. These attacks are not well aimed, but they occasionally hit personnel or equipment. They are often timed during the breakfast rush hour when many people are walking in the open."

"But by far, the most dangerous thing we do in Iraq is ground movement. We go outside the wire when we move from one project site to another. Since we have 2,300 projects, our reconstruction teams must go outside the wire every day."

"Our convoys typically get attacked by IEDs and small arms fire (SAF) or occasionally RPGs. Sometimes it is a complex attack, initiated with an IED explosion to cripple the lead vehicle and block the road, and then immediately followed up by shooting the convoys with PKM machine guns or AK-47s."

"Our forces average over 100 attacks each day throughout Iraq. About half of the attacks involve IEDs. There is so much debris on the road in Iraq - trash and rocks – an IED can be easily hidden in the clutter. The bombers are innovative - placing IEDs inside a dog carcass, a soda can or a section of concrete curbing. Another approach is suspending them under a bridge to blow shrapnel *through a thin-skinned vehicle's roof. There is also the drive-by suicide bomber, who passes a convoy and detonates alongside our vehicles. Lately the enemy has been putting IEDs behind the guardrail. When detonated, a 2-3 meter section of metal rail blows across the road and through a vehicle. Some attacks are complex, initiated with IEDs and followed up with RPGs and small arms fire (SAF) to maximize casualties. Then there is the double IED, where one is detonated, disabling a vehicle. When the reaction force and medics come to evacuate the wounded, a second IED will detonate to kill the responders. There simply is an unlimited number of ways to plant or employ bombs, and the tactics are constantly changing."*

"IEDs are also frequently used to attack critical infrastructure, particularly oil pipelines and electrical power lines. Saddam used 80,000 men to guard his oil pipelines. We have a much smaller contractor guard force (Task Force Shield) to observe and report oil attacks, but they are not authorized to engage the enemy. Ironically, we found it easier to repair oil lines than it is to protect them. However, when a pipeline repair team is sent out, they are often attacked with an IED. This will attrit and demoralize the largely civilian crews. At some point, you run out of willing repair crews."

"One of the biggest challenges is the sheer quantity of munitions in Iraq (mostly artillery shells) which makes acquiring bomb making material easy for insurgents and terrorists. Destroying all the ammo will take years. And we cannot guard it all. Many of the sites where we store captured enemy ammo are being looted at night."

After making the IED situation appear almost impossible to solve, I then threw on my DARPA hat and started to talk about technical approaches that may be part of the solution. *"There is no silver-bullet solution for IEDs, but we can make great progress if we can focus America's best and brightest scientists on this enormous problem. Finding out about an IED as it detonates is a bad situation. We really need to get left of boom. That is, we want to find the IEDs and their associated networks long before they can be used against our forces."*

"Any potential solution must have a low false alarm rate or operators will ignore the system and revert to their own eyes and senses. If the IED detector is so sensitive that it alerts on rocks and trash and does not discern debris from IEDs, it is a non-starter. And the solutions must be simple and easy to train."

Next, I proposed 5-6 potential technical and tactical approaches that needed to be explored. The general approach for a few of these ideas included: looking for pixel change detection in imagery, using robotic vehicles in convoys as decoys to flush out enemy forces, and using novel approaches for tagging and tracking IED materials. All of these ideas were strongly considered and some were immediately implemented as classified projects. I will not detail these ideas further here, as it could possibly give the enemy information that they may be able to counter.

At this point in the workshop, I had covered all my main objectives. I briefly summarized my key points, and took questions from the technologists in Rosslyn. It was a good exchange, and I clarified some technical and operational issues raised by the participants.

At the conclusion of the call, I reiterated that we needed their help immediately. We were counting on them to come through for us. Then I made a request of the attendees – "keep the beer cold and the stock market hot because I am coming home in another 5 months." That line got the entire workshop fired up.

With that, I concluded the call and dropped the satellite link. I paused for a moment and took a deep breath. It was unbelievable that I made it through the entire 30-minute presentation without being interrupted by some urgent tactical issue. I felt good. It lasted a few seconds, but then the training kicked back in. "OK Ranger, go to the GRD Operations Center and get an update on the mission. Move out." It was after 21:00, and I still had a few hours of work ahead of me.

The following day, Pete Bata and several others sent me a note thanking me for the "firsthand account". I was told that the VTC was the highlight of the workshop, and the "presentation was followed by a standing ovation from the attendees." I was glad it made an impact. But the real measure of success, the real reward, would be seeing IED solutions emerge. This wasn't Hollywood. We had more than skin in this game. We had our flesh in it.

Ironically, one week after the IED workshop, my own vehicle was taken out by an IED on Baghdad Airport Road.

IED Attack on Baghdad Airport Road

Every Monday I made a trip to Camp Victory for a strategic planning meeting with Multinational Force – Iraq (MNF-I). I was the GRD representative to the Joint Planning Group (JPG). COL Casey Haskins, my classmate from West Point, typically led the meeting.

Casey had a great attitude and was a wealth of information. Casey, COL Skip Setliff and a few other officers voluntarily left the War College early to deploy to Iraq. It was highly unusual for an officer to interrupt such an important professional development course and Master's Degree program, but duty called, and the mighty Casey was at bat.

Since GRD had an acute shortage of armored SUVs and security teams, we were always looking for more efficient and safer ways to transport our personnel to project sites. MAJ Ball learned there was a daily convoy that left the Green Zone for Camp Victory that provided a security escort service for small units who needed to travel to meetings. The convoy was organized and led by the 2-82 Field Artillery (FA), of the 1st Cavalry Division, that was also called the "Steel Dragon". If GRD requested permission early, and had "priority", we could slip one of our SUVs into the middle of the Steel Dragon convoy. It sounded like a good deal. GRD did not need to send three vehicles and seven men to run a separate convoy. The Steel Dragon would provide HMMWV gunships to escort us and other vehicles to Camp Victory.

At 07:20 on Monday, May 24, 2004, my GRD SUV met the Steel Dragon convoy at an assembly area to get a tactical briefing and then start our convoy movement. "Ben" Benner (Erinys security contractor) was driving the GRD SUV, an armored GMC Yukon. LTC James Hampton rode shotgun on the right side. Barry Williams (Erinys) pulled security on the left side. Other passengers in our vehicle included MAJ Tito Martinez, and LTC Wood, an engineer from the U.K. Army. I was sitting next to LTC Wood.

The Steel Dragon convoy was scheduled to depart at 07:30. We left a few minutes late. The Steel Dragons provided two HMMWV gunships in the front of the convoy and two more at the rear. A mail truck and three SUVs were in the middle of the convoy. The GRD SUV had a huge Codan HF radio antenna mounted on the front bumper that told the enemy we were an important target. An unarmored Ford Explorer was immediately in front of us.

We pulled out of the Green Zone and entered the most dangerous highway in Iraq. The first thing I noticed was how slow we were driving. When riding in a pure SUV convoy, we used speed to enhance our security. A pure SUV convoy typically traveled at 70-100 mph, but we were now pinched in a convoy led by HMMWVs traveling about 40 mph. It felt eerie. Driving this slow seemed unnatural to GRD veterans. The lack of speed and armor made us vulnerable to attack.

About one mile from the entrance to Camp Victory, we drove under the last bridge overpass. It was 08:06. BOOOOM! A large deafening explosion occurred about 10 meters in front of us, on the left side. We drove into the ensuing fireball and blast debris, which engulfed our vehicle. The soft-skinned SUV in front of us was severely damaged and immediately disappeared in the thick black smoke. The last visual I had on it was seeing the glass violently blasted out of all the windows.

I quickly assessed the situation. I still had all my limbs and no obvious shrapnel wounds. I looked across the vehicle and saw that Ben still had his head attached to his body and still had his hands on the steering wheel. He kept cool and continued to drive forward to get out of the immediate kill zone. Good move. Our bulletproof windshield was clearly damaged. The occupants were thrown around in our vehicle by the force of the blast. We were still inside the debris cloud. Ben slowed somewhat to avoid striking the rear of the SUV in front of us. The smoke cleared enough for us to see daylight and, as planned, the convoy dashed out of the kill zone approximately 500 meters forward before stopping to check for casualties and battle damage.

I was now on alert for a secondary attack. The IED detonation may have been just the opening blow. A well-executed ambush could open up on us with PKM machine guns and rocket propelled grenades. If we were going to die, it would be in the next 15 seconds. Military personnel chambered rounds in their weapons, set up a hasty perimeter and scanned sectors for signs of a follow on attack.

I grabbed the only radio I had, a commercial IRAQNA cell phone, and called in a SPOT Report. MSG Spears and MAJ Ball were in the GRD Operations Office and took the initial report. I gave them what little information I had and noted we were still assessing the situation. *"GRD vehicle in Steel Dragon convoy hit by an IED on Route IRISH at 08:06 one mile from Camp Victory. Still assessing casualties and damage. Preparing for potential secondary assault."*

Jim Hampton observed two Iraqi Civil Defense Corps (ICDC) soldiers kneeling with weapons on the right shoulder of the road about 70 meters to the rear of our vehicle.

The Ford Explorer in front of us was completely disabled and a battle loss. The passengers and sensitive equipment were trans-loaded into other vehicles. There were many people with ringing ears and some possible concussions, but I was surprised to learn that our convoy had no major injuries.

The GRD armored SUV absorbed much of the blast and some shrapnel. Fortunately, no high velocity fragments penetrated the interior. The windshield was severely cracked and there were multiple dents and blast marks on the exterior. We accounted for all personnel and proceeded on to Camp Victory.

Because none of us were killed by a blast at such a close range, my initial assessment was that the IED had to be somewhat small, like a mortar round. Jim Hampton thought it was much larger. I figured it couldn't have been a large bomb like a 155mm artillery round. A 155mm round had a 50-meter kill radius and a 100-meter casualty radius. That meant 50% of troops within 50 meters of a blast would be killed, and 50% of troops within 100 meters would be casualties. If the IED was a 155 mm shell that detonated only 10 meters from us, we should have been killed.

We made it through the access control gates at Camp Victory, cleared our weapons and were released. The Steel Dragon escort convoy told us they would escort us back to the Green Zone at 15:00 hours that day. We planned to join them for the return trip. I continued on to Al Faw Palace for my meeting with the Joint Planning Group.

I decided to get a quick situation update from MNF-I Operations first before joining the JPG meeting. I was surprised and irritated when I was told the JPG meeting had been cancelled. *"Bull shit. I almost got blown up coming over here to attend this meeting! So we're going to have the damn meeting!"* Another colleague told me the meeting was delayed until 13:00 hours. That calmed me down a bit. I took advantage of the delay and left to check on the new GRD Headquarters complex that was under construction. I returned to Al Faw in the early afternoon and attended the JPG meeting.

At 15:00, we met the Steel Dragon convoy to begin our return trip to the Green Zone. Before departing, the 2-82 FA convoy commander, LT Clyburn, stated that the IED we hit that morning was fabricated from a 155mm artillery round. It was command detonated, but it was still unknown whether it was hard-wired or radio controlled. Our large SUV with its big antenna was certainly the intended target. It was typical of the vehicles used to transport dignitaries. And it was well before IED jammers became widely available for self-protection.

When I heard the IED had definitely been a 155mm round, I realized how lucky we were to have survived the attack. We were well inside the kill radius. I concluded that our lives must have been saved by a few factors. The first was geometry. Artillery shells are designed to fall to earth nose first, and when they detonate, they disperse a lethal band of razor sharp shrapnel in a radial pattern that is parallel to the ground. The shrapnel will shred anything nearby that is standing between two and five feet from the ground. In our case, the 155mm shell was not oriented nose down. It was probably lying on its side and partially buried to conceal it. So, half of the shrapnel from the blast cut into the earth. The other half of the shrapnel cut an arch through the air. We were lucky we weren't driving through the main shrapnel band, which probably cut vertically between the GMC Yukon and the Ford Explorer. We definitely did take the brunt of the blast, but we were spared being hit with most of the shrapnel.

We were also protected by the factory-installed armor in the Yukon. Most of the shrapnel that did hit our vehicle failed to penetrate into the passenger compartment. Reviewing the photos of the damage, there were at least three shrapnel strikes on the windshield that may have been fatal had they penetrated the bulletproof glass. The metal armor plate had multiple hits, but it also withstood the ballistic impact. And even though I still believe that SUVs suck in combat, this armored Yukon was worthy of some praise.

A Steel Dragon soldier in a rear HMMWV gunship stated that he saw two Iraqi soldiers rapidly depart the attack area in a vehicle immediately after the blast. Either the Iraqi troops were cowards fleeing the bombing scene, or they were "insiders" who planted and detonated the IED. It was obvious there were enemy who had infiltrated Iraqi Security Forces–pretending to guard the road, and when no one was looking, augmenting their salary by planting IEDs.

We were fully alert during the return trip from Camp Victory that afternoon. There were M-1 Abrams Tanks and M-2 Bradley Fighting Vehicles on the main road located every five hundred yards. The combat vehicles were intended to secure the road and to intimidate any enemy forces trying to operate there. It was an impressive sight. All of our senses were immersed in the moment as we drove through the steel gauntlet -- the sight and sound of American battle tanks dominating the highway, the feel of the ground vibrating from the 60-ton armored vehicles, the dust thrown in the air from the crushed concrete, and the smell of diesel fumes hanging over the highway. The 1st Cav Division was enforcing the last 100 yards of American foreign policy.

As we approached each tank on the highway, we slowed down and held up an American flag in our windshield. We did not want the tank crew to mistake us for an enemy suicide bomber! Being ripped apart with a coaxial machine gun or blasted with their 120mm main gun would not be a "good" way to die.

I returned to the GRD HQ, drank some water, and scrambled to prepare my strategic reconstruction comments for the daily SECDEF report. And while surviving the IED attack was strategic to me personally, it was not as newsworthy as the other three IED attacks that occurred on our operations that same day. An 18-inch crude oil pipeline had been sabotaged, a CPA Oil employee and bodyguard were killed during a convoy, and two highway bridges near the An Numaniyah Military Base were damaged.

I later learned that there had been dozens of IED attacks near that bridge in the previous year, and our Yukon was the fourth vehicle hit under that same bridge in the last month. It would have been nice to know about this IED trend before we started the convoy, but we were lucky to have survived the attack, and I'll take it. We all lived to fight another day.

Captured Enemy Ammunition

Iraq was littered with explosives and munitions. Many countries sold Saddam weapons and munitions in return for Iraqi petro dollars. The ammo was stockpiled in storage areas, hidden in schools and mosques, buried in farmers' fields, and stored in housing areas. Upon my arrival, I was informed that the amount of ordnance in Iraq was about ten times that of the rest of the Middle East combined. It was a seemingly inexhaustible supply.

Insurgents and terrorists were using these readily available materials to build improvised explosive devices (IEDs) to attack our troops, the Iraqi authorities, the Iraqi people, and to damage the electrical and oil infrastructure. Artillery shells (155mm) were widely available and easily modified for use as roadside and car bombs.

The coalition strategy was to destroy this ordnance as soon as possible, to dramatically reduce the supply. The Huntsville Center of Army Corps of Engineers, commanded by Colonel John Rivenburgh, had six major sites for destroying Captured Enemy Ammunition (CEA). I worked for John many years earlier at the Army Engineer School. The CEA program was a multi-billion dollar mission that destroyed hundreds of tons of enemy ammunition every day. On the peak day, one thousand tons of ordnance was destroyed across all six sites. Based on the stockpiles that our troops had captured by 2004, it was expected to require three years to destroy all the material. The project actually took closer to five years.

Destroying captured ammo

Captured enemy ammo (just one site)

The captured ammo was not designed for use in U.S. weapons, and much of it was old or unstable, so U.S. forces could not use it. However, some of the small arms ammunition was likely used to equip new Iraqi Army units.

More munitions were found every day. When a cache of weapons was captured, it posed an immediate problem. The military needed to decide if they should "blow it in place" or haul it to a CEA site for later destruction. Destroying the weapons locally with explosives was faster, but it may cause unintended (collateral) damage to nearby homes and injure Iraqi civilians. If the cache were large, it would need to be removed from the village and safely destroyed at a CEA site. Loading trucks with the captured material was a dangerous and manpower intensive effort. And any convoy hauling captured ammo was subject to an enemy attack. This put more of our troops at risk.

Nothing in Iraq was easy. One of the biggest challenges at CEA sites was guarding the explosive material. Large sites required a large guard force working 24/7 to prevent theft. The mission to guard these ammo dumps was an important task sometimes given to our coalition partners. During daylight, our coalition partners could generally be counted on to perform their mission. But at night, some of the guard forces reportedly went back to the relative safety of their garrison. This left the stockpile open to pilfering by our enemies. If these reports were true, this conduct was reprehensible. I heard of several guard force incidents that made me seriously doubt the commitment of our "allies". If an American unit had been guarding the stockpiles and deserted its post at night, that commander would have been immediately relieved. But I am sure that the political value of maintaining coalition partners in Iraq was a major consideration and forced us to quietly tolerate their cowardice. I believe corrective actions were taken, but I wondered how many Americans were killed by IEDs that were stolen from captured stockpiles that were awaiting destruction.

16

Managing Stress and Flying Flags

There was a lot of stress in GRD. The military felt it. The civilians and contractors felt it. The Iraqis felt it. Leaders felt it. Followers felt it. People had different ways of managing stress. Not everyone did it well. Suicides among our larger military force were a major concern, so we looked for simple ways that kept stress in check.

The greatest resource for reducing stress–time off–was not an option. When my team arrived in Iraq, the military strength of the entire Gulf Region Division was about 25 soldiers. We needed about 200. Everyone in the Division G3 shop was incredibly "over-subscribed". Standing up a division in combat, while rebuilding a country, totally consumed every ounce of organizational energy. My staff all worked at least 16-hour days. I often worked 18-20, and it was numbing. Future rotations of GRD personnel benefited from higher staffing levels that permitted a more sustainable work schedule. But for the first wave in GRD, the daily load of work and stress were unbelievable.

The greatest stressor I faced was extended sleep deprivation. I did not have a single day off during my tour, and it exacted a great toll on my mind and body. Alex Dornstauder and I had an unspoken but sadistic competition to see who could live the longest without sleeping. Fortunately, we both learned how to sleep while standing many years earlier during Ranger school.

Coping Strategies

When subjected to daily terrorist attacks, most people's tolerance level naturally increased. After experiencing a few dozen car bombs or rocket attacks, they became somewhat "routine" events. Only the nearby explosions, that put you in imminent danger, were considered a "big deal". Your mental state evolved quickly and your coping strategies improved. You relied more on your senses and less on your fears. During staff meetings, MG Johnson used to put the attacks in perspective for the GRD civilians:

- If you only <u>hear</u> a loud explosion, it can be quickly forgotten – it's "just another one". Explosions just become daily background noise.

- Now if you <u>hear and see</u> the explosion – your level of concern should increase. But you are likely at a safe distance.

- But if you <u>hear, see and feel</u> the explosion – you know you need to take cover and get the hell down.

To manage stress and mark our time during the combat tour, many of us used a simple software program called the "Baghdad Donut". You'd simply enter the start and end dates of your combat tour in Iraq, and the program would calculate the days, minutes and seconds remaining in your tour. It would also graphically depict a donut filling in with each passing day. If you were one third through your tour, it was one-third full. I would check my Baghdad Donut every week to see how far I was into my tour. It was a slow moving donut, but every 10% milestone I reached had a welcome psychological effect.

Another way I marked time was weekly religious services. Scott Lowdermilk often stopped in the G3 shop and reminded me to take an hour off on Sundays to go to a church service in the Republican Palace. We had to keep the Big Ranger in the Sky happy. Given the rising insurgency and danger, we knew we might be meeting Him at any time.

The Pool

One resource we did have was a swimming pool. The two small Palaces that served as the GRD and GRC headquarters had a pool in the courtyard. The pool was in disrepair and sat there full of algae for a few months. With Memorial Day on the horizon, COL Alex Dornstauder gave the directive to get it working so it could be used to improve morale and welfare. An Iraqi contractor made the repairs and had the pool operational in a few days. We officially opened it on Memorial Day. Many of the GRD civilians got in it and started to unwind. Americans were performing flying cannonballs off the diving board. We invited Iraqi maintenance personnel and groundskeepers to jump in as well. They were very hesitant. One of them told me Saddam would have killed them if they used the pool during his reign. It took some coaxing, but we eventually had the Iraqis jumping off the diving board while trying to catch footballs thrown to them. I walked around the courtyard for a few hours in shorts and a T-shirt, wearing my pistol and ammo in a shoulder holster. I fully expected a rocket attack to disrupt the bar-b-que and pool party, but we got away with some fun for four hours, and I actually got in the pool for 10 minutes.

Now that the pool was operational, we decided to let some other personnel enjoy it as well. The Combat Support Hospital in Baghdad was a few blocks away. We invited the doctors, nurses and staff to use the pool. They were always busy trying to keep our wounded troops alive. Occasionally we snuck one of the patients out of the hospital and let him sit by the pool. I'd also invite wounded troops into the Operations Center, where they could sit at my desk for a few minutes and call home. We felt like we were breaking the troops out of jail, but they would have to go back to their cell after a few hours, before the hospital noticed they were missing.

A few tactical units actively patrolled in our area. I think one unit was from the Minnesota National Guard. Jim Hampton and I liked seeing their Humvee gunship randomly loiter around our perimeter, as it enhanced our defenses. It was an active measure we took to make the enemy aware that the GRD sector was not a weak point on the perimeter. After a day of patrolling, some of these troops would get an hour in the GRD pool, as a reward for securing our sector. The unit's first sergeant had to run a duty roster to determine which squad got to patrol our sector to keep his troops from fighting for it.

Combat Reunion

President Thomas Jefferson founded The United States Military Academy in March 1802. Each March, graduates assemble at different locations around the world, for one night, to commemorate the establishment of West Point. Soon after arriving in Baghdad in early 2004, I was surprised to learn that CJTF-7 was holding an annual West Point "Founder's Day" celebration at Al Faw Palace at Camp Victory. It was a combat reunion and an opportunity to renew old ties that I may need in the coming months.

LTC Joe Corrigan and I made a high-speed Red Zone movement in SUVs to Camp Victory to attend the event. Several other officers from GRD also made the trek, including MG Johnson, COL Schroedel, and COL Dornstauder. When I entered Al Faw for the first time, I found it to be a massive and spectacular palace. The dining room was set up with fine furnishings, courtesy of Saddam Hussein. Joe and I soon located two other classmates at the celebration, LTC Joseph McNeill and Mr. Jorge Garcia. Jorge was in civilian clothes, and I asked why. He told me he was with the FBI in Baghdad but did not elaborate further. The FBI was known for investigating criminal enterprises and collecting evidence. They also led the counter terrorism mission inside the United States. The FBI's presence in Iraq made immediate sense, as the enemy we faced was organized and acted more like a criminal and terrorist enterprise than a military force.

LTC Kachejian – LTC Corrigan – LTC McNeill – Mr. Jorge Garcia

    LTG Thomas Metz (USMA 1971) was the senior officer attending, and he cut the "Go Army" cake. LTG Metz was the Commanding General of III Corp, and serving as Commanding General, Multi-National Corps-Iraq (MNC-I).

    Five days later, a second Founder's Day celebration occurred in Iraq. The 1st Armored Division (1AD) held a separate ceremony at the national parade grounds in central Baghdad. Two massive pairs of crossed swords marked each entrance. This famous "Hands of Victory" monument stood 140 feet high, and celebrated Iraq's victory over Iran in the 1980s war (though it really ended in a stalemate).

The hands holding the swords were modeled after Saddam's own. The swords were cast from the melted rifles of Iraqi soldiers. Thousands of captured Iranian helmets were cemented into the base of the monument where Iraqi soldiers on parade could march over them.

"Hands of Victory" monument

Joe Corrigan and I arrived late for the 1AD ceremony and only stayed for about 30 minutes. We found two more classmates, COL Ralph "Rob" Baker and COL Pete Mansoor, who were both Brigade Commanders in the Division. I hadn't seen them in over twenty years. Baker and Mansoor had already been in Iraq for almost a year, and their tours were later extended another three months to quell the Shia rebellion led by Muqtada Al Sadr. We all exchanged greetings on the parade grounds, posed for a couple of photos, and then we went back to the war.

COL Mansoor – COL Baker – LTC Kachejian – LTC Corrigan

Hail and Farewell Ceremonies

The turnover of GRD personnel was so great, that each week we had a one-hour "Hail and Farewell" ceremony to welcome our new employees and to say goodbye to those departing. It provided a brief opportunity to stand by the pool, drink a soda or alcohol-free beer, and socialize. It was a GRD team-building event, and we felt like we were having a small family reunion every week.

GRD Farewell for LTC Hampton

In late July, we had to bid farewell to MAJ Jim Ball and welcome a new officer to the Division G3 shop, Captain Frank Myers. This ceremony was held inside a boathouse along the Tigris River and about 50 people assembled. LTC Stephen Jeselink, LTC Randy Westfall and MAJ Cabell were among the military attendees. BG Bostick was traveling, so COL Dornstauder was the senior attendee.

To prepare for the ceremony, I was given a 3x5 card that outlined CPT Meyer's key information - where he was from, what his new job would be at GRD and what hobbies he enjoyed. The lighting was low and the font size on the card was small. I did not have reading glasses, and my eyes were beginning to fail me. I introduced the new Captain just fine, but when it came time for me to reveal his favorite hobbies, I was straining to see what the 3x5 card said. There was a long pause, and then I stated, *"Well, I am having some trouble reading this card, but it looks like Captain Myers' favorite hobby is .... gynecology."* The entire room began to howl. A couple of the officers almost fell of their chairs. I looked at the card again, *"Or is that genealogy?"* There was another outburst of intense laughter almost to the point of tears—a fantastic way to release stress. Following my flub, we had a great time roasting MAJ Ball, who was going back to California to be with his family. He was a key member of our team, and he had carried a huge load on his broad shoulders.

The Monologue

Military personnel were generally better conditioned to handle stress than civilians. We were trained to endure harsh conditions, and we took an oath to defend our country. Imminent danger and death were risks we accepted as part of the warrior culture. The GRD military tried to help the civilians cope with the stress of this environment. I was particularly concerned about some civilians being paralyzed by fear from the daily rocket and mortar attacks.

During a rocket attack or a car bomb threat, we normally sheltered our civilians in the basement of the White Palace. It was a relatively safe spot because it was protected by soil, and it had few windows so there was little risk of flying glass. Because the civilians frequently rotated in and out of GRD, many of them were inexperienced and somewhat nervous. It was easy to read their body language, and I could see the fear and anxiety in their eyes.

When we had a nearby explosion, I'd check the perimeter defenses and upgrade the alert level. If the initial report was OK, I would make my way to the basement to check on the civilians. It was important that we talked to them during an attack. They needed to know what was going on and to be reassured that they were safe. So one of the techniques I used to cut the tension was "the monologue".

During an attack, I would come down the stairs to join the huddled masses of civilians. I'd stand on the stairwell to overlook the crowd and ask who was from Pennsylvania or Virginia. We'd trade hometowns, and then I'd single out other civilians for more attention. Inevitably, there would be a joke about West Virginia, Alabama or Texas. Then I'd modify some Johnny Carson jokes and continue the monologue. The jokes would cut tension and bring some levity to the moment:

- "Why did the insurgent cross the road?"
- "What do you get when you cross a terrorist with a banker?
- "How many suicide bombers does it take to screw in a light bulb?"

I'd usually get a few smiles, and some of the civilians would offer their own jokes. It was an effective way to kill some time, build social bonds, and take the fear off everyone's minds.

Occasionally, another rocket would explode nearby during the monologue. I'd seize the opportunity to reassure the civilians. "Did you hear that one? They missed again! Man, are they bad shots. They've been trying to get me for six months and haven't come close yet!"

It was a memorable time. It never lasted long, but it helped us all mentally deal with a dangerous situation and to stiffen our resolve. Humor was good medicine and clearly, the best weapon we had to manage the daily stress. Many of my fellow soldiers recognized the power of humor and effectively used it to support each other.

Big Game Hunting

An army of huge rats had infiltrated our palace. LTC Joe Corrigan hated rats. To Joe, the rats were just enemy insurgents that got inside our headquarters. He started placing rat traps in every corner and cabinet he could find. We didn't see them often during daylight, but we heard the traps snapping every night.

Soon, Corrigan and his side kick, MAJ Ray Hart seized the opportunity and entered into a month-long rat-slaying competition. Joe and Ray armed themselves with industrial-size traps, and each day planned where they would set up their nightly ambushes. They experimented with different bait, such as cookies, cheese and peanut butter. There was a large kitchen on the ground floor that was a target rich environment for catching the rats. It was ground zero. The head-to-head competition got serious quickly. All body counts needed to be verified and the dead rats were photographed and posted on the internet so friends around the world could follow their successful nightly hunts.

The competition ended when Joe had to leave Iraq in April. Ray won and was crowned the GRD champion with 29 confirmed kills to Joe's 22 kills. To celebrate his victory, Ray had his final kill stuffed by a local Iraqi taxidermist and mounted in a lampshade. Rumor has it that the final trophy kill was successfully shipped back to the United States as an enduring memento of the royal rat hunt. The month-long competition was entertaining and humorous, and it helped lift our morale. However, I'm sure the hunt elevated the stress level of the palace rat population.

LTC Corrigan   vs.   MAJ Hart

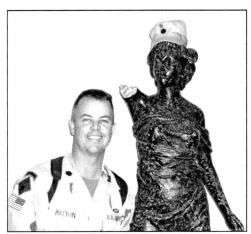

LTC Patton and his Girlfriend

Danny's Girl

LTC Dan Patton was always working hard at the PCO, and he had little time for himself. But luck came his way, and he found a girlfriend, who he introduced me to one day. She was actually a life size female statue that had been pulled from the rubble of Uday's Palace. Petite and wearing something like a Roman toga, she suffered some blast damage from a U.S. bomb and had her right arm blown off. But she had a nice smile, kept quiet, and didn't complain about the mess in Dan's office. I don't recall her name, but I did ask Dan if she had a sister for me.

Panic Button

Not everyone can adjust to the stress of a combat zone. Sometime in my early training, I was told that the fear of death exceeds the fear of punishment. It's very true. If someone is convinced they are imminently going to die, no amount of reassuring them will make them act rationally. We had one notable incident when a civilian totally panicked. He was working on a military installation a few hundred miles from Baghdad in the Kirkuk area. He was new to Iraq and could not take the daily explosions and gun fire. He urgently requested to "go home". The request came to me, and I agreed. If he stayed in Iraq, he would be ineffective and a potential burden on the division. So GRD arranged to pick him up via a convoy that would get to his location in about three days. The convoy would return him to Baghdad where we would get him on a flight out of Iraq.

I guess this plan wasn't good enough for the guy. He had to "get out of Iraq - right now!" He commandeered a government vehicle, without authorization, and just started driving from Kirkuk to Baghdad on his own. No notice. No security. No intelligence. No communications. We had no idea what route he was taking. This was a recipe for disaster. A CPA civilian had been killed under similar circumstances a few weeks earlier. She had no security escort. She was stopped at a false police checkpoint, hauled out of the car, and shot in the head. There was a strong chance this guy's vehicle would be jumped by insurgents, and he would be on the evening news being beheaded.

When I got the word from the Ops NCO, I was in total disbelief. Then I became furious. If a soldier acted this way, it would have been a court-martial offense. Now we had a panicked civilian somewhere in Iraq, and we had to take responsibility for locating him before some Al Qaeda fanatic butchered him. We assumed he was trying to get to the Baghdad Airport, but we had no certainty. Maybe the guy was going to try to drive to Kuwait, Turkey or even possibly Iran.

We organized a Quick Reaction Force (QRF) to try to locate him. We had no vehicles or security teams to spare, so reconstruction convoys would need to be cancelled. I was not pleased about having to divert precious combat resources and put others at risk in order to locate a panicked employee. Putting a QRF on the road in Iraq to find a single American in an SUV was inviting disaster. We weren't sure when the guy actually left, nor what route he took. With no grid coordinate or rendezvous point, the rescue mission would recklessly put seven more men in danger. I decided I would not take the risk and held the QRF until we had a reasonable chance of success.

After a few hours, we received word that the civilian had made it to Baghdad. He beat the odds, but there were a bunch of military guys that wanted a piece of him. I wanted the civilian charged with everything we could legally throw at him. Lucky for him, civilians were not subject to the Uniform Code of Military Justice (UCMJ). I had no idea what authority I actually had, but I thought charges like "theft of a government vehicle", "disobeying a lawful order", "reckless endangerment", and "cowardice" were a good start. The situation was now out of my hands and some other unit was taking ownership of the problem. I really wanted the guy to be dishonorably thrown out of the country. I never did find out what happened to him from a legal perspective, and I never want to meet him.

Scout the War Dog

I saw only a few dogs in Iraq. Man's best friend was not as popular in the Islamic world as he was in America. So when we ran across a dog in Iraq, we often remembered it.

We had a dog called "Scout" that hung around the GRD HQ Palace. I started to notice him in the summer months; he seemed to like our area. Someone thought Scout belonged to the Prime Minister, who was in the process of moving into our Palace. I thought that was pretty cool. He became something of a mascot around the GRD HQ, receiving a lot of attention and some occasional chow.

I never gave Scout much thought until a story broke in The Washington Post, called "A War Dog's Faithful Friend", in October 2005. By then I was a year gone from Iraq. In the article, written by Ruben Castaneda, the true story of Scout was finally told. COL Jim Hampton read the story and connected the dots back to GRD. Jim contacted CPT John Smathers via email and copied me. It was a rare good news story from Iraq.

It turned out that that Scout was not the Prime Minister's dog. Scout was found as a puppy by the 422nd Civil Affairs Battalion at the Baghdad Airport after the invasion. The unit adopted the puppy and named him Scout. The troops took Scout with them when they re-located to the Tigris River waterfront area in the Green Zone. CPT John Smathers and others took care of Scout. They slept and exercised together and when Scout got sick, the unit gave him intravenous antibiotics to keep him alive. But CPT Smathers was injured when his convoy was ambushed south of Baghdad. This happened three weeks before I arrived in Iraq. Smathers was evacuated to the United States for medical treatment where he underwent seven surgeries, and Scout was left behind in Iraq.

Smathers missed Scout and began emailing everyone he knew back in Iraq to find out how he was doing. His unit moved and left Scout behind. It took months to locate the dog. Smathers arranged for Scout to be cared for at the nearby Baghdad Zoo. He then spent a year trying to find a way to get Scout back the United States. U.S. policy does not normally permit soldiers to take animals out of a war zone, so he had to improvise a solution. He had some Iraqi friends help him by transporting Scout almost 300 miles to an animal shelter in Kuwait. Scout was then flown to Dulles Airport in August 2005. Smathers put on his uniform so Scout would recognize him, and he met Scout on the tarmac. Scout immediately recognized Smathers, and ran to him. They lived together in Howard County, Maryland. The confirmation of Scout's identity came in January 2006 in an email from CPT Smathers:

> ----- Original Message -----
> From: "Hampton, James G COL (L)
> xxxxxxxxxxxxxxxxxxxxxxxxxxxx
> Date: Thursday, October 20, 2005 8:57 am
> Subject: Scout
>
> CPT Smathers,
>
> Is this the same "Scout" who hung out around the Palace (King Faisal) on the Tigris there in the Green Zone (this would have been circa APR-SEP 04 when the Palace was the HQ for the U.S. Army Corps of Engineers)?

Wishing you all the best and a full and complete recovery.

-----Original Message-----
From: john.smathers@xxxxxxxxxxxxxxxxxxxxxxx
Sent: Tuesday, January 10, 2006 4:23 PM
To: Hampton, James G COL (L) xxxxxxxxxxxxxxx
Subject: Re: Scout

Hello Sir

Yes, this is the same Scout. Scout and I would run by the
Corps of Engineers every morning. I was injured and left in
FEB 04, Scout was pretty much on the street after that
making new Army friends and wondering where I was.
Lucky for me I was able to get some soldiers to take him to
the Baghdad zoo. They took care of him there for 1 year until I
could figure a way to get him to the States. He's here with me
at my house in Maryland now. It is a real blessing to have him
with me.

CPT John Smathers

Unfortunately, the reunion did not last long. CPT Smathers
died suddenly in February 2006 while running with Scout. His four
bronze star medals and two purple hearts made him one of the most
decorated Reservists to serve in Iraq. He is buried in Arlington
Cemetery. Scout now lives with a family friend.

Fighting Back

For all the stress GRD civilians faced, Iraqi civilians had it far worse.
They lived, ate and slept in the Red Zone every day. And if they spoke
up against car bombers or terrorists operating in their
neighborhoods, they would be quickly targeted. But some Iraqi
civilians had enough, and they were fed up with the indiscriminate
killing. They didn't want their own families to become victims and
decided to fight back.

One incident involved two bombers planting an IED in the
road next to an Iraqi home where small children lived. The father
came out to the street, confronted the bombers and killed them both

with his AK-47. It was the last time this father and his family would be mistaken as victims.

In another incident, a death squad singled out an Iraqi man. He was being searched in the street next to a parked car and knew he faced immediate execution. One of the terrorists laid his AK-47 on the hood of the car to begin the search. It was within reach of the victim, who grabbed it and sprayed his would-be killers with 30 rounds of 7.62mm ammunition. The Iraqi civilian killed them all and in doing so, he probably saved dozens of his neighbors who were similarly marked for death.

Telephone tip lines were introduced, and they were quite successful. It gave Iraqi civilians an anonymous means to fight back by reporting on terrorists that were preparing future attacks. Several car bomb factories were raided, and terrorists were killed and captured. But this was a cunning and adaptive enemy. The terrorists learned to use the tip line to call in false leads and set up an ambush. As a result, Iraqi Police were led to raid houses that were wired with explosives. When they entered the building, it was remotely detonated, killing the entire team.

Stress on the Home Front

Stress was at work on both sides of the Atlantic Ocean. On the home front, wives were without their husbands. The news of death and carnage was plastered all over the evening news. There was no certainty that loved ones were coming home alive. Every knock on the door could be the dreaded visit from a military chaplain.

With soldiers off to war, there were constant demands on spouses, who often had to shoulder the full burden alone. In some cases, women went off to war, and their husbands stayed home. When my team deployed, our wives still had to raise children, ensure schoolwork was completed, take sick kids to the doctors, attend sporting events, participate in church functions, go to work, and care for elderly parents. Bills had to be paid. The grass needed to be cut. Laundry, cleaning, car repairs, and shopping all had to be done – the list went on. Those of us deployed were not there for the holidays, for our children's birthday parties and for our anniversaries. Some spouses, like Constance Driscoll, gave birth while her husband, Charlie, was serving his country.

Active duty military families often live on or near military bases. They tend to have well organized Family Readiness Groups (FRGs) designed to support the families of deployed service members. But my CRU team was part of the Army Reserve. In peacetime, we worked in different organizations and lived in different towns. Consequently, Army Reserve spouses usually don't know each other well.

The Army Reserve made significant efforts to try to organize effective FRGs, but the part time nature of the Reserve force, and the widely distributed living made it a difficult task. For example, the families of CRU members lived scores of miles apart, spread over the Washington, D.C. metropolitan area. The region had some of the worst traffic congested roads in the country. Trying to get spouses and families together often created even more stress at home. There were some extraordinary efforts taken by the CRU that made a difference. For example, the unit sponsored monthly VTCs to unite CRU wives and children with their deployed husbands. It was a huge morale builder for me personally. I could see my wife and kids for an hour each month and try to be a husband and a Dad.

At my home, Alice was busy with all the domestic duties and raising Kent, Kara and Katie. On top of that, Alice also cared for her gravely ill mother, who was on continuous oxygen. We were blessed to have some good friends and neighbors, who prepared some meals and helped to get our kids to where they needed to be. One of our friends, the Planas family, invited Alice and the kids to Ocean City, NJ for two weeks of relaxation during the summer.

Girl Scout Cookies

One of the best ways that Americans could support their country and take care of their troops was to send them a letter, an email or a care package. It boosted morale tremendously, and in turn, it helped us through some really tough times.

The troops that really needed the lift were young soldiers living out in the Forward Operating Bases (FOBs). Their conditions were often the most dangerous and austere. They constantly worked, ate and slept in the Red Zone. Supplies and packages, intended to support the troops, did not always make it to these remote locations.

Of course, good intentions can sometimes go a little overboard. At one point, it seemed like everyone in the United States got the same idea - to mail Girl Scout cookies to American Soldiers and Marines in Iraq. While we all appreciate a box of cookies coming from home, the flood of packages was remarkable. I remember seeing boxes of them stacked all over the G3 shop for about a week. There were probably about 5-10 boxes of Girl Scout cookies arriving in Iraq for every soldier we had. We ate what we could, and shared the rest. That made a lot of Iraqi kids happy.

Gifts for and from Home

I wanted to show my appreciation for the support I received from my friends and my family. But there was little I could buy in Baghdad that was of real value. The Hajji Mart was the local outdoor market, about 200 yards long, inside the International Zone. I went there about once a month for about 30 minutes. It provided a small taste of civilization, and I could pick up some trinkets for the family. The market had rugs, new Iraqi flags, electronics, clothing and anything else an Iraqi family could find and sell. The Iraqis even sold their old paper currency with Saddam's face on it. All of this older Saddam currency was being recalled and destroyed. But the Iraqis counterfeited more of it to sell to the Americans, who valued the expired currency as souvenirs. Ironically, there were other markets in Baghdad where you could buy Iraqi Army and Police uniforms, as well as U.S. Army combat patches. The availability of official uniforms sold on the open market was a huge force protection issue, as anyone could purchase them.

There was also a small Post Exchange (PX) near the Republican Palace. It had basic commodities and a few gifts. My girls liked the stuffed camels. I also bought a box of cigars with an "Iraqi Freedom" label. The cigars were pretty popular even though they were really made in the Dominican Republic. The wooden jewelry boxes for sale were rumored to be made in Syria. I am not sure why the Army Air Force Exchange Service (AAFES) would buy goods made in Syria. The Syrians were thought to be supporting the Sunni insurgents in Al Anbar province. If the boxes really were from Syria, I would not buy one for fear that I might be funding the insurgency. Then I found one of the most popular gifts for my children—a T-Shirt that read, "Where's your Bagh-Daddy?" Kara and Katie really liked that one. Fortunately, we had a small post office that was operating from a nearby bombed out palace that all soldiers could use. The postal team searched every package for contraband before it could be mailed home.

Letters and cards from home

Sometimes the gifts came from home. The letters and food boxes from family, friends, colleagues and school kids were always welcome. I posted several of the letters and drawings on the wall by my desk. They reminded me that there was a life outside of Iraq. I traded letters and photos with Debbie, Ryan and Grace MacDougall while DeAnn and Mike Boehm also sent a few nice surprises. I am grateful to them for thinking of me. Mary and Blake Peck (USMA 1977) were among the numerous friends offering their support to my family while I was deployed. Other friends and relatives in Pennsylvania visited my brother, Kevin, and they wrote to tell me how he was doing. That was a great gift.

Email was the principal means we used to communicate with family and friends. I would get several messages each week asking if I was OK. Email beat the "snail mail" used by previous generations at war. However, the ability to communicate instantly was also a security risk. We had to be careful what information we released.

Flying the Flag

Although I did not get a single day off during my tour, I took a few hours on Memorial Day to attend the GRD Ceremony and the ensuing cookout on the HQ grounds. I was looking forward to it for weeks. I only worked 10 hours that day.

The GRD Command Sergeant Major (CSM), Michael Balch, organized the Memorial Day ceremony. Most of the GRD HQ personnel were sitting in the hot Iraqi sun, on white plastic chairs, holding small American flags and following the program of events. CPT Chris Grose led the prayer. We had a special guest at our ceremony whose presence gave the entire day a much deeper meaning. CSM Balch invited his friend, CSM Ioakimo Falaniko, to the ceremony. CSM Falaniko lost his only son in Iraq the previous October. Pvt. Jonathan I. Falaniko was 20 years old and had been in the Army for only a few months. He and his father were assigned in Iraq, and they were able to spend a few days together. Tragically, Jonathan was killed in action in Baghdad. CSM Falaniko had to inform his family from Iraq during a video teleconference. What an unbelievably heavy burden to bear. Yet here he was, in our presence, on Memorial Day, and still in combat, and I thought, "How many of our fellow Americans would be willing to make the same sacrifice?"

CSM Falaniko visits GRD

Flying the U.S. flag in Iraq was generally against the rules. The United States did not want to look like an occupying power. When the statue of Saddam was toppled in Baghdad in April 2003, a soldier draped an American flag over it. The flag was quickly removed. Since then, we kept the American flag low key, though the U.S. Embassy Annex, that was adjacent to our HQ, flew it daily.

Memorial Day

But this was Memorial Day, and GRD was going to fly the U.S. flag. Period. That's what Americans do. So a week before the event, GRD sent a note to MNF-I asking for an exception to policy. Our senior command did not respond. We called to ask again. There was no answer. We knew their silence was tacit approval to fly it. No real American could ever tell another American not to fly the U.S. flag on Memorial Day. The lack of an official reply was a combat version of "I didn't hear you ask, and I am not going to tell."

After watching the flag fly that day, it struck me that the most precious gift I could give someone was an American flag flown in Iraq. Nothing could strike more pride and emotion in a patriot. This was the gift that I wanted my friends and family to have, so they could share our experience in these difficult days.

Fortunately, the Baghdad PX sold American flags. This begged the question. "What did they expect us to do with the flags once we bought them?" I purchased about 25 flags over a period of several weeks. Several of my comrades also bought some. The word was getting out. I was sure the PX manager wondered why there was a big run on U.S. flags.

Flying Old Glory over Baghdad

If I was going to fly the flag, I would have to be discrete as our HQ was right next to the U.S. Embassy Annex. But after a few seconds of soul searching, I decided that I would just do it and ask for forgiveness later. After all, what was the State Department going to do–drop me for push-ups? So I ran a flag up the pole, let it hit the breeze and saluted it. It was one of the most rewarding things I did in Iraq.

Over a two-month period, I flew all 25 flags within view of the Red Zone. I would often hoist the flag up after a major rocket attack. The flag was proof that we were still there. It was the international language for, "You bastards missed us again."

I mailed the first flags to my sister, Gina and my brother Kevin. I also sent them to Gina's children, Rebecca, Peter and Nathaniel. Peter and Nathaniel were Cadets at West Point. The flags took a few weeks to arrive, and the gift was an instant home run. Gina immediately sent me the most uplifting email I have ever received:

From: Regina Curley
Sent: Wednesday, July 28, 2004 11:07 PM

To: Kachejian, Kerry LTC GRD
Subject: Got the greatest gift!!!!!

Dear Kerry, I can't believe your gift! The flag is AWESOME!!! I cry every time I look at it. So cool..... Received the package Monday PM...(today is Wed) Gave Kevin his yesterday.....he loved his as much......we're deciding what to do with them......Having framed is an option...(don't want them stolen) I'm hesitant about leaving Kev's at the nursing home so I didn't....(he's not there 3 days a week) I've shown all my clients I've trained since Tues. It's the BEST gift I've ever received. Thank you so much. It means SO much. WOW WOW

WOW!!! Thanks thanks thanks...

Thanks again for the unbelievable gift. I will treasure it always.

Be SAFE. Love, Gina

From: Kachejian, Kerry LTC GRD
Sent: Thursday, July 29, 2004 12:35 AM
To: Regina Curley
Subject: RE: Got the greatest gift!!!!!

Gina,

You are the best sister I could have ever asked for.

I knew the flag would be meaningful to both you and Kevin. I sent flags to Peter, Nathaniel, and Rebecca also. Please keep that quiet until they receive them. Let me know if they do not arrive.

Is there anyone else special that you would want to have one?

Love,
Kerry

Flying the flag became the one thing I could do for my family, my friends and my sanity.

* * *

Later that summer, our intelligence reported that the enemy had rebuilt a rocket launcher and was going to hit us.

Left to right: Admiral Nash, BG Bostick, Charlie Hess

Sure enough, on August 7, the Green Zone was hit with 40 enemy rockets. Each one came in about 20-40 seconds apart. That morning, I was in a major theater-wide Engineer Summit held in a corrugated metal building near the Tigris River. The summit was attended by many senior leaders, including Admiral Nash, BG Bostick, Senior Executives Charlie Hess and Robert Slockbower and scores of Colonels and staff officers. General Casey came to help kick the summit off. I realized that if a single rocket came through the thin metal roof, it would have decimated the entire reconstruction leadership. Later that day, we broke from the summit, and I went back to my HQ and hoisted several U.S. flags up the pole again. It was Old Glory saying, "Is that all you got?"

I later learned that August 7 was an anniversary to Al Qaeda. On that day in 1990, U.S. troops arrived in Saudi Arabia, in response to the Iraqi invasion of Kuwait. It is likely the major rocket attack was timed to commemorate that event. So the flags flown on August 7 were particularly meaningful to me.

I made sure three U.S. flags were sent to Kent, Kara and Katie. Each now has their flag on display in their bedroom.

When Gina started showing her flag to her friends, the news got out. It seemed like everyone in West Chester, Pennsylvania wanted one. I couldn't meet the demand. I made it known that these flags weren't Air Force versions - "flown in a C-130 over Baghdad."

These flags were Army versions – "flown in the face of the enemy in downtown Baghdad." These were "Hooah" flags.

I also mailed a flag to my best friend, Mike Willover. He had moved to Florida, but he flew up to Virginia to spend some time with me just before I deployed to Iraq. The war was going badly, and neither of us knew if it was going to be the last time, we'd see each other. Thanks buddy.

I gave one to Dave and Larue Morgan, long time family friends. Mr. Morgan was my elementary school principal and led the school with a unique combination of discipline and humor, which has always inspired me to work hard and enjoy it.

And I brought home about fifteen flags, to give personally to other close friends and colleagues. Presenting each of these flags after I came home helped me decompress from the stress of the war zone and assimilate back into a normal American life.

I presented a flag to Walt and Phoebe Potthoff, longtime friends. Their family visited me while I was a lowly Plebe at West Point. Thanks to their children Debbie, Terry, Mark and Steve, who helped me hang tough during some very lonely days.

Another flag went to Ed Malikowski, an incredibly generous man, who helped my family through many years of hardship. Walt Miller and Nick Gorski at Merrill Lynch each got a flag. I figured that it might help the stock market to stay confident during troubled times. My Homeland Security colleagues at Raytheon, Hugo Poza and Ed Woollen each received a flag for being patriots and holding my job open while I was in combat. Dr. Drew McCausland earned one, a long-time family friend who was always pulling for the troops. If Tip and Tab Bartley were still alive, I would have given them one for all they did for my family through the years. I also saved one for the CRU Commander, COL Walt Chahanovich, which I presented later during his change of command ceremony.

The new school year had recently started. Kent, Kara and Katie all attended Hunt Valley Elementary School in Springfield, VA. Many of the students had parents deployed in support of the Global War on Terror. During the morning announcements, on closed circuit TV, my children and I presented a flag to the school principal, Mrs. Barker, "In memory of those who have fallen, in hope that their children can live in a safer world." Kara told me that Hunt Valley flies the flag on special occasions during the school year. Awesome.

A few days later, I visited VFW Post 106 in my hometown of West Chester, Pennsylvania. I took my brother, Kevin, with me. While there, I gave two flags to the VFW Post President. Both were flown in the face of the enemy. I asked that one of them be kept at the VFW Post. It was my way of honoring the Vietnam Vets, to let them know that the next generation was now following them, fighting to keep our country safe. I asked that the second flag be auctioned and the proceeds used to support a good cause. The President was very enthusiastic and assured me that he would take action, and he asked me to join the Post. I did, as a lifetime member. I also gave several of the men at the VFW some "Saddam" currency and some rubble from the bomb damaged Believer's Palace. Kevin and I stayed for several hours and met some great Vets who had served decades earlier. Things were quite good that day. It was November of 2004, and I felt welcome.

Four years later, after I had completed a second tour on active duty, I returned to VFW Post 106 and was very disappointed to learn that neither flag request was honored. The Post leadership rotated, and it took months to even locate the flags. The VFW, of all organizations, failed to appreciate the meaning of this gift. In fact, when I stopped in 2008, I did not have my VFW card with me, and I was refused service. The barmaid did not even have a member list to look up my name. I was a lifetime member in my hometown, and I was deeply offended. Any pride I had in being a VFW member of Post 106 dumped right on the floor. The VFW desperately needed new blood in its ranks but was alienating its newest members. I wrote a letter to the new Post President, in August 2008, and he promised action. He seemed sincere, but still nothing became of the flags. At this point, I was ashamed to be a Post 106 member and just wanted the flags back. I would proudly give them to some other worthy organization. Anyone who travels to West Chester, Pennsylvania, should stop into VFW Post 106 on Lincoln Avenue and ask them, "Where are the Baghdad flags?" I hope that enough embarrassment will result in the flags either being displayed or returned.

A few months later, I proudly presented a flag to Mark and Carol Reynolds. They were friends of Gina's, and now they were my friends. Mark had asked me what he could do for the troops in Iraq. I told him we had plenty of Girls Scout cookies - probably several planeloads. American Soldiers and Marines didn't need as much as the Iraqi people. I suggested that he send soccer balls or school supplies to the troops, so we could give them out to Iraqi children. That would make Americans look like heroes in the eyes of Iraqi school kids. By helping the U.S. image, it would reduce the number of attacks on us. Mark and Carol donated and shipped dozens of backpacks full of school supplies to Iraq. It was the high-end stuff that I never saw as a kid. They spent thousands of dollars. I asked Mike Donovan, my replacement as the GRD G3, to organize the distribution once they arrived in Iraq. Mike tasked a couple of noncommissioned officers (NCOs) to give these backpacks to needy Iraqi children when GRD opened newly rebuilt schools. Mark and Carol later received a personal thank you letter from the new GRD Commander, BG Michael Walsh, and a Certificate of Commendation from the Assistant Secretary of the Army (Civil Works), Mr. Woodley.

Another flag went to the Raytheon CEO, Bill Swanson. It was a flag flown after the rocket attack on August 7. He earned it. I worked at Raytheon, and unlike many of my Army Reserve peers, I never had to worry about my job while I was deployed. It was waiting for me when I returned home. I wanted to thank the company for having Human Resource (HR) policies that supported Reservists recalled to active duty. Bill later told me he keeps the flag in his office. Hooah.

Presenting flag to Bill Swanson CEO of Raytheon

My brother, Kevin, was a judicial clerk for The Honorable Lawrence E. Wood, Senior Judge, in the County Court of Common Pleas in West Chester, Pennsylvania. Ironically, Judge Wood also wrote me a Letter of Recommendation while I was applying for admission to West Point in 1977. Thirty-two years of quadriplegia took its toll on Kevin's body, and he was gravely ill during the last two years of his life. Kevin's friends at the Courthouse all unselfishly donated personal time and leave to help Kevin through this unbelievably difficult period. Kevin asked that in the event of his death, the flag I flew for him in Iraq be given to Judge Wood. Kevin died in August 2005, less than a year after I returned from Iraq. He was my inspiration in life. And he still is. When Judge Wood learned of the flag bequeath, he decided to share it with the entire community. Judge Wood asked me to speak at a Veteran's Day celebration on the steps of the Chester County Courthouse on November 11, 2005. Afterwards, Kevin's flag was put on display near the Chester County Hall of Heroes. It serves as both a memorial to Kevin and as a tribute to the troops serving in Iraq. Well done Kevin Kachejian. Well done Judge Wood. The inscription reads:

Presented to Chester County on Veterans' Day
November 11, 2005
by
The Honorable Lawrence E. Wood
and the Kachejian Family
as a memorial to
Kevin Kachejian
and as a tribute to U.S. Troops serving abroad.
This flag was flown in Baghdad, Iraq on July 7, 2004, in Kevin's honor,
by his brother, Kerry C. Kachejian, LTC, EN G3
Gulf Region Division

Kevin Kachejian

17

The "Big Ranger" in the Sky

There is a very spiritual aspect to war. Soldiers know they are mortal, and the inherent danger that they face in combat means that their end can come at any time. Given the oath they take and the hardships they face, I believe the average soldier is probably more spiritual than their civilian peers.

War is ugly and unforgiving. The moral issues are often confusing and sometimes contradictory. In GRD, our mission was noble - to rebuild the country and make the lives of everyday Iraqis better. To complete our mission, we needed to be armed and trained to protect human life. But to protect the lives of the rebuilders, we might also need to take the lives of the enemy.

Some of our enemies in Iraq claimed to be fighting for their religion. The truth was they were mainly criminals struggling to gain or retain political power and oil wealth. Many of them were trying to convince everyday Iraqis they were in a religious struggle, hoping to inspire the ignorant masses to fight against the Americans.

In the Army, we often refer to God as the "Big Ranger in the Sky". We seek His guidance, and we pray for His protection. We ask for His help every day, particularly when we are developing strategy, running operations, planning new missions, analyzing intelligence and delivering logistics. We ask Him to provide us with physical strength, courage and wisdom.

I said a silent prayer before every meal, and typically, before I traveled outside the wire in a vehicle or a helicopter. The prayer went something like this:

> *"Dear Lord, thank you for giving me all the blessings in my life. Please forgive me my sins. Help me to be a better leader, father, husband and follower of Your will. Help me set the example. Give me the strength to choose the harder right than the easier wrong. Give me the wisdom to make the right decisions to protect our soldiers and civilians. Bring us all home safely. Please heal my brother Kevin and help him to walk again. Give Alice, my children, and Gina the strength to endure each day. And if I should die today, please accept me into Your Kingdom. Amen."*

On Sundays, when possible, I attended a nondenominational church service, held in a special area of the Republican Palace. Scott Lowdermilk would quietly stop in the G3 shop and remind me that we had a meeting with the Big Ranger in the Sky. Scott was looking out for me, and I appreciated his concern and encouragement. I needed some spiritual reinforcement and found I could easily mark each passing week by attending church service.

GRD held special memorial services inside Essayons Base when we lost a close team member. It was a proper way to remember and honor our fallen. It helped us grieve and to say farewell to our friends. The first special service we held was for Hendrick "Fish" Johannes Visagie. The fact that Fish died on Easter Sunday did not escape me. We held another GRD service for Suna Sabri Hadi, who served as one of our interpreters. Her vehicle plunged in the Tigris River. I tried to save her, but I failed.

As soldiers, we never knew if any given day was our last one on earth. The daily mortars and rockets, roadside bombs, small arms fire attacks and truck bombs were constant reminders of the real risks of operating in Iraq. I had a number of close calls, and I never knew when to give God direct credit for saving me. Being recognized as the all-knowing Creator of the Universe, I liked to heap the praise on Him. The Big Ranger got extra credit for being there the day we hit the IED in our SUV, and the day He delivered the Wer'Wolves to Baghdad.

I wore the same pair of combat boots every day of my tour. By the time I came home, they were dusty, worn and scuffed. Now I keep these boots in my workroom. They are one of my favorite mementos from the war and serve as a visible reminder of how God carried me through the toughest year of my life.

Always There

God doesn't just show up in combat. He is with us every day and tests us throughout our life. The Kachejian family I was born into certainly had more than its share of stress tests. These early physical and mental tests prepared me for Iraq. God was clearly at work in my family.

When I was about fifteen years old, my Dad told me, "*Son, nobody gets out of life alive.*" That statement woke me up, making me quite aware that we are all mortal. At that point, I still wasn't sure what I wanted to do when I grew up, but I sure knew where I wanted to be after I died.

I often didn't recognize when God had intervened in my life until I reflected back over many years. Through the years, I realized that He was always there for my family, helping us get through the toughest of times.

My grandparents survived a mass genocide in Armenia, and God led them to the United States. I am thankful that Aram and Regina Kachejian were not among the more than one million who perished. Out of that tragedy, my family was given the precious gift of American citizenship, which I will always cherish.

On March 6, 1974, my brother, Kevin, suffered a devastating neck injury from a bicycle accident that left him a quadriplegic. At age eleven, Kevin was already a standout student and athlete. He had great potential, but his three broken vertebrae left our family emotionally and financially devastated. Then something transformational happened. Our family became tighter, and we all assumed extra duties at home to adjust to the new reality and to make Kevin's future brighter. The entire community of West Chester, Pennsylvania pitched in with good works. The outpouring of support was incredible. Teachers came to the hospital to help Kevin catch up on his studies. Friends came to our house to build ramps and make it wheelchair accessible. Professional athletes from the Eagles, Phillies and Mets came to visit Kevin. Senator Kennedy wrote Kevin a personal letter of encouragement. The local community held several fundraisers. Despite all of this, our family still faced losing its home due to overwhelming medical bills.

After Kevin's accident, my mother worked for the school district to help pay the bills. At one point, my parents thought they would have to sell our house. But God intervened to help us. On March 6, 1975 – exactly one year to the day after Kevin's accident–my Dad was driving Kevin to physical therapy when he stopped at a convenience store to get his weekly Pennsylvania Lottery ticket. He won $20,000, and we were able to keep the house.

God helped me again in 1976. I took the SAT exam. Soon after, I started receiving mail from dozens of colleges, many of which I had never heard of. I was a pretty good student and athlete, but I knew nothing about college. My parents and grandparents never had an opportunity to attend one. I had no idea, which college was right for me, and I knew my parents could not afford to pay the tuition. But then I received a postcard from the United States Military Academy at West Point. I had heard of that one. I looked at my parents and told them I wanted to apply. I could read their body language. This was a game changer. West Point was the only college I applied to. It was a high-risk strategy, and I had no backup plan. In poker terms, I was "all in". It was West Point or nothing.

I worked toward that goal for two years. The application process was arduous. And although my mother was caring for Kevin and working in the school cafeteria, she was able to drive me to all the interviews, physical fitness tests, psychological screenings and other events. I also wrote several essays and met with Congressman Dick Schultz. A few years earlier, GEN David Rodriguez had also graduated from Henderson High School, and he successfully completed the same application process. Rodriguez was now a new lieutenant from West Point while I was still applying for admission.

And then on April 21, 1978, Mr. Collier, my high school guidance counselor, interrupted my science class. He walked in and said he wanted to be the first to congratulate me. He shook my hand, and told me I had been offered admission to West Point. A rush of adrenaline shot through my body. It was the greatest opportunity I could have ever asked for. That day changed the entire course of my life, and I attribute it to a single postcard that God delivered to my mailbox while I was a high school sophomore.

Kevin walking to receive his diploma

And God was present at Kevin's high school graduation on June 6, 1980. Until that point, Kevin had spent six years in physical rehabilitation. My parents drove him several times a week to different locations. The therapy provided by Dr. Hank Goodwin, in the swimming pool at West Chester University, was particularly effective. In the spring, one of Kevin's friends asked him what he wanted to do at the ceremony. Kevin stated that he wanted to walk up to get his diploma. The news about Kevin hit the community like a lightning bolt. Someone alerted the news media. A TV news helicopter flew to Henderson High School. The stadium was full, and it was standing room only around the field. When Kevin's name was called, pandemonium broke loose among several thousand screaming fans. With the help of two close friends, Kevin unbuckled his seatbelt and stood from his wheelchair. He seemed taller than anyone in the ceremony. Kevin then walked forward several steps, and received his diploma. My knees buckled at the sight of my brother walking. The noise was deafening. It was an awesome, inspiring and unforgettable moment that was captured in the newspapers and on television. Everyone in the stadium was crying. And it was absolutely one of the greatest days of my life.

For many years to follow, God pulled the community of West Chester, Pennsylvania together for a 10-kilometer race to benefit Kevin and another paralyzed youth, Brian Bratcher. The money the "Brian's Run" Committee raised helped to pay for Kevin's first electric wheelchair and handicapped van, as well as his education from West Chester University, and his Law Degree at Villanova.

God also inspired my mother to dedicate the rest of her life to Kevin's care. She even drove 80 miles every day for three years so he could complete his law studies.

I didn't realize it at the time, but I now know that God was there to give me a nudge when I was toughing it out during four years at West Point. And later, He lightened my load at Ranger School, and through several years of night shift work while also working on two advanced degrees.

And during the early 1990s, God was with Alice and me every time our infant son, Kent, was in intensive care suffering respiratory distress. At one point, Kent had been read his last rites. He was there when Kent had heart surgery. Before going into surgery, I put a Ranger Tab in Kent's sock - so the Big Ranger in the Sky would protect my son. He did. And when the surgeon came out of the operating room, he told me he was a former Army doctor, and he gave me the Ranger Tab and my son back.

During every other "character building" experience that I faced, I was not alone. In September 2003, God spared our house from major damage when Hurricane Isabel came ashore in North Carolina. Hundreds of other coastal homes were destroyed. When my mother died that November, God made sure my sister, Gina, and I could step up to care for Kevin. He also stiffened my backbone that same month when my Iraq deployment orders were confirmed.

The day before I deployed to Iraq, He delivered a sign to me. Kevin came off his respirator, letting me know my brother would survive another brush with death. I now knew I could get on the airplane to Baghdad.

And with all the stress and uncertainty that Alice and I faced, He kept us together during the hardest year of my life. Now our relationship is much stronger.

So by the time I got to Baghdad, I knew God had already been at work in my family for many years. He was good to me. I knew I could count on Him to get me through combat. I was on the same team as the Big Ranger in the Sky, and once I had boots on the ground in Iraq, my attitude was, "Bring it on".

18

Yahoo Rescue

As the GRD Operations Officer, I needed to be aware of everything that was going on in the Division. Each day, I received scores of emails on the unclassified USACE account, and I had no means to read them while I was outside the headquarters. At times, routine email was the only means that our reconstruction sites had to let us know about a serious incident or an imminent threat. With little staff and a high operational tempo, critical email messages could easily get lost in the sea of routine ones.

One evening in early May, I was reviewing the long list of emails, and one stood out. It was an urgent message sent to me via a Yahoo email account. The title of the message was bold, in red and all caps. I don't recall the exact title of the message, but the meaning of it was quite clear. It read something like "URGENT FLASH TRAFFIC - PLEASE SAVE OUR ASS". It was clearly a desperate 9-1-1 call. I knew this email was going to rock my world, so I immediately opened it.

The distress message was sent by a contractor working at the Al Numaniya Army Barracks, a major construction project site near Al Kut. I don't recall the guy's name. He was using a commercial laptop, a satellite link and his personal Yahoo email account. Imminently threatened with a rocket attack, the project site was about to be overrun by several hundred Shia militiamen. The only personnel protecting the site were a mixed contractor guard force. There were no U.S. military in the area. He stated that there were 150-200 civilians working and living on the project site - approximately 10 Americans, 15 British, 40 Filipinos and scores of others of different nationalities. Some were U.S. government employees and most were contractors.

The contractor was sharp. His message was direct and factual, and he provided excellent perspective. I learned that he was a former Special Operations soldier and that he spoke some Arabic and Farsi. He was culturally aware. He told me he was personally trying to negotiate a peaceful conclusion to the tense situation with local Iraqi leaders, but if he failed, the construction site may be overrun and all personnel would likely be killed or taken hostage. He requested that the U.S. military respond to protect the civilians.

The message could have been bogus, but the situation in Iraq was chaotic and the facts presented were credible. I knew this message was the real deal.

I recognized Al Kut was a hot spot of enemy activity. There was a recent uprising in Al Kut where the CPA Compound had been overrun. I heard several reports that security contractors were killed during an emergency helicopter evacuation from the rooftop. The description of the action made me visualize the helicopter evacuation of the U.S. Embassy in Saigon.

Al Numaniya Army Barracks project site

The Al Numaniya situation was inflamed when a drunken security contractor drove to a local Iraqi Police station brandishing a weapon and threatened to "kick some ass". The contractor had been shot at earlier in the day, and he thought local police were involved. This incident created quite a backlash against the Americans in the local area, and it was a textbook case illustrating why weapons and alcohol are not a good combination on the battlefield.

I read the contractor's message several times for understanding and replied, acknowledging receipt of the email. He needed a lifeline, and I was it. I told the contractor to hang tough, that I was alerting MNF-I about the situation and would take all actions possible to assist.

I briefed Jim Hampton in the G3 shop about the situation and called MNF-I Operations to alert them. The entire MNF-I staff was immersed in a major fight in Karbala between the 1st Armored Division and the Mahdi Army. I knew I would get little attention on the phone, so I jumped in an SUV and drove to the Republican Palace to make a personal visit.

I entered the Joint Operations Center and approached an Army Lieutenant Colonel, who did not look busy, to describe the dire situation at the Al Numaniya project site. The officer had a completely cavalier attitude. His body language said it all, "What's the big deal? They're just a bunch of civilians and contractors." This officer was a complete waste of human skin and should never have been commissioned. He was obviously quite comfortable with his safe staff job inside a protected headquarters. If I could recall his name, I would publish it here to permanently embarrass him for his reprehensible conduct.

There were only a few times in Iraq when I became really furious, and this was one of them. I mean pistol-whipping mad. But I exercised every ounce of self-discipline and remained professional. Civilians and contractors were humans and many of them were fellow Americans. They were on our team, and we could not succeed without them.

I found another operations officer on the floor who was helpful. He told me we needed to coordinate a military response through MNC-I. He said the Al Kut region was the responsibility of the Ukrainians. He paused and then told me he doubted that they would respond to the rescue mission. His quote was, "Good luck. They refuse to leave their barracks." I was stunned. What kind of coalition was this? The answer hit me like a ton of bricks. They were just part of the coalition for political purposes. They weren't really here to fight. Uncle Sam would have to do this alone.

The operations officer asked me where the project site was. I didn't have a grid coordinate, just the name of the city. He led me to an NCO who was pulling up digital maps of the Al Numaniya and Al Kut area. Since it was a project site still under construction, we could not find a clearly marked Army Barracks on the map. I used terrain analysis to try to determine where the Army base might be. I found what I thought was a potential spot, but a quick reaction force (QRF) would need a confirmed location before they could act.

It was about midnight now, and my next action was to try to locate the Program Manager for the Al Numaniya project, LTC Whit Sculley. Whit worked for the PCO and was residing somewhere in the Green Zone, but I could not find him in the middle of the night, and no one I contacted had his phone number. The minutes were ticking by, and I was gravely concerned that the situation at the project site was getting worse.

At this point at least MNF-I and MNC-I were alerted, but I did not have an identified QRF or a precise grid coordinate for them to go to. I drove back to GRD and sent an email update to the Yahoo account. I told the contractor I was working the problem, but it would take some time due to a lack of U.S. military forces. There was widespread fighting reported in both Karbala and Al Kut. I requested a grid coordinate. I knew that just having the communications link established between the Iraqi Army Barracks and GRD would boost the morale of the besieged civilians at the project site.

Being late at night and having an intermittent satellite link meant it might be hours before I received a reply from Al Numaniya. By then, they may all be captured or killed. The email silence concerned me. I stayed up almost the entire night trying to identify or organize a potential QRF. I was just hoping this situation was not a repeat of the Alamo.

One option was to organize a QRF from GRD assets in Baghdad using our limited military and contractor security teams. All I had was a handful of officers and senior NCOs in the G3 shop and some security contractors. I wasn't sure I could legally direct contractors to engage in a QRF, and their primary mission was to support the Division Headquarters.

Contractually, security of the project site was not GRD's responsibility. The U.S. Government outsourced security for most of the reconstruction project sites to the prime contractor. It was a convenient work-around policy because there weren't enough military forces in Iraq to protect everything. But morally and ethically, I needed to act. It was also a strategic imperative. The loss of scores of personnel at a large GRD project site would likely result in a widespread contractor pull out from Iraq, severely damaging our reconstruction mission.

I studied the situation map in my Ops Center. It was about 150 kilometers each way from Baghdad to the project site. The main roads in the area were considered "Red" because they had frequent enemy activity. I had only two security teams assigned to the Division HQ. One was the CG's. The other one was for transporting the Deputy Commander, staff and key civilians to reconstruction sites. I sized up the tactical situation. Sending a three-vehicle SUV convoy, with only small arms and no military radios, on a potentially offensive mission into a militia stronghold, was a desperate act. That convoy would likely be attacked on the way to Al Kut, and I had no resources left to rescue it. Not to mention the three-vehicle convoy lacked the capacity to adequately reinforce Al Kut and could not evacuate 150-200 personnel from the project site. Realistically, I had nothing with which to respond. I needed another option.

Then an idea hit me. I had just seen Pete Mansoor and Rob Baker at the West Point Founder's Day reunion in Baghdad a few weeks earlier. Pete commanded the 1st Brigade of the 1st Armored Division. Rob commanded the 2nd Brigade Combat Team that liberated Al Kut and the CPA Compound in April. I had Pete's contact information so I called him on the only secure phone I had–a DNVT. I caught him in his command post. Pete confirmed his brigade was ordered to move south from Baghdad to Karbala to quell the Mahdi Army uprising. Karbala is a holy city to the Shia. I was tracking the battle daily in the MNF-I Battlefield Update Assessment and on CNN. From the reports, 1st Brigade was spanking the hell out of the Mahdi Army.

I told Pete about the situation at Al Numaniya, the Yahoo email requesting a QRF, and that the Ukrainian unit was not going to fight. GRD had no combat power and had nothing to respond with. I was hoping Pete had some ability to direct a ground patrol to the project site or fly a helicopter over the area as a show of force. I needed something to discourage the militiamen from overrunning the compound and provide hope for our civilians on-site.

I knew getting any support was a long shot, but I had to try. Pete told me he had everything committed to the current fight. He asked me for a specific location, but all I could give him was a city. I was still working on getting a coordinate. He immediately recognized the big issue, "That's 150 kilometers out of sector." I knew what that meant. Not even an offer of cold beer was going to help. It was just too far, the QRF mission was too vague, and all 1st Brigade's forces were fully engaged in combat in Karbala. I noted that the project site did have some armed security contractors, but most of them were untested. I felt I made some progress by at least alerting Pete. I told him I'd call back if the tactical situation at Al Numaniya further degraded.

I waited for the next email message from my friend at Al Numaniya. It eventually came, and the contractor noted that he was making some headway during his discussions with local Iraqi leaders. He was trying to convince the local officials to side with the coalition against the Mahdi militia. He was drinking tea and discussing the economic benefits that the Numaniya project had on the local economy. There was a lot at stake for the community if the local

Iraqis did not stop the planned militia attack. The news was encouraging, and I prayed he would succeed. He seemed like the right guy who could turn the situation around.

The standoff at the Al Numaniya Army Barracks lasted for three sleepless days. The former SOF contractor succeeded. He convinced the Iraqis that hundreds of local laborers would lose their jobs if the project site was attacked, and the American Army would come into the city and destroy it. The local Iraqi leaders pressured the militiamen not to attack the project site. It was classic carrot and stick diplomacy combined with a little knowledge of local customs and language that made the difference. I regret I don't remember his name, but that contractor deserved great credit for keeping his cool and single handedly defusing a potentially disastrous situation.

I never heard anything more from the guy. The Yahoo email went silent and the war continued on. The Al Numaniya incident was just a small blip that was soon forgotten, but it could have easily become a major international catastrophe.

The important tactical lessons reinforced during the Al Numaniya standoff were:

- Alcohol and guns are not a good combination
- Coalitions are only skin deep
- Reconstruction operations needed to be better aligned with combat forces
- Cultural awareness is important
- Employment is an effective weapon when combating an insurgency
- Sleep is for mortals

* * *

Shortly after the Al Numaniya incident was resolved, I received another interesting email. This note was from Mike Keebaugh, my General Manager at Raytheon, and he delivered some welcome news. Mike told me that the company was holding my position and waiting for me to come home. It was a well-timed shot of adrenaline. There was a light at the end of the tunnel.

19

Death in the Tigris

Fatal accidents were a frequent occurrence in Iraq. Most involved vehicles. In May 2003, my classmate, LTC Dominic Baragona was tragically killed on his last day in Iraq when a tractor-trailer jackknifed and collided with his HMMWV a few miles from the Kuwaiti border. He was the beloved commander of the 19th Maintenance Battalion.

Every week, I read a report about a drowning that occurred in the mighty Tigris River. Many of these accidents involved a U.S. vehicle that plunged into the water, and one or more of the occupants were unable to escape. Little did I realize that GRD would soon suffer a similar loss, and I would be at ground zero.

On July 17, 2004 at 15:15 hours, I was working in the operations office. A few minutes earlier, I had put on some shorts, a T-shirt and sneakers to go out for a short run in the 100-degree heat. I needed the exercise to relieve the physical and mental stress of protracted combat operations. I was starting to stretch before leaving the office, when I heard a loud shout for help. "A car with Iraqis had gone into the water." I ran outside to the balcony overlooking the Tigris River and initially saw nothing. I wondered how a car with Iraqis got inside our perimeter. Several other GRD personnel joined me on the balcony. Then, I saw a white vehicle racing southbound along the riverfront below. I realized the vehicle was heading to the scene of the accident. This was clearly not a drill, so I sprinted to the site.

I arrived at the scene approximately two minutes after the accident. I met Fraser Brown, a senior official at Erinys, who told me what happened. An SUV had driven through the razor sharp concertina wire, off the concrete bulkhead and into the Tigris River. The vehicle was already submerged, and according to Fraser, the current rolled the vehicle over as it entered the river. A USACE employee, Mr. Mike Jaroski, was below us, still in the water with a shocked look. He was one of the two occupants, and he had escaped the vehicle as it was sinking. Mr. Jaroski said there was one person (later determined to be Suna Hadi, a Titan Employee and Iraqi interpreter) still inside the vehicle. Jaroski pointed to where the vehicle went into the river.

It took five seconds to size up the situation. There was perhaps three minutes left to make a rescue. The far shore was Red Zone - if we stood around, we were exposed to enemy fire. The river had a high stream velocity and was toxic. I read about Americans drowning in this river each week, and I knew I swam like a rock. To attempt a rescue, I would need to climb through the concertina wire on the embankment, jump into the river upstream of the wreck, sink underwater and then let the stream wash me down to the vehicle. Not to mention the upside-down vehicle was now wrapped in concertina wire that it dragged into the river.

LTC Jim Hampton stepped up with an M-16 and chambered a round to provide covering fire, if needed. He was scanning for targets. Good move, buddy. One less thing for me to worry about. Thanks.

Fraser wrapped his hands in an old shirt, and we began to pull the razor sharp wire out of the way so we could access the riverfront. Several others joined us at the scene. After a few attempts, I was able to climb through the concertina and stand on the concrete embankment about four feet above the river. I picked my impact spot, a few feet upstream. We were down to maybe two minutes and change. I knew if I did not jump right then, the person inside the vehicle would die, and I couldn't live knowing that I didn't try. Then the training kicked in. I whispered to myself, "Move out, Ranger." And I jumped.

I hit the water not knowing the depth or if there were any objects beneath the surface. Immediately I felt the strong current. I came to the surface and grabbed a taut strand of concertina wire—one end was attached to the embankment and the other was being pulled under the water by the vehicle. I tried an improvised French commando crawl down the wire to work my way to the vehicle. Every movement I made on the wire snagged my clothes and cut my arms and legs. I began to submerge again, but the river current was forcing my head and neck into the wire. I was being "clothes lined" on a razor wire. I had no way to stabilize my position, and I didn't know how much more concertina was under the water. Opening my eyes was little help. The water was turbid, and I had no visibility. It was a bad situation, and I released the wire. I started to wash downstream, but quickly swam to the near shore and ran back upstream.

I jumped in again. I tried to feel for the SUV with my hands and my feet while washing by. My head would snap on some concertina wire. It looked so damn easy before I jumped, but in Iraq, everything is hard.

More people were arriving at the scene of the accident and were watching from the concrete retaining wall. I saw some white tubing and had someone throw it to me. I tied it around my body and had them hold the other end from the shore. I was hoping to stabilize my position. I jumped in again and now found that I was also tangled in tubing.

I made 7-8 attempts to reach the vehicle. The current remained strong, and it kept sweeping me past the likely spot where the vehicle was. Several more times I was caught in the concertina that was under the surface of the water. I was able to touch a metallic object twice with my feet, but I could not grab anything before being swept away again.

A few minutes later, Wayne Morgan (Erinys) and MAJ Jim Ball jumped in. MAJ Ball said he hit a tire with his feet. After 15 minutes in the river with no success, I knew it was no longer a rescue operation. It was a recovery operation. I made one last try, hoping there was an air pocket in the vehicle and that I might still succeed.

I climbed out of the river reluctantly. The Chief of Staff (COL Dornstauder) contacted the GRD Commanding General, BG Tom Bostick, by cell phone, who was enroute back from Camp Victory. He directed us to complete a Serious Incident Report (SIR), which was promptly done by Rene Lopez in the G3 shop. At some point, a crane and ambulance arrived on scene. Some medics pulled me aside and gave me some quick treatment for several cuts.

I looked around and saw about twenty people now involved in the recovery. CSM Michael Balch was there, Scott Lowdermilk and MAJ Bob Cabell also. All of them pitched in. I was encouraged to see that we had our "A team" on site.

BG Bostick arrived on scene, and I briefed him on the situation. He inquired about dive teams in the area. I went back to the G3 shop and called MNF-I Operations to see if a dive team was available. It took about 10 minutes to get the answer—a team was in Balad (Anaconda), about 50 miles north of Baghdad. I called 1LT Marshall who commanded the 86th Engineer Team (Dive). I gave him the location in grid coordinates, vehicle type, vehicle orientation and site conditions at the accident site (depth, velocity, bottom soil and slope). I called LTC Bryan Eckstein to arrange a helicopter to transport the dive team to Washington Landing Zone (LZ), about one mile away from the accident site. While in the Operations Center, I asked Fraser Brown to write a statement on what he witnessed. After I received confirmation that the aircraft and dive team were airborne and enroute to Baghdad, I went back down to the accident site.

In parallel, someone at the accident scene had also requested help from local Iraqi authorities. An Iraqi Fire Department dive team said it would respond. Jim Hampton was directing actions at the recovery site and taking photos for evidence. The Iraqi team arrived on site at 18:30 with a small boat. They were able to attach the crane to the submerged vehicle, a Nissan Pathfinder, and began to lift it out of the river. I asked the GRD counsel to come to the accident scene to give an opinion on who had authority–U.S. military or Iraqi officials. The counsel did not arrive, but we did not let this delay the recovery.

When the vehicle surfaced (18:45-19:00 hrs.), Suna's body was hanging partly out of the window. Concertina wire had wrapped around the side view mirror and had entangled in her hair. Wayne Morgan went into one of the small boats and pulled her body out of the vehicle. She was lifted onto the bulkhead and covered with a blanket. It was obvious that Suna tried hard to escape the vehicle. The windshield had been partly kicked out, and the heels of her shoes were broken off.

So there it was. While Suna was trapped underwater, I was on one side of the windshield, and she was kicking from the other. And I could not get to her. I started to question myself. Did I do everything I could have? If it were my brother trapped in the same vehicle, would I have tried harder?

I went to the Ops Center and contacted MNF-I to report that the vehicle had been recovered. I called off the mission for the military dive team just as they landed at Washington LZ. I thanked them for their quick response.

I returned to the accident site and directed the military ambulance to take the body to the 31st Combat Support Hospital and then release it to the appropriate authorities. Suna's family was notified, and her personal belongings were collected to be returned to them.

I went back to the GRD Operations Center to update the Serious Incident Report (SIR). I walked in the door looking for Rene Lopez. Before I could say a word, Rene came up to me and told me, *"It was the bravest thing I ever saw."* I was stunned. I almost cried, but I bit my lip instead. There was no bravery here. There was nothing to celebrate. I had a moral obligation to try to save another human. Suna was part of our GRD team. I failed to save her, and it felt awful. I thanked Rene for his kind words, and then began to update the SIR with him. Several years later, I learned that Rene named his newborn daughter Suna in memory of our lost Iraqi friend.

When things settled down, I walked a few blocks to the 31st Combat Support Hospital to get checked out. I didn't know what kinds of microbes were living in the Tigris River. I had some open cuts and swallowed a few Iraqi bugs with the water. I was somewhat embarrassed to go to the hospital, but I was prodded by several people. My superficial injuries paled in comparison to other soldiers who were seriously wounded by enemy fire. I apologized to the nurses for taking them away from helping others, but I wanted a quick screening so I could return to duty. They cleaned and bandaged the cuts, and told me what symptoms to look for if I became ill. I slithered out of the hospital, and returned to GRD to get a hot shower.

At this time, I lived in one half of a trailer—a rare privilege to have half a trailer to live in by yourself. I had enough room for a bed, a desk, and a wall locker. I called this little dwelling my "hooch". I got back to my hooch late in the day. My clothes and shoes reeked. I wanted to wash the river mud and stench off my body. I put my muddy sneakers outside my door so they could dry out in the hot summer sun. I took a quick shower and changed into a clean combat uniform. When I stepped outside and looked down for my sneakers, they were gone. Unbelievable—my only pair of sneakers. I rarely used them in Iraq, but I needed them to workout. They were stolen by an

Iraqi worker who must have seen them in front of my door and thought they were a gift from Allah.

Sandbagged trailers – each opening is the entrance to a trailer

While I was cleaning up, electronic reports were flying back and forth across the Atlantic Ocean. I was emotionally and physically taxed but came back to the operations office because it was my place of duty. I checked my email and found a note from Scott Lowdermilk, reporting on the accident and the attempted rescue:

From: Lowdermilk, Scott GRD
Sent: Saturday, July 17, 2004 5:20 PM
To: Tonsing, Bill HQ02

Sir,

LTC K just made a heroic effort to pull one of our Iraqi interpreters out of the Tigris. She was practicing driving near the embankment and she lost control of her vehicle and plunged into the water. He was on scene immediately and jumped in to try and find the vehicle. The current was fierce and the visibility was zero. Finally, after about 15 minutes of trying, we had to force him to get out.

He gave it his very best effort. A crane is down there now pulling the vehicle out. LTC K sustained several cuts from the concertina wire that was all around the scene of the wreck. That is what the vehicle drove through on the way into the river. He is fine and the medics cleaned him up.

See attached SIR. I tried to send a video clip on the first send but it bounced. It is 8MB.

V/R,
Scott
Scott Lowdermilk
Reachback Coordinator
Gulf Region Division
Baghdad, Iraq

And LTC Joe Schweitzer, my CONUS battle buddy running the HQ USACE Operations Center, jumped in:

From: Schweitzer, Joseph P LTC HQ02
Sent: Saturday, July 17, 2004 7:24 PM
To: Kachejian, Kerry LTC GRD
Cc: Lowdermilk, Scott GRD
Subject: SIR

Kerry,

I'm sorry to hear of the latest incident. We're informing the CoS and COL Fritz.

Awfully proud of your response and hope your cuts are not too severe. Sorry to hear of the loss of another member of our contracting team. Hope the head injury to our USACE employee proves to be nothing too severe.

Continue to be well and have such a profound impact on our operations.

Joe

I was really down, but the words of encouragement from Scott and Joe gave me a greatly needed lift. Yeah, I failed to save Suna, but maybe I would be able go on knowing that I tried. At least I could now keep my chin up. Thanks guys.

The next morning, several Iraqi interpreters thanked me for trying to save their friend. While I appreciated their comments, I felt no joy and apologized to them for failing.

Later, LTC Steve Jeselink asked me for a statement to be used as part of the accident investigation. I replayed the events both in writing and again during a personal interview.

A short time later, I had a live video telecon scheduled with my wife and children. It had been planned for over a month. I didn't share many bad stories about Iraq with my family, as I did not want them to worry. On this day, I was concerned that my body language would betray me. LTC John Wagner set up the VTC in Washington D.C., and escorted Alice and my children into the USACE Command Conference room. I tried to spend most of the time talking about the kids and what they were doing for the summer, but my head was elsewhere. I received a complimentary note from John later, telling me that the VTC went well.

From: Wagner, John H LTC HQ02
Sent: Monday, July 19, 2004 7:11 PM
To: Kachejian, Kerry LTC GRD
Subject: RE: Family VTCs (17 JUL)...

... and thank you. We all here know how helpful it is for your wives and kids to get visible contact. I was impressed that you were actively involved in rescue with injuries earlier, and then put on the happy dad face just a couple hours later.

Memorial Services

CSM Balch led the planning for a Memorial Service for Suna that was held on July 24. We had some experience now, having also planned a service for Fish when he was killed a few months earlier.

At first, Suna's parents were reluctant to attend, believing that their family was in trouble with U.S. authorities. They were finally reassured and decided to attend, but they were quite guarded. When Mr. & Mrs. Hadi arrived at our headquarters area, they were shocked to see hundreds of Americans at the service to honor their daughter. The entire ceremony was conducted with great dignity and respect.

We had also learned that Suna's job, as an interpreter, was a major source of income for the Hadi family. To offset the financial loss, GRD and GRC personnel donated several thousand dollars to give to her family. I regret that I never personally spoke to Suna's parents. I wanted to tell them what happened and to apologize for my failure, but I chose to remain silent, as it did not seem to be an appropriate time to disturb them during their grief.

Later, BG Bostick sent a note to all GRD employees, sincerely thanking the entire Corps team for their generosity and teamwork. *"Both the CSM and I spoke with the family. They were moved by our show of love and respect for their daughter. Every interaction we have with the Iraqi people makes a difference in their outlook on us and our nation."*

Suna Sabri Hadi

20

Breaking News

The sensational news reports that Americans saw every night on television about Iraq were often true, but they were only part of the story. The persistent and selective reporting of car bombings, prisoner abuse, and U.S. casualties gave Americans a skewed and deeply negative perspective on the entire effort. It hurt the morale of troops, played in the favor of our enemies, diminished the credibility of our military and our nation, and turned public opinion so negative that it nearly cost us the war.

The total picture was misrepresented. Reporting was not balanced. There were few reports of U.S. tactical successes and little of the valor demonstrated every day by our fighting men, our allies and our security contractors. Only rarely was there a report on the reconstruction program, and few of these accounts were portrayed positively.

All soldiers in Iraq knew we were in a tough uphill fight. The war was taking far more time and blood than our nation anticipated. Severe policy mistakes inflamed and deepened the insurgency and terror campaign. Major errors included the inadequate troop levels, the complete "de-Ba'athification" of the government and the disbanding of the Iraqi military. The use of bureaucratic peacetime acquisition rules delayed the start of major reconstruction for months—breaking the U.S. promise of immediate jobs for Iraqis. Pile on the inadequate armor protection for many troops and there were plenty of issues for the media to feed on. History will judge many of these difficult decisions, made by well-meaning leaders, in a volatile, uncertain, chaotic and ambiguous (VUCA) wartime environment. No question—for a few years, Iraq was very, very ugly. And in 2008, a close advisor to GEN Petraeus bluntly told me that the U.S. initially *"had the wrong team and the wrong strategy."*

But no one I was serving with in Iraq in 2004 thought we were going to lose the war. We were clearly frustrated. It was taking us too much time to get our act together. The enemy, who had no operational restrictions and used ruthless and evil tactics, knew and exploited our vulnerabilities, often because our limitations were widely reported. The media held the United States to a gold standard of accountability while the terrorists had none.

Long ago, I heard that the press was the one profession not accountable for its actions. They could always hide behind the first amendment. I think there is much truth in this statement. While the media always seemed skeptical of the actions and intentions of our Government, I think most Americans fear our real enemies far more than our own Government. The mainstream media is an industry. It is in business to make a profit. It makes a profit by selling sensational headlines. Blood, gore, sex, and scandal have always been a good recipe for improved ratings. In 2004, "Breaking news, massive car bomb explodes in Baghdad", helped with ratings. When I returned to Iraq in 2007, I never heard a commentator lead with, "Breaking news, no car bombs again today in Baghdad".

My high school football coach, Mike Hancock, was a distinguished Navy veteran who stood ready during the Bay of Pigs invasion of Cuba. I enjoyed hearing his stories and respected his opinions. During my final season, I heard Mr. Hancock emphatically claim, "Today's newspaper is tomorrow's toilet paper". It was an interesting perspective. Of course, we only won three of eleven games that year.

I often saw broadcasts from Baghdad where a "talking head" gave their report with a large mosque prominently framed in the background. The reporters made it appear that they were courageously standing on a Baghdad street, broadcasting from the Red Zone. I would just shake my head. They were actually standing in a secure area and giving a false impression of bravado. Many reporters just hired local Iraqis to go out and get video shots of bombings and visceral attacks.

Iraq wasn't just car bombs going off every day. There were many good things happening, particularly with the reconstruction mission. Hospitals and schools were opening, and electrical power plants were coming on line. But everything in Iraq was hard. One "Oh Shit" would wipe out ten "Atta-boys", particularly when the ten Atta-boys were never reported by the media. The Abu Ghraib abuse was dominating the headlines at the expense of all good news, but that was tame compared to the daily torture inflicted by Al Qaeda and the Shia death squads on their fellow Iraqis. The media unrelentingly treated America as if it were the criminal, while the brutal actions of the enemy were conveniently overlooked. Few reporters had the guts to question directly an Al Qaeda cell or a local death squad. It was far easier to rip into Uncle Sam.

I have beaten up on the media quite a bit, and frankly, they deserve it. But there were honorable and gutsy members of the media that traveled into the Red Zone and risked their lives alongside the troops to get the real story. I greatly respect them and salute their genuine efforts. Only there can you really get the inside story—both the good and bad. And that's all soldiers wanted. The full story. The facts. Presented in the proper perspective.

Qudas Case Study

GRD welcomed reporters to our project sites so they could see the Herculean efforts being made to rebuild the country, but some reporters came with a hidden agenda. In one case, LTC Dave Press, the Restore Iraqi Electricity (RIE) Director, personally escorted a reporter to several sites to provide a firsthand look at all the reconstruction activity. The story that was published conveniently ignored all the good. Goodness doesn't sell.

Qudas project site

One of the most telling incidents about the bias in the press occurred at Qudas, a few miles northeast of Baghdad. Qudas was one of Iraq's largest projects for electrical power generation. A new plant was being opened, and it was a major milestone for the reconstruction effort. The press was invited to cover the commissioning ceremony, but GRD was told, *"It wasn't newsworthy."*

Our Public Affairs Officer informed the press that the new Iraqi Prime Minister was going to attend and "cut the ribbon" to open the facility. This was still not considered newsworthy. We also arranged to have the U.S. Ambassador at the ceremony. The answer was, *"Sorry, this was still not newsworthy."*

We offered to give the press a ride to the project site. The answer was, *"That's too dangerous. We want to fly in helicopters."* So we offered to divert precious helicopters from the war effort to fly the cowards to Qudas. And the press said *"OK. Maybe."* I was surprised they didn't ask for champagne on the flight.

At the last minute, the helicopters fell through. We couldn't get them, and the reporters wanted to bail out. In the end, some press did make it to Qudas. But the amount of energy and coddling it took to get them to a major project site revealed their biased motivations and intentions. The adverse behavior of the mainstream media was not lost on the GRD leadership, but I doubt the average American had any idea how much bias was built into the reporting.

Open Source Intelligence

Our military forces had robust capability to collect and report battlefield information, but for security purposes, access to this information was limited. At this point in the war, GRD was not well connected and lacked access to military information systems. So we compensated by acquiring good civil communication systems. Little of the commercial equipment we had was secure, but it was what we needed to Git'r Done. Besides our Intelligence Officer, LTC Vance Purvis, the best source of information in my Operations Center was a commercial satellite receiver feeding us both CNN and Fox News. The military calls these media and public feeds "open sources". Collecting this information and analyzing it is referred to as "open source intelligence" or OSINT. These media sources are usually fast to report, but not always accurate. But speed counts in combat ... and in network ratings.

When we heard an explosion in downtown Baghdad, we could sometimes find out what happened by watching the CNN / Fox News feed. I thought it was a bit embarrassing that the greatest Army in the world was so dependent on outside news sources for tactical information.

On May 30, GRD needed to transport some engineers and project managers to a power plant project at Tadji, about 20 km north of our HQ in Baghdad. We conducted some detailed planning for the convoy, and the Kroll security team departed from the GRD / GRC HQ in the late morning. An hour or so later, I heard a breaking report on Fox News. There was an attack on a convoy just north of Baghdad. Live video was coming in. Two machine guns on a bridge overpass were raking a three-vehicle contractor convoy. One of the SUVs was disabled and the crew abandoned it on the highway. Some of the personnel commandeered another vehicle to escape from the attack site. I realized it was our convoy that had just dropped off the civilians and was returning from Tadji. Fortunately, only our security personnel were engaged. They were earning their paychecks the hard way. Eight HMMWVs from the U.S. military also responded. One of our men was killed and another was wounded in the attack.

Modern communications can be a double-edged sword. Everyone in the U.S. was paralyzed watching Baghdad car bombs on the TV news every night. And every time there was "breaking news" about another massive car bomb in Baghdad, someone would call my panicked wife and ask *"Is Kerry alright?"* After a week, Alice stopped watching the news and stopped answering the phone. She and many other spouses were being tortured by the continuous reports of chaos.

WMDs in Iraq

This brief section is not going to add a lot of new information to the body of knowledge about Weapons of Mass Destruction (WMDs) in Iraq. But I do want to make some observations and provide some perspective and thoughts.

Before and during the war, there was a raging debate about whether there were WMDs in Iraq. The definition of a WMD that I was accustomed to included Chemical, Biological, Radiological, Nuclear and Explosive (CBRNE) weapons.

I am not a WMD expert. I was not directly involved in the search for WMDs. I am familiar with WMDs through my previous training on the use of atomic demolitions (ADM), as well as chemical, biological and nuclear self-protection. I have worn chemical suits, decontaminated personnel and equipment, and have been exposed to riot control agents (CS gas). Thousands of other soldiers have conducted this same training.

I am a man of science, and I believe in facts and evidence. WMD evidence that was well documented included the fact that

Saddam was building a nuclear reactor (the Israelis attacked it in 1981). Saddam also had stockpiles of chemical weapons and used them against the Kurds, the Shia and the Iranians. Thousands were killed in these attacks, and the Iranians took the brunt of the losses.

The Iraq Survey Group (ISG) was in the country searching for WMDs. I had no direct engagement with them but was present at many coalition briefings to senior leaders.

The media kept asking, "Are there WMDS in Iraq?" From what I saw and observed in Iraq, the technical answer would be "yes", but this was really the wrong question to ask. I think the question should have been, "Were there WMDs that were stable, available in meaningful quantities, and that posed an imminent threat to U.S. Forces or interests?" Another question that was more relevant was, "Did Iraq have an active program to build WMDs?" The answer to both of these questions (in 2003-2004) was probably "no".

Why "yes"? Saddam kept large stockpiles of chemical munitions in Iraq. From what I understood, the U.N. destroyed the majority of them. Given the massive amount of ordnance in Iraq, it is likely that many chemical artillery rounds were not accounted for. There was looting during and immediately after the war, and there were concerns about intrusions at chemical stockpile areas.

I recall two reports of suspected chemical IEDs detonating on U.S. convoys. One of the attacks was Sarin gas, a nerve agent. I reviewed GRD's force protection procedures after this incident, as many of us had grown complacent to the potential chemical threat. Other chemical rounds were probably used as IEDs, but they were likely ineffective due to their age and their use was not reported as a chemical attack. No one died from their poison.

The rounds that were used against the U.S. were old and less potent. They were probably stolen from a chemical weapon storage bunker. The storage sites existed, and in fact, GRD had a mission to secure them. I checked open sources and found the solicitation on the internet. That's probably all I can say without further authorization.

I heard a television news report that the last nuclear material had been removed from Iraq and was now safely in Canada. I believe this report is quite credible. Any nuclear materials from Saddam's earlier program would be subject to theft and would need to be very quietly removed. Our convoys and project sites were being attacked every day. We did not want to alert the enemy about our activities and draw attention. Maintaining "operational security" about an effort to remove nuclear materials would be absolutely the right thing to do.

What were Saddam's motivations? Why did he say he had no WMDs, but refused to allow inspectors in the country? I think it was a case of strategic ambiguity. Saddam befriended an FBI agent, George Piro, while he was in captivity. Over time, Saddam revealed some of his thoughts to his American friend. When asked why he did not allow U.N. inspectors full access to his facilities to certify that he had no WMDs, Saddam reportedly said he could not let Iran know that he no longer had WMDs. When I heard this, the light bulb went on. Saddam pretended to hide what he no longer had. Iraq and Iran were in a bitter war for eight years. Saddam killed thousands of Iranians. He hated Iran and saw that nation as Iraq's top enemy. I saw evidence of this—hundreds of helmets of dead and captured Iranian soldiers embedded in the parade field under Saddam's Swords. The information derived by George Piro would have been worth a billion dollars before the war. Perhaps more.

Saddam also fooled his own people about WMDs. When I inspected the National Command and Control Bunker under Believer's Palace, I found direct evidence of Iraqi preparation for chemical warfare. Chemical protection suits, rubber boots and empty atropine injectors were scattered on the floor. The Iraqis in the bunker would have only injected themselves if they believed that a chemical environment already existed outside the bunker.

Chemical protection and atropine injectors

One final thought. Terrorists in Iraq began mixing ammonia with their car bombs to cause mass casualties. Ammonia is a toxic chemical. If this weapon were used in the United States, it would likely be called a WMD attack.

21

Coming Home

The reality that I was going home finally hit me when my replacement showed up in theater. The arrival of LTC Mike Donovan, my replacement as the GRD Operations Officer, was one of the most memorable events of my entire tour. To my utter amazement, Mike showed up a few weeks early to be sure to have a solid handoff of the G3 duties. It was a welcome relief. The standing up of a Division in combat, along with the rampant insurgency, the severe shortages of personnel and equipment and prolonged sleep deprivation had drained every ounce of energy from my body. At this point, GRD was finally getting more staffing and equipment, but my body was flat-out-of-gas. GRD still had a long way to go, but Mike was now going to take the handoff, and I was a happy dude. There will always be a cold beer in my refrigerator with Mike Donovan's name on it.

For a long time, going home seemed like a distant and theoretical event, but I knew it would eventually happen. Every day in Iraq was intense, and it physically felt like a week. After Mike arrived, the replacements for the rest of the CRU team were also identified. Chris Kolditz, Hal Creel, Bob Cabell and Charlie Driscoll were all going home - on the same day and on the same aircraft. Each replacement officer was somewhat of a VIP immediately upon arrival in GRD. No one wanted anything bad to happen that would delay going home.

Mike and I worked on a right seat-left seat ride for several weeks. He shadowed me every day. He began to understand the battle rhythm, meet all the key personnel, learn about our operational procedures, and he quickly started to take on some of the responsibilities. He was smart, confident and calm. I knew the Division Operations staff would be well served under his leadership.

In late August, I gave Mike the right seat. It felt like the weight of the world was lifted from my shoulders. The Division was always busy, but at the end of Mike's first week in charge, he was responsible for the upcoming GRD HQ move. The entire headquarters had to pack up from the Brown Palace and move to a new building about half a mile away. It was a major effort, and Mike's execution was flawless. I was relieved that I dodged that bullet.

Hail and Farewell

Two weeks before our departure, GRD held a "Hail and Farewell" ceremony on the lawn of the Brown Palace. BG Bostick made some remarks about the accomplishments of each departing person, and the departee would have a chance to make a few comments to the GRD team they were leaving behind in Iraq. It was a good bonding experience for the Division HQ. We would roast those departing and toast them with soda and alcohol-free beer. I had a lot of comments prepared for my departing speech. I planned to roast a few of my colleagues, particularly the "Rock of Baghdad", COL Alex Dornstauder.

But it was now getting dark outside, and I didn't have my reading glasses. The reality that I was going to be giving my own farewell remarks finally sank in. The humor that I had carefully prepared did not seem right. So when my time to speak came, I put down my notes and got more serious. I talked about the circumstances of how I got to Iraq, about the paralyzed brother and family that I left behind. Part of my message that night was that adversity and personal sacrifice were relative to one's perspective. Few of our fellow Americans were willing to volunteer to deploy to Iraq to support the reconstruction effort, but I was proudly looking at my GRD comrades who stepped up to serve their country, both in uniform and out. While my tour in Iraq was quite difficult at times, I always knew that any adversity that I faced paled in comparison to what my brother constantly dealt with. Kevin inspired me every day, and I credited him for getting me through these difficult times. Now I was going to go home and thank Kevin and my incredible sister, Gina, who carried the full burden in my absence. I then thanked the crowd for the honor of serving with them.

Alex Dornstauder came up to me after the Hail and Farewell to jokingly tell me I should have stuck to my notes. I told him that I wouldn't let him off the hook next time.

Cigars and Fireworks

Later that evening, I climbed out of a top floor window and walked onto the flat roof of the Brown Palace. I sat on some sandbags and watched the gunfire all around Baghdad. It was probably a Thursday, the beginning of the Iraqi weekend. There was a lot of celebratory fire happening that was usually reserved for Iraqi wedding celebrations. Hundreds of tracer rounds were flying up from the city like an erupting volcano, and it looked pretty cool. COL Dornstauder made it to the roof. Joe Schweitzer and a couple of other guys were there too. We broke out cigars. I didn't hang onto the lit match for too long, just in case some sniper was eyeballing us. I ducked below the top of the sandbagged wall until I got my stogie going. Life was good.

Of course, whenever there was a lot of celebratory fire in Baghdad, the enemy would take advantage and lower their guns at us. So we'd take some incoming small arms fire. There were so many muzzle flashes in Baghdad, it was hard to sort out who was having a wedding and shooting upwards and who was trying to kill us by shooting at us. When a clear enemy target emerged, I'd see our troops return fire - sometimes with heavy-duty .50 caliber machine gun rounds. The .50 cal rounds would really spank the enemy. So there were hundreds of tracer rounds flying up, scores coming inbound, and dozens going outbound. I was with my battle buddies on the roof of a palace, with a spectacular view of Baghdad, smoking cigars while watching it all unfold live and in 3-D high-definition. It was surreal.

Short Timer's Syndrome

When I was within ten days of my departure, I caught the infamous "short-timer's syndrome". Nobody wants to die during their last few days in a combat zone, and I was getting noticeably more cautious with my actions. Tragically, my West Point classmate, LTC Dominic Baragona, died on his last day in Iraq. At this point, I had already survived more than my share of dangerous situations, and I didn't want to become the victim of dumb luck. During my final days, I laid on the floor in my hooch during the morning rocket attacks. I became one with the earth and stayed on my belly for almost a full minute after the last rocket exploded. You just never knew if there was one more rocket on the way. In the evenings, I slept with my body armor lying on my chest. I didn't want a stray bullet or some shrapnel coming through the roof and spoiling my trip home. One night, I even tried sleeping with my helmet on. I felt a bit foolish, but no one was watching, and I lived to talk about it.

Exit Strategy

About this time, MAJ Charlie Driscoll came back to Baghdad. It was the first leg of his return trip home. Charlie served as our liaison officer (LNO) to the 82nd Airborne and later to the Marines at Multi-National Force – West (MNF-W) in Ramadi, about 30 miles to the west of GRD. Charlie was a squared away officer with a good tight Airborne haircut. Even the Marines he served with loved him. Earlier that summer, the most senior Marine officer in Iraq, LTG Conway, promoted Charlie from Captain to Major in combat. It was good to see Charlie, and he had a few days to decompress. Charlie and I made one last run to the Hajji Mart, the outdoor market inside the International Zone. I'm not sure if we bought anything, I think we just wanted to have the Hajji Mart experience one last time.

Captain Driscoll promoted to Major (combat promotion)

A couple of weeks after Charlie and I departed Iraq, suicide bombers struck both the Hajji Mart and the Green Zone Café. As a result, the Hajji Mart was permanently shut down. MSG Breitbach reported that part of the bomber's body was recovered next to the new GRD HQ building. His description of this was very graphic.

The GRD Headquarters relocation was in full motion during our team's last week in Iraq. The White and Brown Palaces we vacated were returned to the Iraqi Government. The new GRD HQ was in a large home across the street from the Baghdad Combat Support Hospital.

There were quite a few administrative actions to complete before I left Iraq, but one stood out as important. Mr. John Shanahan was the team leader for Erinys. He asked me if I would write a Letter of Recommendation for him, and there was no doubt in my mind. I worked with John daily during protracted combat operations. I trusted him and his team to protect the lives of over 200 U.S. civilians involved in the reconstruction of Iraq. They played a central role in the most dangerous operations conducted by the Division - ground movements. I made the letter a personal priority, and I gladly handed it to him in my final days.

On my last night in the Green Zone, BG Bostick gave me one of his personal cigars. He had an impressive humidor on his desk. I had no idea which one to pick, so I took one that looked manly. In return, I gave him a couple of golf balls. I told him I brought them with me with the intention of driving them back at the enemy in response to a rocket attack. I never had a golf club, so the balls were never used as "return fire". Since he was staying at GRD for a while longer, I thought maybe he could use them. I could read his face. He was looking at me like – "Yep, it's time to ship this burned out G3 home."

That evening, I spent about an hour on the roof of the new HQ in a cigar social with BG Bostick and two of his District Commanders, COL Richard Thompson and COL Roger Gerber. It was one last chance to bond with some fellow patriots. I knew when I departed on the next day I was going to miss both GRD and Iraq. But it was going to be a "good miss".

Later on, I was making one last walk through the new HQ building when an Erinys guard came in and reported a rocket attack. I was puzzled at first, because I didn't hear squat. But seven rockets hit in close proximity to our building and, fortunately, none exploded. A couple penetrated the roofs of surrounding buildings. LTC Dan Patton narrowly escaped injury in the Program Management Office (PMO) building. I was later told that a Sergeant Major and senior officer in an adjacent unit were injured by marble fragments when a rocket hit the floor near them.

The "Last Night"

The Final Gun Run

The CRU "exit plan" called for Bob, Charlie and I to pre-position at Camp Victory near Baghdad Airport the day before our departure flight. That meant we had one final Red Zone movement left in our tour. I'd done it a hundred times. I had one last Mad Max drive through Baghdad—an urban sprint in our SUVs, with guns sticking out the windows. After this run, there would be no more high-speed accelerations or high-G lane changes. No more abrupt U-turns over medial strips. No more convoy planning meetings. No more "dead driver" drills. Once we got back to the United States, we'd have to re-learn how to drive like normal people. Driving on the beltway in Washington D.C. was not going to compare to a SUV thrill ride in Baghdad. Universal Studios should make a Baghdad driving simulator for its amusement park. I'd be happy to consult on the design.

     My last Red Zone movement in Iraq was brief and uneventful. The enemy did not have a surprise "farewell party" planned for our convoy. Once I passed under the bridge where I was previously attacked with an IED, I knew our convoy was home free. I was both thankful and surprisingly disappointed at the anticlimactic finish.

     I spent my last night in Iraq at Camp Victory. MAJ Murray Starkel, the leader of GRC's Victory Area Office (VAO), maintained a few trailers on site to support GRD personnel who were departing the country. Charlie and I shared a trailer. I felt like I was on a vacation. For the next 24 hours, I had no duties other than to get to the airstrip and catch a big iron bird back to the United States of America. I felt guilty that Uncle Sam paid me for that day. I would have paid him.

That afternoon, I attended the farewell ceremony for Bob Cabell and Charlie Driscoll at the new GRC HQ facility. Charlie was presented the Global War on Terrorism Expeditionary Medal. He and the rest of the CRU team would later receive Bronze Star Medals.

That night, Bob, Charlie and I watched a DVD movie called "The House of Rock". It was the first movie I had seen in six months. I couldn't relax and was expecting something to interrupt the movie, but nothing did. I didn't unwind for many more months.

Last Meal

The next morning, Bob, Charlie and I sat at breakfast with MAJ Charles Klinge and another active duty Major who were colleagues from the 1st Cavalry Division. GRC had worked with them on a continuous basis during the last few months. Bob and I were shoveling in some chow, and he casually asked me when we needed to start attending Army Reserve drills again after we returned. I told him I thought we had a few months off. The two active duty Majors at the table looked puzzled. One of them said, "Wait a minute, are you guys Reservists?" I proudly told them, *"Yes, we are the CENTCOM team from the Contingency Response Unit (CRU). The fighting CRU. We are a Reserve unit assigned to HQ USACE."* The active duty Majors were stunned. *"We had no idea."* I told them that was one of the finest compliments we could ever get - to have some squared away active duty officers think Bob and I were also full time soldiers. It struck me that we didn't wear an Army Reserve unit patch on our shoulder, but our team had all previously served on active duty, so we knew the culture well. It was a proud moment and a validation that our team was well trained, professional and performed with distinction.

I then named the CRU members that had deployed together, but had worked as a distributed operations cadre for the GRD: Bob Cabell (GRC Operations), MAJ Charlie Driscoll (82nd Airborne, then 1st MEF LNO), LTC Hal Creel (GRN Deputy Commander) and MAJ Chris Kolditz (GRN Operations). And I was the Division Operation Officer. The CRU also sent an advance party with MSG Tom Jankiewicz and LTC Whit Sculley. Of course, the minute Sculley arrived in Iraq, he was hijacked by Tony Leketa and assigned a different job. We were later joined by SFC Keith Felde, MSG David Breitbach (GRD Operations NCO) and Scott Lowdermilk, who was a Reserve Captain, but deployed instead as a USACE civilian to GRD HQ. LTC George Clarke also deployed on a short tour, as he was scheduled to retire at age 60 in only four months.

Parting Shots

After our last breakfast, Charlie and I went across Camp Victory to a bullet riddled guard tower, near the Al Faw Palace, for some final cool guy photos. We took some scenic photos with the palace in the background. It would be the last quality time we spent together in Iraq and some of the last photos I have of Charlie. He died unexpectedly a few weeks later, back in the United States during a five-mile run.

Big Iron Bird

Bob, Charlie and I reassembled at the GRC HQ building for our final farewells and then started our short ride to the runway. The departure terminal was a huge dusty tent with a few folding chairs and soldiers packed around a small grimy TV. There were a few hundred troops in it, all waiting for a ride out of Iraq. It was baking hot and smelled like sweat. This was the Army's version of flying no frills "coach".

Our C-130 arrived at the airfield, and the procedure was to load as quickly as possible and get airborne. The aircraft was vulnerable on an open airfield. There was no sense hanging around and running the risk of having the aircraft hit with mortar or rocket fire while parked on the runway.

Bob, Charlie and I got in line to board the C-130. We were standing on a gravel parking apron. Before stepping on the aircraft, I picked up a small rock as a farewell token of my tour. It now sits in my office as a reminder of that final day.

I got on the airplane and looked around. I saw Charlie and Bob getting onto a jump seat. Could this be real? Am I really going home? I fell into a seat and buckled in. The interior was like an oven and smelled of sand, sweat and fuel. I said a quick prayer to the Big Ranger in the Sky, asking for the safe arrival of the crew and passengers. The aircraft raced down the runway, and quickly went airborne. The breeze inside the fuselage felt good—and nobody shot at us.

We weren't out of harm's way yet. The C-130 flew on to Mosul, in northern Iraq, to pick up more passengers, including Hal Creel and Chris Kolditz. Then back across Iraq to Kuwait, where we landed and were met by the GRD liaison team. We jumped in their SUVs and drove to a warehouse to turn in our body armor and combat equipment.

Dangerously Safe

We were now in Kuwait and out of imminent danger, but it seemed so unnatural not wearing body armor and to drive so carefully in an SUV. It felt frigging weird. I felt perilously vulnerable driving at the posted speed limit. I wanted to drive 90 mph and stick a gun out the window. Driving this slow, with no body armor or weapon was scary. I kept a sharp eye out for IEDs and still did so for several months after I got home.

After turning in our gear and cleaning up, our team headed for the Kuwaiti Airport. We were in civilian clothes, but we were each shipping our M-4s with us in a weapons case. The Kuwaiti Customs officials wanted to see the weapons and verify the serial numbers matched our authorization documents. They also wanted to confirm we didn't have any ammo with us. So we opened the cases in the airport and confirmed the rifles were cleared. I felt strange wearing civilian clothes and pulling out an automatic weapon while in a major Middle East airport. I almost expected nearby passengers to run for the nearest exits. As tempting as it was, I knew yelling "Allah Akbar" while pulling out an M-4 in the airport would severely delay my trip home!

The team caught a civilian flight through Germany enroute to our demobilization station at Ft. Bliss, in El Paso, Texas. We landed in Frankfurt airport about 07:00 local time. I had my first real beer in an airport lounge for breakfast. Man that tasted good. Life was getting better. There was no finer place to have a real beer than in Germany.

American Soil

When we landed at El Paso, our team was met by COL Walt Chahanovich, the CRU Commander, and his wife Ellen. I was now on American soil, and it was nice to see some familiar faces. COL and Mrs. Chahanovich made the trip from Washington, D.C. just to welcome us home. Hooah.

Arriving in El Paso, left to right: Kachejian – Creel – Driscoll – Cabell – Kolditz

Our team decided there was no way we were going to stay in the noisy CRC barracks at Ft. Bliss. Instead, we found a small Marriott nearby, and we got a rental car - a minivan. I was glad it wasn't an SUV. We were going to control our own destiny for the rest of the trip.

We had to "demobilize" at Bliss. That meant turning in our remaining military equipment, undergoing medical and psychological screening, getting all the required briefings on finances, benefits, submitting a leave request, and getting our final airline tickets home.

Nobody wanted to be a "medical hold". If the doctors found something wrong physically or psychologically, you were going to be held at Ft. Bliss for more treatment. The delay could be days, weeks or even longer. I wasn't sure that I would be able to pass the hearing test. I must have, because I made it through.

The next morning we started with the physicals. They asked some probing questions to try to screen returning troops for Post-Traumatic Stress Disorder (PTSD). "Did you see anyone killed?" "Friendly?" "Enemy?" "Were you involved in direct combat?" "Did you ever discharge your weapon?" At this point, I was getting concerned that if I answered yes to any questions, they'd hold me at Fort Bliss for another week of screening. And I'm thinking, "Screw that. I am going home!" Then they read my medical records from the

IED attack and the accident in the Tigris River. They wanted details. They probably even asked when my last bowel movement was. After about ten minutes of interrogation I told them, there was nothing wrong with me that a couple of beers couldn't fix. Then I got up and started to walk out. One of the female psychologists stopped me and shook my hand. She thanked me for what I had done. Even though I failed to save Suna, I had tried. She told me that Suna would have thanked me for trying. I needed to hear that. Her comment gave me a new perspective on the accident, and the guilt I carried with me. I was very grateful.

The team was moving as quickly as possible to get the rest of the out-processing completed at Ft. Bliss. It was after 16:00, on September 14, and the CRC cadre told us they wanted to hold our team over the weekend. We went ballistic. I thought Hal Creel was going to kill someone. He had that look. I am glad he wasn't armed. He had veins popping out of other veins, and he was turning colors that I had never seen. I jumped right in, *"This is absolute BS. I didn't have a single day off during my entire tour in Iraq, and I am not going to sit around here for the next three days so some staff pukes can get their weekend off. We are getting on an airplane home tomorrow morning. Period. It is my son's birthday, and I am going to be there. I don't care who needs to be inconvenienced. Get somebody back in here and finish the damn job, or I'll put your ass on the next flight to Baghdad."*

It was an intense few moments, but the admin section wisely decided to push us through the final out-processing steps.

Later that evening, the team asked me if we were flying the last leg of our journey home in our Desert Camouflage Uniforms (DCUs) or in civilian clothes. There was no question. It was DCUs. I was very proud of our service, and the mission wasn't over until we hit Washington Dulles Airport. I wanted our families to see us as if we were coming directly from Iraq. The entire team was flying to Dulles, except Chris Kolditz. He would fly straight to Pittsburgh to visit his mother, who was seriously ill.

A "Happy Cry"

It was September 15. One final flight left. Since our team had cheap government airline tickets, our seats were spread out all over the aircraft. That meant we had any seat that was in the center of a row that would not recline. Of course, any seat was a luxury compared to a C-130 ride. We weren't going to let a bad seat or even a hijacker keep us from getting home. We had seen it all, and we weren't afraid of anything. This bird was taking us home. Period.

While on the plane, few passengers realized that the military guys scattered around the aircraft were returning home from combat, because the flight originated from Texas. I sat next to a nice lady who asked who we were. I explained our situation, and that we were itching to get home. But no one was more excited than Charlie Driscoll. He had a newborn baby girl, named Claire, and he hadn't met her yet. The lady started to cry, but it was a happy cry.

The aircraft landed at Dulles airport, and we started to off load. I tried to get the team to assemble on the jetway to come out together, but the boots were moving and so were all the other passengers. As we flowed out into the terminal, we were greeted by loud cheers and "Welcome Home" signs. The knees got weak, the throats got dry and the eyes got wet.

I could see my wife and kids. My five-year old daughter, Katie, broke from the crowd and flew at me like a 40-pound linebacker. She hit me with the greatest hug I have ever had. She was wrapped around me like a slice of cheese melting on a smoking hot hamburger. Then Kent and Kara tackled me. All the families were there. Alice videotaped the return for Connie Driscoll, so she waited a few moments to capture those precious moments where Charlie got to see his daughters, Claire and Grace.

Hal, Bob, Charlie and I stayed in the terminal for about ten minutes, and we met each other's families. Then we headed for the baggage belt. I was trying to carry three kids at one time, and they all wanted to wear Dad's beret. It was a great day. In fact, it was one of the best days in my life.

Dulles Homecoming

Epilogue

It took a few days to re-acclimate to my house in Virginia. There were a lot of friends and neighbors that stopped by to welcome me home, and they all wanted to hear about Iraq. I had a thousand stories, but I wasn't sure I was ready to talk. My head was still in Iraq and would be for many months. Every trash can in my neighborhood looked like an IED. I hated Monday and Thursday mornings when every trash can in the neighborhood was sitting near the curb.

I still had a few more weeks left in my active duty tour, but much of the remaining time was allocated to personal leave or simple administrative actions. I had some time to decompress.

MRX at Ft. Bragg

Before departing Iraq, I was identified as a "subject matter expert" in Iraqi Infrastructure and Reconstruction Operations and was asked to support a Military Readiness Exercise (MRX) in the United States. One week after I returned home, I drove to Ft. Bragg, North Carolina to brief the 18th Airborne Corps Commander, LTG Vines and his Gray Beard panel. The 18th Airborne Corps was going to rotate into Iraq in the coming months, and it needed "experts" from Iraq to train them up.

I arrived at Ft. Bragg and found the exercise area. There were about a hundred military personnel and technicians in the briefing room. The 18th Airborne Corps Commanding General and several other retired generals were in the front row. When it was my turn to speak, I told LTG Vines exactly how it was, and I didn't pull any punches. During the one-hour presentation, I shared with him the hard lessons GRD learned that he would need to keep in mind. I focused on Iraqi critical infrastructure—what it was and why it was important. I described how the reconstruction work was executed and discussed the roles and missions of U.S. and Iraqi authorities. I recounted how attacks on Iraqi infrastructure occurred. I talked about issues with armed contractors on the battlefield and showed him some graphic photos illustrating why SUVs suck in combat.

I also informed LTG Vines that reconstruction progress in Iraq should not be measured by how much money was "currently obligated". That measure gave American maneuver commanders a false sense of accomplishment. Money moving from the government to a contractor was only the start of the reconstruction process. What commanders really needed to ask was *"How much dirt has been turned?"* An Iraqi project that was accurately reported as 40% complete may simply mean that the contract had been awarded, the contractor had ordered materials, a construction crew had been identified, and a survey of the site had been conducted—but not a single shovel of dirt had yet been turned on the project site.

Only real construction progress was important to the Iraqi people and to maneuver commanders. Commanders needed to know how much physical progress had taken place on the ground–not what financial transaction had occurred 8,000 miles away. *"How much dirt has been turned?"* was the question that BG Bostick always asked to get the ground truth on the status of a reconstruction project, and he was dead nuts on target.

The briefing went well. I was asked good questions and gave frank answers. At the conclusion, LTG Vines gave me the coveted 18th Airborne Corps Commander's coin. I was honored and glad to help his unit better understand the dynamics of the battlefield and prepare them for a very tough year in Iraq.

Mexico

Anticipating my return, Alice booked a trip for the two of us to Mexico. I was looking forward to decompressing, and we needed to re-connect our relationship. It was a low key, no stress adventure at the Palladium Resort in Playa del Carmen. We ate a little, slept a lot, hit the local shops, and hung out by the pool on the beach. In the afternoon, I laid in a hammock and drank a couple of beers. Alice and I had a lot of nice, casual discussions about us, the kids, and our goals going forward. Every few minutes, I wondered how much I should or could tell my wife about my experience in Iraq. While the hot Mexican sun, palm trees and sand were visually soothing and relaxing, somehow they eerily reminded me of being back in Baghdad.

Charlie Driscoll

My CRU team performed some of our remaining active duty at the Army Corps of Engineers headquarters in Washington, D.C. Our team had lunch near Chinatown on September 29, 2004. When we finished our meal, I whipped out an Iraqi Five Dinar bill with Saddam Hussein's image on the front. The team all signed it: LTC Hal Creel - Mosul, Iraq; MAJ Chris Kolditz - Mosul, Iraq; MAJ Bob Cabell - "Baghdad Bob"; MAJ Charlie Driscoll - Fallujah, Iraq; and LTC Kerry

Kachejian - Baghdad, Iraq. I pinned it to a corkboard in the restaurant. It stayed fixed there for a few weeks.

Meanwhile, Alice and I offered Charlie and Connie Driscoll the use of our beach house in the outer banks of North Carolina. They took their two small children, Grace and Claire to escape and re-connect as a family. It rained much of the week, but getting out of the Washington, D.C. area was a good break for the entire family. I was glad Alice and I could do something to help the family recover some lost time.

Life was beginning to return to normal when suddenly, shockingly, Charlie Driscoll died during a five-mile run. The most fit and energetic of all the officers in the CRU, Charlie died as a young Army Major after having survived the hellhole of Fallujah and Ramadi.

Alice and I went to see Connie immediately. Her husband was now gone, and she had to raise two small children. It was unbelievably tragic and unfair. Alice watched the two girls while Connie tried to understand the shock of her loss and make some initial arrangements.

MAJ Chris Kolditz assumed duties as the Survivor Assistance Officer and coordinated many of the arrangements. The entire unit was saddened by the loss of such a fine young officer, father, and husband. MAJ Charlie Driscoll had a bright future before him.

Charlie's funeral mass was at Fort Belvoir, Virginia. Some of the Marines he served with in Ramadi attended the service. His burial was at West Point, New York during a freezing November rain. During the funeral, I presented the American flag and several medals to Connie for Charlie's service, knowing they were little consolation for her and her two young girls. Why God chose him so early will always be a mystery, but He took one of the finest Americans I've ever served with, and I want his two girls to know that. Every time I travel to West Point, I visit Charlie's grave and see my teammate.

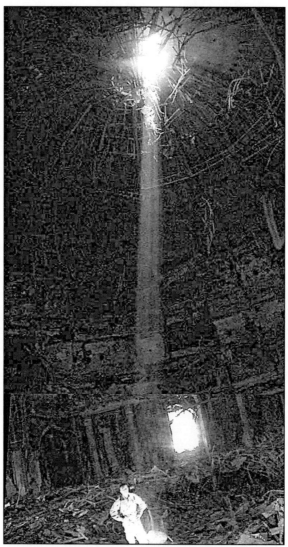

In the Light – Charlie Driscoll

Sometime later, I went back to the restaurant in D.C. to recover the signed Iraqi Five Dinar note. I replaced the currency with another bill that was signed by the four remaining team members. I sent a personal letter and the original bill to Connie.

I returned to my Army Reserve assignment in the Contingency Response Unit (CRU) and COL Chahanovich asked me to assume duties as the Deputy Commander. The first thing I did was to create and post a memorial to Charlie Driscoll in our drill room.

Parachute Jump

A few months later, my brother, Kevin was back in the hospital. I was traveling between Virginia and Pennsylvania to visit him and spend some time in Ocean City, New Jersey with Alice and our kids. For my birthday, Gina, gave me a gift certificate for a high-altitude parachute jump at the Cross Keys Airport in southern New Jersey. I decided to use it in early July. Alice was totally against the idea, but I told her about the outstanding safety record of civilian parachute operations. I had been trained as a paratrooper in the military years before. Military jumping was far more hazardous. We jumped at low level, at night, with combat gear, weapons and hand grenades. We risked hitting power lines, drowning in lakes and rivers and expected to be shot at on the way down. A civilian parachute jump during broad daylight with a trained instructor would be a total cakewalk. I told her, *"No need to fear, honey."*

I was on the Atlantic City Expressway driving to Cross Keys Airport, only five miles from the exit, when my vehicle picked up a nail and got a flat tire. I jacked the car up, but could not break the lug nuts to remove the flat. I called AAA. The repair crew took over an hour trying to remove the stubborn tire. Using a hammer and chisel, we finally succeeded, but I had missed the opportunity to jump that day. I continued to Pennsylvania to visit Kevin in the hospital figuring I could try the jump again the next morning.

The next day, I heard a news report that two parachute instructors became entangled during their jump at Cross Keys and were killed. My flat tire turned out to be very timely. I knew there was no way Alice was going to approve my jump after that news broke, so I gave Gina the gift certificate back. I visited Kevin in the hospital again to celebrate his birthday. A number of family and friends came to wish him well. It was the last time I saw my brother alive.

Kevin

Gina called me a few weeks later to tell me that Kevin was back in the hospital. He was comatose and not likely to survive. I drove to the hospital and saw him. The doctors gave him only a remote chance of recovering, and not fully. With each passing day, his chances declined. It was a one in a million shot. I had played out this scene before - when Fish died in Iraq.

Gina and I knew Kevin's wishes. He had an Advance Medical Directive. He did not want prolonged life support. He wanted to give his last full measure to help others by donating his organs. We contacted "Gift of Life" and arranged for an organ donation. Kevin had been paralyzed for the last 32 years. After a medical review, his liver was determined to be the only viable organ he had to donate. A recipient was located in Ohio. A medical team would fly in to remove his liver, and immediately fly back to Ohio to perform the surgery, but Kevin had to be legally dead before his organs could be harvested. That meant we had to remove him from life support. It was a very hard decision to make, but Gina and I knew it was what Kevin wanted, and it was the right thing to do.

Gina and I arrived at the hospital early in the morning on August 27 and stayed with Kevin. I pleaded with him several times, "Kevin, if you are going to wake up, you need to do it now. Right now, buddy. Right now!" I was hoping for a miracle – that he would open his eyes at the sound of my voice.

At our request, a doctor came in and checked Kevin once again to confirm that he was in an irreversible condition. He was. There was no response to the doctor's physiological and neurological tests. Not even the most primal indication.

That morning, Gina's two sons, Peter and Nathaniel, drove to Pennsylvania from West Point. They arrived at the hospital to spend some final moments with their Uncle Kevin.

The medical team took Kevin back into the operating room, where they removed his respirator. Gina, Peter, Nathaniel and I were then called in so we could stay with Kevin until he died. We gathered around and held him while he gasped for air. I held his hand and prayed. We were pouring tears. Behind us, I could hear the medical team also crying. They too were human. Kevin's heart rate declined and after a few minutes, he crossed the threshold. The doctor declared him dead and shut off the monitor. A few seconds later, Kevin let out one last spasmodic gasp for air. We were only permitted to stay with him for another minute or two. The medical team needed to recover his liver as soon as possible. The four of us said our final goodbyes and started to leave the operating room. On the way out the door, I turned and looked at the team and said, *"Make it count. Please, make it count."*

We were exhausted. The end had come, but Kevin was a believer, and I knew he was in a better place. The way he faced great adversity in life was inspiring. He was no longer confined to a wheelchair and thinking of him still illuminates my day.

We received the news later that Kevin's liver was not suitable for transplant. It hit us like a devastating punch to the stomach. Gina and I felt robbed that his final gift could not be given. We were told that even the medical team was distraught by what they found, but Gina and I both agreed that we would be organ donors to fulfill Kevin's own wish.

For the next month, each time I walked by Kevin's empty wheelchair in our family home in West Chester, I expected to see him in it. The wheelchair sitting by the fireplace was something of a memorial to him. One day, it happened. I walked out of the kitchen, turned the corner, and there was Kevin in his chair, smiling at me. The vision only lasted a moment, and it could have been a mental trick, but to me, it was very real. Kevin was fine, and he was still with us.

Katrina

Kevin's death occurred the same week that Hurricane Katrina came ashore. COL Bob Korpanty had recently assumed command of the CRU, and the unit was alerted to respond. Not surprising, any organization with a name like "Contingency Response Unit" tends to be called first to respond to a contingency operation. My Army Reserve teammates were scrambling to determine what missions we would get as New Orleans was going to take a brutal hit. I returned from Kevin's funeral and put my uniform back on. COL Korpanty immediately deployed to the massive disaster area to get an initial assessment of where the CRU needed to engage. It turned out, we would support the military response provided by Joint Task Force (JTF) Katrina and support the unwatering mission for New Orleans, assigned to the Mississippi Valley Division of USACE. So the CRU swung its focus from supporting military operations in Iraq to a civil response to Hurricane Katrina.

Working with the CRU Operations staff and team leaders, I laid out a plan for five one-month long rotations of personnel. We spread around the burden. Immediately available volunteers were assigned to the first Katrina rotation. MAJ George Stejic and MAJ Jeff Kwiecinski, were among the CRU operations officers that volunteered to unwater New Orleans. Then I started to assign personnel based on their availability, while providing consideration to those with previous hardship mobilizations. Over the course of several months, the CRU provided critical staffing to support our fellow Americans during the worst natural disaster in our nation's history.

Knees

At this point, my body was feeling the toll. My knees were hurting in Iraq, and I had ignored the pain for many months, but they got progressively worse. I went to an orthopedist, Dr. Norman Marcus, to get my knees checked out. I probably could have used the military health care system, but I opted to use my private insurance, and I paid my own way.

It turned out that I had several tears that were eventually repaired with arthroscopic surgery, but I was also missing cartilage on the left knee. I was too young for knee replacement. As a temporary solution, I had lubricants injected in my knee. I opted for an experimental procedure called "carticel", where Dr. Marcus extracted cartilage from my right knee, and a laboratory grew it in a dish for about six weeks. He then transplanted my own cartilage cells back into the left knee. During the procedure, the surgeon had to fracture the bone. I wound up with about 35 staples in my left leg. I was on crutches for a month, and used a cane for a few more months. After a series of four knee surgeries and a year of physical rehab, I finally started to get my legs back under me. The carticel procedure worked.

MOAA Award

About this time, COL Bob Korpanty, nominated me for a national Leadership Excellence award from the Military Officers Association of America (MOAA). At the time, I honestly wasn't exactly sure what MOAA was, but I was honored that COL Korpanty considered my service worthy of nomination. He spent several hours of his time preparing the justification. There were so many good soldiers giving so much for their country, I was proud just to be among them. COL Korpanty would keep me informed periodically as the nomination package made its way through approval channels. Each step of the process, I was surprised I was still in the running.

Then it happened. I received letters from both LTG Jack Stultz, Commander of the U.S. Army Reserve Command, and from

MG George Read, Commander of the U.S. Army Reserve Readiness Command, congratulating me for being selected for the award. My first thought was, "Holy cow, what happened?" I immediately went to the internet to look up MOAA, and found out the association had 360,000 members. I figured that I should probably join MOAA immediately, before I accepted the award. But I was told the award came with a lifetime membership. Still surprised, I asked COL Korpanty for a copy of what he submitted to the Board to see exactly what had been written in the justification. He did a nice job. A few weeks later, I flew to Atlanta to receive the award from the Chief of the Army Reserve, LTG Stultz, and the MOAA President, VADM Norb Ryan Jr, USN (RET), at the Army Reserve Senior Leader Conference.

I had my three minutes of fame, and I was deeply grateful for being selected. But somehow, it felt hollow. It was great Americans like my brother Kevin and my teammate Charlie Driscoll that inspired me to go the extra mile, and they weren't with us any more to get their share of the credit.

Public Speaking

Given my recent Iraq tour, I was invited to speak at numerous public and private events, some officially (in uniform) and some not. I tried to educate and inspire Americans about our Reconstruction efforts in Iraq, particularly when the only news they were hearing everyday was about another car bombing in Baghdad. I found that speaking about my Iraq experience was somewhat therapeutic.

I put together a briefing on "Lessons Learned" that I presented to both military and industry audiences. Every time I talked publicly, I gave my personal opinion and not the official views of the Army or Department of Defense. I was asked to brief the Assistant Secretary of the Army for the Manpower and Reserve Affairs in the Pentagon on the subject of "Contractors on the Battlefield". I also spoke at several Veterans' events, Patriot Day and security conferences. I continued to push for solutions to the IED threat. I provided insights on improving joint force protection and my perspectives on Stability and Reconstruction Operations.

Afterward

Based on my experience with standing up the Gulf Region Division in 2004, I was recalled again to Active Duty in 2007 to help create a new Army Corps of Engineers (USACE) Division supporting the U.S. Central Command (CENTCOM). The new organization was called the Transatlantic Division (TAD), and its mission was to unify and align all the USACE construction efforts in Iraq, Afghanistan and the rest of the Middle East.

At this point in my career, I was a Colonel assigned at the Transatlantic Programs Center (TAC) in Winchester, VA. As part of the planning for the new Division, I made a trip with LTC Don Johantges, the Deputy Commander at TAC, through several countries in the Middle East to get their "boots on the ground" perspectives on the how TAD should be organized, staffed and equipped. The stops we made included Qatar, United Arab Emirates, Afghanistan, Kuwait, Iraq, Egypt and Germany (AFRICOM).

Reconstruction Update – Afghanistan

Don and I landed in Kabul, Afghanistan on October 6, 2007. We didn't realize it at the time, but that day was the sixth anniversary of the U.S. invasion that overthrew the Taliban. We planned to meet with Colonel Miroslav Kurka, Commander of the Afghanistan Engineer District (AED), and other officials, to get their perspective on the new Division structure.

We arrived on a commercial flight and had to wear civilian clothing to maintain a low profile. The AED security team was supposed to meet us at the airport, issue us body armor, helmets and weapons and then escort us to the AED compound in downtown Kabul. Ironically, the AED headquarters, called the Qalaa House, occupied the former Iraqi Embassy in Afghanistan.

We came through the immigration control point and grabbed our bags off what was probably the only baggage carousel in the entire country. We looked around for our security team. There was none. It was a combat zone, and no plan was perfect. I recalled our explicit instructions were not to leave the airport, under any circumstances, without meeting our security team. They must have known we had arrived – the plan was clearly communicated. I was feeling a bit naked standing in the Kabul Airport with my bags and no weapons, no body armor, and no security team in sight. It was a screw up, but the situation was not desperate. I didn't like standing inside the large glass terminal that would shatter into a thousand pieces of shrapnel if a VBIED detonated outside. Don and I speculated for a few minutes as to where the security team could be. Perhaps they stopped at a Starbucks.

After waiting about twenty minutes, I tried dialing out on both of my Blackberries. I had a military one and a civilian one. Each was on a separate network. One Blackberry was dead. No signal. On the other, I got a recorded message from an operator speaking in some central Asian language that I did not recognize. The message probably translated into something like, "Please insert another fifty cents" or maybe "Yankee Go Home." I just wasn't feeling the love.

While I was trying to place another call, the activity level in the airport increased dramatically. Dozens of armed Afghani police/military were sweeping the airport terminal. Several vehicles pulled up, just outside the terminal, in the restricted area. It was clear that some Afghani VIP was coming through the airport. Rumor was that it was President Hamid Karzai's security detail. Maybe Don and I could get a ride with him, if we asked nicely.

After waiting for thirty minutes, with no communications and no security team, I was starting to consider some contingency plans. It was getting late in the afternoon, and we had to do something before nightfall. Like a good troop, I was mentally developing courses of action: Option 1, wait it out – those were our instructions. Don't be a hero. Option 2, take the initiative and find a ride to the compound, but I didn't have a map or a grid coordinate. That scenario made me feel like a new Second Lieutenant. Option 3, we could throw our bags over our shoulders and run a couple of miles toward the U.S. Embassy. That plan could go really bad really fast. Option 4, ... answer the friggin phone – it's ringing.

It was a poor connection and the message was quite broken, but definitely in English. "*SGM .... (garbled), from AED. We know you are there. ... (garbled) ...on the way.*" I confirmed we were at the Kabul Airport terminal and would stand fast. Course of action 1 was clearly the best one. We stayed put. It took another ten minutes for the two-vehicle security team to arrive. I immediately concluded that the security situation in Kabul was better than in Baghdad, as the Kabul convoys only had two SUVs.

I met the security team, and they explained the delay. The Taliban had marked the 6th anniversary of the U.S. invasion by exploding a car bomb on the main road between the U.S. Embassy and the Kabul Airport. A soldier was killed just before we landed. This incident caused delays due to increased security measures and re-routing of traffic. Don and I threw on our body armor and helmets and started the road movement toward the AED HQ.

On the way out of the airport, our driver locked up his brakes after astutely spotting another car with license plates on the suspected VBIED list. Some of our guys dismounted the vehicle. There was a terse discussion and confusion as a local Afghani Policeman claimed the suspect vehicle was his. We handed the situation over to some local security officials to resolve and moved out again.

We made it to the AED HQ without incident and had an office call with COL Kurka, who gave us a command briefing. We also engaged a series of meetings with his Deputy, LTC Karen Otto, and several senior military and civilian staff. We got a good feel for the country, and how Afghanistan compared and contrasted with Iraq. Afghanistan was much larger and much poorer. While Iraq had oil, Afghanistan was the fifth poorest country in the world. It had no natural resources to fuel its economy. Each Afghan province had a separate warlord. The reconstruction effort in Afghanistan was focused on building a road network that tied all the provinces together to promote commerce. There was a local saying, *"Where the road ends, the Taliban begins."* Each provincial warlord would get his own National Army Brigade and National Police Brigade. That would help to maintain the balance of power. President Karzai was really the warlord for Kabul, which explained why he did not have great influence outside the capital.

New road network

In the following days, we toured a few project sites for the Afghan National Army, including a barracks complex and a major hospital. We also conducted a road trip to Gardez Resident Office, near the border with Pakistan. The office managed over sixty construction projects in four provinces: Paktia, Paktika, Logar and Ghazni. Located near the end of the world, the terrain was rugged and barren. It was clearly Taliban country. Our SUV convoy attracted a lot of hard stares. We traveled with a Navy Captain, who shared responsibilities in the reconstruction effort.

One of the project sites near Gardez was an Afghan National Army Brigade Headquarters. We met the local Afghan Colonel and asked him what his needs were. It was a frank discussion, and the translator was busy supporting the dialogue. We moved around the installation to assess the construction progress. The barracks were completed, the dining facility was under construction, and the wastewater treatment system was being installed. There was a plan to better protect the fuel storage area that was completely exposed to enemy observation and attack.

The existing Afghan prison on the base was a small wooden building with several rows of concertina wire wrapped around the outside. Our guide pointed out a new prison that was being built about three hundred meters away. The new prison was being modified to meet the needs of the Afghan Army. We went inside to look. One of the requested modifications was to make a large room with a high ceiling and a sloped floor. The Afghans were ambiguous about the purpose for the modified room, but we believe the intent was for indoor executions by firing squad.

I left Afghanistan with a healthy respect for the challenge that our nation faced bringing security and stability to this region of the world. I asked myself, "When will we know when the conflict in Afghanistan is over? How do we know when our mission is complete?" The best answer I had was, "*We will know the Taliban has been defeated when the first McDonalds or Burger King opens in downtown Kabul.*" Even more compelling evidence of a complete victory against terrorism will be the opening of a "Hooters" in Kabul or Baghdad!

Reconstruction Update – Iraq

While enroute to Iraq, Don and I stopped for a few days in Kuwait to meet with COL Judd Cook, the forward TAC Deputy Commander. We toured an Army hospital under construction, a Kuwaiti Naval Base and a military crossing site on the Kuwaiti-Iraqi border (K-Crossing). MAJ Tim Vail, a squared away officer from the Kuwait Area Office, escorted us to Ali Al Salem, a remote Kuwaiti airfield, to catch our flight to Baghdad.

MAJ Vail issued us weapons and body armor before departing. A C-12 aircraft was waiting for us on the parking apron. I felt reassured when I learned that the two pilots on the plane were from Kennett Square, Pennsylvania, which was about ten miles from my hometown of West Chester.

I was returning to the Gulf Region Division (GRD) three years after I left it. I wondered what had changed. The "surge" in Iraq was reportedly making great progress with security. I would believe it when I saw it firsthand.

While airborne, I could see the trench and barrier system that formed the Kuwaiti-Iraqi border. About two hours later, we landed at Baghdad International Airport (BIAP) without incident.

We were met by the GRD contractor security team at the Distinguished Visitors Terminal. It was a simple building, but a marked improvement from the tent that I departed Iraq from in 2004. I noticed that the security teams and their vehicles were different. The GRD security contract had been consolidated, and Aegis had now completely replaced Erinys. Both the military and the contractor security teams were equipped with better vehicles, radios and had Quik-Clot® readily available to treat the wounded.

We departed the airport and entered the highway leading to downtown Baghdad. Years earlier, this highway had earned a reputation as the most dangerous road in the world. All the vegetation on the shoulders of the highway had been cleared to eliminate hiding sites for the enemy. This convoy moved in a series of short bursts; very different than the 100 mph sprint I was used to. Our speed would be 5 mph one minute, and 70 mph the next. It was a new movement technique, intended to throw off the timing of an attack. I couldn't quite figure out why this technique was now preferred, but I didn't want to distract the driver by asking a bunch of questions while he was trying to perform his mission. I had an eerie feeling while driving under the bridge where I hit an IED on my last trip.

When I reached the GRD HQ, I dropped my bags and began my mission. I met with multiple staff elements to get their inputs on the design of the new USACE Division. Jack Holly was the logistics chief when I left Iraq and incredibly, he was still there. COL Gary Pease had deployed from HQ USACE to serve as the GRD Chief of

Staff. Gary had plenty of opinions to offer on how and when we should form the new Transatlantic Division. COL Dale Adams was Deputy GRD Commander and COL Mike Aberle served as the Strategic Plans Officer (G5). Both were from the North Dakota National Guard, which provided some key military staffing.

GRD and the Reconstruction Operations Center (ROC) were now well staffed and robust. The ROC was supported by contractor teams from Aegis. There were enough personnel to man multiple shifts. Intelligence and operations were better integrated, providing improved awareness and security for reconstruction convoys. LTC Steven Roemhildt was now the Operations Officer (G3). At full strength, the G3 office had thirty assigned personnel: 16 officers, 7 enlisted, and 7 U.S. civilians. When GRD first stood up, the G3 section peaked at eight personnel: 4 officers, 3 NCOs and one civilian.

I met briefly with Brigadier General (BG) Jeff Dorko. He had recently assumed Command of the GRD from BG Michael Walsh. Coincidentally, BG Dorko and I completed a five-day course on "Dynamics of International Terrorism" and "Security Driving" about six weeks earlier in West Virginia. The course taught offensive driving techniques to tactically and psychologically prepare us for our deployments. We drove at high speeds while dodging ambushes, threw scores of "Starsky and Hutch" J-turns, performed dozens of pit maneuvers and rammed cars that blocked our escape path. We also conducted counter surveillance exercises and live fire weapons training. At the end of this excellent course, we felt well prepared for deployment in a combat zone.

Ironically, BG Dorko was seriously wounded by an IED a few weeks after I left Iraq. He was riding in an SUV. The circumstances made me believe he was specifically targeted by an insider. To my knowledge, he was the only General Officer to be wounded in Iraq.

Don and I also met with Mr. Jim Proctor who gave us an updated tour of Saddam's National Bunker under the rubble of Believer's Palace. After three years, the air in the massive bunker was more vile, and foul water had filled many of the areas.

Everywhere I looked, there was good news. In fact, there was great news. The bottom line was the "Surge" was working. Iraq was in the midst of an amazing transformation. From a relative perspective, peace was breaking out in Baghdad. During a period of three days, I only heard one bombing, one local rocket attack and one small arms fire incident. It was strangely quiet. Again I thought, "Is that all you got?" We had more than that before breakfast each morning when I was here. This ain't a war no more. If nobody was gonna shoot at us, let's just pack it up and go home."

There was a light now shining over Iraq. I thought it was over, but there was one more chapter to be written in my family history.

The Next Generation

In the summer of 2009, my two nephews deployed to Iraq. CPT Peter Curley was an artillery officer and supported a Provincial Reconstruction Team from FOB Warhorse. 1LT Nathaniel Curley was a combat engineer assigned to the 82nd Airborne Division in Ramadi. He cleared IEDs off the roads.

Gina and I prayed for their safe return.

Our prayers were answered in the summer of 2010.

Mission Complete

In June 2012 I retired from the military. My family and friends joined me for a farewell ceremony in Winchester, VA. We reserved an empty chair in the front row to remember our brother, Kevin.

It had been 12,396 days since I first put on a cadet uniform on July 6th, 1978 at West Point. It was a long and rewarding journey that took me around the world, to dozens of nations, in both war and peace. I never imagined that my last day as a soldier would finally arrive. While I celebrated reaching this important milestone, I also knew that I would miss wearing the uniform. I would miss being a soldier.

But that day was not just about me. It was about the hundreds of people who I served with and shared experiences that shaped our lives. Throughout my career I was honored to work with many great people who put the national mission ahead of their personal convenience.

I want to thank the American people who have been so supportive to our military during the past decade of war. We can feel their deep gratitude, and it truly helps our soldiers and their families get through some very tough days and long deployments.

May God bless our great nation, and all the men and women who proudly serve it, and the families that support them.

At West Point: COL Kachejian, his sister Gina and her sons, Cadet Nate Curley and 1LT Peter Curley

Retirement Ceremony: Kara, Katie, Kerry, Alice and Kent Kachejian

Lessons Learned

Throughout this book, I've stated my personal opinions and perspectives. The "lessons learned" that follow are based on those opinions and do not reflect the official positions or views of the publisher, U.S. Army Corps of Engineers, Department of Defense or any U.S. Government agency or personnel.

* * *

After I returned to the United States, I compiled a list of lessons I learned from my deployment. The blood, sweat, and tears that we shed should be documented for the benefit of future generations. Fortunately, as the war progressed, the U.S. military learned how to overcome many of the problems that it experienced in the early days. But we need to always remember these issues as we design, equip and train our future fighting force.

EQUIPMENT

We had the wrong tactical wheeled vehicles for counter-insurgency operations.

The lack of adequate armor protection was pervasive in non-combat units. The HMMWV was an administrative vehicle hastily modified into a poor fighting vehicle. Enemy forces hid among civilians and were able to get up close and take the first shot. We need to survive the opening blow during an engagement, and that requires better physical protection. While DOD moved aggressively to fix the problem, it took several years to adequately respond to the urgent need for better armor.

GRD had equipment issues far worse than other military units. The unit was stood up and equipped during combat operations. It never participated in peacetime training exercises. We had no military vehicles, no crew served weapons, no tactical radios and few military shooters. To Git'r Done, GRD leased 200 SUVs, of which only 12 were armored. Half of them were broken from being ridden hard and shot up. The other half were taken from GRD to protect the new Iraqi leadership. There was no question about it - SUVs suck in combat - particularly the unarmored ones. Their slow acceleration and distinctive look made them bullet magnets.

GRD expended an incredible amount of energy trying to fix the problem. We improvised and adapted, buying and installing after-market armor kits. We tried to buy mine-resistant vehicles that were commercially available, but we were repeatedly told it was illegal to the purchase them. This policy was probably well intended for peacetime operations, but in Iraq, it resulted in the unnecessary loss of human life.

If the United States is going to engage in stability and reconstruction operations in the future, then these forces need to be identified, manned, trained and equipped in peacetime. Acquiring the right vehicles going forward will be an important task for the Army procurement system. We have to assume that we will operate in close proximity to an enemy hiding among the civilian population, and they will get the first shot. The implications for counter insurgency need to be foremost in the minds of those developing the next generation of Army equipment.

Combat aircraft have to be immediately responsive to ground forces.

No surprises here. When troops are in contact with the enemy, air power has to be available in seconds because the fight is over in minutes. Remember, the enemy often gets the first shot. Fighter aircraft are of little use to troops in contact if they can't get into the ground fight within seconds to minutes of a fire support request.

Loitering ground attack platforms are best suited to support stability and reconstruction operations, but slow and low fliers are more vulnerable to hand held anti-aircraft missiles (MANPADS) and small arms fire (SAF). Ground combat forces often have their own attack helicopters that serve as guardian angels, watching over their maneuvering troops. These generally provide a faster response, but since early reconstruction operations were not integrated in with the tactical forces, they had no priority for air support, nor the ability to communicate with them. There is still work to do. Reconstruction teams in Afghanistan have been misidentified as Taliban and attacked by our own aircraft.

Ships need to reach further with their combat capabilities.

In Iraq, ships and their aircraft could not reach 90% of the fight. That's my opinion based on observation, not on hard empirical data. Flying naval aircraft farther inland meant burning more fuel traveling to the mission area. This reduced the time available to support ground forces.

Ships were effectively used in littoral areas to observe and interdict the smuggling of oil and weapons. Their aircraft were used to "fly pipelines" to report new oil attacks, but I am not convinced an aircraft moving at 400 knots and at 5000 feet can prevent an attack. How can a pilot see, much less distinguish, normal civilians from those intending to put IEDs on the pipeline?

OPERATIONS / TRAINING

We need to develop and rapidly evolve tactics, techniques and procedures (TTPs) to combat asymmetric attacks.

Adversaries know they will lose in a big way if they attempt to slug it out in a conventional military fight with the United States. Instead, they will attempt to weaken and defeat us by using every available hit and run means that avoids a decisive engagement. They know the rules that U.S. forces must work within, and they freely operate outside these boundaries to provide an advantage. They understand that U.S. forces will comply with the law of Land Warfare, so they will constantly try to make it appear that we are violating it. Our enemies have also studied our tactics, equipment and capabilities. They know that our vulnerabilities are broadly reported in the mainstream media, which unwittingly or self-servingly acts as a surrogate intelligence arm for insurgents and terrorists.

Our enemies are ruthless and evil. They use human shields to protect themselves and willfully create civilian casualties when attacked. They use schools, hospitals and places of worship as "safe zones" to store weapons, plan attacks and use them as defensive positions. They use ambulances and taxis for command and control and to transport their weapons, personnel and logistics. If the U.S. responds, damage to the school, hospital or mosque is used as evidence of U.S. aggression and our hostile intent against civilians.

The enemy will falsely report and intentionally cause civilian casualties to constantly keep U.S. forces off balance and on the defensive in the global media. The harder we are pounding them, the more outrageous and theatrical their claims. A single unfortunate incident of a U.S. attack that kills civilians will outplay twenty successful attacks on enemy forces in the global media. The United States is held fully accountable, while terrorists and criminals get a free pass.

Trust me. The United States does not intentionally attack wedding parties. When forty insurgents are killed in the desert on a Tuesday night by an AC-130 gunship, the enemy will try to inflame the world press by screaming that the United States killed an innocent wedding party. Yet only fighting age males and lots of weapons are found among the dead, while there are no females and no gifts. Weddings traditionally happen on Thursday nights, not Tuesday nights and the nearby village was a known insurgent staging area in an IED hot zone.

We need to be staffed and trained to aggressively respond to false allegations in the media, to publicly expose the true nature of this cunning and unethical enemy. The truth needs to be delivered at network speed. It can be done. U.S. political candidates respond to allegations in minutes to hours as each November approaches. Asymmetric war has a huge political and information dimension that combat forces are not well trained to deal with.

Embedding Iraqi authorities with U.S. forces during an attack proved valuable in Fallujah. Iraqi officials were able to see and confirm when a mosque, school or hospital was being used for military purposes. Once the Iraqis physically saw the evidence, the building lost its protected status, and it became a legitimate target.

We have become heavily dependent on civilians and contractors. We need to better protect them and their identities, as the enemy will coerce, kidnap or kill those that cooperate with us. For example, our heavy reliance on local interpreters provides an opportunity for the enemy to threaten an interpreter's family to gain insider information and plant misinformation.

Our forces need better cultural awareness. Simple gestures and language skills can go a long way to demonstrating respect and building trust. We have gotten much better at this, but we still have a long way to go, as these skills can degrade over time.

We need to rapidly distinguish which civilians we can trust. Americans tend to trust others to a fault. Police are generally good at determining when someone is lying. But many of us are unsure when a civilian is lying, withholding information or providing false tips. The widespread use of biometrics (fingerprints, facial recognition, and iris scanning) has helped to sort out the good guys from the bad actors.

I had an opportunity to visit the National Training Center (NTC) in the California desert. Brigadier General Abrams (pictured on the right) was the commander. He has fully integrated many of the lessons he learned from Iraq into the training. Full-scale Iraqi villages and hundreds of actors are among the many innovations used to provide realism. It is a world-class facility.

Maneuver forces and reconstruction efforts must be fully integrated.

Engineer command and control (C2) and reconstruction operations during the early years of Iraqi War were fragmented. Part of the reason for the disconnect was that many engineer units were eliminated or gutted in the previous two decades to provide more slots for combat forces. Many of the Engineer brigade headquarters, that provided overarching engineer C2, were eliminated from the force structure. That decision caused some unforeseen secondary and tertiary effects when it came to the reconstruction effort. There is no single boss to organize, prioritize and align scores of simultaneous engineering projects.

Most military engineers start out as tactical engineers. That means they train on how to help U.S. combat forces move freely on the battlefield and to restrict the enemy's movement. Tactical engineers breach minefields, build bridges, clear roads of IEDs, build field fortifications and austere airfields, and blow up enemy obstacles. When I was a Lieutenant, tactical engineers even had an atomic demolition mission – to use a small nuclear weapon to quickly blow up an entire airfield or a port to prevent it from being captured by the enemy.

The U.S. Army Corps of Engineers (USACE) provides another breed of engineer on the battlefield that designs and builds major construction projects and permanent facilities. Its division in Iraq was GRD. USACE is led by a thin cadre of military officers, but most of the technical experts are civilians. They don't normally operate in combat zones, so they don't train with their tactical counterparts or use common information systems. The two communities speak different languages. Throw on top of that the fact that Navy and Air Force engineers and USAID were also in Iraq, and you can quickly see the potential for inefficient operations – with redundancies and gaps in reconstruction efforts.

My hat is off to the 1st Cav Division, led by MG Chiarelli, and to Colonel Ken Cox, the 1st Cav Engineer. Along with BG Bostick, the GRD Commander (and former Deputy CG for 1CD), they were able to start pulling the command and control together. The 1CD model worked. We successfully integrated the GRD's Area Offices into the BCT structure, and the 1CD provided much needed security escorts for GRD personnel.

The establishment and evolution of Reconstruction Operations Centers was a major leap forward, successfully integrating the projects, logistics and security into a common reconstruction picture. Colonel "Rock" Donohue, the MNC-I Engineer in 2008-09, reported that ROCs were now fully integrated into the Engineer Brigades. This solution needs to be adopted into our warfighting doctrine.

FORCE PROTECTION

IEDs are an enduring threat.

IEDs were a pervasive problem across Iraq. We can safely assume that IEDs will be an asymmetric weapon of choice for many years to come. There is no silver bullet solution to solve the problem. Avoiding IED attacks is a combination of good armor, good techniques and procedures, good radio jammers, good intelligence and good luck. There was seemingly an inexhaustible supply of IED material in Iraq. It eventually took five years to destroy the massive supply of captured enemy ammunition that was locally available. IED jammers were such a new capability that not a single one was available to GRD during my tour. I was recently told there have now been over 40,000 of these devices produced.

Protecting a garrison is more than just perimeter security.

In Iraq, we owned islands of land called garrisons or Forward Operating Bases (FOBs). Most perimeters of these garrisons were protected with large concrete walls and concertina wire. While we know how to provide decent perimeter security, we still need to improve our capabilities at entry control points (ECPs) or "gates". Hundreds of military, commercial and private vehicles need to enter and exit the gates of a garrison each day. Each vehicle requires multiple layers of screening, and many require a complete physical search.

Preventing a car bomb or enemy combatant from entering an FOB is crucial, but we must be able to screen these vehicles much faster. We need both high security and high throughput at the gates. Current security procedures are manpower and time intensive. In combat, hundreds of vehicles and personnel often line up outside our largest installations waiting to be inspected. While the garrison is secure, the personnel standing outside in line become highly vulnerable to enemy attack. Mortars, rockets, car bombs and small arms fire are easily used to kill and injure the exposed personnel. The gate guards conducting the screening earned respect from me for performing this dangerous assignment.

Automated vehicle inspections are needed. The best would be non-intrusive ones that can quickly identify potential threat vehicles, personnel and equipment. Sensors need to detect hidden explosives, weapons and personnel. Each person needs to be biometrically identified and assigned a risk level. Many other sensor modalities could be used to reduce the risk of false alarms and improve the confidence level of the finding.

When perimeter security is effective, the enemy cannot get their personnel and car bombs inside our facility. Indirect fire, such as rockets and mortars, become the enemy's preferred means to attack a garrison. Many of these systems were set up with batteries and timers, so they were fired well after the enemy left the launch site. Many new systems were introduced in Iraq to counter rockets and mortars. I will not comment further as I do not want to educate our enemies. However, detecting crews in the act of setting up mortar tubes and rockets would be a useful step forward.

Waterside security is generally not as well understood. Perimeter walls and concertina wire can be quickly overwhelmed by rising rivers and floodwaters. Diver detection sensors and surface radars are needed to provide early warning, particularly at night. Suicide boat bombs are a relatively new threat, and they should be considered in the local security plan.

INFRASTRUCTURE & BORDER SECURITY

Point facilities, such as garrisons and power plants, can be reasonably well protected with walls, fences, sensors and security forces. It is much harder to protect linear infrastructure, such as pipelines, power lines, roads, rail, fiber optics and international borders. Security for these is very difficult in remote and non-permissive areas, such as the Red Zone. Linear features need to be monitored with a 24/7 staring capability, and quick reaction forces (QRFs) need to be able to respond in time to prevent the attack or at least interdict the attackers.

But the "insider" is one of the greatest threats that can defeat the best physical security measures. In Iraq, insiders could be easily bought. When border guards make only $3-5 per day, anyone offering a $100 bribe can easily smuggle personnel and contraband through a Port of Entry. It was an insider that planted the IED that took out my SUV along the most dangerous highway in Iraq. Insider threats related to cybersecurity are another major issue that we must face in future conflicts.

OUTSOURCING

The U.S. military has become increasingly dependent on contractor support during wartime. We simply cannot succeed without them. Contractors provide our forces with a broad spectrum of services, such as food, fuel, communications, medical supplies, technicians, engineers and even security.

Outsourcing these services also has real limits. Our enemies successfully exploited our dependence on contractors, who were particularly vulnerable when they worked outside the wire without adequate security. Contractors and foreign drivers were threatened, kidnapped and killed while driving logistics convoys to U.S. troops. While contractors were well paid, the fear of death can quickly shrink the pool of available drivers. In one notable case, the Government of India convinced the Kuwaitis to refuse to let Indian citizens drive convoys into Iraq due to the imminent danger.

Contractor security forces were essential to the early reconstruction mission, but there were no uniform standards among the dozens of contractor security forces. There was no integrated approach to register, equip and train the thousands of armed contractors. There was ambiguity with issues related to the Law of Land Warfare. How did these laws apply to armed security contractors? And the disparity in the training and professionalism among different armed contractors led to many fratricide incidents. Policy and training solutions are needed.

C2 / INTELLLIGENCE NETWORKS

There has been a lot of investment to make our DOD information networks "joint", enabling the Army, Navy, Air Force and Marines to see a common operating picture. There have also been successful efforts to make our networks accessible by other federal agencies and coalition personnel. However, military networks did not support or interoperate with contractors and host nation personnel involved in reconstruction. (This situation improved greatly over time with the standup of Contractor Operations Centers and Reconstruction Operations Centers).

Civil-Military Ops and Reconstruction Ops were heavily dependent on contractors that were not integrated into the military's command & control (C2) structure, and they lacked situational awareness (SA). The coalition network, CENTRIX, was not widely available. Furthermore, many contractors lacked security clearances, meaning they would not be authorized to receive classified intelligence or see the common operating picture.

To work around the situation, contractors used ad hoc communications (Iraqna cell phones, commercial HF/VHF) that were not interoperable with military radios. Requests for Quick Reaction Forces (QRF) and MEDEVAC helicopters had to be coordinated through special arrangements. When things got desperate, even Yahoo email accounts were used to relay tactical information.

Until the standup of CONOCS and ROCs, military commanders had limited visibility on attacks on reconstruction contractors. Contractors were tracked as "neutrals", so little attention was paid to them. The primary focus of the military was on friendly and enemy casualties. Contractors were considered neither. The Significant Activities (SIGACTS) database recorded all reported attacks, but it did not provide adequate visibility on attacks on reconstruction personnel. If these attacks were even entered in SIGACTS, the reports were often entered many hours or possibly days later. Only current attacks (less than 12 hours old) were brought to the attention of the operations team and the commander. Thus, many attacks on reconstruction personnel arrived late and then went straight to a historical file without notice.

Human Intelligence (HUMINT) was extremely valuable but difficult to collect. Due to insufficient Arabic speakers in the U.S. Army, we were heavily dependent on local interpreters. That raised some doubts about what translators we could trust. A loyal translator can be turned against us if their family is held hostage or threatened.

I believe a great source of intelligence could have been harvested from hundreds of daily situation reports prepared by reconstruction contractors. Analyzing these unclassified documents would have greatly enhanced our understanding of local threats and issues.

NEED FOR A COMMON ID SYSTEM

Trying to figure out who everyone was in Iraq was a big challenge. I sat in a Force Protection meeting one day and an officer announced that there were 43 different types of identity badges associated with coalition forces. It seemed like every military command and government agency had a different badge.

On top of that, we needed to better distinguish who the Iraqis were – military, police and civilians. Trying to sort it out was a mess. There were cases when Iraqi Ministers were denied entrance to military bases because the gate guard did not recognize their ID card. The Minister could sit in his vehicle in the Red Zone waiting in line for quite a while. One of those SNAFUs would hit the diplomatic channels real fast and real hard.

U.S. Forces, government civilians and their supporting contractors often had common access cards (CAC). The CAC was the "gold standard" identity passport for the battlefield.

We really needed a biometrics based identity system for Iraqis – to quickly sort out who had a background check and was considered a non-threat. A biometric identity management system would let trustworthy Iraqis receive less scrutiny and get faster access to facilities. The ID system would need to be able to enroll thousands of people quickly. Furthermore, it would need analytic software to identify anomalous trends that will automatically alert a security operator for further investigation. I don't want to go into too much detail here about how the system would work – it may educate potential adversaries, but the use of biometrics in Iraq did start to take off. However, it was mainly used to find bad guys involved in IED attacks, and it was not routinely used for access controls.

NEED TO BUILD CIVIL CAPACITY

After the invasion, the Iraqis were dependent on the United States for just about everything. Their trained government and industry leaders (principally Ba'athists) had been removed from power. Rebuilding civil capacity was an essential step to reduce dependence on the U.S. and to enable sustainable security. Instead of giving the Iraqis a fish to eat every day, we needed to teach the Iraqis (and Afghanis) how to fish. Establishing a stable Iraq was essential to our exit strategy. Fundamental elements of civil capacity include:

- establishing the Rule of Law
- having effective governance
- economic development
- restoring essential services

Building civil capacity required a broad interagency effort between the Departments of State, Defense, Justice, Homeland Security and Treasury. GRD provided only a piece of the total effort, and it contributed by employing Iraqis and restoring essential services. It soon became clear that GRD needed to train the Iraqis how to build, operate and maintain their own infrastructure. At one point, COL Schroedel proposed standing up an Iraqi Corps of Engineers. That would enable Iraqi engineers to stand up as the U.S. stood down.

The Interagency environment can operate better by building trust and bridging cultural and language gaps to achieve better unity of effort. Military forces rarely conducted peacetime exercises with civilians from the State Department, USAID, armed security contractors and other agencies. This hurt us in Iraq, as we went into the Super Bowl of reconstruction without practicing as a team. Fortunately, there were efforts moving in this direction, such as those recently led by LTG Caldwell at Fort Leavenworth.

Peacetime acquisition rules are lethal in combat.

Speed is security. Our initial strategies won't always be right. We need to be able to rapidly respond and adapt to win against an insurgency.

Our obscenely burdensome peacetime acquisition rules were lethal in combat. The United States needed streamlined ways to start reconstruction projects sooner. Our acquisition processes and the emphasis on big projects caused a major lag time in getting real work started. Fortunately, some of this delay was offset by the proactive USACE effort to get TF RIE, TF RIO, and the FEST teams stood up and executing Iraqi projects early. The slow process of soliciting and evaluating bids, followed by months of contractor mobilization and staffing, delayed the hiring of Iraqi men. This fueled and deepened the insurgency.

Employing Iraqis was one of our best tools to improve the domestic security situation. Iraqis were promised jobs that did not quickly materialize, and they became disillusioned. We needed to start more of the smaller decentralized projects sooner to keep the 18-35 year old Iraqi men employed before they became insurgents. There initially was a great imbalance of resources toward big "American led" projects. It took more than a year to reallocate some of these funds toward smaller projects. We could have probably hired 100 local Iraqis for the price of hiring one deployed American contractor. And we could have hired the Iraqis in a week rather than waiting up to a year to select and deploy a single American contractor. So we need faster and more agile rules to be able to quickly shift resources and priorities.

But the fear of potential contract abuse paralyzes American bureaucrats and adds more rules and delays. Those delays worsened the tactical environment. We need to have prudent controls to mitigate the risk of contract abuse. Combat Contracting Officers need to have high integrity, and perhaps be subject to pre and post screening by polygraph exams. We need to let them get the job done. I believe the financial cost of potential contract abuse pales in comparison to the cost (human life and capital) caused by the lack of acquisition speed. The war was worse and more prolonged because we tended to be idealists and not realists.

One way to accelerate reconstruction is to pre-select contractors in peacetime before a contingency conflict happens. Fortunately, USACE did have some pre-existing contracts in place. These were used from the outset of the war, and they provided some ability to accelerate reconstruction. Without them, the situation may have been even more grave.

OTHER LESSONS

While I have recounted some of the larger lessons that I learned from Iraq, there are many more that I missed. I will leave the task to expand the "lessons learned" list to others.

But let me briefly mention two more lessons that I learned from experience and observation.

- Rule #1 in the Ranger Handbook applies to all combat operations: "Don't Forget Nothing."
- The wounds in this war were not all physical.

GRD Commanders

Name	Date
MG Ronald Johnson	2004
BG Thomas Bostick	2004-2005
MG Thomas McCoy	2005-2006
MG Michael Walsh	2006-2007
BG Jeffrey Dorko	2007-2008
MG Michael Eyre	2008-2009

Early Organization

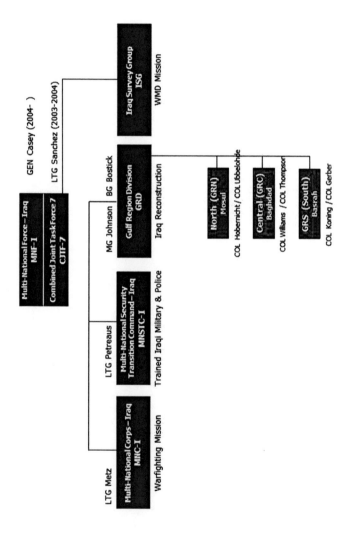

(Does not reflect Embassy Organization, IRMO, PCO)

ACRONYMS

1CD	1st Calvary Division

1CD	1st Calvary Division
1ID	1st Infantry Division
1LT	First Lieutenant
1MEF	First Marine Expeditionary Force
1st CAV	First Cavalry Division
2LT	2nd Lieutenant

A

AED	Afghanistan Engineer District
AAR	After Action Review

ADM	Admiral
ADVON	Advance Party – Early team sent in to prepare for the arrival of the rest of GRD
AFCEE	Air Force Center for Engineering and the Environment
AIF	Anti-Iraqi Forces
AIRP	Accelerated Iraq Reconstruction Program
AK	AK-47 automatic rifle carried by the enemy and some coalition troops
AQI	Al Qaeda Iraq
ARRK	Automated Route Reconnaissance Kit
ASAP	As Soon As Possible
ASIS	American Society of Industrial Security
AT/FP	Anti-Terrorism / Force Protection

B

BCT	Brigade Combat Team
BFV	Bradley Fighting Vehicle
BG	Brigadier General (1-star)
BIAP	Baghdad International Airport
BMW	Bavarian Motor Works
BOHICA	*Classified:* contact the author or publisher (or most veterans) for the definition
BUA	Battlefield Update Assessment
BUB	Battlefield Update Brief

C

C2	Command and Control
C7	Corps-level Engineer (The MNC-I Engineer officer)
CA	Civil Affairs
CAC	Common Access Card
CEA	Captured Enemy Ammunition
CENTCOM	U.S. Central Command
CENTRIX	Coalition Computer Network
CERP	Commander's Emergency Response Program
CFLCC	Combined Forces Land Component Commander
CG	Commanding General
CJTF-7	Combined Joint Task Force 7 (Predecessor to MNF-I)
CMOC	Civil Military Operations Center
CNN	Cable News Network
CODELs	Congressional Delegations
COL	Colonel
COM	Chief of Mission (Ambassador)
CONOC	Contractor Operations Center
CONUS	Continental United States
COS	Chief of Staff
CPA	Coalition Provisional Authority
CPR	Cardio-Pulmonary Resuscitation
CPT	Captain
CRC	CONUS Replacement Center
CRU	Contingency Response Unit
CSM	Command Sergeant Major (E-9)

D

DARPA	Defense Advanced Research Projects Agency
DCU	Desert Camouflage Uniform
DFI	Developmental Fund for Iraq
DHS	Department of Homeland Security
DNVT	Military Secure Phone System
DOD	Department of Defense
DOS	Department of State

DV   Distinguished Visitor

E

ECM   Electronic Counter Measures
EOC   Emergency Operations Center
EMI   Electro Magnetic Interference
EOD   Explosive Ordinance Disposal
EPSS   Electrical Police Security Services

F

FBI   Federal Bureau of Investigation
FEST   Forward Engineer Support Team
FOB   Forward Operating Base
FOC   Final Operational Capability
FRG   Family Readiness Group

G

G1   Division Personnel Officer
G2   Division Intelligence Officer
G3   Division Operations Officer
G4   Division Supply / Logistics Officer
G6   Division Communications Officer
GEN   General (4-stars)
GNP   Gross National Product
GPS   Global Positioning System
GRC   Gulf Region Central District (Baghdad HQ)
GRD   Gulf Region Division (Baghdad HQ)
GRE   Gulf Region Engineer
GRN   Gulf Region North District (Mosul)
GRS   Gulf Region South District (Basrah)

H

HEBENATOR   Mysterious device known only to COL
                            Dornstauder
HF   High Frequency
HMMWV   Humvees
HQ   Headquarters

HR   Human Resources

I

ICAF   Industrial College of the Armed Forces
ICDC   Iraqi Civil Defense Corps
ICU   Intensive Care Unit
IDF   Indirect Fire
IED   Improvised Explosive Device
IIG   Interim Iraqi Government
IRMO   Iraqi Reconstruction Management Office (State
                            Department)
IRRF   Iraq Relief and Reconstruction Fund
IOC   Initial Operational Capability
IPC   Iraqi Provisional Command (later became
                            GRD)
IP   Iraqi Police
IRAQNA   Iraqi Cell Phone

J

JASG   Joint Area Support Group (military mayor and
                            landlord)
JCMEB   Joint Civil-Military Engineering Board

K

KIA   Killed in Action
KPH   Kilometers Per Hour
KV   KiloVolt

L

LT   Lieutenant
LTC   Lieutenant Colonel
LTG   Lieutenant General (3-stars)
LMCC   Logistics Management Coordination Cell
LNO   Liaison Officer

M

MAJ	Major
MANPADS	Man Portable Air Defense System
MEDEVAC	Medical Evacuation (Helicopter)
MEF	Marine Expeditionary Force
MG	Major General (2-stars)
MIG	Soviet made fighter aircraft
MILCON	Military Construction (Congressionally funded basing projects)
MNC-I	Multi-National Corps—Iraq
MND (CS)	Multi-National Division – Center South (Al Kut region)
MND (SE)	Multi-National Division – South East (Basrah region)
MNF-I	Multi-National Force—Iraq
MNSTC-I	Multi-National Security Transition Command—Iraq
MOAA	Military Officers Association of America
MOD	Ministry of Defense
MOE	Ministry of Electricity
MOI	Ministry of Interior
MOO	Ministry of Oil
MPH	Miles Per Hour
MPV	Mine Protected Vehicle
MRAP	Mine Resistant Ambush Protected Vehicle
MRX	Military Readiness Exercise
MSC	Major Subordinate Command
MSG	Master Sergeant (E-8)
MUC	Meritorious Unit Citation
MW	Mega Watts

N

NDU	National Defense University
NCO	Non-Commissioned Officer
NCOIC	Non-Commissioned Officer-in-Charge
NGO	Non-Governmental Organization
NIPR	Non-classified Military Computer Network

O

ORHA	Office of Reconstruction and Humanitarian Assistance
OSD	Office of the Secretary of Defense

P

PAO	Public Affairs Office
PCO	Project and Contracting Office
PGM	Precision Guided Munitions
PM	Prime Minister
PM	Program Manager
PMO	Program Management Office (later called PCO)
PSD	Private Security Detail (security contractors)
PT	Physical Training
PTSD	Post Traumatic Stress Disorder
PX	Post Exchange (military shopping store)

Q

QRF	Quick Reaction Force

R

RIE	Restore Iraqi Electricity Directorate (formerly Task Force RIE)
RIO	Restore Iraqi Oil Directorate (formerly Task Force RIO)
ROC	Reconstruction Operations Center
RPG	Rocket Propelled Grenade
RSO	Regional Security Officer

S

SAF	Small Arms Fire
SAM	Surface to Air Missile
SATCOM	Satellite Communications
SAW	Squad Automatic Weapon

SEAL	Sea, Air, Land (Naval Special Operations)
SECDEF	Secretary of Defense
SES	Senior Executive Service
SF	Special Forces
SFC	Sergeant First Class (E-7)
SIGACTS	Significant Activities database
SIPR	Secret (Classified) Computer Network
SIR	Serious Incident Report
SITREP	Situation Report
SOF	Special Operations Forces
SPOT Report	Timely intelligence or status report
SUV	Sport Utility Vehicle

T

TAC	Transatlantic Programs Center (Winchester, VA), now called Middle-East District (MED)
TACOM	U.S. Army Tank-automotive and Armaments Command
TAD	Transatlantic Division
TFO	Task Force Olympia (Mosul)
TTPs	Tactics, Techniques and Procedures

U

UCMJ	Uniform Code of Military Justice
UK	United Kingdom
UN	United Nations
UPO	USAID Program Office
USACE	U.S. Army Corps of Engineers
USAID	U.S. Agency for International Development
USAR	U.S. Army Reserves
USMA	United States Military Academy (West Point)
USMC	United States Marine Corps
USN	United States Navy

V

VADM	Vice Admiral
VBIED	Vehicle Borne Improvised Explosive Device

VFR DIRECT	"Communications Protocol" used by COL Dornstauder
VFW	Veterans of Foreign Wars
VHF	Very High Frequency
VIP	Very Important Person
VTC	Video Teleconference
VUCA	Volatile, Uncertain, Chaotic, Ambiguous

WIA	Wounded in Action
WMD	Weapon of Mass Destruction
WVANG	West Virginia National Guard

USMA 1982 In Iraq, Afghanistan and other Forward Deployed Locations

I would like recognize my classmates that went into harm's way during the Global War on Terror. Many stepped out of their civilian careers to return to duty and serve their country.

This is an unofficial Service Record based on best information available. Thanks to the 1982 Scribe, Jay Jennings, for assistance putting this list together.

Many classmates served in CONUS or in prior conflicts, including Grenada, Panama, Desert Storm and Bosnia. Their service is not reflected in this list.

Each one has a story to tell.

Combat Tours in Iraq and Afghanistan (incl DOD Civilians)

First	Last	Tour Rank	Country	Years
Robert	Abrams	COL	Iraq	2004 - 2005
Robert	Abrams	MG	Afghanistan	2011 - 2012
Brian	**Allgood ***	COL	Iraq	2006 - 2007
Frank	Asencio	LTC	Iraq	2008
David	Aucoin	COL	Afghanistan	Nov 08 - Oct 09
David	Aucoin	COL	Afghanistan	2011 - 2012
Rob	Baker	COL	Iraq	2003 - 2004
Rob	Baker	BG	Iraq	2010
Rob	Baker	MG	Horn of Africa	2012
Art	Ball	COL	Iraq	2007
Dominic	**Baragona***	LTC	Iraq	2003
Rick	Bassett	COL	Iraq	2008
Jim	Bowen	COL	Afghanistan	2012
Jim	Brown	COL	Iraq	Nov 04 - Nov 05
Jim	Brown	COL	Iraq	Sep 07 - Feb 08
Jim	Brown	COL	Afghanistan	Jun-Jul 09, Jan 10
Margaret	Burcham	COL	Iraq	Jul 08 - Jul 09
Paul	Calbos	COL	Afghanistan	Jul 06 - Jul 06
Paul	Calbos	COL	Afghanistan	2010 - 2011

First	Last	Tour Rank	Country	Years
Ed	Cardon	COL	Iraq	Jun-Aug 2003
Ed	Cardon	COL	Iraq	Jan 05 - Jan 06
Ed	Cardon	BG	Iraq	Mar 07 - Jun 08
Ed	Cardon	MG	Iraq	2010 - 2011
Robert	Carlson	COL(P)	Afghanistan	2011 - 2012
Joseph	Coleman	COL	Iraq	Dec 05 - Jan 06
Joseph	Corrigan	LTC	Iraq	2004
Jim	Creighton	COL	Afghanistan	2009 - 2010
MaryAnne	Cummings	COL	Iraq	2006 - 2007
Craig	Currey	COL	Iraq	2007
Harry	Dabney	LTC	Afghanistan	Sep 02 - Apr 03
Kenneth	Dahl	COL	Iraq	2005 - 2006
Kenneth	Dahl	BG(P)	Afghanistan	2011 - 2012
Tom	Devine	MAJ	Afghanistan	2006
Matt	Duban	COL	Iraq	2005
Bo	Dyess	COL	Afghanistan	2009 - 2010
Ron	Dykstra	COL	Iraq	2005 - 2006
Todd	Ebel	COL	Iraq	2005 - 2006
Bryan	Eckstein	LTC	Iraq	2004
Tom	Faupel			
Celia	FlorCruz	LTC	Iraq	2009 - 2010
Randy	Fofi	LTC	Iraq	2003
Randy	Fofi	COL	Iraq	Sep 08 - Sep 09
Robert	Forrester	COL	Iraq	Mar 10 - Mar 11
Erik	Fretheim	LTC	Iraq	2004
Ozzie	Gorbitz	COL	Afghanistan	2004 - 2005
Brian	Groves	COL	Afghanistan	2011 - 2012
Dan	Grymes	COL	Iraq	2003
Casey	Haskins	COL	Iraq	2004
Scott	Henry	COL	Afghanistan	2008
Steve	Hill	COL	Iraq	Jul 07 - Jul 08
John	Hornick	LTC	Iraq	2009
Steve	Jackan	MAJ	Iraq	2009
Steve	Jarrard	LTC	Afghanistan	May - Nov 2006
Steve	Jarrard	LTC	Afghanistan	Jul 08 - Jan 09
Jay	Jennings	DA Civ	Iraq	2005 - 2006
Jay	Jennings	DA Civ	Afghanistan	2008 - 2009
Jay	Jennings	DA Civ	Afghanistan	2010 - 2011
Thomas	Juric	LTC	Iraq	2005 - 2006

First	Last	Tour Rank	Country	Years
Kerry	Kachejian	LTC	Iraq	2004
Ole	Knudson	COL	Iraq	2010
Tom	Kula	COL	Iraq	2006
Tom	Kula	BG	Afghanistan	2012
JC	Kuttruff	COL	Iraq	2006
Craig	Langhauser	LTC	Iraq	2004
James	Lashe	LTC	Iraq	Apr 04 - Apr 05
Brian	Layer	COL	Iraq	
Ken	Lewis	LTC	Afghanistan	Aug 04 - Sept 05
Ken	Lewis	COL	Iraq	Mar 09 - Jan 10
Michael	Loew	LTC	Iraq	2007
Thomas	Lynch III	COL	Afghanistan	Jan - Aug 2004
Brian	Malloy	LTC	Iraq	2006
Kevin	Mangum	COL	Afghanistan	2007
Kevin	Mangum	BG	Iraq	2009 - 2010
Peter	Mansoor	COL	Iraq	2003 - 2004
Peter	Mansoor	COL	Iraq	2007 - 2008
Bill	Mayville	COL	Iraq	2003 - 2004
Bill	Mayville	BG	Afghanistan	2009 - 2010
Bill	Mayville	MG	Afghanistan	2011 - 2012
Dave	McBride	COL	Iraq	2008
Everett	McDaniel	COL	Iraq	2005
Joseph	McNeill	LTC	Iraq	2004
Mike	McNeill	COL	Iraq	2005
Raymond	Millen	LTC	Afghanistan	Jul - Nov 2003
Raymond	Millen	LTC	Afghanistan	Aug 06 - Aug 07
John	Moore			
Robert	Moore	CPT	Iraq	2009
Joseph	Moravec	COL	Afghanistan	Aug 09 - Aug 10
Thomas	Morgan	LTC	Afghanistan	2006
Matthew	Moten	COL	Iraq	2005
Dan	Mulligan	MAJ	Iraq	Mar 08 – Feb 09
Bob	Nakamoto	SGT	Iraq	2005 - 2006
Roberto	Nang	COL	Iraq	2005
Casey	Neff	LTC	Iraq	2003
Mick	Nicholson	COL	Afghanistan	2006 - 2007
Mick	Nicholson	BG	Afghanistan	2008 - 2009
Mick	Nicholson	MG	Afghanistan	2011 - 2012
James	North	COL	Iraq	2004

First	Last	Tour Rank	Country	Years
Brian	O'Leary	CW4	Iraq	2006
Brian	O'Leary	CW4	Iraq	2010
Andrew	Osborn	MAJ	Afghanistan	2005 - 2006
Andrew	Osborn	MAJ	Iraq	2007 - 2008
Mark	Palzer	COL	Iraq	2007 - 2008
Mark	Palzer	BG	Afghanistan	2011 - 2012
Michael	Peffers	LTC	Iraq	2003
Greg	Perchatsch	COL	Iraq	Jul 07 – Sep 08
Warren	Phipps	COL	Iraq	2005 - 2006
James	Polo	COL	Iraq	Oct 05 - Oct 06
Bobby	Rakes	LTC	Iraq	2005
Karl	Reinhard	COL	Iraq	2006 - 2008
Dan	Roper	COL	Iraq	2007
Dan	Roper	COL	Afgh. & Iraq	2008
Sean	Ryan	COL	Iraq	
Steven	Salazar	COL	Iraq	2006
Steven	Salazar	BG	Iraq	2009
John	Schatzel	LTC	Iraq	2006
John	Schoen	LTC	Iraq	2005
John	Schoen	LTC	Afghanistan	2008 - 2009
Robert	Scurlock	COL	Iraq	2005
Robert	Scurlock	LTC	Afghanistan	2002
Lewis	Setliff	COL	Iraq	2004
Dan	Shanahan	COL	Iraq	
Eugene	Skinner	COL	Iraq	2010
Robert "Powl" Smith, Jr.	Smith	COL	Iraq	Jul 04 - Aug 05
Susan	Sowers	COL	Iraq	2005 - 2006
Rick	Stevens	COL	Iraq	2005 - 2006
Rick	Stevens	COL	Afghanistan	2007 - 2008
Dean	Stodter	COL	Afghanistan	2005 - 2006
Douglas	Strock	SSG	Iraq	Mar 04 - Feb 05
Jeff	Terhune	COL	Iraq	2006 - 2007
Rocky	Tyler	COL	Iraq	2008
Tom	Vandal	BG	Iraq	2010
Chris	Valentine	MAJ	Iraq	Mar 08 - Jan 09
Rick	Waddell #	LTC/COL	Iraq	2004 - 2010
Ricky	Waddell	BG	Afghanistan	2011 - 2012

First	Last	Tour Rank	Country	Years
Mike	Wadsworth	COL	Iraq	2006
Steve	Walker	COL	Afghanistan	2007
John	Wasson	LTC	Afghanistan	2009
Bryan	Watson	COL	Iraq	2008
Brian	Watson	BG(P)	Afghanistan	2011 - 2012
Tony	Wickham	COL	Iraq	2005
Mike	Winstead	COL	Afghanistan	2005
Tezeon	Wong	LTC	Iraq	2005
Paul	Wood	COL	Iraq	Nov 06 - Feb 08
Chuck	Yomant	COL	Iraq	2005 - 2009

* KIA
** Former member of USMA 1982
# Five deployments ranging from 1-5 months each.

Travel to / Service in Iraq and Afghanistan or Region (Military, USG Civilian, Contractor)

First	Last	Tour Rank	Country	Years
Mark	Biehler	COL(R)	Afghanistan	2008 - 2009
John	Boler	Mr.	Iraq	2006 - 2007
Thomas	Bryant	MAJ	Iraq, Kuwait	Jul 00 - Aug 01
Thomas	Bryant	MAJ	Turkey	Sep 01 - Feb 06
Robert	Croskery**	LTC	Various	Brief Trips
Mike	Davidson	LTC (R)	Iraq	2004
Michael	Dixon	LTC	Kuwait, Iraq	2003
Randy	Fofi	COL	Afghanistan	2011 - 2012
Jorge	Garcia	Mr.	Iraq	2004
Cindy	Glazier	COL	Iraq, Afghan.	Brief Trips
Rhys	Johnson	Mr.	Iraq	2006
Rhys	Johnson	Mr.	Afghanistan	2008
Thomas	Juric	LTC	Qatar, Iraq	Sep 03 - Oct 04
Kerry	Kachejian	COL	Iraq, Afghan.	2007
Arthur	Kane	LTC	Kuwait	Feb 2004
Terrence	Kelly	Civ SES equivalent	Iraq	Feb - Jun 2004
Terrence	Kelly	Civ SES equivalent	Iraq	Feb 06 - Apr 07
Mark	Kimmey	LTC	Iraq, Kuwait	2003 - 2004
Thomas	Lynch III	COL	Qatar	Sep 04 - Jun 05
Thomas	Lynch III	COL	Qatar	Jul 05 - Aug 07
Raymond	Millen	CIV	Afghanistan	Sep 08 - Sep 09
Randy	Odom	LTC	Kuwait	Jun 02 - Jul 04
Michael	Peffers	LTC	Qatar	2005
Greg	Perchatsch	COL	Afghanistan	2010
Dan	Roper	LTC	Kuwait	2002
Dan	Roper	LTC	Kuwait	2003
Anthony	Smith	Mr.	Iraq	
Mark	Supko	MAJ	Qatar, Iraq	2003 - 2004
Mark	Tilllman	COL	Qatar, Iraq, Afg,	2003 - 2005
Marcus	Weldon	CIV	Iraq	2007
Mike	Woodgerd	CIV	Afghanistan	2008 - 2010
Mike	Woodgerd	CIV	Afghanistan	2012

** Former member of USMA 1982